WORLD WAR II CAMPS IN JAMAICA

WORLD WAR II CAMPS IN JAMAICA

Evacuees, Refugees, Internees, Prisoners of War

Suzanne Francis-Brown

The University of the West Indies Press
Jamaica • Barbados • Trinidad and Tobago

The University of the West Indies Press
7A Gibraltar Hall Road, Mona
Kingston 7, Jamaica
www.uwipress.com

© 2022 by Suzanne Francis-Brown

All rights reserved. Published 2022

A catalogue record of this book is available from the National Library of Jamaica.

ISBN: 978-976-640-925-8 (print)
978-976-640-926-5 (ePub)

Cover photograph: The main entrance to Gibraltar Camp (1940-1941), The National Archives, CO 1069-371-6. UK

The back image is from The Daily Gleaner, March 25, 1946, page 10

Cover design by Robert Harris

The University of the West Indies Press has no responsibility for the persistence or accuracy of URLs for external or third-party internet websites referred to in this publication and does not guarantee that any content on such websites is, or will remain, accurate or appropriate.

Printed in the United States of America

Contents

List of Figures / vii

List of Tables / x

Preface / xi

Acknowledgements / xiii

List of Abbreviations / xv

Introduction / 1

1. The Jamaican Context during World War II / 18
   Background / 19
   Society / 22
   Nationalist Agitation / 31
   Defence Regulations and Implications for Freedoms within the Colonial Frame / 38
   Impact of War / 45
   Local Perceptions of the War / 54

2. A Camp for Free Europeans in Need / 61
   Evacuees / 64
   Refugees / 70
   Other Groups / 80
   Evacuee-Refugee Relationships / 82
   Location, Layout and Administration / 85
   Regulating the Camp and Residents / 97
   Living in Gibraltar Camp / 101
   Responses to Camp Conditions / 107

3. Internment Camps / 115
   3.1 Male Internment Camp / 117
      Locally Interned Enemy Aliens / 123
      Jamaican Detainees / 130
      Merchant Seamen / 132
      German and Italian Internees from West Africa / 134
      Finns / 138

   Inter-Group Relationships and Divisions / 138
   Location and Layout / 141
   Administration and Oversight / 146
   Conditions of Daily Life / 147
   Work and Play / 151
   Health / 157
   Changes to the Camp Population / 161
   Long-Term Detainees / 165
  3.2 Women's Camp, Hanover Street / 167
   Living Conditions / 173
   Challenges / 177
  3.3 Mona Family Camp/Married Families Camp / 183
   Layout and Conditions / 188

4. Isolation and Interaction in Colonial Jamaica / 195
 Isolating Friends / 196
 Securing Enemies / 200
 Media Interface / 201
 Physical Interface: Impact of Gibraltar Camp on the
  Immediate Community / 204
 Economic Interface / 208
 Interface and Interaction – Employment / 212
 Social Interaction / 219
 Interface and Interaction: Birth, Death and Marriage / 228

5. Traces in Heritage / 232
 Material and Cultural Remains / 235
 Lived Heritage / 246

Notes / 257

Selected Bibliography / 304

Index / 307

Figures

Figure 1	Postwar UCWI students process from Gibraltar Camp building / xi
Figure 2	Sources of World War II incomers / 2
Figure 3	Imperial camps in Jamaica / 14
Figure 4	Location of World War II Camps in and around Kingston, Jamaica / 16
Figure 5	Timeline of Arrivals and Departures at Gibraltar Camp / 65
Figure 6	Map of Gibraltar Camp within the Papine and August Town area / 86
Figures 7, 7A, 7B	Gibraltar Camp under construction / 88
Figure 8	PWD Layout of Gibraltar Camp / 90
Figure 9	Annotated Plan of Gibraltar Camp showing approximate living areas for different groups of residents / 95
Figure 10	Contemporaneous sketch layout of refugee section of Gibraltar Camp / 96
Figure 10A	Sketch of barracks and bathroom layout in refugee area of Gibraltar Camp / 97
Figure 11	Gibraltar Camp warning notice in *Gleaner* newspaper / 100
Figure 12	Gibraltar Camp cultural group / 112
Figure 12A	Dutch refugee family Schpektor in Gibraltar Camp refugee section / 112
Figure 12B	Ticket aboard SS Serpa Pinto for Polish refugee Manne Eckstein / 113
Figure 12C	Dutch refugee children in Gibraltar Camp 1943 / 114
Figure 13	Annotated map of Up Park Camp Kingston showing estimated location of Male Internment Camp / 143
Figure 14	Internee walking around the outer edge of the recreation field, close to the barbed wire perimeter fence, while others play a match in the distance / 144

viii | Figures

Figure 14A	Recreation area adjacent to the barracks buildings which accommodated the male internees / 144
Figure 14B	Fencing between two segregated areas of the male internment camp / 145
Figure 14C	Guard on duty at one of the guideposts along the perimeter of the male internment camp / 145
Figure 14D	Football team coached by Gerhard Zitzow at the Male Internment Camp gives a rare glimpse into camp life / 154
Figure 14E	Band from Male Internment Camp, which would also visit and play at Mona Family Camp / 155
Figure 14F	Image of Newcastle Hill Station from 1940s postcard / 162
Figure 14G	Military Detention Barracks at Up Park Camp / 167
Figure 15	Outline Drawing of Women's Internment Camp / 171
Figure 15A	Zitzow family on visiting day at the Women's Internment Camp / 172
Figure 16	Plan of Mona Family Camp / 185
Figure 16A	Index to Plan of Mona Family Camp / 186
Figure 16B	Frau Berger layout of the Mona Family Camp / 187
Figure 17	Painting by German internee from Zitzow verandah at Mona Family Camp / 191
Figure 17A	Photograph of residents of Mona Family Camp / 192
Figure 17B	Photograph of young children at Mona Family Camp / 192
Figure 18	Staff at the Gibraltar Camp hospital / 213
Figure 18A	Staff in the refugee camp kitchen / 214
Figure 18B	Staff in office at Gibraltar Camp / 214
Figure 19	Photograph of Aileen Mansfield, her cousin Fernando and his friend Orville around 1944 / 223
Figure 19A	Lara family at Gibraltar Camp / 224
Figure 20	Bustamante monument inside Up Park Camp / 238
Figure 21	Gibraltarian Anthony Lara and UWI Mona Campus Principal Elsa Leo-Rhynie with the Gibraltar Camp monument in 2007 / 239
Figure 21A	Gibraltar mayor Kaiane Aldorino Lopez in 2019 beside a heritage sign marking the entrance to Gibraltar Camp / 239
Figure 21B	UWI heritage sign marking site of Mona Family Camp / 240
Figure 21C	Gibraltar Camp building remaining on UWI Mona site / 241
Figure 22	Briggs Park Military Cemetery adjacent to the National Stadium whose lights can be seen above the graves / 243

Figure 22A	Joan Arnay Halperin places a stone on the grave of her sister Polish refugee Yvonne Krakowiak at Orange Street Jewish Cemetery / 243
Figure 22B	Grave of Elizabeth Epsworth Lara at St Andrew Parish Church cemetery in Kingston / 244
Figure 23	Concrete benches / 245
Figure 23A	Concrete benches originally made by Italian ex-internees and now an unquestioned part of the local landscape / 245
Figure 23B	Painting of Mona landscape by Italian internees Umberto Cattaneo / 246
Figure 24	Gibraltar Evacuation monument / 252
Figure 24A	Presentation of replica of Our Lady of Europe to the UWI Museum in 2019 / 253
Figure 24B	Gibraltarian and Jamaican officials at the site of Gibraltar Camp on the UWI Mona Campus / 253
Figure 24C	Gibraltarians born in Jamaica during World War II at the official twinning of Gibraltar and Kingston Jamaica / 254
Figure 24D	2015 Lecture at the Gibraltar Library / 254
Figure 24E	Gibraltar Camp church bell now the centrepiece of a park honouring Caribbean leaders who are graduates of the university / 255
Figure 24F	Original Gibraltar Camp tank still serves the UWI Mona Campus / 255

Tables

Table 1   Population of Male Internment Camp 1939–1947 / 118

Preface

Gibraltar Camp lurks like a half-forgotten memory between modern buildings on the eastern side of the Mona Campus of the University of the West Indies, on the outskirts of the Jamaican capital city of Kingston. The low, board barracks, mostly overborne by concrete classrooms and residences, beg a question which may or may not actually be asked – what are these structures and why are they there? Few know the answer that stands in plain sight on signs indicating the names of intersecting main roads on this side of the campus – Gibraltar Camp Way and Gibraltar Hall Road. One refers to the World War II camp that rested its persistent footprint on a site already marked to the west by brick and stone remains of eighteenth-century plantation structures; the other identifies its subsequent reincarnation as the cradle of a West Indian university, on the heels of World War II. Together they reflect the continuities and discontinuities that jostle on a site with plantation, wartime and postwar footnotes.[1]

Figure 1 Postwar UCWI students process from Gibraltar Camp building (Source, UWI Museum).

An academic quest for the history of now-weather-beaten structures uncovered the earlier reality of a modern wartime enclave for white, southern European but still British colonial evacuees from the Rock of Gibraltar and – separate but overlapping – many hundreds of eastern and northern European refugees. They lived in a fenced and guarded community set down amid the black and East Indian agricultural labourers of two nearby poor, semi-rural communities – buffered from them and from the wider Jamaican community. This, in a time when issues of race, class and gender shaded labour and political challenges to long-standing local colonial conditions. This also in a time when these local concerns, amplified by a denial of avenues to engage in the clash of armies on land, at sea and in the air, contended with the war for imperial attention.

Though a haven for free Europeans, Gibraltar Camp shared many conditions with internment camps also established in Jamaica's capital to house Europeans who had been designated as enemy aliens – many of them brought for security from West Africa – as well as prisoners from enemy vessels captured in nearby waters. Virtually nothing material remains of three internment camps: one of them belatedly established in a space carved from the northern extremity of Gibraltar Camp; another, adjacent to the main garrison some four miles away; a third in the heat and inconvenience of miscellaneous repurposed buildings in downtown Kingston. Their contribution to the Allied cause during World War II is largely unacknowledged. Their absence from Jamaican historiography deserves to be addressed – not only to provide added nuance to the understanding of the period but also to question how such a significant intrusion on the local space could leave such a light footprint and such slight traces.

Acknowledgements

The inspiration for this work is the languishing heritage of Jamaica's interface and interaction with historical events of the colonial period, and specifically of World War II. Of primary importance, then, are the repositories of information – the many archives and archivists, libraries and librarians, with specific acknowledgement of the Jamaica Government Archives, the National Library of Jamaica and The National Archives of the United Kingdom to which I had direct access, as well as the Swiss Federal Archives, the Archives Division of the International Committee of the Red Cross and the Archive of the American Jewish Joint Distribution Committee which were among those providing important assistance at a distance. Media houses provided another type of chronicle for everyday events and occurrences, with the online archive of the *Jamaica Gleaner* and the microfilmed editions of the *Public Opinion* offering published access to unofficial elite and non-elite voices and to developing events of the past. In the present, both the traditional and the online media enabled communication with a wide number of involved persons who might otherwise have been much less accessible.

Because this work started life as an MA and then a PhD thesis at the Mona Campus of the University of the West Indies, there are thanks to be offered to the Department of History and Archaeology and, especially, to Professors Patrick Bryan and James Robertson. As it has moved into this new form, I acknowledge those who reviewed the manuscript and the staff of the UWI Press, especially the late Dr Joseph Powell who initially agreed to the manuscript proposal.

The many individuals who became involved as this work evolved include persons whose personal histories overlapped with aspects of the story. Uwe Zitzow, who lived in internment camps in Jamaica until he was seven, reached out in 2002 through the UWI Library's West Indies Collection, in an effort to find out more of his own story. He has been a sterling resource and support with regard to the Women's Camp and Mona Family Camp – sites which he and his older sister Gisela would revisit. Anthony Lara was put in touch through the UWI Marketing and Communications Office in 2006. He had come to Jamaica to find the grave of his grandmother who died in 1944 while living at Gibraltar Evacuee Camp, and his ongoing interest has facilitated research at a distance in Gibraltar and collaboration on heritage commemoration at Mona. Regina Inez Baker neé Schpektor, who was one of the children of the first Dutch refugee group in December 1942, became a generous contributor of her knowledge and contacts from 2004. Gibraltarian Aileen Mansfield Gordon, who visited Gibraltar Camp in 2015 to connect with the place where she was born in 1943, had a hand in my own visit to Gibraltar in 2015 as a guest of the Gibraltar government for the seventy-fifth-anniversary celebration of the evacuation of the civilian population. Ram Ragbeir gave me a window into the Papine area near the city of Kingston as it was when first Gibraltar Camp and then the University College of the West Indies were established and led me to Harold Ramdeen, one of the very few remaining local voices from the time. They and everyone else whose story is interwoven into this history of World War II camps that became a point of connection between a British colonial outpost and a global conflagration deserve and have my acknowledgement, even if I do not have the space to name them all. Finally, thanks are due to my family and friends who have accompanied me on this journey.

Abbreviations

BITU	Bustamante Industrial Trade Union
CDW	Colonial Development & Welfare Act
CO	Colonial Office
DO	Dominion Office
FO	Foreign Office
HO	Home Office
JAS	Jamaica Agricultural Society
JLP	Jamaica Labour Party
JOINT	American Jewish Joint Distribution Committee
JPL	Jamaica Progressive League
PNP	People's National Party
PWD	Public Works Department
UCWI	University College of the West Indies
UWI	University of the West Indies
WO	War Office
YMCA	Young Men's Christian Association
YWCA	Young Women's Christian Association

Abbreviations for Job Positions

CS	Colonial Secretary
Gov	Governor
NCO	Non-Commissioned Officer
OAG	Officer Administering the Government
OCT	Officer Commanding Troops
SoS Colonies	Secretary of State for the Colonies

Abbreviations for Primary Document Collections

AICRC	Archive of the International Committee of the Red Cross

Catholic Archives	Archives of the Archdiocese of Kingston, Jamaica
JARD	Jamaica Archives & Records Department
NLJ	National Library of Jamaica
SFA	Swiss Federal Archive
TNA	The National Archives of the UK
WIC UWI	West India Collection, UWI

Introduction

During World War II, an array of displaced persons from both sides of the European conflict found themselves in Jamaica, based on decisions by the British government and its colonial representatives. On the Allied side were evacuees from the British colony of Gibraltar who eventually shared a facility built to accommodate them, with various groups of mainly Jewish refugees – some accepted for short stays in transit to more permanent locations and some for the length of the war. These were free civilians, accommodated in a camp run by Colonial Office functionaries, but with set conditions for residence and employment (see Figure 2: Sources of World War II Incomers).

From the other side of the conflict, many hundreds of men, women and children were interned in gender-differentiated camps – with interned families belatedly accommodated together after nearly three years apart. These groups exemplified some of the complex dynamics generated or underscored by the war. They included German and Austrian natives – many but not all Jewish – who had left Europe prior to the outbreak of war, seeking to escape discrimination and danger which were foreshadowed from the early 1930s. There is clear irony in their internment, sometimes for years, in the same category as and literally alongside German and Italian supporters of the Nazi cause. Most of the active Nazis were merchant mariners, captured by the British and Allied navies as they tried to run vital goods through a British blockade of American ports. These sailors formed the largest group within the Male Internment Camp, adjacent to the military headquarters. Most were brought into Kingston Harbour in 1939–41, aboard vessels that they had tried to scupper when the British or their allies closed in. Other merchant mariners and enemy aliens were sent from British West Indian territories that lacked the facilities to hold them over the long term. Next, numerically, within the internment camps were German and Italian civilians – men, women and their children interned in British West African territories and sent to Jamaica for safekeeping in late 1940. A small group of Finns, interned at a time when Finland was allied to Germany, added even greater diversity.

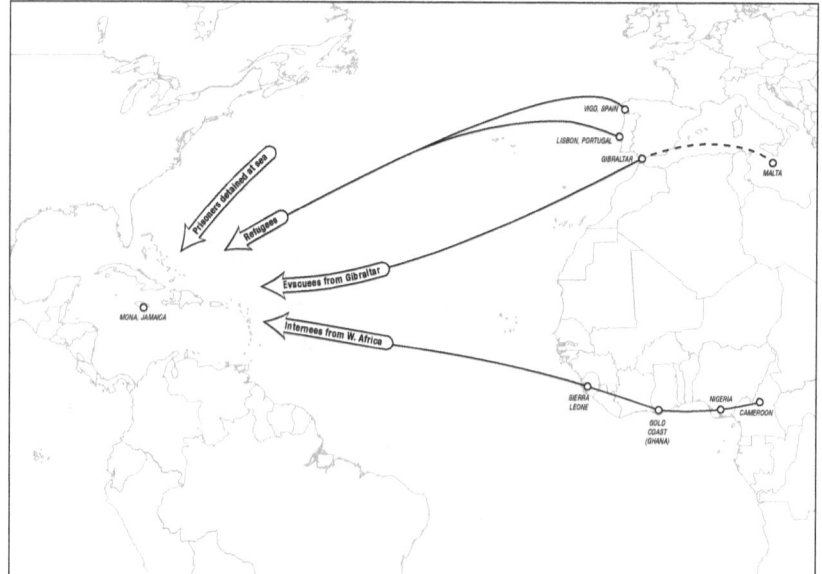

Figure 2 Sources of World War II incomers. Graphics for Figures 2, 3, 5 and 9 were created with the kind assistance of Mr David Williams.

The locations for these camps around Jamaica's capital city reflected the approach of the colonial government as well as its perception of the security risks involved – the colonial population in a camp on the outskirts of the city; the male internees and prisoners of war adjacent to the military garrison, and the female internees and their children, belatedly, in a jerry-rigged facility in Downtown Kingston. A facility for interned families would be carved out of a far end of Gibraltar Camp, in mid-war.

This study evolved from my PhD History thesis, "Gibraltar Camp 1940–1947: Isolation and Interaction in Colonial Jamaica", which explored the Gibraltar evacuee and refugee camp in the context of the wider wartime camp environment.[1] What was striking were the similarities as well as the differences between camps for free and unfree populations. It was clear that the colonial government was concerned not only to secure these various populations but also to buffer them from the Jamaican host community in which the incoming groups were placed. It appeared that the aim was to create what I have described elsewhere as holding tanks and then return them, essentially unchanged, from whence they came.[2] In this way, the colonial government would significantly support the Allied effort but would avoid disrupting the colonial status quo. This may have been considered particularly desirable in Jamaica – one of the British West Indian territories that had seen significant political and labour disruption during the mid- to late 1930s, related to poor socio-economic conditions. The Royal West India Commission, appointed in 1938 to investigate the situation in the region, would produce a report with such negative connotations that the British government declined to publish it in full until the end of World War II for fear of providing propagandist fodder to the enemy.

Sir Arthur Richards, the colonial governor sent to Jamaica in 1938, "to restore order", would have a generally fractious relationship with the island's political and labour activists – his arsenal included defence regulations more restrictive than those in place in Britain. So much so that he found himself at odds with the Colonial Office by 1942–43. But, despite criticism by local activists and civil libertarians, the colonial government had a cadre of local supporters who found the restrictions perfectly acceptable, arguing that local people and conditions were "politically, economically, socially and morally . . . vastly different" from those in the United Kingdom.[3] Within this traditional colonial frame, the government in Jamaica did little to engage the local population with the European incomers displaced by a war that many Jamaicans considered distant.[4] Indeed, it made clear that its only requirement was that the population remain at arm's length.

The perspective of the colonial authorities on the initiation of the camps and the management of their residents as well as the local community was authoritarian, paternalistic, race and class conscious, with a view to maintaining existing power dynamics. It is arguable that the efforts to buffer the incomers may have stemmed from concern over possible undercutting of long-standing perceptions of white superiority – especially if the mainly black population was exposed to the sight of white Europeans doing labouring jobs. The introduction of a range of European groups, some from working-class backgrounds and therefore arguably with some natural commonalities to many Jamaicans, had the potential to inadvertently upset this aspect of the local colonial context. This is reminiscent of René Maunier's observation that "outsiders" inserted into a relatively stable colonial situation might, by their presence, generate a different colonial response or confirm some essential colonial attitudes.[5] Maunier had in mind the impact of nations that were rivals in the imperial stakes. However, this study suggests that even groups without actual power might have the potential to disrupt the status quo just by their presence, without making efforts at sabotage. Hence the sight of the poor or working class, white visitors, operating outside of the usual norms and without the power normally associated with Caucasians in the colony had the potential to draw attention and spark thought among members of the colonized population.

The notion of race and class superiority fell in line with broad colonial perspectives teased out by mid-twentieth-century authors like Aimé Cesaire and Albert Memmi, as well as Franz Fanon, writing out of – albeit the French – colonial experience. Memmi described racism as "a consubstantial part of colonialism", one which established fundamental discrimination between colonizer and colonized as well as laying the foundation for social immobility. These authors identified attitudes, nurtured by colonizing administrations and colluded by the colonized, including Memmi's "mechanisms of debilitation" and Cesaire's "cunning instillation of fear and a sense of inferiority".[6] More contemporaneously, Jürgen Osterhammel noted the absorption of European cultural stereotypes "through education, habit, lack of alternatives, and identification with the aggressor", with the result that a sense of inadequacy inhered in the basic mental outlook of every colonized people.[7] By extension of this perspective, colonial people were not perceived to be actors. This could also explain the lack of effort at engagement – a non-involvement of the local population in the decision-making on and hosting of these displaced European groups that extended even to the locally elected legislative representatives.

This does not deny the colonial government's positive intent – to generate some local short-term employment and revenue – beyond direct support for the Allied effort. And there was a consistently stated concern to protect local employment from foreign job seekers, especially in the face of local labour activism. However, given the age, gender, socio-economic and language profile of those camp residents who had a degree of liberty, there is room to interrogate this concern as it applied to most local working-class jobs. What is also true is that there were concerns over protecting local British jobs and industries, and this may help to explain why interest in establishing new industries in Jamaica, expressed by some refugees, was dismissed. Such refusals also applied to any incomers seeking to remain in Jamaica after the war and were in keeping with policies on immigration – into Britain itself and by extension to the empire.

Early expressions of loyalty, and the desire to volunteer for active service, faded in the face of ongoing denials by the authorities and a gathering understanding that direct participation by local black and coloured men, was not wanted. It would be the news reports on those local men – and women – who found their own way to Canada or the United Kingdom to volunteer, and the belated recruitment of thousands of Jamaican and other Caribbean persons as Royal Air Force ground crews and munitions workers in 1943 and 1944, that re-fixed the interest of many local people in the war. The government appears not to have considered that the camps and their residents could offer locals another direct, visual and human connection to the war.

There was consistent daily information on the progress of the conflict, which was most accessible to those with newspaper subscriptions or shortwave radios. Literacy was also a factor, but it was common for people to read newspapers aloud in public parks, and this was also done, over a microphone, in some factories.[8] Nonetheless, it was not the battles and strategies so much as the increased economic hardship, including price spikes and shortages, that marked the wartime recollection of the majority. Especially in the early years of the conflict, many believed that the war remained far away from the Caribbean. Yet the backstories of the mainly German merchant mariners who were brought in for imprisonment at the Male Internment Camp in Kingston in late 1939 and 1940 illustrate efforts by the British Navy and its allies to stop German and Italian merchant vessels breaking a trade blockade and getting needed supplies to military outposts and the Reich. Many of these encounters took place in the Caribbean, including several in the Northern Antilles. More significantly, for Allied trade and local supplies, was the period in 1942 and early 1943, when German – and to a lesser extent, Italian – submarines ranged successfully throughout the Caribbean and along the continental waters. In his *U-Boat War in the Caribbean*, Gaylord Kelshall exploded the misconception that the Caribbean remained far from the conflict. He showed that while the direct physical impact of the successful German campaign concentrated on the southern Caribbean and continental coastline, near the British oil-producing island of Trinidad and the Dutch refineries in Aruba and Curacao, there was also activity in the northern Caribbean, not far from Jamaica.[9] Survivors of at least one vessel sunk close to Jamaica would be taken to the capital, Kingston, for succour. Also relevant, though never proved, may be common stories told by Jamaican interviewees, of spies overlooking Kingston Harbour and of German seamen – or submariners – who would come ashore along the island's extensive and largely unsecured shoreline for occasional rest and recreation. Such citizen concern that the island might attract enemy attention increased with the siting of American bases in south central Jamaica in 1942. However, no attacks were ever reported.

In addition to reporting on the war, the local media helped to assuage interest in the camp residents while simultaneously conveying the message to stay away. Some newspapers and news magazines also reported local concerns where there were divergences between the needs of the camps and local interests. This occurred in relation to perceived racial discrimination in decisions on job placement, as well as charges regarding the diversion of some scarce local food supplies for the camps. And while the enclave approach, even for the Allied evacuees and refugees, created a significant buffer, there is some evidence that Jamaicans, across different classes, went beyond distanced interest in the incomers – initiating or responding to some level of interface and interaction. Beyond suggesting a level of agency within a disapproving colonial context, such wartime encounters left some written and oral traces, which research could uncover. But the recall of the wartime camp experiences was generally greater on the part of the displaced, for whom the experience was life altering and for whom these experiences were connected to some level of commemoration. Even where individual Jamaicans retained some recall of the camps and their residents, those memories remaining after seven decades were often conflated and imprecise.

This work sets out to shed light on this period in Jamaican and wider wartime history, through a discussion of the people who lived behind the camp fences during the period 1939–1947 and the local context within which these camps were placed – including instances of discouraged interaction. While a direct contribution to Jamaican historiography, the events chronicled are also part of a wider Caribbean, British colonial, European and American story. As such, parts of the story were addressed in a chapter within Karen Eccles and Debbie McCollin's *World War II in the Caribbean*, published in 2017.[10] That volume recognized and sought to illuminate the region's contribution to the Allied effort which, it noted, has been underestimated in war and conflict-related historiographies.[11] In addition to Kelshall's extensive analysis of the German maritime offensive in the Caribbean, which helped to refocus attention on the region as a theatre of the war, there has been some acknowledgement of the Caribbean volunteers who contravened official advice and crossed the ocean to fight, as well as later recruits to an underutilized Caribbean Regiment and to British munitions factories and Royal Air Force (RAF) ground crews. The use of Caribbean colonies in bargaining with the United States, leading to the placement of bases in eight British colonial territories, six of them in the then British West Indies, was another part of the contribution, discussed by Humphrey Metzgen and John Graham in *Caribbean Wars Untold*.[12] And Bridget Brereton's *History of Modern Trinidad, 1783–1962* addressed Trinidad's additional importance as a location from which the United States deployed resources to the various theatres of war.

This study seeks to build on previous work, exploring the role that the British West Indian colony of Jamaica played by providing detention facilities for Europeans deemed safety hazards, away from shifting battle lines. It also looks further at examples where events in these facilities could have a far-reaching impact – as when reports of conditions among German women and children interned in Jamaica, conveyed through civil society and neutral reporting on the camps, impacted German treatment of British internees in Germany. And, through those same reports, a clear sense of life within the internment camps can be conveyed. The make-up of the camp populations, the interface between them and the changes brought by developments during the war are all addressed. These camps were always framed as holding tanks, as the chapter in Eccles and McCollins proposed. There was no intent to allow permanent settlement, even after the end of the war. Indeed, most internees were held within a closed facility until they could be repatriated – which for some was more than a year after the end of hostilities. Shifts in wartime alliances and developments, such as the 1943 Armistice with Italy, did lead to adjustments in camp populations and, in some cases, the civilian camp became home to persons formerly categorized as internees. Those groups that managed to gain additional freedoms – specifically "cooperating" Italians and some of the refugees housed at Gibraltar Camp – were a source of irritation to the colonial government.

With respect to the evacuees at Gibraltar Camp, significant Gibraltarian context was recorded by T.J. Finlayson in *The Fortress Came First* (2000), as well as *They Went to War* (2004) by Eric Canessa and *We Thank God & England – A Collection of Memorabilia about the Evacuation of the Gibraltar Civilian Population, 1940–1951* by Joe Gingell edited by Dennis D Besio. *Mona Past and Present: The History and Heritage of the Mona Campus, University of the West Indies* (2004) by Suzanne Francis-Brown looked at Gibraltar Camp as part of the legacy of the Mona campus site. These studies focused on the civilian evacuation for which Jamaica was briefly central – plans to accommodate between seven and nine thousand of the estimated thirteen thousand Gibraltarian civilian evacuees, in camps on the island, which were disrupted by fears of transporting civilians across the North Atlantic. Gibraltar Camp, Jamaica, eventually accommodated around sixteen hundred Gibraltarians, with some of the excess accommodation that had been prepared being later assigned for refugees. This work shines added light on the experiences of the evacuees in Jamaica and their interactions with Jamaica and Jamaicans, despite official discouragement.

It also contributes to the Jamaican case, within an increasing understanding of the role that some Caribbean colonies played as havens for groups of Jewish refugees. Along with articles by several other scholars, Joanna Newman's *Nearly the New World: The British West Indies and the Flight from Nazism, 1933–1945* addresses aspects of the policies related to refugee groups such as those who ended up in Gibraltar Camp, Jamaica, during the period 1942–1947, as well as groups of self-exiled individuals who found their way to various West Indian territories.[13] My own 2008 thesis, "Gibraltar Camp 1940–1947: Isolation and Interaction in Colonial Jamaica", gathered interviews with several camp residents, including refugees from the Dutch group. And there are memoirs published by Polish refugee Miriam Stanton and Dutch refugee David Cohen, which help to enliven camp reports.[14] A detailed exploration of the stories of some of the refugees within the camp was made by Diana Cooper-Clark in *Dreams of Re-creation in Jamaica*.[15] Even more complex than the cases of the Eastern European and Dutch groups, accepted as refugees by the British imperial and colonial administrations and brought to Jamaica for succour, were those of the individuals and families identified and interned as enemy aliens after fleeing Nazi repression in the early to mid-1930s. These persons were Jewish, anti-Nazi or otherwise non-conformist, but of German and Austrian birth – some even naturalized British citizens or persons in the process of achieving that status. German Jews among the refugee groups were also separated out and interned, though some efforts were made – soon or late – to provide some separation from non-Jewish compatriots within the internment facilities. Newman, as well as Christian Cwik and Verena Muth, have discussed the ways in which such refugees found their way into Caribbean territories, having escaped the conditions that forced them away from Europe in the 1930s.[16]

Less frequently addressed are the Italians who sought new lives in the region before the start of the war, a handful of whom would also end up in detention after Italy entered the war on the German side, in June 1940. Some of these traders, mechanics, planters, professionals and businessmen had either become or sought to become naturalized British citizens during the late 1930s. The little known about them often emerges from legal notices challenging detention, but it may be assumed that like others seeking greater freedom or opportunity, they came to the British West Indies due to relative ease of entry before the war. An article on migration from fascist Italy during the inter-war period noted that many Italians who left in the

1920s and early 1930s were political refugees with anti-Fascist positions – many of whom returned to Italy after the war – while Italian Jews sought refuge abroad after the government of Benito Mussolini enacted anti-Semitic laws in 1938. Poverty was also a factor in the decisions to leave.[17]

This study is also unique in its consideration of the heritage of these camps. It recognizes that among Jamaicans, there is a low level of recollection and memorialization of the camps and their residents, and other aspects of the wartime period, and considers some of the relevant factors. It provides information to enrich the historical roots of some local heritage that is not generally linked to this period.

World War II Camps in Jamaica draws on an extensive range of primary sources, buttressing official records from several archives with media reports and oral testimony to create a focus that is as much about the people who experienced this period as the policies that framed their actions. Media reports from consistent publications generated information within accepted professional norms, guided by an editorial perspective. During this period, the *Gleaner* was the main media house, though the *Jamaica Times* published on a weekly basis and the *Public Opinion* moved from weekly to daily. The monthly *Spotlight* newsmagazine was launched by journalist Evon Blake in 1939, and the *Catholic Opinion* was published monthly as the conservative voice of the Catholic Church in Jamaica. Availability of consistent runs of these publications was a factor in their use. Newsprint restriction during the war was one limiting factor in consistent publication during the period in question, and subsequent discontinuation of publication may also affect current availability. In the case of the *Gleaner*, which began publication as a newssheet in 1834 and has been published consistently as a daily paper for more than a century, its archive is now available online. Analysis of its output through two world wars respectively underlined its conservatism – revering private property, free enterprise and limited political franchise – and its loyalty to the empire despite occasional willingness to pressure the colonial government.[18] Beyond the paper's consistent editorial and reportorial output, public views were accepted through letters to the editor, which also helped to broaden the input on local perceptions.

Journalistic style has changed significantly over time – wartime articles were often longer and more narrative and might also be more evidently reflective of the proprietor's perspective than later reports, which made more conspicuous effort at balance. However, the journalistic pursuit of factual information remains clear, and these reports have the advantage of being contemporaneous. They therefore provide a good counterbalance to oral testimony and memoirs which, while rich in human detail, immediacy and emotion, were often incomplete and prone to conflation. The ability to access other contemporaneous material such as diaries or drawings was also helpful in this regard. In one case, a correspondent who was seven years old when he left Jamaica had later interviewed his older sister and parents to corroborate and add detail as well as an adult perspective to his own recollections. In another instance, the written memoir of a young teenager, as a school project, provided a detailed, coherent narrative with verifiable information that had been treasured in a family archive. Access to more than one source from specific groups or periods was important for supporting testimony or nuanced analysis. One example relates to the provisioning of the camps, which is well covered in reports and the source of some comments in the media. Allan Rae, son of the Gibraltar Camp commandant, Ernest Rae, recalled that people living within the facility were never without scarce items like bacon, butter and eggs – though at a time fresh eggs were replaced by powdered substitute. In his late teens when the family moved on to the camp, Rae would have been keenly aware of the comparison between what was provisioned for the camp and what Jamaicans outside were able to access, especially from 1942 when trade routes were under siege by the German submarine force. However, his recollection did conflate a period which ended after the departure of the Gibraltarians in 1944. The Zitzow family's recollection of the food in generally well-provisioned internment camps was rather one of adequacy than of bounty, especially with regard to scarce items. This memory, expressed by the youngest member of the family, reflects the experience of himself, his sister and mother who lived at the Women's Camp, his father at the Men's Camp and the overall positive experience of the reunited family at the Mona Family Camp from late 1943. They had no basis for comparison outside of those three camps – and perhaps, through correspondence, to family or friends elsewhere. Interpretation requires a balancing of such sources and experiences over the course of time.

The wartime camps created a major interface between the small colonial island of Jamaica and the European conflict which exploded into a global conflagration, in a period of growing anti-imperial tensions. This study's inside-out approach to the wartime experience inverts the usual centre to periphery perspective, to suggest that relevance is not a one-way street and to join in the production of evidence on wartime contributions by the island and its immediate Caribbean context. And while this focus on wartime is not a military history, it does have some overlap with the activities of the British garrison which oversaw the internment camps, often through deployed Canadian troops, as well as the US bases that were briefly active in southern Jamaica.

Chapter 1 therefore focuses on the Jamaican context into which the camps and their residents were introduced at various points during World War II. The background to Jamaica's wartime experience was one of long-standing colonial status, under the British flag, including poor socio-economic conditions and recent labour and political activism – in common with other Caribbean territories. Issues of social context are explored, including the part played by increased racial consciousness, which would be raised with respect to the internment camps on occasions during the war. Race was a visual factor and class a consideration in relation to the camp populations placed among the mainly black and brown Jamaicans, and there were instances where it was clearly on the mind of local colonial authorities who sought to maintain separation. All other things aside, Gibraltar Camp inadvertently indicated to many Jamaicans that white people were not inevitably privileged, cultured nor of a higher status. Here were many hundreds of Caucasians, male and female, who were similar in interests and income to many of the local people. Who is to say what impact this may have had on the thinking of many "ordinary", non-privileged individuals in a country already beginning to think out of the traditional colonial box? Enough reason, perhaps, for the camp administration, supported by colonial regulation, to discourage interaction.

Developments in Jamaica during World War II were framed by the experiences of the 1930s, which had seen labour riots in Jamaica and across the British West Indies. In Jamaica, there was also a push for greater self-governance within the context of demands for more respect as well as more socio-economic development. Detailed treatments of these developments are offered elsewhere – in *Strike the Iron* and *Arise Ye Starvelings* by leftist political scientist Ken Post and *Towards Decolonisation. Political, Labour & Economic Development in Jamaica. 1938–1945* by Richard Hart, left-wing activist and historian, who was himself among the Jamaican political detainees in the Male Internment Camp, Kingston. This chapter touches on the activist context and the issues of civil liberties raised by the way in which the local defence regulations were implemented.

It also looks at the broad impact of the war and the way Jamaicans broadly perceived it, as context for local impressions of the camps and their residents. Decisions leading to the placement of thousands of Europeans in Jamaica for periods even beyond the end of the war, as a contribution to the imperial effort, were made without reference to this local population – even at the nascent legislative level. This despite the scale of the effort: Gibraltar Camp alone was designed to hold up to nine thousand evacuees – virtually the population of Montego Bay, Jamaica's third largest conurbation.[19] The year 1940 also saw the agreement to accept several hundred interned enemy aliens. By early 1941, while it was clear that far fewer evacuees would arrive in Jamaica than had been planned for, colonial government correspondence indicated a willingness to accommodate many times more than the three or four thousand who were eventually accounted for across the various camps. The year 1941 saw active consideration of a War Office request to host ten thousand Italian prisoners of war,[20] as well as a proposal to transfer a large group of British evacuees from Portugal. While neither came to pass, an undetermined number of British individuals and families spent the war in Jamaica on their own recognisance.[21] There was no official effort to convey to the public the notion of a local contribution and connection to the war, through the hosting of the evacuees and refugees or the securing of the internees and prisoners. Indeed, the main message conveyed was that these people were the business of the authorities and that any interference would be punished – despite the spontaneous public welcome received by the first contingent of Gibraltarian evacuees. A *Gleaner* editorial comment just after the arrival of the first group recognized that Jamaica's furnishing a home for evacuees "proves distinctly useful to the Mother Country in this war".[22] It suggested that providing safety for displaced persons would be balanced by the active participation of young Jamaican men fighting in the RAF, "bringing destruction upon those who have forced men and women to flee in their thousands from the danger of suffering and death". Neither element of this dual perception received any official acknowledgement or support. The most accepted means of broad public support, for some time, would be a contribution in cash or kind to a series of successful campaigns, including those to underwrite the cost of RAF bombers and canteens.

Despite angst over the refusal of local efforts to volunteer for the war, leading to some disengagement and the ploughing of energies into local political and labour developments, Jamaicans positively supported the Allied cause. There were no disagreements over decisions to establish the camps, though there were some local complaints and comments over the manner in which decisions were taken, as well as the impact on the local population, especially in terms of scarce food items. In most instances, these debates were really rooted in local responses to aspects of the colonial condition, including the desire for more respect and more participation in local decision-making.

Chapters 2 and 3 focus on the camps and their residents. While internments and other imprisonments in the Male Internment Camp took place from the very start of the war in September 1939, it can be argued that the framing of camps as a contribution to the imperial war effort – within official circles – came in 1940: first with the offer of what would be Gibraltar Camp and then with the internment camps for civilian enemy aliens. These camps were provided on the basis that the British government would provide or reimburse funding for the building materials and construction as well as ensuring that the expenses for commissioning and administration were guaranteed. It, or another agreed source, would also repay the accommodation and maintenance of the various accepted populations. The term often used was "imperial obligation", and it applied to all but one of the categories accepted for accommodation in camps during World War II – the mainly Jewish refugees. These groups were accepted for specified periods and were funded respectively by the US-based JOINT Distribution Committee and the Dutch government-in-exile.

Chapter 2 therefore focuses on Gibraltar Camp, which both housed and held groups of free Europeans in need of haven, and Chapter 3 focuses on the various internment camps that were established to detain Europeans designated as enemy aliens, including several hundreds brought for safekeeping from British colonies in West Africa (see Figure 3: Imperial Camps in Jamaica). The Male Internment Camp was also designated a Prisoner of War Camp, for German and Italian men detained as part of the war effort – most of them mariners taken during Allied operations in the northern Caribbean and near Atlantic waters. However, this group of men was eventually designated as internees rather than prisoners of war.

Within the controlled environments of the camps, the treatment of the residents was largely positive. Their accommodation was simple but adequate. They had electricity and running water, often to a far greater and more consistent degree than the local population; their food was generally plentiful and included many items – reportedly including beef, eggs, ham and bacon – which became scarce delicacies during the war. They had recreational facilities and materials, and they were not required to work beyond assisting in their own care. Only one camp, the Women's Camp on Hanover Street in downtown Kingston, generated consistent complaints relating to physical and social conditions – and this situation generated negative resonances in Germany which ultimately impacted British women interned in two German camps. Overcoming this situation forced the belated creation of a family camp for the married civilian internees and single women, despite previous resistance by the local colonial authorities.

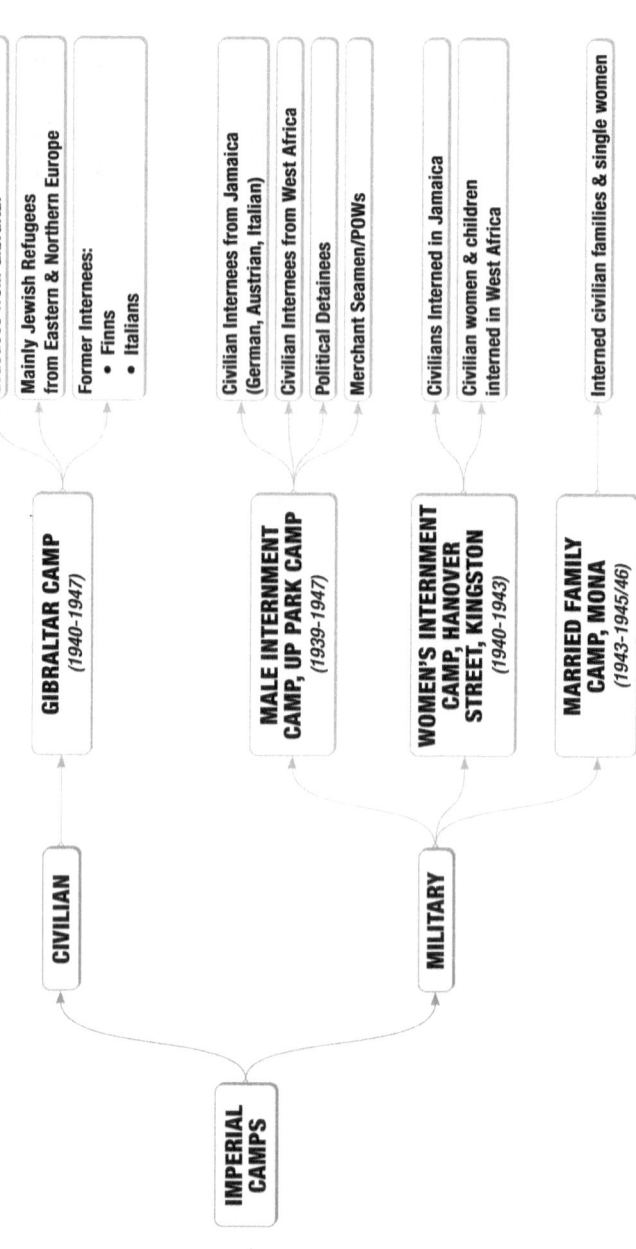

Figure 3 Imperial camps in Jamaica.

In both chapters that focus on the camps, a range of sources were mined to explore the physical conditions of the camps as well as the day-to-day provisions for the persons living within fences for periods from months to several years. The composition of these various groups was considered as well as inter-group relations within the camps and the changes throughout the war. Reports generated by several parties, generally considered neutral, were valuable in understanding developments within the camps – with importance attached to the organizational sources as well as the individuals involved in compiling the information. In the case of the internment camps, significant detail emerged from regular reports by the Swiss Vice-Consul in Jamaica, Rudolf Waeckerlin, a businessman running the local Coruba Rum office. By the middle of the war, under the Swiss mandate as Protecting Power for German and Italian interests, he undertook regular visits to the Male Internment Camp and later to the Newcastle Hill Station where some Italian internees were moved after the Armistice of 1943. For the Women's Internment Camp, this task was taken up by Mrs Helen Waeckerlin. The pair later visited the Married Families Camp at Mona.

Other formal reports were generated, less frequently, by the Young Men's Christian Association (YMCA)s War Prisoners Aid office and the Young Women's Christian Association (YWCA), as well as the American Jewish Joint Distribution Committee (JOINT). These sometimes addressed specific situations, but also provided perspectives on the camps and the outlook of their residents. Sometimes these could also raise or lower tempers in the countries of origin and impact relationships between the countries of origin and the detaining country – in this case, Britain or Britain's colonial authority in the colony. In the case of complaints from residents of Gibraltar Camp, over imposed conditions, respective reports from Gibraltarian investigators sent from New York and the JOINT's Charles Jordan in Cuba helped to calm concerns. On the other hand, there was a report, in correspondence, suggesting that reports by an official of the YMCA's War Prisoners' Aid might have helped inflame German concerns over conditions in the Women's Internment Camp in Jamaica in 1942. The YMCA and YWCA, both of which started as youth service organizations in the mid-nineteenth century and both headquartered in Geneva, Switzerland, maintained an active interest in the impact of the war. As it had during World War I, the YMCA activated a War Prisoners' Aid office. During World War II, it focused on supplying Allied and German prisoners of war with non-essential goods including reading material, musical and sporting equipment and stationery supplies.[23] During visits to Jamaica, YMCA official Conrad Hoffmann Jr visited the internment camps but also spoke to groups of Jamaicans, such as the rural Manchioneal community in January 1941. He told his audience that he was collecting bibles and hymn books for interned Germans in the hope that captured Britons in Germany might be treated as well.[24]

Chapter 4 focuses attention on instances where interest, interface and interaction emerged during the war years between the camp residents and Jamaican people, as well as the broader socio-economic context into which these residents had been placed. Any such connection occurred despite physical, administrative and social structures designed to separate the camps from the external contexts. In the case of Gibraltar Camp where the residents were free and not detained, the structures nonetheless strictly regulated access. Social focus, especially for the Gibraltarian population, was internalized with all facilities from school and church to shops and hospitals, provided within the fence. Limited group forays outside the camp, and the occasional invitation of a team or group to play or perform inside the camp, were monitored and directed by the priest and nuns who had oversight of this group. The less homogenous, and in some cases less conservative refugee groups who eventually shared the camp facilities, also retained group cultural and language connections but had fewer social

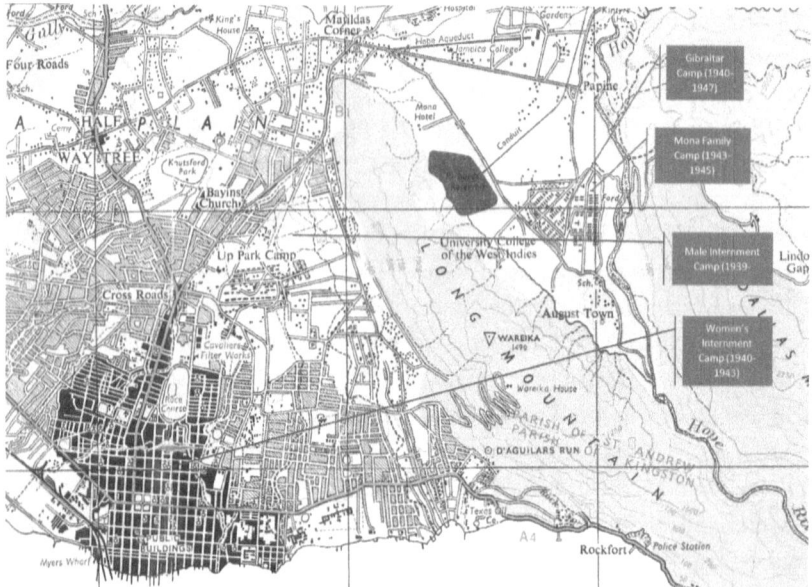

Figure 4 Location of World War II Camps in and around Kingston, Jamaica (locations identified on detail from Jamaica 1973, 1:50000 sheet L, Map & Image Library, Department of Geography & Geology, UWI, Mona).

constraints and sometimes fewer resource constraints. And despite the requirement that they live only within the camp, these persons did make frequent forays into the wider community. There was also a degree of active interaction with the geographically local population around Gibraltar Camp and with various communities of interest.

Despite regulations preventing general access to the camps by Jamaicans, a few persons did gain access. In most cases, though, relationships which developed did so in the spaces outside the camp. Some regulations relating to camp residents not taking local employment were also disregarded. The fact that connections were initiated, in various instances, by both the incomers and the locals, and in the face of disapprobation by colonial officials, suggests a degree of agency by subaltern populations, especially on the part of the local population. Nonetheless, the consistent effort to maintain physical control of the wartime incomers was largely successful and is one of the reasons why so little remains, in the island's material and cultural record, to mark their passage, despite the uniqueness of their wartime presence.

This light imprint on local heritage is the subject of the final chapter. In Jamaica, where a few thousands of free and detained Europeans were shipped in and accommodated in camps from 1940 on, the government was largely successful in buffering them from the local population. This failure to expose the local population to the evacuees and refugees – indeed the deliberate attempts to maintain distance – removed an opportunity to connect the local population to the reality of the war. It also predisposed the local population to retaining little of this experience in memory and heritage. Perhaps as a result, those aspects of World War II heritage which still dot the local landscape are often unrecognized and unvalued.

More consistent recall and memorialization can be identified among the incomer populations, for whom the Jamaican experience was a major stage – sometimes a point of calm – in the disruption of their lives by the war. Not surprisingly, given that the evacuation was an official government decision, the most significant official commemoration of the Jamaica sojourn is in Gibraltar, where there is also recognition of the United Kingdom and Madiera as other evacuee sites. The refugees and the internees/prisoners were more disparate individuals and groups. Nonetheless, some refugees and internees have researched and written about their experiences, and even made pilgrimages to Jamaica to reconnect with their past, of which some retain pleasant memories – often those from the younger generation whose experiences were less overwhelmed by stressful considerations.

Chapter 1
The Jamaican Context during World War II

What was the Jamaica within which British colonial authorities sought to contain a range of European evacuees, refugees, interned enemy aliens and crews of enemy merchant vessels captured in the Caribbean Sea and near reaches of the Atlantic Ocean? Within the British colonial context, Jamaica was summarized as a star of eighteenth and early nineteenth-century sugar production, which had descended into a slum by the 1930s. Within the island, however, this external perception did not diminish the politically activist mindset visible at many levels of the population. Indeed, this vibrancy had been intensified in the wake of World War I, by the return of Jamaicans exposed to racism in service of Britain – and again when the global recession forced the repatriation of many Jamaicans who had worked and been exposed to economic and social conditions, labour activism, work and life experiences in the Americas.[1]

Political and labour organizations were evolving, and riots in Jamaica in 1938 topped off a decade of protest across the region, spurring the appointment of a West India Royal Commission to investigate conditions. It's negative findings would spur constitutional reform and limited development projects even during wartime. The events also created a stressful environment within which Governor Sir Edward Denham died suddenly on 2 June 1938, bringing to the island Sir Arthur Richards who would be the first of two wartime governors. The authoritarian approach, words and actions of Governor Arthur Richards quickly undercut initial cooperative approaches which local activists offered on the outbreak of war in September 1939, in the face of Allied peril. The governor's use of the local Defence Regulations to keep a lid on protest and contain protesters meant that the war years in Jamaica were rich with concerns over political and civil rights, and these were often expressed in the media as well as in official correspondence. Indeed, Governor Richards's disagreements with a range of local actors extended to several local media houses, including the local newspaper of record, the *Daily Gleaner*.[2] Mid-war, Governor Richards was reassigned to Nigeria and replaced by Sir John Huggins who oversaw the 1944 implementation of a new constitution, with elections under universal adult suffrage, as well as furthering welfare projects based on the new Colonial Development Fund. These wartime developments in Jamaica were unusual and were aimed at undercutting some of the damming conclusions of the 1938 Royal Commission whose report would not be published in full until after the successful conclusion of the war.

This chapter provides an overview of the Jamaican situation up to and during this period, focusing particularly on the decision-making context, which was being challenged by local activists; the Defence Regulations which were used as a tool of control and under which World War II camps were regulated; and how both these and the war impacted local society. The island's wartime camps operated against this background.

Background

At the start of World War II, Jamaica was approaching three centuries as a British colony. Captured from Spain in 1655, the island became a major sugar producer, using enslaved labour and significantly supporting imperial development over more than a century. An economic slump anticipated the 1838 emancipation of the enslaved population, who faced freedom without any resources of their own, while former slaveholders were compensated by the British government. Efforts to ensure a continued labour force, cost-effective to the planters, included the introduction of indentured labour from China and India. By the 1850s, the British ended their duty preferences for British West Indian sugar exports. In 1865, in the face of poverty and official neglect, there was a peasant uprising at Morant Bay in eastern Jamaica, whose harsh suppression led to the replacement of Governor Edward John Eyre and in the face of which the long unrestrained Jamaican House of Assembly surrendered its rights and privileges and accepted the imposition of Crown Colony government. Some two decades later, an amended constitution provided for a partly elected Legislative Council, based on a limited franchise that enabled only those with significant property or position. Persons standing for office had to be male, with an income of £150 from land or £300 from other sources, who paid annual taxes of at least £300. Those voting for them, similarly all male, had to be over twenty-one years and paying at least £1 in annual taxes – a severely limited franchise estimated at 7 per cent of the population.[3] In February 1939, Jamaica's electoral roll was some seventy-three thousand men.[4]

At the start of the war, the island's modified Crown Colony system provided only one elected member for each of the island's fourteen parishes. They sat with nominated members representing various interests and the administration, with the governor holding absolute veto power. Many of the elected members were from the small but growing black and coloured middle class, and while sometimes outspoken, they had little power and were, in many ways, invested in the status quo.

The governor's power was even more far-reaching during wartime. Analyses of the operations of the Colonial Office during wartime indicated that while there was tightened central control over activities in economic and some other fields, colonial governors also gained greater authority over decisions that did not immediately affect the war effort.[5] In Jamaica, Governor Arthur Richards particularly used the special wartime Defence Regulations for administrative, social and police convenience. Indeed, correspondence between the foreign and colonial offices regarding the internment of enemy aliens in Jamaica included a note that the governor's use of the regulations might be "an unnecessary departure from the normal British traditions of justice and administration".[6] In a memoir of Richards, Richard Peel said that the governor – asked to "proceed to Jamaica and restore order" after the death in office of Governor Edward Denham – instructed the colonial secretariat that there should be no more communication with London than was absolutely necessary as "I wanted a free hand". Peel also quoted Colonial Office (CO) Permanent Under-Secretary Sir Cosmo Parkinson in a letter to Richards which acknowledged that the governor would not tell the CO what he was proposing to do in Jamaica but asking that he at least tell them what he had actually done.[7] Peel said that the governor "was convinced that what Jamaica needed was strong but just government".[8]

Early political agitators on the island included men who had served abroad in World War I, many of whom experienced racism but were also exposed to wider conditions and ideologies. In *Caribbean Wars Untold*, Graham and Metzgen argued that this wartime experience included a sense of alienation and rejection by the empire's white establishment, a devaluation of their contribution and the imputation that any white man was more important than even the most able black man. These, they said, were "the Caribbean's real and lasting legacy from the First World War".[9] They argued that most who were returned to the region and demobilized there found themselves facing unacceptable levels of poverty and lack of opportunity. Similar frustrations were expressed by returned migrant workers, forced home by the worldwide economic depression of the early 1930s and, often, accompanying anti-alien and anti-migrant feelings.

These experiences, and local impacts of the global recession, contributed to the new consciousness, especially in the urban areas of Jamaica. Howard Johnson also tied the social and economic hardships to surging race and class consciousness throughout the British Caribbean, "as the working class increasingly recognised that economic status and race were inextricably linked".[10] The work of Marcus Garvey and his United Negro Improvement Association (UNIA) was a major factor in this consciousness which also sparked the emergence of Rastafarianism in Jamaica in the early 1930s. Garvey had formed Jamaica's first modern political organization, the People's Political Party in 1929, but it was the late 1930s and 1940s that really saw the burgeoning of local political and labour organization and disaffection over parlous economic and social conditions across the then British West Indies.

From 1935, academic W.M. MacMillan bemoaned conditions in the British West Indies, urging transformation of the "settler ideology" and a "considered policy of expenditure to make up for past neglect".[11] Alexander Grantham, who served as Colonial Secretary – head of the civil service – in Jamaica from 1938 to 1941 analysed the island's economy as having bogged down by the 1930s. He said that despite the development of the banana industry – itself challenged by blight – and some related tourism initiatives, the population had outstripped its means of support, especially given limited markets for sugar and bananas. "Britain now gave tariff and quota preferences up to a certain amount, but there were limits beyond which she could not go, whilst in world markets, Jamaica had difficulty in competing." With the economy in decline and unemployment rising, the senior colonial government official acknowledged that riots which broke out in Jamaica in 1938 were "the culmination of a series of crises".[12]

The riots in Jamaica were in keeping with labour and social unrest that swept through the British territories in the late 1930 – from British Guiana, through the eastern Caribbean islands and north to Jamaica. By 1938, Jamaicans experienced protests at the Frome Sugar Factory in the west of the island, followed by a dock strike in Kingston. Howard Johnson argued that they became "unprecedented in their scope and scale", with a heightened impact on public consciousness "because they occurred with disquieting regularity".[13] Governor Edward Denham requested a visit to the island by the British cruiser HMS *Ajax*, to provide a show of strength in the face of the labour troubles. However, within days, Denham died of a heart attack and was buried at sea by the crew of the same vessel.[14] On the heels of his death, the Colonial Office appointed Sir Arthur Richards, previously governor of Fiji, with Colonial Secretary Sir Charles Campbell Woolley acting as interim governor until Richards' arrival in August.

The British government also established a West India Royal Commission, chaired by Lord Moyne, to examine conditions underpinning the unrest. Hearings started in Jamaica in November 1938, continuing in 1939 until its work was disrupted by World War II. In February 1940, a report from London said that the commission had made searching criticisms of British administration in the West Indies and far-reaching proposals for reform. It said that concern over the use that enemy propagandists might make of the findings meant that the War Cabinet was giving serious consideration to postponing publication. Indeed, the British government declined to publish the full report until after the end of World War II – nearly five years after the inquiry was concluded. Nonetheless, the Colonial Secretary "strongly urged that cleaning up colonial administration cannot be delayed ... (and) that social reform and the development of industrial conciliation machinery must go on during the war".[15]

The commission distinguished between early "blind protest against a worsening of conditions" and the recent riots which, the commissioners affirmed, represented "a positive demand for the creation of new conditions that will render possible a better and less restricted life".[16] The British government therefore passed the Colonial Development & Welfare Act, in 1940, seeking to address a range of Moyne Commission recommendations, specifically concerns with land ownership and use, land settlement, the reorganization of agriculture for greater food production and social welfare. Under the act, the British government, during wartime, unusually allocated £5 million annually, mostly for programmes in the West Indies.

Uniquely for wartime, the government also acted on commission recommendations for constitutional change in Jamaica. These aimed to increase the low level of political representation for the majority of the population and drew in part on submissions relating to local governance that had been made by the newly formed People's National Party (PNP) and by the US-based Jamaica Progressive League (JPL). Debates relating to these recommendations would colour political activity in Jamaica throughout the war, and constitutional changes would come into effect in 1944.

Society

By 1943, Jamaica's population was somewhat over 1.2 million, just under 600,000 men, nearly 638,000 women, with 395,403 under 21 years. It was a population divided by overlapping distinctions based on colour and class, with impacts extending into the political and economic spheres. Fernando Henriques, writing in 1946, put the population at 78.1 per cent black, mostly labourers and peasants. While the coloured and black middle-class controlled government clerkships and elementary supervisory jobs and predominated in shopkeeping and teaching, the whites and fair-coloured people of the upper class monopolized executive positions, such occupations as planter and the professions.[17] He said that race-related factors – including colour, hair type, features and skin texture – and geographical location in town or country had a greater impact on social status than did economic status, even though the economic and prestige value of a person's employment was also important.

Henriques, a social anthropologist, also identified a "white bias" in the society, which continued to apply despite the race consciousness of Marcus Garvey and the UNIA earlier in the century, and some working-class activism in urban areas. Political Scientist Ken Post went further, arguing that many of these local movements that aimed at improving the condition of black people – from Bedward in the 1920s to Leonard Howell's Rastafari and Marcus Garvey's dreams of repatriation to Africa – actually diverted the attention of the lower classes from economic realities.[18] Most Jamaicans, across the classes, appear to have accepted the existing social structures just as they accepted most colonialist strictures. Henriques wrote that "government at the highest level, orthodox religion, education, are all associated with white superiority".[19] He added that efforts to revolt against the "white bias" were checked by constant reinforcement and that while there appeared to be a strong constraint about openly expressing colour feeling or consciousness, it nonetheless existed, especially in areas of private life. Within this context, the emergence of the Rastafarian community in the 1930s would have been disturbing to many. Witness *Gleaner* newspaper coverage of a Rastafarian man and woman who in April 1943 "Shocked Legislators" by standing in the gallery and demanding a Back-to-Africa programme. Evicted from the building, Egbert Charles Smith and Rustel E, Bennett, who gave their address as the "Dungle" or city dump, were nonetheless photographed for the newspaper. Bennett explained that they went to "have a talk with His Excellency the Governor concerning the deplorable conditions under which the black people are living in this country".[20]

Education remained limited for most of the population, and even those who could access secondary education had few career options. Colour impacted access to jobs in retail establishments and offices, even for years to come. The heights of the civil service were reserved for British officials posted overseas, with lower managerial and supervisory levels often the purview of light-skinned Jamaicans. In his autobiography, Jamaican Royal Air Force (RAF) airman, Pan-Africanist lawyer and later government minister Dudley Thompson commented on the social barriers of race prejudice, especially in the capital city:

> White Englishmen held most of the senior posts and often did not equal the ability of black Jamaicans placed under them. In fact, the colonial system provided a convenient dumping ground for many second-rate officials who were not quite suitable for the home service. There were, of course, exceptions to the rule. At the time, I, like most Jamaicans, accepted this situation as normal, that the best jobs were reserved for Englishmen. Our resentment to this was, at the most, muted and not widespread. Colonial compliance was the order of the day.[21]

The governor and all colonial officials and heads of department were, unquestioningly, British, white and male. Attention was called to exceptions: When coloured Jamaican Ernest Rae was appointed as the new acting head of the evacuee camp in March 1941, succeeding Englishman J.L. Worlledge who had also been Jamaica's auditor general, the newspaper story specifically mentioned that the decision was on the recommendation of Worlledge "who has always adopted a policy of giving Jamaicans their chances".[22] Rae had been deputy to two white Englishmen between the start of the camp in October 1940 and his acting appointment in March 1941.

The racism intrinsic to colonial systems was largely unchallenged by British officials, though the editors of *British Documents on the End of Empire* said that some "found distasteful, the extent to which colour prejudice existed in the colonies and they admitted that the Colonial Office had not done more, 'by precept and example', to combat it".[23] MacMillan's *Warning from the West Indies* also mentioned the preoccupation with colour wherever European imperial interests were present. And Kenneth Blackburne, the island's last British governor, in a memoir noted significant prejudice across the region.[24] Race was a frequent subtext in Jamaica in the early 1940s, with media coverage of various incidents as well as related speculation even among elected members of the legislature – despite this being distasteful to president of the Legislative Council and Governor Arthur Richards. Incidents raised with the governor by the Colonial Office, in 1942, included the segregation of coloured RAF candidates from their white compatriots, aboard a US transport *en route* to the United Kingdom.[25] In Jamaica, racially tinged clashes between American soldiers and contractors, and local police as well as civilians, included incidents at the popular and traditional upper-class Bournemouth Bath in Kingston. These incidents overlapped with efforts by the Kingston & St Andrew Corporation (KSAC) to democratize and diversify the facility while retaining an air of respectability. In January 1942, following a "major disturbance" in which bottles, sticks and other missiles were thrown between "uniformed men and civvies", the KSAC promised new regulations which, the *Gleaner* observed, might "serve to remove any prejudices that may have existed in the past in the minds of social top-notchers". The facility was also placed out of bounds to Americans linked to the bases. The Americans opened a United Service Organizations (USO) Canteen on Old Hope Road in Kingston to cater to the American troops and their friends. In December 1943, an advertisement from the USO in Jamaica invited interested white men and women to apply for jobs as soda fountain clerks, office help, store managers, typist-stenographers, senior clerks and store clerks. It caused an angry response from the KSAC which passed a resolution expressing resentment and public dissatisfaction, for dispatch to the secretary of state for the colonies and the American president. Expressing vexation that the KSAC had escalated attention to the incident, the US Base Commander in Jamaica Col John Dallin said that the action of the official involved was unauthorized and against the policy of the Jamaica Base Command, the USO or the US government and that it gave Jamaica an "erroneous impression of American policy". He apologized and declared the matter closed.[26]

During this period, articles in the media increasingly called attention to racial discrimination in other aspects of life, hand in hand with a push towards greater local involvement in government and the economy. When PNP propaganda secretary Samuel Marquis was detained under the Defence Regulations, the party noted that he had been highlighting the colour line in the Jamaican constabulary – as reflected in a page one headline in the *Public Opinion* newspaper: "Social and Colour Barriers Operate Against Maximum Efficiency of Constabulary".[27] The editorial from the same edition of the newspaper carried the headline "Can Such Things Be?" over a story highlighting racial discrimination inside Up Park Camp and efforts to entertain white enemy aliens. From mid-1941, *The Gleaner* had carried reports that questioned efforts to provide outings for interned women and children, held in close quarters on Hanover Street in Downtown Kingston – referencing race discrimination practised by the German regime.[28] *Spotlight* newsmagazine, in a review of 1943, included the item that Phillip Rose and Samuel Bailey had become the first "native Negroes" to be appointed police sub-inspectors, adding pointedly: "all whites moved up and out of the 'sub' class".[29]

Richards was certainly disturbed by such reports, representative of rising race consciousness, increasingly expressed in public fora during the early 1940s, though W.A. Domingo overstated for effect when he described racial segregation as "Sir Arthur Richards's Legacy to Jamaica".[30] Domingo, a political activist and *Public Opinion* columnist, had just spent nearly two years interned at Up Park Camp at the governor's behest, having been detained as he landed in Jamaica to assist the PNP.

The governor's distress at the foregrounding of concerns over racially rooted discrimination was communicated to the Colonial Office in London from as early as 1940–1941 when he wrote to the secretary of state for the colonies that there was fundamental disloyalty in urban Jamaica and growth in racial feeling, which he linked with the demand for constitutional reform.[31] This concern would become more urgent in letters of 1942 and 1943 when he wrote about "a skein of racial hatred . . . skilfully woven into the pattern of the incompetent Englishmen in selfish and autocratic control for his own good and the people's detriment".[32] Greater acknowledgement of the "racial barriers and colour prejudice in Jamaica" would be publicly expressed by Lady Molly Huggins, the flambouyant wife of Richards' successor Sir John Huggins who said that they were anxious that this should be brought to an end, according to Lady Huggins' published memoir, *Too Much to Tell*.[33] She recalled a revolutionary decision to invite "leading coloured citizens" to an evening cocktail party hosted during a visit by Eleanor Roosevelt; unusual because, "in the past, most of the coloured community were asked only once a year to the large King's House Birthday Garden Party".[34]

Concurrent with his nervousness about racial consciousness in Jamaica, Governor Richards also consistently telegraphed traditional class awareness, querying the class status of the various groups being considered or accepted for refuge or detention, within camp accommodation. It was a consciousness which permeated the colonial society and was widely accepted. As Petrine Archer-Straw found in a thesis on the development of cultural nationalism in Jamaica, the middle class of the period shared upper-class cultural aspirations and white-oriented educational values – upholding the concept of empire and being willing to work within the colonial system.[35] This was, after all, the route to success. Indeed, many criticisms of the system were not meant to overthrow it, but to make it more workable for a wider group of people. It could be argued that a gradualist agenda was the preference of leading local activists, including some elected members as well as politicians and labour leaders like Norman Manley and Alexander Bustamante, and that they were sometimes thrust along by outpourings of working-class energy spilling into labour and political action on the streets.

While several elected members of the Legislative Council were coloured or black, they were also from a local elite – inevitably, given the financial and property requirements that persons standing for election had to meet. The line between representation and class politics was a fine one for members to walk, and there was not necessarily a common approach – even regarding the policies and approaches of the colonial government. Indeed, criticism of the government did not equate with wanting to change it. During the 1941 legislative season, several elected members criticized government's approach to decision-making on Gibraltar Camp the previous year, among a raft of other issues. Elected member J.A.G. Smith expressed amazement "that any island could have been treated in the way that Jamaica has been treated in regard to this camp". This was Gibraltar Camp, which had recently received two groups of evacuees, totalling more than one thousand five hundred persons. He argued:

> Now sir, you bring people coming from Gibraltar to this colony. We only hear that it is the Imperial Government sending them: only hearsay, what we hear on the streets. We didn't know anything whatever about it, don't know the financial arrangements; nothing whatever is told to the country through the elected members or otherwise through some elected source, and yet even if the Imperial Government eventually finds the money, we have to vote money by way of advances, so it touches directly expenditure of the money of this colony . . . Now, is that right? . . . it is not justifiable, the acts that took place in bringing people though under government supervision and care and protection, as a question for the Governor of the colony and officials only. It cannot be right.

Elected members also raised concerns that race was a factor in decision-making related to the internment camps. Regarding the Women's Internment Camp, there was concern that a brown-skinned Jamaican Matron, in charge of the camp when it was opened in June 1940, had been replaced by a white Englishwoman ahead of the arrival of German and Italian internees brought from West Africa in December 1940. Three members spoke on this matter, questioning whether it constituted racial discrimination within the government service, which was considered especially unacceptable in the broad context of Nazi racism. A fourth member extended the concern to the guarding of the internees, wondering whether a recent decision to replace local forces with Canadian soldiers at the Male Internment Camp, was also a matter of discrimination.[36]

However, when barrister and elected member for Clarendon, J.A.G. Smith, sought to censure the government over several issues, including the lack of consultation on Gibraltar Camp, he could not generate any significant support among his fellow elected members.[37] *Gleaner* columnist G. St C. Scotter suggested that this was partly due to the government's overall record of achievement. But Scotter also agreed with Smith that in its manner of operation,

> The Government, as a whole is too dictatorial and too secretive and does not give the public directly or through its Elected representatives, the information and opportunities for expression of opinion that any free citizenry has a right to expect.[38]

Scotter, an English ex-policeman working in Jamaica, argued that this was true of the government as a whole but that the negative effects were exaggerated by one or two individuals whose manner of dealing with the public was "rude and overbearing". While not naming Governor Sir Arthur Richards, Scotter made it plain that he was one of these persons by excluding him from a short list of top government officials who had a positive approach. The journalist would later be one of those locals interned by Richards under the Jamaica Defence Regulations.

The insertion of large concentrations of white persons into the small society inevitably helped draw attention to the racial and overlapping class considerations that were generally taken for granted by the existing socio-cultural ecosystem. It can be argued that this potential increased when some of these incomers were of the same class as the majority population, and both might acknowledge class commonalities that were not usual between different races in Jamaica. Indeed, efforts to buffer free incomers from the local society may have aimed to pre-empt this potential challenge. Governor Richards' queries relating to the various displaced groups, free or interned, being assigned or considered for accommodation in Jamaica regularly included "all possible information as to social class, etc".[39] When asked, in 1941, to consider taking British subjects marooned in Portugal, he offered information about classes of accommodation available, including the possibility of camp accommodation for those not able to afford hotels – adding that he did not favour this, nor putting them in Gibraltar Camp, but wanted "further particulars regarding this group e.g. are they European professional or labouring class".[40] In the case of persons who were neither British by birth nor British subjects, camps were the only option offered, with free incomers subject to accommodation and employment restrictions. This may have been an effort to subvert inadvertent social and cultural missteps by white refugees and former internees who had neither familiarity nor commitment to the existing British colonial norms.

The impact of undermining the local association of white with higher social status was underlined by RAF airman Dudley Thompson, when he recalled his experiences in England during the war. While struck by racial discrimination against black colonials fighting for the Allied cause, he was even more astounded by the sight of poor white Englishmen carrying coal on their backs. He wrote that the sight:

> totally destroyed the myth of the white superman of the colonies. The class system, both at home and in England, revealed itself dramatically before my eyes. . . Wartime in England was a great university to the uninitiated colonial.[41]

Hence, aside from the possibility of creating opportunities for local working-class confraternity with white working-class incomers, there may have been a concern that the presence of large groups of white persons in detention or with limited resources could pose a visual and conceptual challenge to the hegemonic position of the local whites as a mainly upper-class elite. This type of anxiety was not limited to Jamaica. In 1939, a Trinidadian Jew expressed concern about European immigrants "going on the roads of the Colony as peddlers and doing work that hitherto has been done by the coloured people". He was determined that the "prestigue [sic] of the white race should be maintained" and that the government should act to this end.[42] A telling comment from the United Kingdom in 1943, when consideration was being given to the release of Italian internees after the Armistice, acknowledged the "difficulty of employing white persons in labour gangs" in the colonies.[43] And the Swiss Consul in Jamaica would similarly recognize that white persons were not normally employed in agricultural labour.

Gender joined race and class considerations with regard to the management of Gibraltar Camp, which was designed and initially run solely as a haven for fellow British colonials of European and Mediterranean descent – a majority of them female, working class and Roman Catholic. The civilian evacuation of Gibraltar had privileged elders and children as well as women, including the parents, wives and children of working-age men who remained in Gibraltar when the first groups of evacuees left.[44] Concern over the vulnerability of this population in Jamaica, especially in the absence of its traditional male decision-making supports, would have been deepened by the potential of relationships developing with Jamaican men, especially black and coloured men. This mix of concerns was made clear in September 1942, when there was strong resistance to a British War Office proposal that a distant section of Gibraltar Camp be repurposed for a "battalion of local (coloured) militia", which was being embodied for full-time service. Governor Arthur Richards objected that Gibraltar Camp contained a:

> large proportion of adolescent girls and quartering of coloured troops in such close proximity is likely to give rise to considerable reactions in Gibraltar. Military proposal to build unclimbable fence and to make relations with other camp military offence does not seem to meet situation. Gibraltar women and girls would inevitably be using same roads of approach.

He said that the Father Superior of Jamaica's Catholic Church, which had oversight of the social aspects of the camp, was also apprehensive.[45] The governor of Gibraltar agreed and was explicit in his strong objection to "the suggested proximity of coloured troops to my refugees. Effect on morale here would almost certainly be deplorable".[46] In canvassing opinion, the Colonial Office also spoke with colonial administrator Mr Worlledge, who had charge of Gibraltar Camp for a brief time before relocating to the United Kingdom, and who "felt that the possibility of serious incidents could not be ruled out". The Colonial Office refused the military request; however, its refusal reflected concern over possible external perceptions that there was racist thinking within the imperial service: The Colonial Office official said he had been asked to make it clear that

> though the Governor refers in his telegram to the proximity of coloured troops to Gibraltar evacuees our objection to the proposal is not, in any way, based on the ground that the troops are coloured. We should feel bound to take the same line if white troops were involved, and if they were recruits without any training or discipline, as we understand the Jamaica troops will be.[47]

Instead, £50,000 was approved to build an alternative camp for the local troops, though this does not appear to have been followed through.[48] And seven months later, a proposal to repurpose the northern section of the camp for interned German and Italian families was pushed through despite some objections from the camp administration.[49] Beyond such flurries, there was a consistent effort to protect the camp population through restricting entry of Jamaicans to the camp, dissuading contact, physical barriers and the full-time Catholic social administration in place within the camp from the start, at the request of the Gibraltarian governor.

In several instances, then, the various wartime camps became actual touchstones for the airing of these issues of race, class, gender and even broader issues of respect for the views and desires of the colonized – even those at the highest representative levels.

The official church in Jamaica from the early years of British colonial authority had been the Anglican Church, which continued to have primacy despite its separation from the ruling authority in 1870. The Catholic Church was even older, originally introduced under Spanish rule in the late fifteenth and early sixteenth centuries. By the early twentieth century, the Catholic Church in Jamaica was anti-communist and conservative and catered mainly to the merchant class. Official church perception was that it "occupied, at best, an inferior place in civic and social life" secondary to the Anglican Church, reinforcing "a caste mentality in the colonials".[50] Like the Anglican diocese, the Catholics established several prominent secondary schools, especially in Kingston. Many other churches were represented across the island, with the Baptist, Methodist and other "dissenter" denominations that gained traction during the late eighteenth and early nineteenth centuries playing an especially significant role for the black majority.

The small Jewish community in Jamaica was of long-standing, with a community of some one thousand three hundred persons in 1943, more than half of them in Kingston.[51] Uniquely, the Jamaican Jews developed a United Congregation which pulled together members of former Ashkenazi and Sephardic congregations after those synagogues were destroyed in a city fire of 1882. Unlike the Catholics, who were officially requested to be involved in Gibraltar Camp, the local Jews had no official position with either the Jewish Gibraltarians or the Jewish refugees who arrived later. However, the camp administration did arrange for the Gibraltarians to visit and worship at the synagogue in Kingston, and a report noted that the local rabbi visited them periodically.[52] While the first Jewish refugees did not develop a relationship with the local rabbi, arguably over issues of orthodoxy, various camp residents attended the local synagogue. An Ashkenazi synagogue was improvised in the refugee section of the camp, and some local Jewish businessmen also played a significant role in facilitating the refugees.

Nationalist Agitation

Richard Hart, a former political detainee, communist trade union activist, lawyer and historian, identified the following aspects of 1930s Jamaica as giving rise to working-class rebelliousness and nationalistic aspirations:

> The low level of wages; the subservient attitude of a majority of the workers; the restrictions on trade union activities; the poverty and distress of the peasantry; the widespread acceptance of the concept of white superiority and black inferiority; the intention of British imperialism to perpetuate this state of affairs.[53]

Except for a tiny though active communist group, and Rastafarians still angered by British betrayal of Abyssinia in 1935, Jamaicans remained essentially pro-Britain and pro-Empire. The sentiment was expressed verbally and through the media, as well as through common acts as simple as displaying images of the royal family in many rural homes.[54] The colonial system was as old as the native population, the indigenous population having been decimated prior to the British arrival, and the British had been in charge, with their language, laws and culture, for more than two centuries. Most people, including the mainly middle-class activists who were seeking greater political and economic independence, favoured retaining British parliamentary and legal systems. Howard Johnson noted that "the emergence of incipient national consciousness in Jamaica and other West Indian territories" had not been accompanied by "the intense nationalism and anti-colonialism which marked the African and Asian colonies". He argued that the efforts of the West Indian colonies were towards the modification of Crown Colony regimes and eventual self-government within the British Commonwealth, which did not conflict with the protection of British economic interests in the region, and that the British government therefore regarded this colonial nationalism as "non-threatening and compatible with metropolitan interests".[55]

Nonetheless, arriving in Jamaica in August 1938, two months after the death in office of Governor Edward Denham, Governor Arthur Richards was disconcerted at the political – even more so than the labour – activism in Jamaica. With war already threatening, he may have been anxious to lower the temperature of debate and action on the island, but his authoritarian approach won few friends. He quickly came to verbal blows with the various sectors of Jamaican society that were pushing for a share of power – whether legislative, political or economic – especially the small group of communist and socialist activists whose views he actively despised. Within a few months of his arrival, in February 1939, Richards tartly assessed the extent of activism in Jamaica as being:

> largely of the half-educated middle classes – clerks, teachers, small traders and so forth – professional politicians, labourers who have been to Cuba, Panama and America, professional agitators with a foreign training and a sprinkling of educated idealists, fanatics and men with a colour complex.[56]

When war was declared, the governor welcomed the outpouring of loyal sentiment, acknowledging a "wave of loyalty which passed over the country and the way in which all domestic differences were set aside in order to face the calamity of war with united faith".[57] The local political organizations pledged to suspend their activism – specifically the push for constitutional change – until the return of peace. However, the lull did not last. The governor enforced stringent Defence Regulations under which general elections, due in 1940 were postponed until after the war, citing the "virtual impossibility" of combining "the political strife and agitation, inseparable from elections, with an unqualified support of Government in its efforts to meet war emergencies".[58] He discouraged the desire, by local activists, for a greater part in governance and sought to damp down any political activity. The governor simultaneously and over a long period urged patience on the many eager to volunteer – an eagerness variously stemming from a loyal desire to fight or from a desire for greater opportunity in a time of increasing scarcity and price inflation. While he did not acknowledge it, Governor Richards was certainly aware that recruiting of Blacks was still subject to unofficial discouragement in the United Kingdom – a reality that would come to inform local rhetoric and attitudes. His own rhetoric disparaged local agendas as disloyal – further feeding a downward spiral in his relationship with the political intelligentsia and their followers. In this limbo, political activism re-emerged and with it, the inevitability of friction. Governor Richards deplored criticism of the colonial government, arguing that it undermined respect for authority and spread distrust, and rejected criticisms of the constitution, suggesting that its inefficiencies were mainly due to the length of debates. He rejected demands for greater self-government until the "capacity was informed by the desire".[59] And he was deeply uncomfortable with any criticism to the status quo rooted in class or race. The governor was also publicly dismissive of locally generated proposals for political and financial change. In December 1940, while recognizing that political aspirants should have opportunities to learn, he declined to hand over "the lives and welfare of Jamaicans", without adequate safeguards "to the prentice hands of every platform politician and every fireside financier who confuses the aspirations of the people with a personal craving for power". The PNP executive read this speech as "a slap in the face for every intelligent group of people in Jamaica . . . which has taken an interest in the welfare of the country and for every individual who has dared to speak a word for the country's future". And *Public Opinion*, a PNP voice, commented that the government did not provide the tactful, sympathetic leadership that Jamaica needed for unity, indeed, that the government did not wish disunity to end.[60]

In 1941, the governor publicly dashed cold water on PNP proposals for constitutional change, stating in the Legislative Council that "self-government by Dominion Status is so distant a goal and so impracticable in present circumstances as to remain little more than a pious aspiration for a far-distant future".[61]

Internment of political and labour activists during 1941 and 1942 raised concerns for civil liberties, which extended across many strata of Jamaican society and beyond, to the United States and the United Kingdom. At the same time, Jamaicans continued to be excluded from active personal involvement in the distant war and consequently developed a sense of distance, as several interviewees averred. In February 1942, in the Legislative Council, the governor deplored the "growing tendency of certain groups to attribute all ills, even the inevitable hardships attendant upon life on earth during a World War, to the present Government of Jamaica". He said that the incessant discrediting of authority was sowing the wind to reap the whirlwind and charged critics with trading in the unhappiness of the people.[62] In October 1942, *Public Opinion* headlined a report of an interview which the governor did with the American news service United Press (UP): "Plain Facts Give Lie to Governor's Claims in Fireside Interview". The governor was reported to have been positive about the situation in Jamaica despite issues relating to unemployment and to have said that Jamaicans neither wished for self-government nor thought themselves capable of coping with the problems of the times.[63] Indeed, *Public Opinion* had consistently challenged the governor and his "small circle of bureaucrats who have shut themselves off from the public mind and agitation" and whose concern appeared to be "to stifle legitimate criticism and foster internal dissension".[64]

Specifically, Governor Richards appeared to sow division between major local political and labour actors, especially cousins and early collaborators Norman Manley, president of the PNP, and Alexander Bustamante, leader of the Bustamante Industrial Trade Union (BITU) – and later also of the Jamaica Labour Party. Bustamante was detained in 1940 under local Defence Regulations for seditious speech and spent some seventeen months in internment. On his release, the labour leader was bitingly critical of his former ally while reports suggested a rapprochement with the governor; another report quoted Manley charging that Bustamante had been enticed to denounce the PNP as a condition of release from detention.⁶⁵ An intelligence report quoting Colonel Stratton of MI5 seemed to offer some support for the idea of deliberate manipulation:

> Sir Arthur Richards' recent release of Bustamante from internment had been based on the hope that Bustamante's rivalry with Mr Manley would divide the forces of opposition. Bustamante and Manley were certainly at logger heads at present but there was always the risk of a combination between the two which would add the full strength of the Trades Unions to the Peoples National Party.⁶⁶

Though Richards later denied that this had been his intention, his memoirist referred to the governor's use of *divide et impera*, while in Jamaica.⁶⁷ While he targeted political activists and media owners for most of his salvos, the governor was also critical of the population at large. In a private letter to the Colonial Office in 1942, he referred to Jamaicans as "very ignorant and emotional people", "of an envious, jealous and spiteful nature", that "always listened with avidity to abuse of Government".⁶⁸

Even in the middle of the war, concerns about labour unrest, political activism and civil liberties in Jamaica were the subject of questions in Parliament, newspaper articles and lectures or discussions at Fabian and other societies – especially after the detention of political activists under the island's Defence Regulations. As the war progressed and hardship increased – rooted in high unemployment, high prices and food shortages – the governor became seriously alarmed over the possibility of disturbances. This alarm was reflected in speeches and in accusations and actions under the wartime Defence Regulations and communicated to the Colonial Office, especially in a series of handwritten letters in 1942. He noted that the causes of the hardship being experienced were "not properly understood by those affected" and charged that the time was ripe for agitators to make trouble based on recent political agitation which had "created the belief that all troubles due to local Government and British administration".⁶⁹ Measures to alleviate the situation included relief work, augmentation of the police force to meet any disturbances and a parade of the armed forces in Kingston to provide a "much needed emotional outlet" as well as a warning to "subversive elements".⁷⁰

Some Colonial Office officials clearly had reservations regarding the basis of these complaints about the Jamaican population. A minuted note on the governor's letter suggested:

> that considerable responsibility rests with the local Government for having failed to emphasise sufficiently the potential dangers of the situation, thereby failing to get an active popular interest in the remedial measures which are possible

and at the same time giving an opportunity to the opponents of the Government to make profitable capital out of the situation when it reached a stage when it was impossible to conceal the seriousness. I was given to understand that the policy pursued has been influenced, if not dictated, by the attitude of the security authorities who feared the effect on morale of publishing the dangers to West Indian supplies. This attitude has not of course been confined to Jamaica . . . The general attitude of all the West Indian Governments seems to be too much influenced by the desire to comfort people by telling them that everything will be all right.[71]

The year 1942 also saw an active discussion between London and Kingston, on constitutional change for Jamaica, following up on recommendations of the Moyne Commission report. Proposals went through several stages during the period of the war. Issues included whether to grant universal adult suffrage; whether to have a bicameral or a unicameral chamber; the appropriate membership of the country's executive council; how to allocate numbers of nominated, elected and ex-officio members; as well as the powers of the governor. Lord Moyne, author of the Royal Commission report and secretary of state for the colonies from February 1941 to February 1942, sought to keep elected members in one chamber with nominated and ex-officio members, arguing that this would support tutelage – a position roundly rejected by local activists. In February 1942, the local Federation of Citizens' Associations criticized efforts to force Lord Moyne's proposals on the local Legislature, especially in context of the August 1941 Atlantic Charter, whereby Britain and America set out their post-war global perspective, including an affirmation of the right of peoples to choose their preferred form of government. In a newspaper article which also criticized the role of the governor, the Federation charged:

> Opinion in the country is of vastly less importance than the thoughts of officials without. Our political aspirations are not to be encouraged, nor the rate of progress fixed in discussion with the Secretary of State acting as umpire for the political organisations in the Colony; but it is always to be decided by that official regardless of the judgement of our own representatives, because, according to the Governor, "Democracy is dangerous", – too dangerous for Jamaicans.[72]

The Federation rejected the notion that the average elected member needed association with ex-officio and nominated members, to qualify him for "higher responsibilities". It said that just as Britain had advanced without this tutelage, "so can Jamaica or any other country where the seed of Democracy is allowed to take root and its growth is encouraged and aided".[73]

Though British prime minister Winston Churchill would, in November 1942, dismiss any interpretation of the Atlantic Charter that might presage the liquidation of the British Empire, the British government would approve a new, 1944 constitution for Jamaica – the major constitutional advance recorded in the British Empire during the war. Uniquely for a colonial constitution of that time, especially a largely black country, the new constitution featured universal adult suffrage, a lower chamber containing only elected members – the House of Representatives with thirty-two elected members, up from fourteen – and a new Legislative Council of fifteen members nominated by the governing administration. There was a requirement that all bills must be passed by both Houses and an Executive Council including five members selected from the lower chamber and five nominated members. However, the governor retained both a casting vote and veto power though he could exercise his reserve powers only with the consent of the Executive Council.[74]

W. Adolphe Roberts, president of the JPL, ascribed the Jamaican developments to three factors: a "determined fight for self-government, well timed and well led . . . by Jamaicans since 1936"; Downing Street's readiness "to alter a hitherto immutable policy and try universal suffrage in a colony with a preponderantly Negro population"; and vitally, "a drift toward autonomy for West Indian colonies, growing out of the joint policy of Britain and the United States as allies today".[75] Roberts considered the 1944 constitution "a considerable advance beyond what we have now", though he found the governor's retention of an absolute veto "objectionable". He argued that provision should have been made for the over-riding of the veto, if a two-thirds or three-quarters majority to that end could be obtained in the Legislature. Nonetheless, he noted that the new constitution would be reviewed after five years and hoped to see liberalization of the veto power at that time.[76] Roberts added that the fifty-fifty composition of the executive committee represented a small step towards dominion status. "It is not pointed towards independence – no!" he said in answer to a query, "for dominion status is the highest type of self-government you can get and still stay in the British Empire".[77]

Dominion status may have been the desire of Jamaican activists at that time, melding the desire for greater self-assertion with a generally pro-mother country attitude. However, there is no indication that colonial or imperial officials seriously considered offering it.

Richard Hart, like Roberts, an active participant in the struggle for constitutional change, underlined the important part played by the US push for a trusteeship and decolonization agenda. Hart said that there was, in general, a different response to colonial demands by Britain's Foreign Office than the Colonial Office which hoped to resist constitutional concessions. However, veteran colonial administrator Sir William Battershill urged the secretary of state for the colonies to proceed vigorously towards a new constitution, thus proclaiming British good faith to the world and avoiding "perpetual references to Jamaica in both Houses of Parliament" which were "disturbing to good government in that Island". He argued that Britain would "at least appear to give some constitutional advance willingly instead of having it dragged out of us".[78]

Defence Regulations and Implications for Freedoms within the Colonial Frame

Wartime Defence Regulations affected Jamaican society in a range of ways throughout World War II, and their stringent application – so far from the main conflict and in a situation where the population was generally encouraged to feel that the war was far away – was severely criticized. Governor Richards asked for and was granted emergency powers, through the Public Security (War Emergency) Law 1939, as early as 2 August, a month before the outbreak of war. This was replaced by the Emergency Powers (Defence) Act, which was passed in London on 25 August and applied to the colonies by Order in Council. This was when the local forces were mobilized – the Jamaica Infantry Volunteers to Up Park Camp, the Jamaica Engineer Corps and Jamaica Militia Artillery to forts – and the British garrison, then the 2nd Battalion of Kings Shropshire Light Infantry, was put in defence position.[79] The 25 August defence act, which would be amended in England to remove areas of concern, remained the foundation for the Jamaica Defence Regulations – regulations in some regards thereby stricter than those in the United Kingdom itself and one of the wartime developments considered uniquely Richards's legacy. Gordon Lewis, in *The Growth of the Modern West Indies*, argued that the colonial power "in the shape of Sir Arthur Richards' administration, became more authoritarian than ever under the pressures of the war". He noted that after 1940, this administration would be characterized by wholesale internment, repressive censorship legislation and use of the law of seditious libel to silence his loudest critics.[80] It is arguable that this authoritarianism really peaked in 1942 and 1943, with the reality of Germany's successful Caribbean submarine campaign at sea and harsh economic realities hitting a fractious population which the local administration kept significantly uninformed and unengaged.

The Defence Regulations governed the economy, including the supply of goods and their prices, covering the appointment of a Banana Board; Imports & Exports and Prices (Foodstuffs) Board; Imports and Exports and Prices (Hardware, materials, fuel, etc.) Board; Food Production Board; Currency (Finance & Exchange) Board; and Food Controller. It oversaw security including naval control measures, harbour regulations, the institution of censorship, the internment of alien enemies, the registration of neutral foreigners, the institution of coast guards, special customs arrangements, arrangements for the guarding of vital points, call up of local forces, creation of a register of reserve officers and submission of names of suitable applicants for commissions in the British Army to the War Office.[81] An order restricting the importation and sale of "seditious literature", including any works related to socialism and communism, found support from *Catholic Opinion*, the monthly voice of the conservative Catholic Church, which argued that this prohibition rightfully removed a danger from the "ill-instructed and half-educated".[82] The Defence Regulations would also be applied to the dampening of opposition or potential opposition through regulation of gatherings and marches or other processions, as well as through detention without trial or much by way of explanation. The governor used detention orders to silence and deactivate several labour and political activists between 1940 and 1943, beginning with labour leader Alexander Bustamante in September 1940. Others were PNP propaganda secretary Samuel Marquis who was interned in March 1941, as was longshoreman and vice president of the Maritime arm of the BITU, Wilfred A. Williams, English journalist G. St.C. Scotter who wrote for the *Gleaner* newspaper and who was interned in May 1941, political activist W.A. Domingo who was detained on arrival in Jamaica from the United States in June 1941, as well as left-wing activists Richard Hart, Arthur Henry, Ken Hill and Frank Hill. In later work on the period, Richard Hart wrote that after Marquis's detention, the party executive only received a general allegation that he had made speeches that contained matter considered prejudicial to the war effort – which, party leaders concluded, referred to Marquis pointing out that all rank and file police were black and all officers were of white or very light complexion.[83] This issue – the lack of specific charges which could form the basis of a defence and of a robust defence procedure – was a sore point for many and applied not just to the detainees but also to those of enemy origin who had been interned.

The year 1941 saw a verbal and written debate on the impact that Jamaica's Defence Regulations were having on civil rights. Indeed, the use of Defence Regulations to put a lid on trade union and political activism and any race-related narrative in the West Indies was already on the agenda of a conference on Civil Liberties in the Colonial Empire, held in London in February 1941. One resolution drew public attention:

> to the basic fact that the essential and fundamental ideas of law, justice and administration which are generally regarded as inherent in the British tradition and are therefore popularly assumed to apply to all peoples under the British flag, do not in fact apply to the colonial subjects of the British Empire.[84]

Commentary and letters to the editors of the local media houses carried the debate, with the *Gleaner*'s coverage of the topic appearing to increase after Scotter, one of its columnists, was interned in May 1941. That month saw the formalization of a Jamaica Council for Civil Liberties, which "held a number of enthusiastic public meetings of protest and conducted a campaign in Jamaica and England" – efforts reportedly involving "pressure of general public opinion of all classes" and taking place "despite opposition and even abuse from some surprising quarters including high government officials and some Elected Members".[85] A major point of issue between local liberals and the colonial government related to the difference between the regulations in force in Jamaica and those in England, as they related to the power to detain suspected persons. These distinctions were underlined by *Gleaner* director and wealthy local solicitor Leslie Ashenheim in a newspaper article which noted that safeguards contained in equivalent British legislation were omitted from the local regulations. He pointed to two major differences in the colony compared with the imperial centre: one relating to the requirement for reporting actions under the regulations; the other to the powers and duties of the advisory boards and appeal tribunals – including a requirement that detainees know what was alleged against them.[86] Indeed, a June 1941 editorial, in *Public Opinion*, charged that the local Defence Regulations allowed persons to be interned if two or three persons made a charge against them, and it was hard to establish evidence to the contrary, making people disinclined to discuss the war.[87] A key aim of the council was to have the government recognize the principle:

> that the detention power was not a convenient substitute for ordinary criminal prosecution and was only to be utilised when there was a genuine and compelling reason why the matters complained of could not be brought before the courts of law – in other words in cases where ordinary prosecutions would give away information of value to the enemy or would hamper the government in the investigation and suppression of espionage or sabotage or similar action on the enemy's part or in the enemy's interest.[88]

Legislative Council minutes for June 1941 recorded that Elected Member J.A.G. Smith was defeated when he sought the replacement of the Jamaica Detention Order Regulation with the corresponding English regulation, noting serious differences which prejudiced the rights of British subjects in Jamaica and arguing that "widespread fear and unrest have arisen as to the consequences following the said . . . Regulation . . . and the inadequate provision provided in favour of civil liberty".[89] This fear was reflected at the popular level in a poem by Louise Bennett, who wrote that under the governorship of Arthur Richards, if a poor man made a mistake, he would be sent to jail. "Me did bex wid him bout dat fe true", she wrote in Jamaican patois, "for talking not noh crime". (English translation: I was really vexed with him over that, for talking is not a crime.)[90]

The debate hit a new high after the June 1941 detention of activist W.A. Domingo on his arrival in Jamaica to work with the PNP. The JPL of New York, which had supported Domingo's trip, launched a protest campaign that included a strongly worded cable to Lord Moyne, then secretary of state for the colonies, "declaring in effect that Great Britain cannot be fighting Hitlerism in Europe and at the same time support it in Jamaica".[91]

In mid-July, the *Gleaner* newspaper published a letter from poet and writer Roger Mais, who ironically would later be prosecuted and imprisoned under the Defence Regulations.[92] Mais responded to a previous letter by civil engineer Braham T Judah, who had argued that local regulations needed to be stronger than those in force in England, "because conditions, politically, economically, socially and morally are vastly different in Jamaica to those in England".[93] Mais responded:

> the obvious implication [is] that it is justifiable for Government to extend the scope of these Regulations (that have to do with the defence of the realm solely) to "take care" of those who might oppose Government's policy as it relates to matters political, economical, social and moral.[94]

Weighing in a week later, local solicitor Ansell Hart expressed apprehension at "the undue exercise of power and authority" which he saw in the recent history of the government of Jamaica and which he perceived in the exercise of the Defence Regulations without reference to pre-existing regulations. Hart said that the government in Jamaica had "taken powers which have not been taken by the Government in England, and that provisions which were regarded as obnoxious by the British Parliament are in force in Jamaica." He contended that the local colonial government did not explain, defend or palliate, and in the face of criticism or question, "the official batteries are turned on the opponents who are charged under a now established formula with disloyalty, treachery and personal motives". He charged that no other government had "done so much to denigrate Jamaican effort and Jamaican independence of thought as this Government has done".[95] Ironically, Hart's son Richard, who espoused communist views, would soon be among the political detainees.

A response titled "Criticism of Mr Hart's Recent Letter" admitted that there were abuses under the Defence Regulations but argued that more drastic regulations were necessary for Jamaica than in England, because of "the rotten reputation which Jamaica has acquired in the Empire in consequence of recent happenings here". The writer especially blamed labour disputes which disorganized work in the ports and sugar estates, suggesting that such mass action was disloyal. He argued that "if the Imperial Government thought the regulations were oppressive or too drastic, it would have ordered a change long ago". Reflecting conventional upper-class opinion, the letter suggested that public sentiments such as those expressed by Ansell Hart could do incalculable harm, because they were "entirely above the heads of the common herd and are for the most part misunderstood by them".[96]

In August 1941, at its third annual conference, the People's National Party was scathing in its assessment of how the colonial government had used regulations that were enacted to deal with special public safety and defence conditions that the war might create:

> The use of the regulations to create a special body of law to deal with the ordinary peacetime incidents which are unaffected by any war risk however remote goes beyond the intention and scope of the Legislative sanction from which the above regulations derive force . . . so clear an instance of the illegitimate use of the powers involved.[97]

In November 1941, CO Under-Secretary George Hall was challenged in Parliament by Labour MP Arthur Creech-Jones regarding the operation of Defence Regulations in Jamaica since the start of the war. Hall refuted any suggestion of injustice in the administration of the regulations but advised that some provisions had been amended to conform to existing provisions in the United Kingdom.[98] The local Defence Regulations were amended to require that detained persons should be advised of the grounds of their detention.

Nonetheless the concerns over the use of the regulations continued. Richard Hart wrote that the Jamaican regulations also did not contain the English requirement of showing reasonable cause to believe that the detainee is "of hostile origin or associations or that he has recently been concerned in acts prejudicial to the public safety or defence or in the preparation or instigation of such acts", before detention.[99] Hart documented the Colonial Office response after Governor Richards, in 1942, used them to pre-empt efforts by PNP left-wingers to unionize the government railway and post offices. The governor created Authorised Associations (Government Departments) (Defence) Regulations, making the relevant unions illegal, nullified related proceedings in the courts and ordered police raids on the homes and officers of suspected subversives: four of whom – Hart among them – were later detained while several other PNP executive members were served with restriction orders. Only afterwards was the Colonial Office advised of these actions. Fearing that the governor's actions might be construed as anti-union and noting that the new regulation had no counterpart in English law and no roots in the Jamaica Trade Union law, the Colonial Office urged the governor to explain his actions diplomatically and to withdraw the regulations – which Richards did after protest.[100] It is arguable that Governor Richards' intransigence may have played some part in his reassignment from Jamaica to Nigeria in 1943.

While most of the concerns expressed locally regarding the Defence Regulations related to the detention of political and labour activists, there was also reference to the management of information and, by extension, to prejudices within the society. *Public Opinion* commented on the government censor's requirements that war news must be presented in an optimistic frame, strikes and disputes of a disruptive character must not be reported until they had been settled, and no matter likely to raise colour or racial feeling was to get into headlines on the grounds that it might weaken national unity; yet people could advertise in newspapers for clerks, typists, companions, lodgers and so on who were "white" or "fair" – and the Press Censor's position was that stopping them would comprise unnecessary interference with individual liberty.[101] An example from the *Gleaner* was a classified advertisement asking, "Will white family living near Halfway Tree offer accommodation to English refugee schoolgirl aged fifteen attending day school?"[102]

The Defence Regulations were also used to intern Germans, Austrians and eventually Italian-born persons who had been living in Jamaica before the war and who were classified as enemy aliens. This included some who had been granted British citizenship. Initially interned at the outbreak of the war, several of these persons were released but subsequently re-interned for months or even years in the wake of a British order in May 1940.[103] Though this order was soon rolled back in Britain, the colonial government in Jamaica continued to hold, in detention, many "whose opposition to the Nazi or Fascist regimes appear(ed) to be genuine" and whose continued detention therefore caused "a good deal" of criticism in the United Kingdom as late as 1943.[104]

Orders establishing the various camps in Jamaica during World War II were also made under the Defence Regulations, which directed the conditions applying to persons living inside the camp and anyone who might seek to enter it without direct permission. Criticisms of these conditions, made in the newspapers, were framed in terms of hospitality and civil liberties. Former Alderman John Soulette, in a newspaper column discussing the abrogation of civil liberties, cited the restrictions on the Gibraltarians who were "kept apart from the rest of Jamaica as if they were interned rather than given a refuge".[105]

One basis for the application of strict conditions of access to the camp and for discouraging egress by residents was the need to ensure their security. A young Finnish man who lived in Gibraltar Camp in late 1942 and 1943 said that this concern was stated or implied to discourage wandering widely and to explain the strict regulations but that he nonetheless visited widely outside the camp and never encountered any difficulties.[106]

Many Jamaican interviewees recalled this as a time when people did not lock their doors and could walk the streets at all hours without being harassed.[107] However, government departmental reports make it clear that there was criminal activity, though the wartime increases post-dated the regulations aimed at keeping residents safe within the camp boundaries. *Public Opinion* newspaper, which went from a weekly to a daily during the period, had one or two stories each year between 1941 and 1944, dealing with burglaries and robberies in urban and suburban areas. In 1942, stories of recent robberies included two incidents on Lindo's Gap Road, near Gibraltar Camp – one involving a taxi driver who was held up at knifepoint and the other involving an officer from the camp who was also held up and robbed. Another story, a month later, stated that criminal assault on women was on the increase.[108] Research on crimes prosecuted in the Circuit Court during the war years, 1940–1945, and reported in the *Gleaner*, indicated between 61 and 96 cases annually for Kingston & St Andrew (KSA) and between 157 and 212 annually for the entire island, including KSA. Interestingly, the figures for 1942, the period when Governor Richards expressed the greatest concern, were the lowest of all the war years.[109] However, a CSO circular of February 1942 did invite the attention of Resident Magistrates to an "alarming increase in the number of serious offences committed with the aid of firearms" in many parts of the island, resulting in "a real menace to the safety of law-abiding citizens and their property".[110] Statistics suggested that the highest number of offences were those against the revenue, municipal, road and other laws "relating to the social economy of the Colony". These included praedial larceny and other offences against property – such as theft, and offences against the person – such as assault. Convictions in the Superior Courts were also highest for offences against property.[111]

During the period when the camps operated, there were no reports identified of attacks on those evacuees, refugees or former internees who had the liberty to be out in the community during the day and evening. Court reports relating to the camp, outside of the rash of early prosecutions for vendors seeking to breach the camp perimeter and sell to residents, involved one evacuee charged with disorderly conduct, a runaway couple, an elderly evacuee's death by falling from a bridge in Gordon Town – judged suicide or accident – and a labourer who died while working on the camp – again with no suspicion of foul play.

Impact of War

The fear and destruction of the frontline of war never reached Jamaica, except via overseas radio broadcasts and the constant coverage across the front pages of the *Gleaner* newspaper – though armed conflict came closer than was generally acknowledged. From the start of the war, British authorities classified the island as liable only for occasional light raids by aircraft from naval ships and shelling by armed raiders – as stated in the Jamaica Defence Scheme of 1939.[112] Its original designation as a convoy assembly point for the Caribbean theatre was terminated in 1939 because of the incorrect assessment that no German naval offensive was likely against Caribbean Sea lanes. However, the offensive that did come focused mainly on the south, where Trinidad was an assembly point for convoys of trading vessels with military escorts.[113] Nonetheless, there were incidents in the waters close to Jamaica, even before the German submariners began their consistent and destructive hunting in the Caribbean and adjacent Atlantic waters in 1942 and 1943. These involved efforts to intercept German merchant ships that operated as blockade runners from the start of the war, seeking to get past British patrols and take supplies to German navy vessels as well as to Germany itself. Traditionally, if they were intercepted by British or Allied ships, the German merchant mariners sought to scupper or sink their vessels, so as to deny the cargo and future use of the ships to their captors. This was sometimes done by setting fire to the vessel and cargo or by seeking to let in water so it would sink. The crew would then take to their lifeboats, in an effort to escape.

As early as October 1939, the Up Park Camp War Diary noted the arrival in the Male Internment (and Prisoners of War) Camp of German merchant seamen taken prisoner when their vessel, the *Emmy Friedrich*, was intercepted by a British cruiser near Jamaica.[114] This would be the first of many such crews held in the camp until well after the end of the war. Indeed, several would be from vessels which had been holed up in neutral ports for long periods. A report in late December 1939 said that Germany had ordered five hundred merchant vessels to return to the Reich and scupper their vessels if they were in danger of capture.[115]

In November 1942, while the threat of enemy invasion to capture the island was considered negligible, the Command Headquarters assessed the threat of sabotage raids by two to three thousand well-armed and trained specialist troops to be a reality. This was at the time when the German navy was hunting effectively in the Caribbean waters, especially to the south but with some strikes in the northern Caribbean also. For the colonial government in Jamaica, the concern at that time related to potential threats linked to the fractious civil situation, with the authorities fearing that any raids "might be synchronised with civil disturbance". This explained the particular concern over the activities of the small communist group within the PNP, especially when their trade union activities targeted the island's railway and post office systems. A November 1942 report on the situation in Jamaica by commander of the Northern Caribbean Area, D. Denis Daly, said that it was:

> impossible in this Island to separate the Civil and Military situations for the direct threat against which the Military must be prepared is sabotage, internal disorders, riots, strikes, or a combination of all of these factors together.[116]

Threats at sea were documented in Kelshall's *U-Boat War in the Caribbean* and he recorded activity north-east of Jamaica, between Cuba and Hispaniola and at least one incident close to Jamaica. This was the July 1943 loss of the Dutch vessel *Poelau Roebiah*, torpedoed by German submarine *U-759*, thirteen miles off Morant Point in eastern Jamaica, while in *Convoy TAG-70*, going from the Panama Canal Zone to Guantanamo. Two men died and three boatloads of survivors – some sixty-eight persons – were rescued and taken to Kingston. The greater focus, however, remained to the south and along the continental shelf where the German U-boat campaign in the Caribbean was both intense and offensively cost-effective – especially between February 1942 and August 1943, when Kelshall analysed that for each of seventeen U-boats sunk, the Allies lost more than twenty-three merchant ships.[117] In July, the British intelligence forecast was for more submarine activity in the Caribbean, though the German focus would soon shift to the Mediterranean.[118] However, Fitzroy Baptiste, in his thesis on European possessions in the Caribbean during World War II, argued that the British gave relatively low priority to German threats in the region, even when these could have affected colonial Trinidad's important oil reserves. He said the British correctly assessed that the United States would defend the Caribbean for political and strategic reasons – even before it entered the war in December 1941.[119]

The intensity of this naval conflict in the region had little resonance for general populations ashore. For the British Caribbean overall, Kelshall commented that the general public remained in almost total ignorance of the seriousness of the Caribbean conflict, "with the result that all they could remember was the restrictions that this so-called war had imposed on their lives".[120] This could certainly be said of Jamaica, the exception being when locals were on torpedoed ships. An interviewee recalled an occasion "when a ship was torpedoed, and people were killed – a Manley and a Kelly . . . local 'aristocracy'. I remember reading that and my aunt crying".[121]

Even though there was no expectation of Jamaica being involved in significant enemy action, the war's impact was felt through shortages and loss of employment opportunities, through changes in lifestyle and increased regulation, through the loss of individuals who fell in the fighting, even though these were far fewer than wanted to volunteer to go and fight. The few Jamaicans and other Caribbean men who would fly in RAF crews were those able to find their own way to points in Canada and the United Kingdom where they could volunteer for the Royal Canadian Air Force and Royal Air Force, and young women similarly volunteered to join the Women's Auxiliary Air Force (WAAF). Many Jamaicans recalled reports of deaths and soldiers missing in action, printed in the local newspaper as well as posted in the public square in Downtown Kingston.[122]

Many interviewees mentioned anxiety at night-time blackout drills when all lights were to be covered, vehicular traffic was paused and Air Raid Wardens patrolled to ensure compliance or threaten prosecution. Blackouts were meant to frustrate bombing threats, especially from the air, and were instituted in many British colonies when such threats were being experienced in Britain – where nightly blackouts were endured through most of the war. A Black Out Order was initially made in Jamaica under the Jamaica Defence Regulations, at the beginning of 1940, with a first trial blackout advertised and held a few days later, on 15 January. A few more trials were reported in 1940 and 1941, and a new official order in 1942 preceded a consistent period of practice blackouts and greater emphasis on compliance, with a few newspaper reports of prosecutions for breaches. In the case of an alarm – or when blackout practice was held – the signal was ordered by the Officer Commanding Troops and a siren of a "fluctuating or warbling pitch" sounded. Church bells would take up the signal in case any had not heard it. Reports said that blackouts would last between one and two hours after which a siren "of steady pitch" would sound the "all clear". The order forbade churches to ring their bells at other times to avoid confusion. While many of these practice blackouts were localized, especially to the metropolitan area of Kingston and St Andrew, there were also blackout drills in various towns, and an all-island blackout was ordered and held on 21 May 1942. Newspaper reports provided details of practice blackouts throughout 1942 and early 1943, not surprisingly the period when German submarines were most active and successful in the Caribbean region.

In a March 1942 broadcast on the local station, *ZQI*, republished in the *Daily Gleaner* newspaper, the Chief Warden's Assistant for Air Raid Precautions (ARP) P.M. Sherlock said that the war which had initially seemed so far away from Jamaica and the West Indies had moved closer:

> The war moved nearer still to us in Jamaica as we heard more frequently of the sinkings of ships that came to our shores; as we saw young Jamaicans going abroad to join the forces and to work in factories; and then, swiftly, the war embraced all the vast areas within which we live. The United States was also an ally and West Indian islands were being attacked – Aruba and Trinidad and St Lucia.[123]

There were frequent rumours of German infiltrators among foreign sailors and submarine crews landing at various local ports for late-night recreation – in St Thomas, but also around the area of East Queen Street in Kingston. This East Queen Street story may have been connected to a location where it was said that the owner of a "cold supper shop" would regularly play German propaganda broadcasts. Additionally, there were urban legends about spies among sailors from ships in Kingston Harbour. An interviewee who lived near the popular Bournemouth Bath in Kingston recalled a German named Dietrich who was:

> always over at Bournemouth with the boys, and of course when the sailors came in, they were always entertained over at Bournemouth Bath, so it was a very good way of finding out information . . . He wasn't interned, and he used to mix among everybody.[124]

He also repeated a frequently told story that equipment, later found at a house in the hills above Kingston, could have been used for signalling convoy information to German submarines.[125] One interviewee linked a "Herr Dikkers" to the story of signalling from Flamstead, the location in the hills most frequently connected to this story. The value that could have accrued from information on shipping movements is undoubted but, unlike harbours in the southern Caribbean, Kingston's strategic and well-protected harbour was never attacked, and stories of recreational stops by submariners were never confirmed, though Jamaica's long coastline would certainly have offered many opportunities.[126] The conflated stories may also have connected to an actual person, who would have had reason to pursue German interests, though in the pre-war period. Theo A. Deters, a merchant operating from Harbour Street in Kingston, arrived in Jamaica in 1934 and lived in several different locations before his 1939 residence on Hermitage Dam Road, an area overlooking Kingston Harbour. He was to have been formally appointed honorary consul for Germany in Jamaica and was among those interned as enemy aliens in September 1939. A German flag and other instruments of office addressed to him arrived in Jamaica in November 1939, having been posted before war was declared. An appeal against his detention was not entertained, and it appears that he remained in the internment camp. However, in September 1940 he was reported to have been exchanged for an Allied prisoner as part of a general exchange and returned to Germany.[127]

A post-war report on the colonial empire acknowledged that the West Indies "suffered from enemy submarine activities by which their food supplies and communications were at times seriously dislocated".[128] In Jamaica, the economic dislocations included mid-war shortages as well as massive hikes in the cost of living. The island's Cost of Living Index was 100 in August 1939, 115.31 in January 1940 and 141.41 in September 1941.[129] Shipping-related shortages worsened in 1942 and 1943, concurrent with the German naval attacks in the Caribbean and Atlantic, leading to further cost increases. In July 1942, official security reports highlighted recent "severe food shortages affecting the style [sic] diet of the population, acute transportation *(word obscured)* resulting in petrol shortage and high increasing level of unemployment". Also reported was an increase in labour unrest, sporadic attacks on grocery stores and some outbreaks of lawlessness which, it was feared, could lead to organized riots.[130] In 1942, efforts were put in place to manage the distribution and allocation of scarce items, especially protein sources such as meat and eggs, and to subsidize the prices of certain basic items including imported salted fish. Gasolene was also rationed. Substitution was encouraged and included the development of various types of flour.

Shortages of food and other supplies were complicated by the need to guarantee supplies to the evacuee/refugee and internment camps, as well as the military establishment. Indeed, *The Colonial Empire* acknowledged that maintenance of British and US military garrisons strained supplies of food, supplies and men in some colonies.[131] Information on the camps makes it clear that they were generally well and consistently provisioned – the main exception relating to the Women's Camp for a period during the early months of 1943. Gasolene shortages did affect visits between families separated in the men's and women's camps. While the general population appears to have generally accepted the requirement to provide scarce items to the camps, there were some negative mentions in the press, especially in relation to the relative allocation of scarce beef supplies, between late 1941 to early 1943.

Imports and exports were among the economic spheres falling under Defence Regulations put in place at the start of the war. Significant cutbacks in the island's exports, due to shortages of shipping for other than essential items, had a negative impact on the economy and on employment. While cargo space continued to be found for sugar, which was deemed essential to the British consumer, the island's bananas were virtually given away locally or rotted, though the United Kingdom continued to pay a subsidy to prevent the total collapse of the industry.[132] Imports were scaled down based on reduced shipping allocations, and there was a particular focus on eliminating luxury imports and developing maximum local production of essential food items. The consequent reduction in earnings from import duties was a major factor in reduced revenues. By mid-1942, Governor Sir Arthur Richards wrote to the Colonial Office in London that the cumulative effect of war controls was beginning to show in diminished trade, based on "the shipping shortage and the absolute necessity to cut down our imports to a minimum, gasolene rationing and the re-organisation of all transport on a lower level of service".[133]

Up to the war, a wide range of products had come from England. Retired *Gleaner* Advertising Consultant Imelda Williams Howell recalled that "in those days, Jamaica hardly manufactured anything" and that imports from Britain included "all sorts of medicines, jams, jellies, soaps, for example".[134] Axis countries, Germany and Japan, had also been significant suppliers of manufactured goods to Jamaica before the war. With wartime diversion of imperial production capacity as well as shipping-related shortages, the local production of foodstuff for domestic consumption became a focus and even manufacturing was, to some extent, officially encouraged.¹³⁵ In his autobiography, then Colonial Secretary Alexander Grantham noted that the government built a cornmeal factory, using locally grown corn, to replace imported wheat flour: "Other projects of a similar nature had also to be undertaken in the war-time emergency."¹³⁶

Indeed, relevant factors included the allocation of British government funds following the passage of the Colonial Development and Welfare Act of 1940 and the appointment of Sir Frank Stockdale as Comptroller for Development and Welfare. Jamaican businessman, James F. Gore, listed local endeavours, in a September 1940 newspaper article. He included the manufacture of matches from imported material, the production of meal from local corn, a factory to produce condensed milk, manufacture of butter substitute, lard compound and edible oil from coconuts, production of laundry soap and biscuits, refining of sugar and manufacturing of ice.¹³⁷ A Clay, Tile & Brick factory was also among the initiatives which generated some media coverage after it was taken over by the government in May 1945.¹³⁸ However, not all reports on local industrial development were sanguine. A report towards the end of 1941 cited abandonment of a rice-growing project, refusal to sanction the establishment of a flour mill, partial abandonment of the cornmeal project, failure to develop land settlements or to provide factory facilities to use up surplus bananas, failure to establish a coir factory as a subsidiary to the coconut industry and failure to utilize cheap cane alcohol for industrial and domestic purposes. One local newspaper *Public Opinion* challenged: "Do these omissions represent development? Uplift of the masses and the middle classes?!"¹³⁹

Indeed, Gore's effort to establish a cement factory highlighted policy issues involved in decisions that pitted colonial development efforts against imperial business interests. Richard Hart documented how Gore's efforts were resisted in favour of British interests then supplying cement locally. He quoted Colonial Office papers which indicated collusion with the British suppliers who were not inclined to make the investment in a Jamaican plant but wanted to ensure that no foreign company was allowed to construct a factory.¹⁴⁰ In addition, Hart noted that there was objection, in London, to any tariff being put in place that would provide protection for local manufacturing. The colonial government also refused to countenance wartime proposals from refugees or internees living in camps in Kingston, who expressed interest in establishing businesses in Jamaica.¹⁴¹

The shortage of jobs in Jamaica, and the context of the recent labour riots, made it important and politic for the government to rule against any of the incomers being allowed to work during their time on the island. Indeed, local legislators had called on the government, in June 1940, to prohibit the entry of non-Jamaicans who gained employment to the detriment of natives.[142] Large-scale construction projects helped to fill the local employment gap, especially for male jobseekers. Some three thousand men from Kingston and surrounding areas were employed during 1940 in the construction of Gibraltar Camp and the Palisadoes Aerodrome – which would eventually become the Norman Manley International Airport. The construction of US bases at Fort Simonds on Goat Island, in the southern parish of St Catherine and Vernamfield across the border in the parish of Clarendon, also helped to fill the local employment gap, with five thousand men reportedly engaged in the naval base construction.[143] Jamaican workers at the American base took limited industrial action over low wages, unsatisfactory food and inadequate transportation to and from work – a US representative agreeing to ameliorate the conditions of labour and food but not to increase wages.[144] Similar complaints occurred in Trinidad, with the issue of rates similarly considered to have been in keeping with the desires of local industries who did not want to see wages rise.

In Jamaica, unemployment was significant, and the fear of labour unrest was real, especially in the wake of the 1938 riots, and subsequent strikes in 1941 and 1942 were reported in the media and in Colonial Secretariat documentation. In August 1941, more than two thousand men reportedly gathered at various points in St Catherine demanding work.[145] By 1942, employment at the bases was severely reduced and the construction of the Mona Reservoir in Kingston – officially named Richards Reservoir – was brought on stream to ease the job drought. In *Strike the Iron*, Post quoted official estimates, in December 1942, which showed that between 150 and 200,000 Jamaicans were seriously affected by unemployment or underemployment. The figures indicated that 30,000 people had been affected by the curtailment of transportation and that relief work was up from 3,577 jobs in mid-July to 10,611 four months later.

Efforts were also put in place to find labour contracts overseas. In 1941, it was reported that three thousand workers were employed in Panama. The year 1943 saw the start of a programme to employ Jamaican farmworkers in the United States, replacing men recruited for the war effort.[146] Tens of thousands of Jamaicans were among more than fifty thousand West Indians eventually recruited to work in agriculture and war industries, most of them in the United States.[147]

Hopes that a significant number of Jamaicans would be employed at Gibraltar Camp after it opened were dashed by the relatively low number of arrivals compared to the size of the camp, and more so by a decision to offer jobs to camp residents, who were forbidden to seek employment in the wider community. Consequently, there were many more disappointed job seekers than there were jobs. A wartime poem titled "Po' Mufeena" (Poor Mufeena) by Jamaican poet and folk commentator Louise Bennett also illustrated some of the challenges, especially for applicants from the lower economic class. As a summation of the poem states: "May seeks a job in the new camp at Mona, without success. The whole matter of rigorous screening of employees is too much for her."[148]

Low levels of employment were underscored by low wages for most Jamaicans – denominated in British currency as in other British West Indies territories. In January 1941, the Labour Department noted that pay rates for labourers were 3/9 per day, and this was the rate which the Americans paid to workers on the US base construction sites, despite local protest. Many persons earned far less. A bus conductor was being paid, on average, 2/1 per day or 12/6 up to a possible 17/- per week. Nearly two years later, a newspaper report noted that the government had fixed the "absurd" minimum wage of 2/6 per day for male sugar workers and 1/6 for their female counterparts.[149] This at a time when even at government subsidised prices, consumers were paying 8–10 pence/lb for pickled meat, 6pence/lb for salt fish, 2 ½ pence/lb for flour and only a little less for rice, and at least 6 pence for a bar of soap.

In 1943, Britain's RAF began recruiting in the West Indies – finally offering an opportunity that Caribbean people had clamoured for from the start of the war. Some 6,400 men were signed up, of whom some 800 served as aircrew.[150] Many more men volunteered for service but were rejected on the grounds of being unsuitable, including some who were not medically acceptable. Subsequently, local newspaper advertisements offered the opportunity for other men to sign up as tradesmen or workers in munitions factories. But even when Jamaicans and other West Indians were formally accepted, they faced prejudice: a Caribbean regiment, raised in 1944, was rejected by British military authorities in India and Italy before finally serving in Egypt and Sudan.[151] The regiment included hundreds of local soldiers previously serving as infantry volunteers. While offered fewer wartime opportunities, a few women travelled to England to join the Women's Auxiliary Air Service (WAAF) and the British Auxiliary Territorial Service belatedly began recruiting in the West Indies in 1943 – having been in operation from 1938. A Jamaican unit was formed which serviced local military facilities.

Service in the military establishment aside, Jamaicans contributed significantly to efforts to purchase aeroplanes for the British war effort: £75,000 and £13,700, respectively, for the *Gleaner*'s Bombing Plane Fund and Churchill Tank Fund; £167,594, up to February 1944 for the Empire War Fund, in addition to various donated comforts – significant contributions, especially from a country with severe economic and social constraints.[152]

Local Perceptions of the War

The war was consistently reported in the local media – a daily offering on the front page of the main local newspaper and often the main story. Persons traditionally read the newspaper aloud, in parks in Downtown Kingston as well as in some factories, for the benefit of the illiterate – estimated at some 25 per cent of the population over seven years of age, in the census of 1942.

Yet the foreign news aside, Jamaican interviewees recalled the war for its inconveniences and occasionally for excitement or fear. Many said that it had little impact on the local population, except for people who joined up or who knew others that had done so. Of three interviewees who were schoolgirls during the war, one remembers it as "a lark", especially when there was air raid practice during school, though she noted that she felt some connection when the headmistress, in assembly, spoke about past students who were in the services or who had been killed. She also noted that, being poor, her family's light came from kerosene lamps which had to be doused if the siren signalling a blackout was heard – an event that her aunt turned into storytelling time. Another recalled being terrified when the siren went off while a third said the war's main impact was taking away her boyfriends – middle- and upper-class youth who had volunteered for service abroad. Many interviewees remembered the blackouts and air raid drills as well as shortages, especially gasolene rationing that resulted in the widespread use of bicycles and buggies.[153]

An interviewee who lived in the parish of Portland in the island's northeast recalled life being "tough", with shortages of kerosene, which most rural people and the urban working class used for light and cooking, as well as a shortage of gasolene, and difficulty getting staple food items like rice.[154] He said that he and his wife would make candles using wax and kerosene, and "things that we called floaters that we put on oil to get light". Jamaica's post-Independence First Lady, Lady Gladys Bustamante also mentioned floaters as an important wartime innovation. These additional recollections were listed by a correspondent:

All the ships, which were usually painted white, all became grey or camouflaged and sometimes convoys would assemble in Kingston Harbour. England bought our bananas, but they were not shipped. You could buy a bunch for about a shilling. Most cars were jacked up on blocks (for lack of gasolene to run them). The few remaining were either "essential vehicles" or owned by scufflers who tried to beat the rationing system. Jamaica was self-sufficient. We had cornmeal in abundance. We had hominy corn, arrowroot, banana, and rice porridge – no dry cereal and such.[155]

While some young men joined the ARP unit and others trained with the Home Guard or joined the local forces, several interviewees said that Jamaicans did not take the war seriously, did not discuss it specially and did not feel connected – though this may have been more common in rural areas with less access to news. One interviewee mused:

People wake up one morning and hear, "war declared!" The question is how it affects you. The average young man or woman didn't have any special interest except where they saw it could help them or they felt loyal enough to volunteer . . . War, far away, didn't mean much to us. That was the general position of most people I knew. We didn't specially discuss it.[156]

A correspondent who worked in the lower ranks of the civil service, in Kingston, argued that the average Jamaican saw the war as "backra fighting backra" (white people fighting among themselves) and that people were very aware that their colonial status would remain the same, regardless of the outcome. He argued:

All the heads of government departments, police above the rank of sergeant, bank clerks, and most parsons, were white. Governor Richards locked up Bustamante, who was very popular, and we could do very little about it. The few patriots were white folks. Those of us who wanted to join the RAF, were only looking for adventure.[157]

Another interviewee, light-skinned and from the middle class, who was a young lieutenant in the Jamaica Battalion at the end of the war, felt that people were proud to be part of the British Empire and that upper-class and propertied Jamaicans wanted to defend the empire. He added that he and his colleagues only realized in 1947, after the war, "that our prospects for promotion, beyond captain, were pretty much nil unless you were very, very good. That was about as high as you could get in the colonial set-up". He agreed that for the working class, the issue was not loyalty to empire so much as "an escape route to a better life".[158] It was also recognized that people who joined the army in Jamaica mostly stayed there, while those who joined the RAF were sure to leave, "and that is something that every young person wanted to do, was to leave Jamaica".[159] Reviewing reasons why Jamaicans wanted to join the fighting forces, historian Patrick Bryan included: fighting Hitler's racism, a family tradition of military service, attraction to the uniformed services, vengeance and the search for economic opportunity abroad.[160]

The complex attitude of Jamaicans to the war, including the pursuance of an activist agenda during wartime would be a significant source of difference with the island's governor for much of his time in office in Jamaica. At the outset of the war, Governor Richards saluted the patriotism of men who offered their services to the military authorities, asking them to exercise patience until their services were required.[161] This "exercise of patience" would become one of several points of bitterness and eventual disinterest during the war, as he himself recognized. Reporting on *The Colonial Empire at the Outbreak of War*, the secretary of state for the colonies said:

> The Governor of Jamaica, in common with other Governors in the West Indian area, reports that there has been a wave of intense loyalty among all sections of the community. He has added a warning that this state of affairs may not be maintained unless suitable openings can be found for utilising the numerous offers of service for military and other duties. This question is now under consideration.[162]

Although the colour bar in the British armed services was formally abandoned in October 1939, the Colonial Office told the colonial governments in January 1940 that non-European British subjects should not come to Britain for enlistment.[163] Nonetheless, some West Indians went to Canada – one of six countries considered autonomous dominions within the British Empire – to join the RAF there, as a sure route to Britain and war service. In 1940 and 1941, *Public Opinion* newspaper charged that Britain's disinterest in offers of Jamaican manpower had killed personal interest in the war.[164] And the newspaper's columnist Morris Cargill defended Jamaicans who became disproportionately concerned with local problems, in wartime, saying that this was rooted in factors beyond local control:

> Jamaicans on the whole are tremendously patriotic . . . when the poorer class demonstrates its belief in the Empire and all it stands for, they do so not for the material profit that they have made out of it in the past, but because of a deep instinctive understanding that their future is safer as part of a great liberal Empire.

He added that Jamaica had been told "often and clearly" that its help was not required.¹⁶⁵ This perception was mirrored further afield: A 1941 article from the *Economist* magazine observed little attempt to take advantage of the "wholehearted wish of the coloured peoples to serve the empire as a whole". The article noted that a "proposal to recruit West Indians in special West Indian regiments has been refused; and little has been done to raise a civil defence service or local defence corps".¹⁶⁶ In 1942, *Spotlight* magazine reported that Legislative Council member for St James, A.B. Lowe, had brought a resolution asking local officials to lobby the Imperial Government for Jamaican regiments that would fight for king and empire. He said that the lack of opportunity was "having a bad effect on the minds of the people. People are saying: 'It's not our war . . . they don't want us'".¹⁶⁷ The local publication blamed "misguided Jamaican patriots who think their first duty is to Britain instead of their own country". And it took note of a report which the *Gleaner* had reprinted from the *Manchester Guardian* which said that West Indians in uniform in England, many of whom had paid their own passage to get there, were being referred to as "monkeys" and "niggers".¹⁶⁸

The issue of Jamaica's loyalty to Britain had already become political since Governor Richards equated the local campaign for greater self-government, and growing opposition to his style of rule, with a lack of patriotism and disloyalty to the British Empire. In an Empire Day speech in 1941, the governor publicly charged Jamaicans with defeatism, drawing the ire of *Public Opinion* columnist, Morris Cargill. Cargill said that he was "not aware of any considerable body of defeatist opinion in Jamaica"; indeed, he pointed out that Director of Education B.H.M. Easter had recently attacked Jamaicans' over confidence.¹⁶⁹ The same issue of *Public Opinion* noted the "instant and sincere response" of Jamaicans to news of the sinking of the British battlecruiser *Hood* by Germany's *Bismark* and to the determined pursuit which also ended the German battleship's sensational career.

> Anyone walking the streets and hearing the talk on street corners, in bars, on park benches and in homes, would have dispelled once and for all the stupid idea that any class of Jamaicans is hostile or indifferent to the issue of this war.¹⁷⁰

Governor Richards averred that Jamaicans had "no background of real patriotism or willingness to bear hardship for the sake of victory". Instead, he found "lip-service with no real intention to help even amongst those who are not openly disaffected – and they are an unpleasantly large number".¹⁷¹ Richards's memoirist, Richard Peel, explained that the governor was "frustrated at the lack of realisation of the needs of the United Kingdom and of the Free World in their struggle to the death against the totalitarian states". He said that this exasperation, along with weariness, "would sometimes cause him to lash out at critics of his fiscal policies and the programmes of his government".[172]

For many Jamaicans, the war did present a mix of opportunity and traditional loyalty. But the issue of loyalty was complex, rolled up in the increasing acknowledgement and critique of the long-standing colonial condition – though the majority of people remained compliant. An interviewee who was a school leaver working in a junior government post during the war noted this duality: "Jamaicans were at the stage of (political) awakening, but the loyalty (remained). There were patriotic songs – 'There'll always be an England' – and people sang this with gusto."[173] Persons who had been schoolchildren during the war recalled the ongoing colonial requirements of singing "Rule Britannia" at elementary school, using British schoolbooks and learning British history. Some said that people frequently sang the hymns "Land of Hope & Glory" and "For Those in Peril on the Sea". Several interviewees recalled standing for the imperial anthem at cinemas: One of Jamaica's early soldiers said that anybody sitting down would be pulled out, "or something like that". He added that people "kind of respect the British, you know, because, technically, the British army was in camp there".[174]

Patriotic poetry, reflecting an educated, British sensibility, was fairly common in newspapers and other publications, typical examples including "To America. A Jamaican's Appreciation" published in the conservative *Catholic Opinion* in 1941, and "London Stands" by the headmistress of Westwood High School in northern Jamaica, M. Jeffery-Smith, published in the *West India Committee Circular*: "We are far away, we listen in/We hear the bellow and the blasts of hate –/Still LONDON STANDS."[175]

The complexity of the local perspective was also tied up in attitudes to Germany and Japan, which had been recognizable trading partners before the war. A correspondent who worked in a government office in Kingston said that while there was no pro-German sentiment locally, many people were familiar with German products from a barter trade agreement in place during the 1930s: "So, they may not have been as evil to us as they were to others."[176] Two sources referenced a "cold supper shop" at the corner of East Queen Street and Gold Street in Downtown Kingston, where the proprietor regularly played Lord Haw Haw's German propaganda broadcasts in English; one contending that "half the population here was pro-German, not British; pro-Garvey and all that".[177] Activist and later historian Richard Hart attributed favourable response to the German broadcasts, among a section of the urban masses, to resentment caused by distressing economic conditions, leading to "a sentiment of satisfaction at Britain's reverses". He said that "in the rural areas, for the most part, the traditional loyalty to Britain did not diminish".[178]

The general approach of the colonial government was to avoid alarming the population and to depress any desire to become actively involved, and, in relation to the groups of Europeans brought in as evacuees, refugees or internees, to discourage or outright forbid any interface which might disrupt aspects of the status quo.

Information officers were in place to disseminate informative war propaganda so as to keep morale high and maintain "loyal confident interest in the Allied Cause", and the Legislative Council was assured that efforts were being made to keep the public informed.[179] Keith Jeffery, in "The Second World War", said that the imperial publicity message in 1940 was that the British colonies were loyal and happy and helping as much as they can.[180] Yet, in the colonies – specifically in the British West Indian colony of Jamaica – the evidence suggests that there was a general lack of effort to connect the general public to the war or keep them updated on its likely impact. In the early years, this may have been partly to avoid fuelling any desire to take an active part through volunteering for combat or other jobs which were not being offered.

The lack of significant information on the local implications of the war was slightly addressed by the commissioning of a government broadcasting station, *ZQI* in 1940, though there was criticism on the limited reach of the transmission equipment under consideration for the station.[181] Music was the major offering but *ZQI* also brought a start to local news: a five-minute daily news package within the one – later two – hour broadcast each evening.[182] Persons with radio receivers, many of whom became the centre of wide circles of listeners, could already access *BBC* broadcasts and transmissions from several American stations, for news on the war as well as musical and theatrical entertainment. The *BBC*'s regional West Indies radio newsletter, broadcast from the United States, was established in 1942.[183] Despite government information machinery operating from London, with information officers in the colonies, it was not until July 1943 – with a new constitution announced, a change of governor in progress and the beginning of the recruitment of Jamaicans for war jobs – that a Jamaican newspaper reported a significant improvement in local information flows. The report said that initiatives included slides at movies urging people not to repeat rumours and to "Open the Offensive on the Home Front"; displays in the foyer of the new Carib movie theatre in Kingston; war-related displays in windows at Nathans department store on the corner of King and Barry Streets in Downtown Kingston, the *Jamaica Times* building on Kings Street and Nelson's Drug Store in Cross Roads; a big sign along South Camp Road by Issa Park, loaned by Coca-Cola; boards at Rockfort Gardens and the junction of Hagley Park and Spanish Town Roads (covering major entrances/exits to and from the city); boards also in the chief country towns; maps to help the public follow the big military campaigns; a weekly war commentary published in the *Gleaner* under the pseudonym Veritas; British newsreels in the cinemas; and a nightly news service on a screen mounted at Cross Roads and known as Information Junction.[184]

Chapter 2

A Camp for Free Europeans in Need

Gibraltar Camp was one of four fenced, gated and guarded camps that were established in Jamaica over the period of World War II. Unlike the others, Gibraltar Camp was not established under the aegis of the security forces. It was a civilian facility, underwritten by the Colonial Office in London, and matters relating to the camp normally passed through the local colonial secretariat. Yet, despite this unique aspect, there were several commonalities with the internment camps that were concurrently established with a view to ensuring local and imperial security during a time of war. Indeed, the rigidity of Gibraltar Camp conditions led them to be described as "semi-internment" conditions.

Like the internment camps, Gibraltar Camp was ringed with barbed wire, in addition to which cautionary signs warned locals to stay out. Further, the camp was designed to be an enclave – beyond accommodation and meals which were provided, it had its own places of worship, shop, school, hospital, workshops, fire and police stations – removing the need for residents to seek services in the wider community, beyond the fence. Residents could go out on day passes, though they were initially discouraged from doing so.

Regulations relating to the camp were established in mid-October 1940, under the Jamaica Defence Regulations. The nomenclature of commandant, deputy commandant and commissary officer underlined the military appearance. Barracks structures, laid out in seried rows, were rapidly constructed to meet deadlines for evacuation of the Gibraltarian population, though efforts were subsequently made to connect rooms within the buildings in a way that created family spaces.

Also like the internment camps, Gibraltar Camp was created virtually by *fiat*; in this case by decree of the governor. Once Gibraltar governor Sir Clive Liddell accepted the offer of haven from the governor of Jamaica, the development of the camp proceeded on two tracks – physical development of the facility and its social structure. At the request of the governor and the Catholic bishop of Gibraltar, Governor Richards visited the Winchester Park headquarters of the local Catholic Church to ask that the church run the educational, religious and social aspects of the camp. This necessitated the assignment of a resident chaplain as well as the recruitment of a community of nuns. Fr William Feeney, Roman Catholic Chaplain at Gibraltar Camp, 1940–1943, said that no one religious order could spare eight religious sisters for Gibraltar Camp, without crippling ongoing work, hence a community was formed made up of two Franciscans, two Sisters of Mercy, two Dominicans and two Native Sisters.[1]

The government order to proceed with the construction of a camp for four thousand evacuees was received by the Public Works Department (PWD) on 19 July 1940, sparking immediate work to select the site, prepare plans, import materials not available locally and parcel out the work to several local contractors. Work on site began on 25 July; the camp was ready to receive residents by September.[2]

At the beginning of August, the local military was asked to supply the camp with bread, on repayment, and the Officer Commanding Troops in Jamaica wrote the War Office: "Jamaica government accepting 4,000 evacuees from Gibraltar. One half expected to arrive about 20th August balance two months later. All costs chargeable to imperial funds."[3] These would have been Gibraltar's early evacuees who were sent to Britain in July and who were to have been re-directed from there to the British West Indies, but who ended up staying in London due to the challenges of the North Atlantic crossing.

Neither wartime regulation nor pre-existing colonial condition required Governor Richards to refer his decision on Gibraltar Camp to the local legislature or to the municipal authorities nor, indeed, to communicate it to them or to the population in general. Nor is there any indication that the colonial government in Jamaica issued any pre-emptive announcement to the local population, their few elected representatives, unelected activists or leaders of society – advising or seeking engagement with respect to this contribution to the war effort. However, once the Gibraltarians arrived, it was made plain, through signs, advertisements, prosecutions and occasional other communication, that the local population was expected to take a polite but "hands-off" approach, leaving the camp to exist in a virtual bubble, largely separated from its local environment.

The omission of any reference to the local elected members was raised in the 1941 Spring Session of the Legislative Council and reported in the *Gleaner* newspaper, which routinely gave full reports on political, constitutional and legal matters. Elected member for the parish of Clarendon, prominent local barrister J.A.G. Smith, averred that information on the camp had only come to members by hearsay and that arrangements for the supervision and care of the evacuees had been kept as a matter for the governor of the colony and officials only.⁴ The mayor of the capital city would also confirm, in May 1941, that the Kingston and St Andrew Corporation had not been "officially informed about the creation of the new Gibraltar Camp 'township'".⁵

Newspaper reports on the camp began to appear in September 1940, just weeks before the first group of evacuees arrived. Reporters may have been tipped off by advertisements for key temporary posts and the resignation of Kingston's deputy mayor Ernest Rae to take up the position of manager at the camp. Media enquiries and subsequent reports appear to have been the major means by which people at all levels of the society, outside of the administration, gained knowledge of plans for the camp, though government officials may have supplied some requested information. News reports published in early October advised that the camp was being constructed to hold up to nine thousand people from Gibraltar and Malta, up from an initial plan for four thousand.⁶ The reference to evacuees from Malta reflected a plan to include, in the camp, a large group from Britain's other Mediterranean fortress colony, Malta. Indeed, many Jamaicans still hold that the Maltese did come as well as the Gibraltarians. However, the Maltese refused to leave their ancient home – convinced that they could weather the storm there.⁷ In the end, only a single handful made the journey.

The arrival of fewer evacuees than planned meant that there was significant surplus accommodation. In 1940 and 1941, the government entertained suggestions that the camp be given over to housing Italian prisoners of war, moving the Gibraltarians into another, smaller facility. After some investigation, the idea was eventually dismissed based on broader strategic decisions concerning the placement and guarding of various categories of prisoners, their potential use for labour elsewhere and shipping availability.⁸ The existence of spare capacity also drew the eyes of organizations and governments seeking havens for wartime refugees, with two groups of Eastern European Jews and various groups of mainly Jewish Dutch refugees occupying a section of the camp from 1942. Additionally, as the war moved through its various stages and enemies became Allies, there were groups of internees who were given greater freedom through reassignment to Gibraltar Camp.

Within Gibraltar Camp, the upper level, geographically, was sometimes known as Camp I to distinguish it from the lower plateau – Camp II. On occasion, the differentiation also applied to the various populations, with the evacuees in Camp I and the refugees in Camp II – or even a further differentiation with the Polish refugees in Camp II and the Dutch refugees in Camp III.

In 1943, the camp's northern extremity would be fenced, buffered and repurposed as a military facility to accommodate interned families who had previously been in separate, gender-specific camps. In October 1944, as the

Gibraltarians were repatriated, most of Gibraltar Camp was taken over by the military, to accommodate various local units. Indeed, the process appears to have begun as early as 15 September 1944, on the lower level of the camp – with the relocation of some five dozen refugees remaining in that section, to the upper level. This facilitated the military taking over Camp II, which was initially used for the reception of Royal Air Force (RAF) recruits, while a Transit Camp was being established for them at the Palisadoes military facility east of the city. Beginning 25 October 1944, some three weeks after the departure of the Gibraltarian evacuees, "#2 Transit Camp Gibraltar" on that same lower level was handed over to the embodied units of the Jamaica Home Guard, which had been under canvas at Briggs Park, near to the Male Internment Camp. Their proposed move into unused accommodation at Gibraltar Camp had been stalled two years earlier, due to concerns over locating coloured soldiers next door to Gibraltar's daughters and wives. Concurrently, the Jamaica Battalion, formerly the Jamaica Infantry Volunteers, which had been at Palisadoes, moved to the upper level of Gibraltar Camp, a move completed on 11 November 1944.[9]

The new military facility was fenced off from the remnant of the evacuee camp, where the remaining refugees lived in accommodation clustered near the original entrance to the camp. The military used what is now termed the Post Office Gate, entering on Hermitage Road at the south of the camp's main thoroughfare. A lieutenant in the Jamaica Battalion, at Gibraltar Camp, in 1945, recalled a camp next door, with Europeans, including young women. He said that soldiers wishing to visit that camp had to request permission and that at least one soldier in his unit did so on several occasions. Other military interviewees, one a non-commissioned officer, recalled strict regulations regarding the nearby "Women's Camp".[10]

Gibraltar Camp formally closed in 1947. In December, the military handed the facility to the PWD which passed the camp buildings, along with some six hundred and fifty acres of the combined Mona and Papine estates, over to a new University College of the West Indies. The Gibraltar Camp Committee was finally dissolved a year later, in December 1948.

Evacuees

The establishment of Gibraltar Camp was reported, privately, in this quite startling fashion by the local Catholic Church:

> About 1,500 evacuees, practically all Spanish speaking, have taken refuge in the Island Mission of Jamaica. They constitute one of the largest cities of Jamaica and certainly the largest exclusive Catholic Settlement of the island.[11]

A Camp for Free Europeans in Need | 65

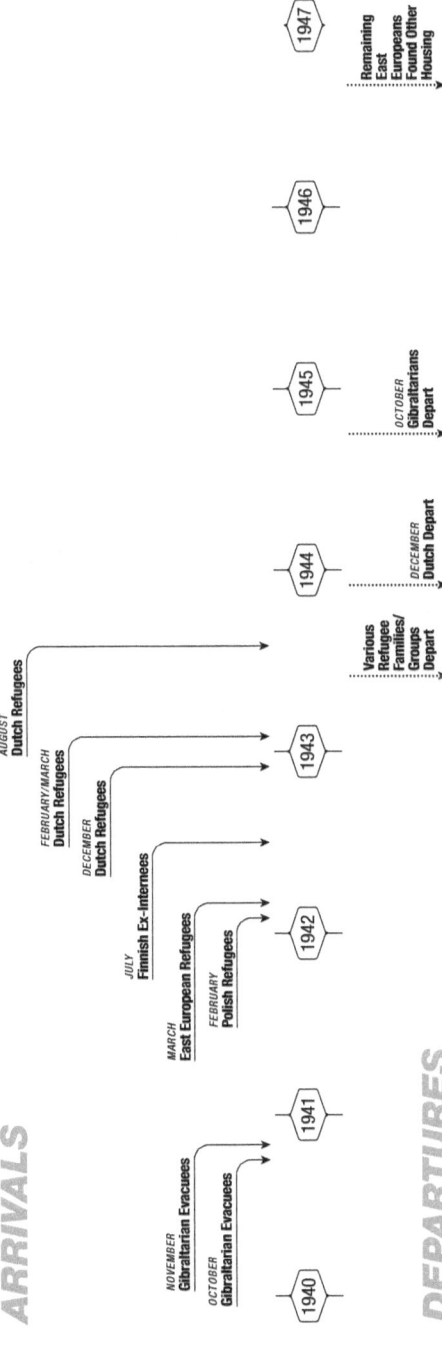

Figure 5 Timeline of Arrivals and Departures at Gibraltar Camp.

This closed community of white, mainly Catholic, southern Europeans was created at the end of 1940, in a precisely laid out enclave, with good infrastructure, guaranteed food supplies and all facilities – located in semi-rural Jamaica between two poor communities of mainly black and East Indian descent. The nature of the decision to create Gibraltar Camp would have pre-determined some of its elements. British governor of colonial Jamaica, Sir Arthur Richards, had volunteered to establish the camp, at imperial expense, as a contribution to the British war effort. He was responding to an urgent appeal broadcast to governors across the empire, from the governor of Gibraltar – a strategically crucial British colony and military complex at the entrance to the Mediterranean. Tiny Gibraltar's civilian population was increasingly seen as a hindrance, taking space and resources that could be used by fighting forces. T.J. Finlayson's *The Fortress Came First* detailed the initial evacuation of more than thirteen thousand civilians to French Morocco, in June 1940 – a move almost immediately reversed after the fall of France to the pro-German Vichy regime. By this time, Italy had entered the war on the side of Germany, and concern began to emerge over a proposed German operation codenamed Operation Felix, which threatened to attack Gibraltar through neighbouring Spain, still neutral under the heavy hand of fascist leader, General Francisco Franco.[12] Evacuation of the Gibraltarian civilians began again in July, with some eleven thousand sent to the United Kingdom, based on a plan for subsequent transfer to Jamaica and Trinidad. Another two thousand, many of whom could afford their own economic costs, were evacuated to Madeira by agreement with the Portuguese authorities.

In October, after heavy air raids in Gibraltar, two groups were shipped directly to Jamaica: 1,093 aboard the SS *Neuralia*, leaving Gibraltar on 9 October, and 393 on the SS *Thysville*, sailing on 31 October.[13] The *Neuralia*, a re-arranged troop ship with huge red crosses painted on port and starboard, which carried 185 men – mostly teens and over 45s — 673 women and 246 children, arrived on 26 October. A report recorded that from 3.00 p.m. until 11.00 p.m., "auto-busses [sic] poured the first contingent of 1,000 evacuees into Camp Gibraltar".[14] As was often the case, the totals showed some discrepancies, as the numbers of men, women and children above added up to 1,104 persons, not 1,093. The second group, nearly three-fourths of them women, with the youngest arrival aged one month and the oldest about eighty years old, arrived three weeks later.[15]

In fact, the Gibraltarian population in Jamaica was about 90 per cent women, children and elderly adult males, many of them without trades or professions. A camp report noted that "they lack for the most part able bodied men"[16] and another that "several received Pensions and Separation Allowances from home, but that many were without consistent means of support".[17]

The Gibraltarian evacuees told the monthly *Catholic Opinion* newspaper that they had been unwilling to leave home:

> We did not want to leave the Rock. We believe it is impregnable from sea and air. The only way it could possibly be taken is from land, and we feel that General Franco will neither move against it himself, nor allow the Germans passage through Spain, unless his hand is forced by superior military might.[18]

The plan to re-evacuate Gibraltarians from London to the West Indies foundered in the face of intensified attacks in the North Atlantic, especially after a German submarine sank the SS *City of Benares*, a vessel evacuating British children to Canada, in September 1940. On 25 October 1940, the First Lord of the Admiralty advised the War Cabinet that threats to shipping from German U-boats made it impossible to transport evacuees until a new and more effective convoy system could be put in place. In late November, the secretary of state for the colonies advised the governor of Gibraltar that they would not proceed with the re-evacuation plans in the near future.[19] In the end, the Gibraltarians in the UK spent the war there, billeted in London during the Blitz and eventually transferred to Ballymena in Northern Ireland where many spent up to a decade before finally being allowed to return home.[20] A War Office document noted in Spring 1941 that the reason for wishing to send Gibraltarians to Jamaica rather than keep them in Britain was largely a health question, "but as it happened shipping did not allow many to be sent to Jamaica and we have got over the winter without any disasters".[21]

By mid-1941, it was decided that further groups of evacuees leaving Gibraltar, most of them able-bodied male civilians who could be released from their tasks, should be sent to Britain rather than Jamaica. The availability of work in the United Kingdom, the presence of many of the wives and families there and the shorter journey from Gibraltar were major factors in the imperial decision, despite the availability of space at Gibraltar Camp in Jamaica.[22] A footnote to this decision came in a letter to the Colonial Office in June 1941: it said that recent arrivals from Gibraltar included about thirty men and women anxious to re-join wives or husbands in Jamaica – some of them stating that they were told in Gibraltar that this could be arranged.[23] Permission was denied, and it was suggested that Gibraltar be asked not to hold out any such hope to subsequent evacuees. Hard on the heels, the *Gleaner* of 29 July 1941 carried a story headlined: "Five Gibraltarian Evacuees Here." The male evacuees had left Gibraltar on their own and taken ship to Trinidad, from whence they were sent on to Jamaica.[24] There were also at least two transfers from Curacao – one, a group of three Spanish refugees who had been living in Gibraltar and the other, Alfred Mansfield, a young Gibraltarian man following his family and sweetheart. Medically discharged from his dockyard job, he took the first available ship to the West Indies, signing on to an oil tanker as a cabin boy. In Curacao, he abandoned the ship and found his way on to a ship sailing for Jamaica, where he asked to be admitted to the camp. Mansfield and Dominga Busuttil were married at Gibraltar Camp on 14 September 1940, and their daughter, Aileen, was born at the Victoria Jubilee Lying-In Hospital in Kingston in July 1943.[25] She would be one of the youngest of some one hundred babies born to Gibraltarians while in Jamaica. Many of the others had been conceived before their mothers left home. Births at the camp would be balanced by deaths, most of them among the many older residents. An unconfirmed reference, rooted in a school project in Gibraltar mentioned "other cases in which certain numbers of Gibraltar civilians were sent to Jamaica in the [troopships] *Aurelia* and *Athens*".[26] No records of these arrivals have been found.

For the period November 1940 until October 1944 when most of them were repatriated, there were over fifteen hundred evacuees living in Gibraltar Camp, including a group of some three dozen Jewish Gibraltarians.[27] This population also included various individuals or small groups who arrived in the ensuring year, petitioning to join the camp community. These evacuees, who were settled on the upper level of the camp in the closest proximity to all its facilities, had the camp to themselves for just over a year before the first set of refugees were moved into barracks on the lower level. They would remain in Jamaica for another three years, until 10 October 1944, when they were among the earliest Gibraltarian evacuees repatriated, aboard the SS *Duchess of Richmond*. A census of the population was taken in December 1943; however, the record is incomplete.[28] Only a few Gibraltarians, most of them young men who had joined the military auxiliary Pioneer Corps but also a few women who had married Jamaicans, would remain behind.

The Gibraltarian presence in Jamaica sparked an ongoing semantic confusion between *Evacuees* – persons sent away from home for their own safety on orders from their governments, often despite protest; and *Refugees* – persons who escaped religious or political persecution by gaining permission to stay in another country. The evacuees pithily reminded Jamaicans of their identity in an article in the *Catholic Opinion* newspaper, shortly after their arrival in Jamaica:

> Just the other day two of our girls from the Camp were shopping in Issa's, when they heard a voice behind them saying: "There's two of those Spanish refugees, now!" Ofelia and Eulalia turned around, and Ofelia said: "First of all, we are not Spanish, we are British. And secondly, we are not refugees, we are evacuees."[29]

The Gibraltarian group did include dozens of Spanish refugees from General Franco's Spain, which was only a causeway away from Gibraltar. Many thousands of Spaniards had long worked – and some lived – in the British colony where the residents spoke at least as much Spanish as English. Some of these residents became refugees from the Spanish Civil War of 1936-1939, and some of them arrived among the evacuees in 1940. A *Gleaner* report numbered thirty-four Spaniards among the second group of Gibraltarians evacuees, though in general there was little reference to the presence of Spanish refugees among the Gibraltarian evacuees, perhaps in acknowledgement of the unstable relationship between General Franco's Spain and the Allies.[30] In June 1941, a further three Spanish citizens from Gibraltar landed in Curacao, asking to be sent on to Gibraltar Camp, Jamaica. Permission was granted on the condition that "if admitted, they will be accommodated in the Gibraltar evacuee camp, and will be subject to the rules under which the camp is administered".[31]

The sensitivity of the position of the Spanish among the evacuees was hinted at in newspaper coverage in November 1943. Following a brief report on a performance by young ladies of Gibraltar Camp, which also referred to this "Spanish nation", the newspaper ran a retraction. It said that the evacuees at Gibraltar Camp were all British citizens, "none of them are Spanish nationals as might be inferred from a paragraph in Wednesday's Gleaner".[32] Official correspondence also made clear the continuing delicate balance in the relationship between Spain and Britain with respect to Gibraltar, as the war in Europe wound towards an end. The time was not propitious for Gibraltarians to live on the Spanish mainland, nor for Spanish refugees among the Gibraltarian evacuees to return to Gibraltar. At the end of 1943 when a Plan for Returning Evacuees suggested that evacuees in Jamaica be given priority for repatriation, it added that "Spanish evacuees who might have to be sent back to the Colony would be relegated to the bottom of the priority list". The document went so far as to ask the Colonial Office, if no undertakings to the contrary had been given, to ensure that "no Spanish evacuee from Gibraltar should be allowed to return to the Colony" – a position eventually modified.[33] A 1944 Gibraltar Resettlement Board document listed eighty Spanish refugees among the Gibraltarian civilians in Jamaica.[34] The governor of Jamaica, by then Sir John Huggins, had a slightly higher estimate, perhaps on the basis of the Gibraltar Camp census carried out in December 1943. He said, in 1944, that there were ninety-eight Spanish or other alien evacuees classified as political refugees and technical aliens, long resident in Gibraltar, among the group scheduled to return to that colony. And, in response to a suggestion that the governor of Gibraltar might only be prepared to receive some of these persons back in Gibraltar, Governor

Huggins stated that he would not allow any of them to remain in Jamaica.[35] It should be noted that there was a Spanish vice-consul in Jamaica from 1941, menswear manufacturer David Sabio, though official correspondence regarding these refugees has not been located.[36] A *Gleaner* newspaper report of December 1944 suggested that a special solution might have been found for at least some of these refugees. It said that the vessel repatriating the Gibraltarians made a stop at Casablanca in Morocco where some fifty of the Spanish refugees were landed before the vessel carried on to Gibraltar.[37]

Refugees

The Gibraltarians had been in Jamaica for just over a year, and the British government had decided that the larger group of Gibraltarians still in London would stay there rather than risk crossing the North Atlantic, when the decision was taken that would bring the second group of residents into Gibraltar Camp. These were Jewish refugees from Poland and other Eastern and Central European countries who had escaped ahead of Nazi occupations in central and southern Europe. Many had hidden and hiked long distances – stories which some of the refugees would write for personal history and others for publication.[38] They had gotten as far as Portugal, some of them by the grace of Portuguese consul in Bordeaux, France, Aristides de Sousa Mendes who famously defied Portuguese government orders to cease issuing visas or passports to Jews fleeing the Nazis – a decision that ended his diplomatic career.[39] With so many refugees already in Portugal, the authorities professed themselves reluctant to issue onward transit visas for Poles and Czechs in unoccupied France who had qualifications that were valuable to the war effort and whom the Allies were anxious to extract from the continent.[40]

Pragmatism and serendipity may each have played a part in the decision to allow some of the refugees entry to Jamaica. Certainly, in early November 1941, correspondence was already taking place between the Polish Embassy in London, the British Foreign Office, and later the Colonial Office, with regard to rescuing this group. Some of the refugees also claimed that they sent British prime minister Winston Churchill a birthday telegram on 30 November, in which they appealed for his help.[41] Whether or not this was a factor in the decision-making is unknown, but the British Foreign Office did request that the Colonial Office "ask Jamaica whether they could accommodate them temporarily either in an existing camp or by building additional huts". The Colonial Office agreed to forward the request but said that there would have to be a guarantee of removal after the war, as well as a guarantee of expenses, and "the refugees would probably all have to be accommodated under semi-internment conditions". It said that this might mean confinement to camp at night and that the refugees would not be allowed to engage in any business without special permission from the colonial government: "That Government would reserve its right to make such conditions in this respect as it deemed fit and also to intern fully any refugee whom it deemed fit to intern."[42]

Governor of Jamaica Sir Arthur Richards concurred with these arrangements in December 1941 and, in January, enquired whether the refugees would need interpreters or a kosher butcher – both of which the Colonial Office answered in the negative.[43] Jamaica also agreed to accept up to twenty Allied refugees from Portugal under the same conditions as the Polish Jews, to a total of two hundred and twenty persons.[44]

During wartime, policies guiding the acceptance of the refugees in the colonies reflected imperial concerns. Louise London, in *Whitehall and the Jews*, argued that Britain was determined to operate, where necessary, as a country of transit for Jewish refugees and hence wanted to be sure that they had an ultimate destination. London recognized British anti-Semitism as a factor but also concerns regarding unemployment and social services.[45] This perspective would have informed a discussion within the Colonial Office on the possible – even likely – Gibraltarian objection to sharing their camp with Jewish refugees, though there was no evidence of the Gibraltarians in the camp actually expressing any such objection. It was decided to provide some spatial separation between the Gibraltarians and their new neighbours – something easily achievable given the camp layout and the significant amounts of accommodation standing empty.[46] These refugees, and eventually other non-Gibraltarian groups, were accommodated in what was sometimes termed Camp II on a lower escarpment within the camp. The accommodation, sanitation provisions and dining halls were the same as in Camp I on the upper level where the main common facilities – hospital, police post, canteen and recreation hall – were located. The sections shared the same entrance and the same regulations applied.

The first group of 153 refugees arrived in Kingston aboard the SS *Serpa Pinto*, on 7 February 1942, two weeks after sailing from Lisbon, and were moved to Gibraltar Camp. Of them, 147 were Polish men, women and children, three were Dutch, one Belgian, one German and one American. The American, Bertrand Jacobson, was representing the American Jewish Joint Distribution Committee (JOINT), which had agreed to underwrite the group's maintenance, and subsequently left.[47] Jacobson wrote that members of the group had been stranded in Lisbon for between six and eighteen months. He said that they had appealed to the Polish government-in-exile which negotiated with the British government, and which negotiated with the JOINT for a guarantee to cover their transportation to and maintenance in Jamaica:

They had been able to get only as far as Lisbon; the broad Atlantic seemed an insuperable hurdle. Their situation in Portugal was precarious. Not permitted to work, they were being supported by the J.D.C. together with other stranded refugees in Portugal. They had nothing to look forward to except an imminent German invasion of Portugal.[48]

In March, a telegram notified the governor of Jamaica that a second group, under the same agreement, would leave Lisbon around 15 March 1942. The eventual numbers landed in Jamaica from the SS *San Thome* were fourteen Poles, nine Czechs, four Dutch, seven Luxembourgers and one Austrian – a total of thirty-five persons. This would have brought the total number of Polish and Eastern European refugees at Gibraltar Camp to 188 persons out of a possible 220 agreed for acceptance.[49] Paul Bartrop, "From Lisbon to Jamaica. A Story of British Refugee Rescue during the Second World War", argued that the number was as high as five hundred. While there were requests for acceptance of subsequent groups, neither official correspondence nor camp estimates appear to support other arrivals.

On arrival in Jamaica, a few of the refugees, identified by the authorities in Portugal, were segregated for questioning prior to being allowed to join their colleagues. One man from the first group, the German, was sent to the military internment camp in Kingston – one of the cases of Jews interned in the same camp with Nazis, which would raise concerns near and far.[50] The other refugees were moved to Gibraltar Camp, where many were quarantined due to a suspected case of typhus aboard the SS *Serpa Pinto*.[51] This was prolonged when a camp resident contracted dengue fever, and it was eight weeks before the refugees were actually allowed to take trips outside the camp.[52] Businessman Maurice Tempelsman, a guest at the sixtieth anniversary of the UWI in 2008, recalled arriving in the camp from Portugal as a twelve-year-old boy with his parents and younger sister. He explained how the war disrupted their lives in Belgium, "when the German panzers crashed through the borders of Belgium, France and neutral Holland, nine months after the start of World War II in September 1939". Between May and June, the Allied forces were overwhelmed, and the remaining British fighters were evacuated from Dunkirk. Tempelsman recalled how, in Jamaica, he started learning English in a wooden barrack classroom, "alongside the children who previously had been evacuated from Gibraltar". His family remained just seven months at Gibraltar Camp before leaving *en route* to a new life in the United States.[53]

These refugees at Gibraltar Camp would be subject to the same freedoms and restrictions as the Gibraltarians, including a ban on taking up employment outside the camp. The restrictions would be a consistent bone of contention. While the Colonial Office had clearly conveyed these conditions of entry to the

Foreign Office, it appears likely that they were not shared with the group until they were *en route* – perhaps even on arrival in Kingston Harbour. Tomasz Potworowski, who researched the evacuation of the Poles from Portugal, was of this opinion.⁵⁴ A Committee of the Polish Group at Gibraltar Camp, writing to the JOINT in mid-1942 went further, stating, "most categorically", that they were told "that we would have the right to work and to reside freely in Jamaica". The signatories said that it was on arrival, while still on board ship, that they were told they would be housed, temporarily, in the camp – the final truth about the impossibility of working or living outside the camp being communicated by the JOINT representative a few days later.⁵⁵ Some have argued that this timing reflected security concerns including fears that these groups might become infiltrated by German agents.⁵⁶ However, it seems possible that the failure to convey the conditions of entry might also have reflected anxiety to get this group out of Portugal, clearing the way for the technically qualified refugees whom the Allies considered useful to the war effort.

The Poles at Gibraltar Camp were frustrated with their living conditions – especially the inactivity – as well as with a lack of representation in Jamaica by the Polish government-in-exile and connected difficulties in gaining visas to other, permanent destinations. These concerns were aggravated by transport challenges, given the distance of the camp from the city, as well as the personal circumstances of many of the refugees. Stories, spread abroad, that they were being held in poor conditions at Gibraltar Camp may have sought to force interest in their situation, but did not endear them to local officials. The JOINT, which provided the economic guarantee for the Poles, said that while the British authorities "stressed that the refugees were treated as guests of a friendly power . . . the Polish refugees were disposed to compare camp conditions with those of a concentration camp".⁵⁷ These complaints surfaced in the United States and were communicated to the Colonial Office, which wrote to the governor for clarification. In this context, it was perhaps unsurprising that Governor Richards roundly refused to relax the restrictions. The governor acknowledged that there was some unrest among the Polish Jews in the camp, "who claim that they were brought to Jamaica under false pretences and were given to understand that they would be free to work and to live where and how they chose". He said that it suited these persons to allege that they were interned and that references to a concentration camp were aimed at persuading the American authorities to grant the refugees entry permits. Recalling earlier correspondence with the Colonial Office, which had established the basis of entry, the governor refused to "review the arrangements under which these persons were permitted to come to Jamaica, or to consent to their accepting employment or engaging in business", but said that those who could get visas were at liberty to leave the island.[58]

This unhappy relationship between the colonial authorities in Jamaica and the Polish refugees at Gibraltar Camp may have doomed any chance of a positive response to queries about sending other Polish refugees to Jamaica. Two such efforts were documented. One was in 1942 seeking the evacuation of a group of Polish Jews in Tangier, Morocco, who were threatened with repatriation to Poland at a time when the German authorities were already sending Jews to concentration camps. An initial query of May 1942, by the Polish Embassy in London, had elicited the response that the Jamaican quota for Jewish refugees was full. At the end of August, around the time when the governor was responding to charges by the Polish Jews already in Jamaica, there was a second attempt to raise the matter, asking for entry under similar conditions as the group already in Jamaica. In 1943, another enquiry about the evacuation of Polish refugees from Gibraltar to Jamaica may have referred to the same group – Gibraltar being a mere stone's throw from the Moroccan coast. However, there is no record of further arrivals of Polish refugees in Jamaica, at the Gibraltar Camp facility.[59]

The second set of refugees and third major group resident within Gibraltar Camp during World War II comprised several contingents of Dutch refugees, who stayed for varying periods from December 1942. The original correspondence involving the Dutch government-in-exile and the British Foreign Office, and then the Foreign Office and Colonial Office, was over the possibility of temporary asylum in Trinidad for Dutch nationals who urgently needed to leave Spain, *en route* for Dutch Guiana – Surinam. The Foreign Office told the Colonial Office that it was particularly anxious to oblige the Netherlands government, "as a *quid pro quo*" for having accepted a batch of Jewish refugees at Curacao, the previous year – a group that the British had not finished withdrawing, despite overstaying the agreed time. The Foreign Office argued: "Unless we can help them over their party of Jews for Surinam, they will certainly be averse to turning a favourable ear to any appeals we may make to them in the future."[60]

The Colonial Office responded that Trinidad was grossly overcrowded, with over fifteen hundred seamen rescued from ships sunk in Caribbean waters, in addition to British and American service personnel. As early as June 1940, Trinidad's governor Sir Herbert Young told the Legislative Council there that the island had a population of fewer than half a million people, but some ten thousand Allied, neutral and foreign aliens and scores of naturalized British citizens. Officials said that in July 1943 there were three camps operating in Trinidad – a Prisoner of War Camp, a rest camp and an internment camp with some fifty-one internees and thirty-four detainees of all nationalities, including women and children.[61] This was in addition to active American bases. British officials suggested Jamaica or British Guiana as alternatives.[62] Follow-up communication resulted in arrangements for a party of one hundred and fifty to two hundred Dutch subjects to be transported to Jamaica on board a ship of the Spanish Steamship Company, *Transatlantica*. A subsequent letter from the Foreign Office asked permission to extend the stop-over permission to cover 75 Dutch Jews from Unoccupied France, making 225 in all, and advised that they were hoping to all travel on the Spanish ship, *Marques de Comillas*, which should leave towards the end of October.[63] A telegram to the governor of Jamaica on 5 November 1942 advised that currency limitations would be applied to these refugees but they "are not *(repeat not)* to be searched for other unauthorised valuables".[64] These unauthorized valuables included diamonds sewn into hems of garments or otherwise concealed.

The first group from Vigo, Spain, arrived in Kingston at the beginning of December 1942, and documentation suggested that a second group followed soon after.[65] A member of that group recalled:

> Our first group was fortunate to be able to arrive in Spain before the Germans occupied Vichy France. The second group, still consisting of Jewish refugees, had to cross the Pyrenees on foot. . . . The third group consisted almost entirely of young, non-Jewish, mostly very blond men who had escaped in order to evade being sent to Germany to work. I only recall one Jewish family of four (husband, wife, parents of the woman) being in that group.[66]

The second group may be one whose arrival in March 1943 was reported in the *Gleaner* – described as being "comparatively small, including some seventy persons only".[67] Five months later, in August, there was a request for a group of fifty Netherlands refugees to be admitted in Jamaica, *en route* to Surinam.[68] Subsequent correspondence between the secretary of state for colonies and the officer administering the government of Jamaica indicated that a party of fifty to sixty Dutch refugees was scheduled to sail from Spain around 22 August 1943 on the SS *Marques de Comillas* and that these would form part of a quota agreed at a conference on Jewish refugees in Europe, held in Bermuda in 1943. It was agreed that up to four hundred refugees of Allied nationalities who were then in Spain could proceed to Jamaica. "They will be vouched for by the Joint Distribution Committee, the Allied

Authorities, and the Passport Control Office Madrid."[69] However, it was also noted that the development of a camp in North Africa to take refugees from Spain and Portugal could lessen the need to send persons to Jamaica.

In November 1943, the Netherlands consul-general in Jamaica, C.M. Dozy, provided the *Gleaner* with an overview of efforts to move Dutch refugees to safety after the German invasion of the Netherlands in May 1940. He said that Dutch citizens who fled to France were initially to have been moved to the Dutch East Indies – a plan delayed by shipping difficulties and then abandoned when the war spread to South-East Asia. The switch to the Dutch West Indies colonies – Curacao and Dutch Guiana (Surinam) – was slowed by a lack of adequate accommodation. Some refugees were moved to Curacao, mostly *en route* to other countries, and just over one hundred were sent directly from Portugal to Paramaribo, Surinam, in December 1942. Mr Dozy said that a group of 173 persons had been sent to Kingston in December 1942, with another group of 79 brought temporarily to Jamaica from Spain in March 1943. By the time of the interview, some 154 of these Dutch refugees had already moved on or identified jobs to which they would go. He said that several of the refugees, some of whom had lived at Gibraltar Camp for more than a year, had made private arrangements to go to Cuba, the United States or other locations. Another eighty-one would go to Curacao, and some young men had gone to join the armed forces.[70] Mr Dozy, who was seconded to Jamaica for one year from his post of consul-general at the Netherlands Embassy in London, left Jamaica shortly after the interview. A subsequent newspaper article reported that the Dutch refugees who had been living at Gibraltar Camp, some for more than a year, had left Jamaica for Surinam, on the order of their government, during Christmas week 1943.[71] An interviewee whose family was among those Dutch refugees allowed to move to Cuba said that they flew to Havana via Santiago de Cuba, leaving Jamaica on 17 December. She said that they spent two years in Cuba and then returned to the Netherlands.[72] A letter of 19 January 1944 from the commandant of Gibraltar Camp to the colonial secretary, regarding the payment of wages in refugee camps, noted that Polish and Dutch refugees in the camp were employed, where relevant on the same basis as the evacuees.[73] This might have suggested that some of the in-transit Dutch refugees remained at the camp in January. However, it might also relate to four Dutch refugees who had arrived with the Eastern European group.

Joanna Newman, using data from the American Jewish Joint Distribution Committee, identified five groups of Dutch Jewish and non-Jewish refugees as having arrived at Gibraltar Camp: two in December 1942, of 250 and

175 persons respectively, one in April 1943 of 305 persons, one in October 1943 of 60 persons and one in December 1943 of 300 refugees.[74] This is a significantly higher number than either the Dutch Consul or the Gibraltar Camp administration admitted.

Figures prepared by the commandant of Gibraltar Camp in relation to reimbursement for these and other refugees for the 1942–1943 financial year stated that 173 Dutch were maintained from 5 December to 31 December 1942, 174 Dutch from 1 January to 10 March 1943, 254 Dutch from 11 March to 31 March.[75] This would tally with the figures given by the Dutch Consul. Subsequent correspondence referred to arrangements for the reception of different batches of these Dutch Jewish refugees "on their arrival in Kingston on the 5th of December, 1942, the 11th of March, 1943, and the 20th of September, 1943, by the SS *Marques de Comillas*".[76] A Dutch correspondent who lived at the camp for a year recalled that the first two groups – one of 172 and a second of 110 – were Dutch Jews, while a third group was mainly non-Jewish young men.[77] This could be the planned group of some fifty to sixty persons, referred to earlier. It is possible that a fourth Dutch group arrived in Jamaica after Mr Dozy's departure: Gibraltar Camp Estimates of Expenditure for 1944–45, submitted in December 1943, assumed the presence of 165 Dutch residents.[78] However, these may equally be the Dutch who left during Christmas week on order of their government. Certainly, it appears that the Dutch had all departed by early 1944. In June 1944, the *Gleaner* newspaper reported that a course in social welfare for twenty-five Caribbean students, funded by the West Indies Development & Welfare Scheme, was using the **former** Dutch barracks in the lower level of Gibraltar Camp.[79]

The Dutch group, many of whose members were wealthy, also expressed frustration over the requirements to live in the camp and to refrain from creating or accepting business opportunities. However, unlike the Poles, these refugees were aware of efforts by their government to move them to permanent locations, and many of them established links outside of the camp or took advantage of opportunities for recreation.

As the varying estimates for the numbers of Dutch refugees portend, there is significant variation in the overall numbers of refugees claimed to have lived on the lower level of Gibraltar Camp – sometimes termed Camp II and sometimes further distinguished as Camp II (Poles) and Camp III (Dutch). As was discussed in a chapter on Jamaica in *World War II and the Caribbean*, several estimates have been made on the number of Jewish refugees provided with haven inside Gibraltar Camp, though some appear out of step with evidence provided within the camp records. Looking back in 1989, Fr William Feeney, Roman Catholic Chaplain for the Camp from 1940 to 1943, estimated that "as many as two thousand Jewish refugees" were accommodated in the "surplus barracks" at Gibraltar Camp.[80] A 1996 article by Claus Stolberg and Katja Füllberg-Stolberg estimated that up to "four thousand eight hundred refugees of various nationalities" were in the camp, as at April 1943. They argued that "many more Jewish refugees from Holland were accommodated in Camp III than had been recorded in the documents at hand" and preferred to rely on the recollection of eyewitnesses from the period.[81]

In her memoir, *Escape from the Inferno*, Polish refugee Miriam Sandzer Stanton said: "We had, with the Dutch refugees, over three thousand people living in the refugee section of Gibraltar Camp and about one thousand employees working there." But she also wrote of the "dead silence, hardly a soul walking about except a handful of people in the lower camp" when, in October 1944, "the Gibraltarians, all two thousand of them, left together on one big ship".[82] Stanton's estimate of the Gibraltarians was also overstated by some four hundred, and her other references to the camp as a "bustling and lively little town" were to the facility as a whole, not just to the refugee section. Hence it may be that she was really estimating three thousand persons in the entire camp.

Colonial Office files referred to two Eastern European – mainly Polish – groups arriving from Portugal, the first in February 1942 and the second in the first quarter of 1943, to a total of 188 persons. This appears to tally with the Gibraltar Camp records, including a detailed record of arrivals, births and departures among the Polish group up to the end of March 1943.[83] Three Dutch contingents could be confirmed: one of 173 arriving in December 1942, a possible but not proven group of around 110 persons arriving in February 1943 – which could overlap with the reported group of seventy or eighty persons in March 1943, and a group of fifty to sixty persons referenced in August 1943. A list sourced from a Dutch Archive referenced just three sailings to Jamaica by the SS *Marques de Comillas* from Vigo between November 1942 and August 1943.[84]

These documented arrivals would suggest a total of 533 at minimum and around 880 refugees at maximum. Of course, it is possible that more refugees arrived after these first groups had moved on, though no evidence of that has been confirmed through camp or Colonial Office records. An October 1944 report on measures taken by the British Commonwealth to provide asylum for refugees referred to Jamaica maintaining "approximately five hundred refugees" in addition to some fifteen hundred evacuees from Gibraltar.[85]

The estimates of expenditure for the camp, prepared in December 1943, certainly supported the more modest figures, though some of the refugees would already have moved on. These estimates contained a file note indicating that of 1,709 inmates of the 3 camps, 1,530 Gibraltarian and Spanish evacuees were accommodated in Camp I; with an unspecified number of Polish and other refugees in Camp II; and some 165 Dutch refugees in Camp III. There were also 7 Finnish internees, 186 local staff and 446 evacuee staff employed at Gibraltar Camp. A concurrent document detailing the number of Polish and other Eastern European refugees in Camp II between the first quarter of 1942 and the first quarter of 1943 showed a high of 185 persons, falling to 149 by the end of the period.[86]

The estimates for the Dutch and Finnish residents were calculated at 5/- per person per day which, at an estimate of £15,696 for Camp III for 1944–1945, compared with an approved estimate of £14,601 for 1943–1944, works out to some one hundred and sixty persons.[87] The apportionment of expenditure for the Dutch refugees from December 1942 to March 1943 was worked out at 4/2 per person per day, including 1/6 per person per day for dietary costs and 2/8 per person per day for other costs.[88]

Despite speculation to the contrary, an assessment of the correspondence and camp records makes it seem unlikely that the cumulative number of refugees in the barracks on the lower level of the camp ever approached the total number of evacuees on the upper level.

While most of the refugees in Gibraltar Camp moved on to longer-term or permanent opportunities, a few Eastern European residents who were awaiting or had been unable to get visas remained in the camp. There were some sixty-nine persons remaining when most of the Gibraltarians were repatriated, and the military began taking over the camp. These Polish and other Eastern European refugees were moved to the upper level, close to the administration and the main gate. Already, there was "strong objection to continuing to administer the camp for these persons only", but it was still felt that "their release in Jamaica is impracticable". Appeals to London were unhelpful. The Colonial Office commented that the Polish government was in no position to assist, and the UK government was "no more willing than in 1942".[89]

By March 1945, with thirty-three Eastern European refugees remaining in a significantly shrunken camp, the possibility of finding alternative accommodation was investigated, and it was determined that the cost of putting them in private lodging would be greater than continuing to accommodate them.[90] There appears to have been an effort to lobby for them to be employed early in 1945 but Acting Colonial Secretary H.M. Brown confirmed that the Local Defence Regulations did not permit them to practice any profession or carry out any business, occupation, industry or craft without a licence – which the government was not prepared to grant.[91] *Gleaner* columnist Peter Simple publicized the plight of the small group in his column "It Seems to Me", in April 1945. He suggested that either a fund be raised to help them overcome the financial hurdle obstructing their migration to the United States, or they be allowed to become part of the local community. In response, Polish musician Dr Arthur Steigler wrote that after an idle and useless camp life, most of the refugees were ready and willing to place their knowledge and professional experience at Jamaica's disposal and to be of use to the country and would be glad to enjoy "the hospitality and the warm social climate of the Jamaican community". He said that "to solve the problem of 'absorbing' the thirty souls, it would be quite sufficient to find work for the fifteen heads of families which includes the single persons".[92] The authorities remained uninterested. A minute to a 1947 Colonial Secretariat file noted that none of the Poles or Czechs at the Gibraltar Camp wished to return to Europe and that apart from Czechs who were seeking permission to enter Argentina, the remaining refugees had applied for permission to enter the United States. It added: "The prospects of their departure from the Colony is [sic], however, uncertain." It said that the local authorities had requested early removal of the refugees from Jamaica but had been advised that the United Nations Relief and Rehabilitation Administration was being asked to undertake responsibility for refugees in the British Empire "and that those in Jamaica could only be dealt with in connection with negotiations for the general settlement of the problem".[93]

By the time the Camp's 1947/48 Estimates of Expenditure were being prepared, the number of refugees had fallen to fourteen. Though the government still rejected permanent residence, describing the majority as "advanced in years" and "destitute", the matter of moving them to private lodgings was again raised – this time, implemented – and Gibraltar Imperial Camp closed its doors. [94]

Other Groups

Adding to the heterogeneity of the population within Gibraltar Camp, by the middle of the war, there was also a small group of Finnish sailors quartered in Camp II on the lower level where the refugees would be accommodated. These men had been interned in Jamaica at a time when the Soviet Union had become a British ally against Germany, and the Finns had allied with Germany in an effort to regain territories lost to the Russians earlier in World War II. One of the Finns was a cabin boy, taken off a Norwegian ship visiting Kingston Harbour, in December 1941. The others were the crew of a merchant ship seized by British authorities in early 1942.[95] First sent to the Male Internment Camp in Kingston, the men were soon reassigned to Gibraltar Camp when the British policy towards Finnish seamen shifted, based on a Canadian decision to continue employing Finnish, Hungarian and Romanian seamen. The Canadians argued that shortages of seamen would affect shipping and asked for a change of policy in several colonial ports. The official order moving thirty-one named Finns to Gibraltar Camp was dated 16 July 1942. Subsequent correspondence noted that the men were released from internment subject to a Restriction Order and that some of them had since obtained employment and left the island.[96] The Estimates of Expenditure for Gibraltar Camp, prepared in December 1943, made provision for seven Finns.[97]

Italian collaborators were another ex-internee group allowed to take up residence in Gibraltar Camp – in this case, after the departure of the Gibraltarians and all but a few refugees, when most of the camp had been taken over by the military. After the Armistice of 1943, when Italy surrendered to the Allies, Italian internees in the Male Internment Camp had been offered the opportunity to sign an agreement signifying their co-operation with the Allies. Those who did were moved to a military hill station at Newcastle, in the mountains above Kingston, until severe drought forced alternative arrangements. Some of the Italians had already been accommodated at Gibraltar Camp while doing contract work on military construction projects and all of them appear to have subsequently moved there. For a time, three Italian couples were also accommodated.[98]

By April 1946, there were 149 Italians housed at Gibraltar Camp. The Swiss vice-consul reported that because most of the refugees previously in Gibraltar Camp had left Jamaica, the accommodation was available for housing the Italians. It was also reported that they were "treated more or less as refugees. They are given the utmost freedom and allowed to come and go as they please, except that there is a rule that they must be in the Camp by 11 o'clock in the evening, unless a special pass has been obtained".[99] A report from the Swiss vice-consul said that most of the men were working, "employed as brick makers, masons, terrazzo workers, labourers and carpenters. They work at the local standard of pay or at piece work rates". The men had also been allowed to develop "quite a large workshop in the Camp, where a great deal of work is done, which is in turn sold in the local market. In addition, a number of them have been employed in building houses for local contractors".[100] Local interviewees recalled the Italian workshop, which produced ceramic drainpipes, basins, tiles and other items including ornamental concrete items for gateposts and gardens, with lions' heads and pineapples being popular themes.[101] One recalled going there more than once, between 1944 and 1946, with her father who was planning to extend their home and needed fixtures for which the skilled Italian craftsmen were developing a reputation:

> The camp was . . . all enclosed with barbed wire, and there were guards, and one got in with some sort of official permit . . . We walked some distance to the workshops where the Italians had their drainpipes, face basins, bathtubs and such like on display.[102]

Accommodation for the single men was in three long barracks with sanitary conveniences "some distance from where the three married couples and the Camp Supervisor and his Assistant etc are housed". They had a separate bath house and a nearby, airy outside kitchen and received rations which were considered good, but they could also make their own arrangements at the camp kitchen whereby they received extra food for a weekly fee.[103] It is not clear where in Gibraltar Camp the Italians were housed. The reference to the Camp supervisor and his assistant suggests that they were within the refugee section, which was separated from the military compound – however it is also plain that they technically remained under military oversight and subject to reports by the protecting power. By this time, the only earlier camp residents were the remaining Polish and Czech refugees, who may have been accommodated in the old Nunnery, near the administrative housing. There is no evidence of interaction between these groups.

Evacuee–Refugee Relationships

There appears to have been little social interaction between the evacuee and refugee groups within Gibraltar Camp during the period up to late 1944 when the Gibraltarians left. They shared the camp, with its shops, post office, administration and access ways but had their own barracks accommodation, eating and entertainment areas. This enabled the maintenance of language and religious communities, but it also created spatial buffers, rooted in expectations that different groups might resent sharing space. The British officials who, in 1942, accepted the mainly Polish refugees expected the Gibraltarians to react negatively to sharing the camp – perhaps modelling anti-Semitic attitudes found in the heart of the empire. A letter from the governor in Jamaica to the secretary of state for the colonies said that the lower section of the camp had been opened "for racial and religious reasons".[104]

The potential for lack of appreciation may have been mutual. Polish refugee Miriam Stanton, in a memoir of the camp, commented that "the people in the camp left a lot to be desired, but the camp was big enough for privacy".[105] And a Dutch refugee, then a pre-teen, said that there was "practically no interaction with the people from Gibraltar, except with the woman who came to clean our rooms every now and then. These people spoke Spanish only".[106] The Jamaican daughter of the camp manager, who lived in the camp as a teen, saw relations between camp residents in socio-economic terms, based on what their preferences and resources were. Friendly with some of the young Dutch adults, she observed that the Gibraltarians spoke mainly Spanish and developed few social connections with other groups. "But there was no problem", she added. [107]

Hence it was non-physical barriers that effectively separated the co-existing populations – the staunchly Roman Catholic, mainly working-class, British government-protected Gibraltarian evacuees; the business, professional and working-class Polish Jews, many of them bitter at their unsettled situation; and the mainly well-off, middle- and upper-class Dutch who were in Jamaica at the behest of their government, in transit to more permanent destinations. The evacuees spoke Spanish and some English; the refugees spoke their own national languages, and some spoke English and, perhaps, one of the other European languages. Differences of language therefore supported the differences in religion and culture – a factor acknowledged in a newspaper article on Polish refugee, Mavia Bojm, who spoke "several languages and always contributed to everything done for the comfort of the residents at Gibraltar Camp".[108]

Some of the younger refugees attended privately arranged classes in their own sections of the camp, but they could also access the regular school classes established in 1940 to cater to the Gibraltarian children, most of whom were fully educated within the camp. Only a few of the Gibraltarians – those preparing for external examinations – were sent to local secondary school, while many of the refugee children had recollections of attending external schools. Manne Ekstein also spelled Eckstein, a nine-year-old whose father was Polish and mother Dutch, attended school with the Gibraltarian children for a term, to learn enough English to go to a school in the nearby city of Kingston. She recalled that she developed a close relationship with her Gibraltarian teacher and her teacher's sister and would visit their home in the upper level of the camp.[109] However, it appeared that this was unusual and, perhaps, an easier transition for a child.

The unseen barriers extended beyond the evacuee-refugee divide. Despite common faith, the implied and stated issues of class and language also affected relations between various groups of refugees living in the lower section of the camp – some of whom were wealthy while others were working-class people including dressmakers and shoemakers. One interviewee, then a young refugee, commented that the Dutch "did interact with the Polish people, but not too often. I know my sister who was three years older than myself, spent time with other nationalities her age in the camp".[110] Close relations between the Dutch and Poles did develop in at least one case: Jeane Casuto of Holland married Martin Flugelman of Lamberg in Poland at the Duke Street Synagogue in Kingston in 1943, with local Rabbi Henry Silverman officiating. *The Gleaner*, which carried a photograph of the newlyweds, noted that the marriage followed a year-long romance that began at Gibraltar Camp.[111]

One cross-faith marriage, between a Gibraltarian Catholic and a Gibraltarian Jew, may have had roots in Gibraltar. The teenagers ran away from Gibraltar Camp rather than be parted by the Catholic young woman's "stern father's decree". A *Gleaner* report noted that the young man was charged under the Defence Regulations which governed the camp, for persuading his girlfriend to leave the premises without written permission of the Camp commandant. The resident magistrate was sympathetic but said he could not allow the romantic aspects of the case to interfere with discipline. The two were later married by the camp chaplain at St Peter & Paul Church, Toll Gate, after they refused to be separated.[112]

A major factor in the development (or lack) of inter-relationships within the camp would have been timing. The Gibraltarians had full possession of the camp from their arrival in October–November 1940, until February 1942 when the first Polish refugees arrived and were assigned quarters on the lower level where they were quarantined for several weeks. The second group of Eastern Europeans followed. In July 1942, the small group of Finns were billeted nearby. December 1942 saw the arrival of the first Dutch group, followed by at least two more Dutch groups in 1943 – one of these mainly comprising non-Jewish young men. Some of the Eastern Europeans and many of the Dutch stayed weeks or months – some, up to a year. This Timetable of Arrivals and Departures in Gibraltar Camp is reflected in Figure 5. During 1943, various individuals and families left the camp as they received visas to travel on to new destinations, whether to jobs or to join family sponsors. Dutch family, the Schpektors, who had arrived in December 1942, moved on to Cuba late in 1943. Daughter Regina Inez said that when the Dutch government wanted to move the refugees to Surinam, "those that had bank accounts in the free world, or relatives in other countries, tried to go elsewhere – Curacao, Aruba, U.S.A. My mother's uncle was in Cuba and arranged for us to go there". She said that Cuba was "wonderful for refugees, but people were not allowed to work there unless they began a factory or worked for a refugee-owned factory – usually in the diamond trade". She estimated that there were some fifteen thousand Jews living in Cuba at the height of the refugee period.[113] Dutch refugees who did not find their own destinations were sent to Surinam by the Dutch government-in-exile. Also moving from Gibraltar Camp to Cuba were the Polish-Dutch Eckstein family who had arrived in February 1942. Daughter Manne Eckstein wrote that having been required to live in the camp in Jamaica, they were able to live freely in an apartment in Havana, before they gained visas for the United States and moved on to New York.[114] By early 1944, only Polish and Czech – and perhaps one or two other individuals of uncertain nationality – remained in the lower camp.

The Finns, who gradually found work on Allied vessels and left Jamaica, appear to have been the quietest of the camp residents, but also willing to interact. Jamaican camp officials recalled gifts of carved wooden items – Priscilla Harris, wife of the camp's commissary officer treasuring carved wooden boxes, and the Rae family long prizing a carved wooden ship that was a gift from the Finnish ship captain to the wife of the Camp commandant. The small group of Finns were reportedly content with their living conditions. According to one of their number, they received permission to convert an empty wooden building into a community hall and built tables and chairs to furnish it. He recalled that the Jews complained to the camp leader about their conditions and, also, that one of his group did "remodelling and changes for the rich Jews in the camp".[115]

Location, Layout and Administration

The camp into which these groups were placed during World War II and its immediate aftermath was a large, tidy and well-provided facility, with modern infrastructure belying its simple structures, which were built in haste with materials available during wartime. The choice of location

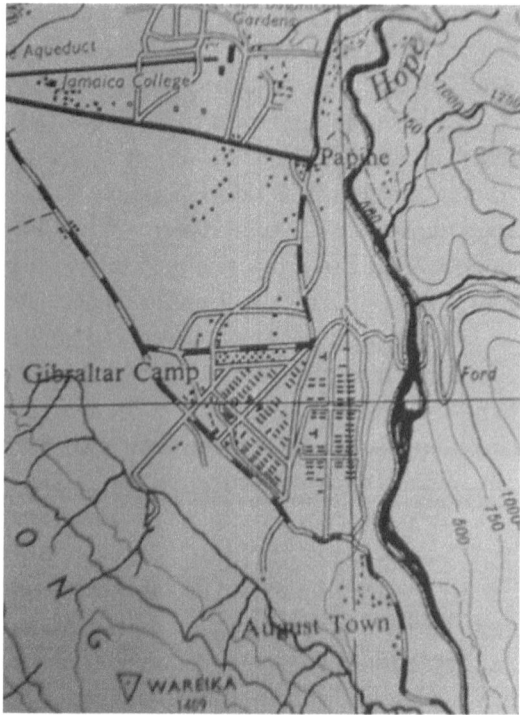

Figure 6 Map of Gibraltar Camp within the Papine and August Town area. Detail from 1:50,000 map of Kingston produced by the Directorate of Colonial Surveys.

would have taken into account the availability of a large and easily buildable site, accessibility to services, favourable climate, but also some degree of removal from the local population. The site chosen was in the parish of St Andrew, seven miles from the heart of Kingston, between the semi-rural districts of Papine and August Town. It was built on land once belonging to the Mona sugar estate, whose eighteenth-century cut-stone aqueduct ran along the western boundary. The actual boundaries of the site leased by the colonial secretariat were the Hope River to the east, August Town Road to the south, the old Mona Estate Works to the west and Lindo Gap Road to the north.[116] Figure 6 shows the camp location.

The main approach to the camp was via the market community of Papine, which lay about two kilometres north of the camp, and which was the terminus for a public tram service – replaced, in 1944, by bus service.[117] This transportation system provided ingress and egress for residents, employees and other Jamaicans with business at the camp and could also be a locale for social interaction. A December 1942 report on conditions for the recently arrived Polish refugee group said that going to Kingston necessitated a fifteen-minute walk "to the nearest trolley stop. The trolley leaves every thirty minutes and takes about three quarters of an hour to Kingston". Charles H. Jordan of the American Jewish Joint Distribution Committee (JOINT) which was underwriting the maintenance of the group found it "quite expensive" and thought that "many people are unable to afford it".[118]

Several Jamaican interviewees noted the distance of the camp from the centre of Kingston, mentioning that it was even beyond Jamaica College, a well-known boys' school considered to be isolated, and also beyond the Hope Botanical Gardens, which was even farther from the city.[119] However, the clearest description of the camp's location came from an interviewee who explained:

> St Andrew was not what it is now. The city was Torrington Bridge to the sea. Torrington Bridge, up, was rural. It's only in the last forty years or so that St Andrew has become a part of Kingston. If you took the tram north, in the night, you would see *peeniewallies* and (hear) toads ... Mona was a mango walk. August Town – the people living there was isolated, country, ruinate, mongoose bush. It only developed after Hurricane Charlie (in 1951).[120]

Another interviewee who visited the camp in 1945, age eight years, with her father, described Gibraltar Camp as a place at the end of Hope Road. "We went to Hope Gardens for picnics, but that was an expedition", she said. "The tram went to Papine, but if you didn't have business there, why go there?"[121]

Construction of the camp fell to the local PWD which, with a very tight time frame, designed simple wooden barracks structures, ordering in materials not already available on the island. Site survey and planning were completed in two days following which the PWD subcontracted several local builders who employed thousands of local men to clear the site, construct roads, erect construction offices and stores, put in water and electricity supplies and telephone service.[122] Fr Bill Feeney, who became the camp's Roman Catholic chaplain, later wrote that three thousand five hundred men, employed by several contractors used six million feet of lumber to erect the barracks and other buildings and that during the building stage, "the place was bedlam".[123] Figures 7, 7A and 7B show views of the camp construction.

It was a massive effort and within four weeks, the first eighteen wooden units were ready and nine more were underway. Each of the barracks units, designed to accommodate the evacuees, was one hundred and fifty feet long and twenty-five feet wide, on hardwood footings, with seven-foot wide verandahs on the long sides. They were sub-divided into cubicles, to provide

Figures 7, 7A, 7B Gibraltar Camp under construction (Images by contractor G.W. Hart, Courtesy National Library of Jamaica).

homes for individuals and families and each block was twinned to another with concrete walkways and a block of sanitary conveniences in-between. Buildings combining kitchens and dining halls, as well as recreation and social facilities, stores and administrative buildings, hospital, fire station, police station and staff quarters were also under construction. Straight asphalt roads bisected the site. Water was drawn from an existing supply fed by the nearby Hope River, with a 10-inch main to a 181,000-gallon steel tank located beside the Commandant's residence near the entrance to the camp.

The PWD reported that by the end of the seventh week, the camp was essentially ready to receive the four thousand evacuees originally planned for. Then, on 15 September, instructions came to prepare for an additional five thousand people. The construction site was expanded from the originally surveyed eighty-one acres to two hundred plus acres and by the end of September, the expanded scope of work was underway. More buildings were being added to the original site with the balance, to house some three thousand people, on a lower terrace, one hundred feet above the Hope River – the section sometimes termed Camp II. The original camp hospital was also being expanded. This work was underway when the first and second groups of evacuees arrived in late October and early November. But on 13 November, word came to cancel any new construction, though work continued until early January to complete buildings already underway.[124] In a local radio broadcast on 28 November, the first official information on the camp to be shared with the Jamaican public, Commandant Mr J.L. Worlledge said that the camp had been occupied and that further work to accommodate an expected total of seven thousand evacuees was practically complete.[125] A 1941 Colonial Office estimate indicated that the eventual camp covered just over 252 acres: 85 acres for Camp I and 114 acres for Camp II and 53 acres for the camp hospital, at a cost of £375,000.[126]

Roads edged the camp boundaries on several sides, but the size of the camp meant that much of it was out of sight of these roads. In any case, traffic was relatively light – a mix of wheeled vehicles, pedestrians and animals, with the motorized traffic severely limited by gasolene rationing as the war progressed. Nonetheless, barbed wire fences enclosed the site. Indeed, in urging the removal of a section of fence which had obstructed the traditional road between August Town and Papine, along the Hope River, the August Town Citizens' Association noted sarcastically that the camp might wish to erect "another wire fence inside and parallel with the first to avoid interference with the Evacuees", as had been done on another side of the Camp.[127] Signs warning against unauthorized entry were also erected along the boundary of the camp. In July 1941, a letter to the *Gleaner*

90 | WORLD WAR II CAMPS IN JAMAICA

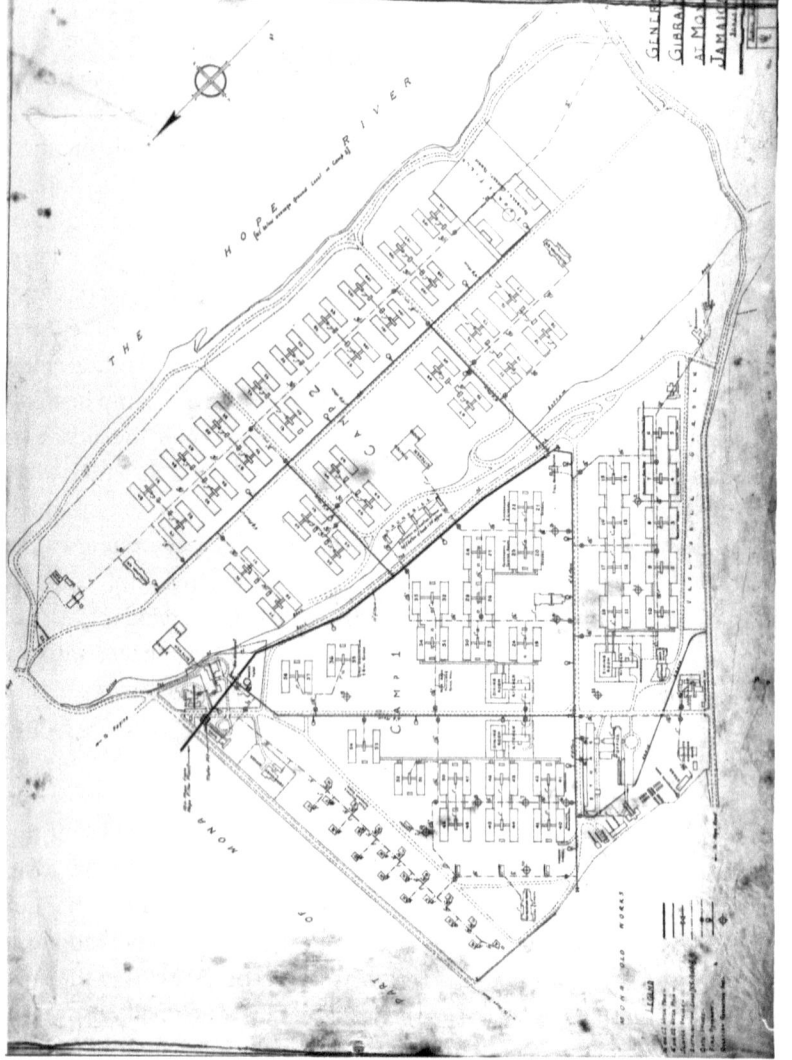

Figure 8 PWD layout of Gibraltar Camp (Source: The Jamaica Government Archives).

said that "yet another sign board has been put up until the state of complete encirclement seems to be near at hand".[128]

One such signboard was visibly mounted beside the guarded main gate, at the northern end of the camp, where both the Union Jack – the British flag – and the flag of Gibraltar flew.[129] Two secondary gates were erected on the August Town side of the camp, but not commonly used by residents – one of them giving occasional, limited public access to the camp's football fields.[130]

The chief guard was Juan Herrera, a Cuban who had come to Jamaica some years before the war and become the island's heavyweight boxing champion, and who wore a sheathed machete at his side. The commandant's son, a young man living in the camp, described Herrera as a charming man who "was dead serious about looking after their [camp residents'] security" and said that the refugees and evacuees, who had to report to him when they were leaving the camp, loved him.[131] There may previously have been a less prepared gateman – a newspaper report in early December 1940 said that a Gibraltar Camp gateman had been admitted to hospital with a fractured arm, received when he refused admittance to a group of men.[132] Jamaican watchmen undertook a regular night patrol, "recording on time clocks at fixed stations".[133] In addition, a Gibraltar Camp police station was established in October 1940 with a strong detachment of local police, and several male evacuees were sworn in as special constables. Records indicate that the station originally had a strength of "forty sub-officers and men, to meet which the government authorised the enlistment of forty extra men ... on 12 November 1940".[134] Even with a government intent to protect the evacuees against any incursions from the local population, this seems a large security contingent, though the numbers would have been estimated based on the expectation that the camp would be filled to capacity – which never occurred. The detachment of local constabulary was lessened over time and numbered some fourteen sub-officers and men when the force was removed in April 1942, leaving the Gibraltarian constables to manage policing on the camp. A "reliable source" explained to a reporter that "things have now so far settled down that it has been found unnecessary to incur the expense of maintaining a regular branch of the constabulary there".[135]

Within the camp gate, the main road ran north to south through a cluster of senior staff residences, including a Nunnery, the only two-storey building on the site. It passed several sets of barrack units and three connected dining hall-kitchen structures, before reaching the post office. An intersecting east-west artery wound from the main recreation hall, past laundry sheds, the canteen and stores buildings, crossed the main road and passed the Sacred Heart Church on the left, the 120-bed hospital, dispensary, dental facilities, police, fire brigade and quarters for the Priest and Matron on the right, before looping down to the lower level. Figure 8 shows features of the camp, laid out on a PWD plan.

The Nunnery was not complete when the camp opened. The nuns who had been seconded from several local orders to assist at the camp lived in three cottages on the site for seven weeks before moving into their own quarters, which included a private chapel.[136] Six of the sisters – two Franciscan, two Sisters of Mercy and two Franciscan Missionary Sisters (also called Blue Sisters or Native Sisters) oversaw the school; while the two Dominican Sisters assisted at the hospital.[137]

The Catholic Church, where mass was regularly sung, was created on the same plan as the camp recreation hall and seated some five hundred persons. It had a "good" organ and a "fine" altar, with statues of the Virgin Mary and the Sacred Heart on either side of the sanctuary, each with a metal candle holder in front. A large clock and a white cross, both electrically lit at night, were mounted over the main entrance, and there was Bahama grass, as well as canna lilies, crotons and roses planted around the church and frequently watered.[138] Sodalities and other church organizations were instituted and well attended. A room was identified for a synagogue as well as one for a kosher kitchen to cater to the small Jewish community among the Gibraltarians, though this kitchen does not appear to have ever been commissioned. Finlayson wrote that the Gibraltarian Jews were generally sent by bus to the local synagogue.[139] Another synagogue space was created on the lower level after the acceptance of the first group of Jewish refugees in 1942. Anglicans in the camp also had a small chapel where services were held by a clergyman who came regularly from Kingston.[140] One such clergyman was Jamaican, Archdeacon Eric Maxwell, who would serve as Chaplain to a Caribbean Battalion later in the war.[141]

Many small details on the organization of the camp emerge from a report of September 1941. Most of the children attended the camp school which opened in January 1941 with some 331 children aged four to fifteen years. Another sixty-six infants were in a separate facility. The few teens who had been preparing for external examinations were placed in Catholic schools, including St Georges College for boys, and Alpha and Immaculate high schools for girls. When the Jewish refugees arrived in 1942 and 1943, most of the teens were placed in local secondary schools, also including St Andrews High School for girls and Jamaica College which were overseen by the Anglican church. These were all secondary schools run on the traditional English public school pattern, most of them under the auspices of religious denominations and with government oversight.

The main recreation room was used as a theatre which could accommodate five hundred people. Motion pictures and occasional vaudeville shows were put on with the collaboration of Jamaican groups, as well as amateur theatricals and concerts organized by camp residents. There were reading rooms with books, periodicals and magazines. There was also a canteen with a dry goods department that sold clothes, shoes, fabric and other items, with an attached restaurant and bar that was "much patronised. Spirituous liquors are prohibited, but beer is permitted". A general store combined grocery, sweet shop, tobacconist and, to an extent, drug store. These facilities were run for the sole benefit of residents, though a local company, Lascelles DeMercado, was eventually invited to take over the running of the dry goods canteen. A barber shop, shoemaker's shop, sewing room, beauty parlour and dry cleaner were provided, all offering work for evacuees, with any profits carried over to the camp's welfare fund.[142]

Meals for the Gibraltarians were served in three dining halls, semi-open to the tropical surroundings, each facility capable of seating one thousand persons. Seat assignments separated young children from the elderly. The meals were cooked in attached kitchens, each with dedicated preparation areas, large wood stoves, as well as electrically operated vegetable peelers and other modern gadgets to speed the work. Meat and other perishables had been stockpiled in cold storage at Up Park Camp, the military garrison, to ensure that there was enough for the evacuees.[143] Eventually, the camp established its own butchery which made hams and other smoked meats, as well as a bakery. Identical cooking and dining facilities existed on the lower level where the refugee groups would be assigned from early 1942. Residents were discouraged from taking their food out of the dining area – a rule which caused resentment, and which seems to have eventually been relaxed.

Residents were allocated rooms in the long, single-storey barrack-like buildings, each with a central passageway down the middle that opened into fourteen rooms on each side. Twelve of these provided two beds each in a 10' x 10' space, with 10' x 12' rooms at each end, holding three beds each. Families were given one, two or three rooms which could be connected into self-contained flatlets, according to the size of the family. They could also partition off their section of the long verandah that led off every room and ran the length of each building on both sides.[144] A Gibraltarian youth in the camp, who was interviewed as a senior citizen, recalled living "like battery hens". He said that "all your possessions had to hold in this confined space" – though there was a separate, large storage facility for trunks and large items.[145] The internal walls did not go all the way to the roof, a design aimed at enhancing ventilation though it also restricted privacy. One effort to address this was by allocating single person to some barracks and families to others. Distinct groups, such as the thirty-six Gibraltarian Jews, could be housed in one barracks block, with the same approach taken to the location of elderly people and invalids.

To differentiate the units and provide street addresses, the numbers 1 to 112 were painted on one side of each neat wooden barracks building. Many of the residents began their own gardens. Journalist and publisher Esther Chapman, who visited the camp early in 1941, "was struck by the contrast between those houses that had been left more or less as the authorities had provided them, and those which had been converted . . . into homes". In an article, she noted that one family had shared up the adjoining rooms assigned to the husband, wife and daughters, to create a dining room and sitting room, where blue silk curtains screened windows, shelves and home-made wardrobes; the beds were covered with attractive spreads and there were photographs and Catholic symbols on the walls.[146]

While there appears to have been an effort to cut doors between adjacent rooms to create connected family quarters for the Gibraltarians, the approach to the refugees may have been somewhat different – perhaps because they were viewed as being in transit. A correspondent who was in the Dutch section of the camp recalled that the parents and children were assigned adjacent rooms, but that there was no internal connection between them. She and her brother shared a room that had a window to the verandah. Their parents' room could access the verandah through a two-part door. "So even though our room was next to my parents' room, we had to go out in the corridor or on the veranda to access our parents. We had just the two rooms and the verandah would have been the only common family space."[147] One of the Polish Jews recalled their accommodation as being "like soldiers' barracks", with partitions reaching three-quarter way to the roof instead of complete walls – impeding privacy but allowing some circulation of air in a hot climate.[148] Figure 9 overlays the sections occupied by the various groups of residents on a PWD plan of the camp.

The refugees' dining room was located between the Dutch and Polish sections on the lower level of the camp. The Dutch correspondent recalled that the Polish contingent was well established by the time the first Dutch group arrived in December 1942:

> Polish Jews ran the kitchen, together with Jamaican help. I suppose the food must have been kosher, because of the religiosity of a number of the Polish Jews. They lived in the barracks on the one side of the open-air, covered dining hall, the Dutch on the other side, so that there was a definite separation of sorts. There was a bar, close to the dining area but "across the road", or rather, to the right of

A Camp for Free Europeans in Need | 95

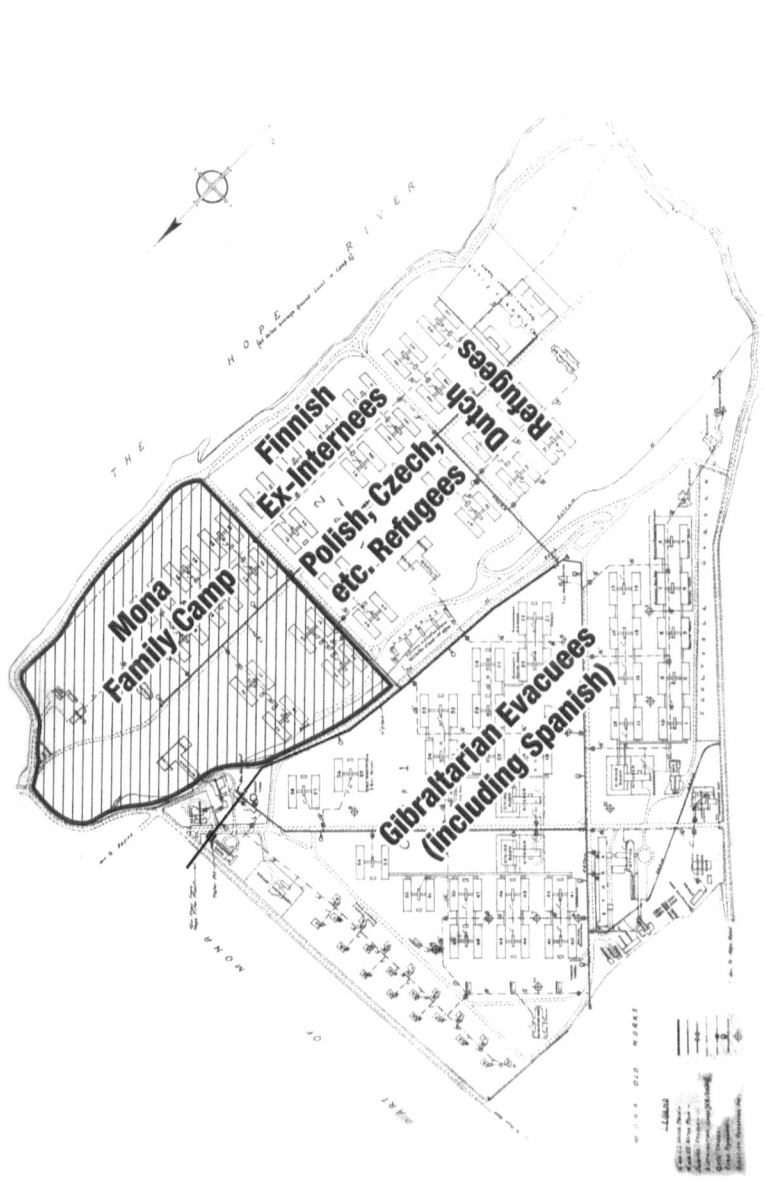

Figure 9 Annotated Plan of Gibraltar Camp showing approximate living areas for different groups of residents and area occupied by Mona Family Camp from 1943.

96 | WORLD WAR II CAMPS IN JAMAICA

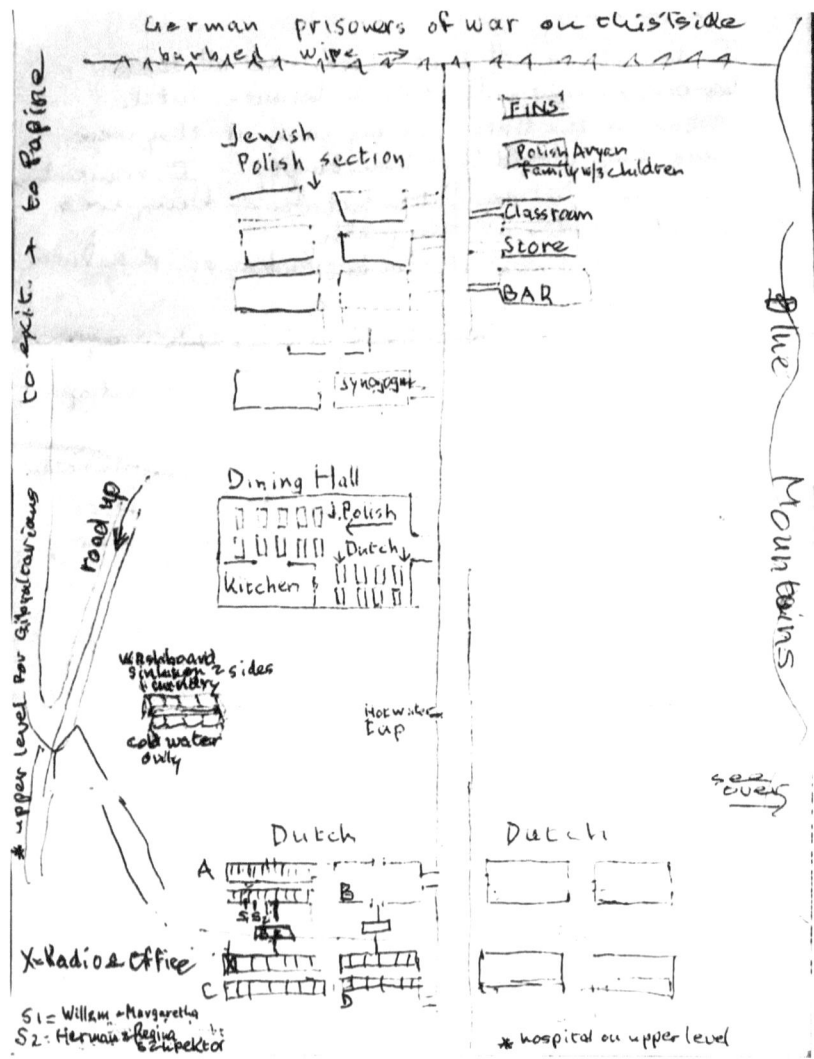

Figure 10 Contemporaneous sketch layout of refugee section of Gibraltar Camp by Dutch refugee Regina Schpektor age eleven years.

the concrete, covered path leading through the camp, whereas the dining area was on the left ... The Finns may have eaten there as well and would have had a table to themselves.[149]

She said that one of the barracks in the Polish section was used as an orthodox synagogue – what another young resident, Polish Jew Manne Eckstein, called "a home-made synagogue". JOINT records include images

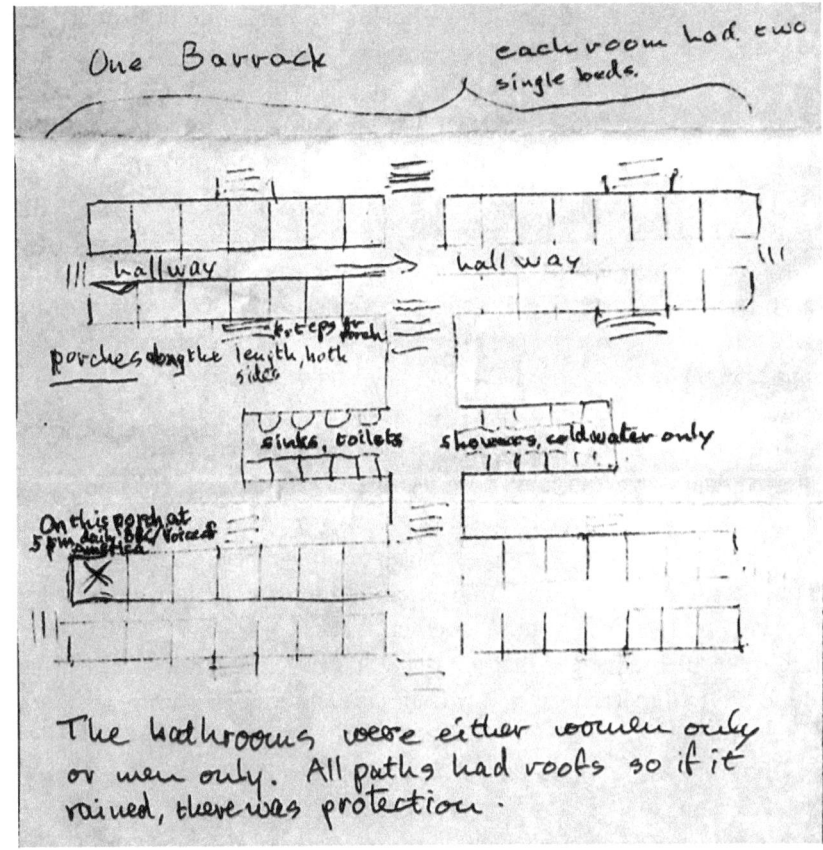

Figure 10A Sketch of barracks and bathroom layout in refugee area of Gibraltar Camp by Regina Schpektor age eleven years.

of the synagogue where the Polish Jews worshiped and of religious items provided to furnish the building.[150] Figures 10 and 10A relate to the layout of the refugee section in Gibraltar Camp.

Regulating the Camp and Residents

The level of priority given to the camp was clear in its administration, oversight of which was in the hands of a high-level executive committee chaired by island food controller Mr F.E.V. Smith, and later by Barclays bank manager Mr P.E.N. Mortimer. Other members were Custos of Kingston Sir Noel Livingston, director of Public Works Mr P. Martin Cooper, Auditor General Mr P.D. McPhail, along with the commandant and the Catholic Father Superior. Two British appointees in quick succession were named commandant – retired military man, Major Henry Simms, formerly director of public works and colonial civil servant J.L. Worlledge, who returned to England in March 1941. Jamaican businessman and sportsman Ernest A. Rae, formerly deputy mayor of Kingston, who had been appointed camp manager before the facility opened and then deputy commandant to Worlledge, became acting commandant – a post in which he was later confirmed. After the end of the war, when Rae left but while the camp remained open, Fabian Lopez, previously head of the Commissary Department, was named commandant. The term commandant was applied to the heads of the civilian evacuee and refugee camp as well as the military-run internment camps.

Given the size and complexity of the operation, and its increasingly international scope, the camp administration was complex – backed up by managers responsible for accounting, commissary, general stores, medical and security functions as well as mechanics, electricians and plumbers, carpenters, chauffeurs and watchmen, groundsmen, farm labourers, teachers, the religious, medical and social staff. Because the Gibraltarian authorities had requested that the Catholic Church be integrally involved in the life of the evacuees, a staff of priests and nuns lived on location – most of them, Americans – with other Catholic nuns, priests and laypeople coming in to assist, as necessary. The resident religious community was involved with the social programmes, including visits outside the camp and oversight of any groups coming into the camp – which also helped to buffer the Gibraltarians from the local population. No equivalent social and religious structure was put in place when the camp population was extended to include significant numbers of Jewish refugees – the governor's initial query, whether special arrangements were needed, having been denied by the Colonial Office in London. However, camp authorities did make a room available for a synagogue on the lower, as on the upper, level. Rabbi Henry Silverman visited the Jewish refugees on at least one occasion but apparently failed to make a connection with them. An anecdote related that the Polish Jews were confused by the Rabbi's "roman collar", which was accepted dress in the local Jewish community, and refused to have anything to do with him.[151] Individual refugees from the Polish group did engage with the local Jewish community, as did some of the Dutch Jews.

The evacuees – and later the refugees – were not allowed to live anywhere but inside Gibraltar Camp and, initially, could only leave the camp on a pass issued by the commandant, which would state the hours for which it was valid. These were some of the strict regulations in effect at the new camp, as reported in a *Gleaner* article of 28 October 1940, a few days after the arrival of the first evacuees. The regulations, made under the Evacuees (Defence) Regulations 1940, also prohibited "any evacuee from practicing any profession or carrying on any business occupation, industry or craft in Jamaica for reward". Offenders could be fined up to £5, imprisoned at the camp prison for up to seven days, be handed over to the police and have their freedom or diet rights restricted – including by being restricted from leaving the camp for up to twenty-one days.[152] The report said that the evacuees' right to entertain visitors could also be restricted or cancelled for a period not exceeding twenty-one days – though the force of this was questionable since they were not allowed visitors from outside the camp. One complaint in this regard was made by an evacuee in London, whose mother was at the camp in Jamaica. While his complaint was clearly made in an effort to have his mother join him in London, his comment on the camp policy of exclusion was nonetheless interesting: "nobody is allowed into the camp so that if some friend comes to take a person in the camp out, he is made to wait at the gate, and one has no right to entertain anybody where it ought to be your home".[153] The Colonial Office asked the local authorities for a response and Governor Sir Arthur Richards explained the policy in a November 1942 letter to the secretary of state for the colonies, in London: "It is not possible to allow evacuees to have their friends to their own huts in the Camp, as the Administration would obviously lose all control of Camp discipline and order if this were allowed in other than very special cases."

Regulations also applied to Jamaicans who might seek to enter the camp without authority: the regulations apply "not only within the precincts of the camp but also within one hundred yards from its boundary".[154] Advertisements in bold type, placed in local newspapers during October and November 1940, as well as signboards near the camp, warned Jamaicans of prosecution if they sought to enter the camp without authority (see Figure 11). The advertisements noted:

> Passes to enter the Camp will *not* normally be granted to members of the public except in special cases where the purposes of the visit are approved by the Commandant of the Camp.[155]

These special cases included the limited number of employees who were, where possible, bussed in and out; sanctioned volunteers to help with classes and bridge language gaps; and strictly chaperoned groups allowed

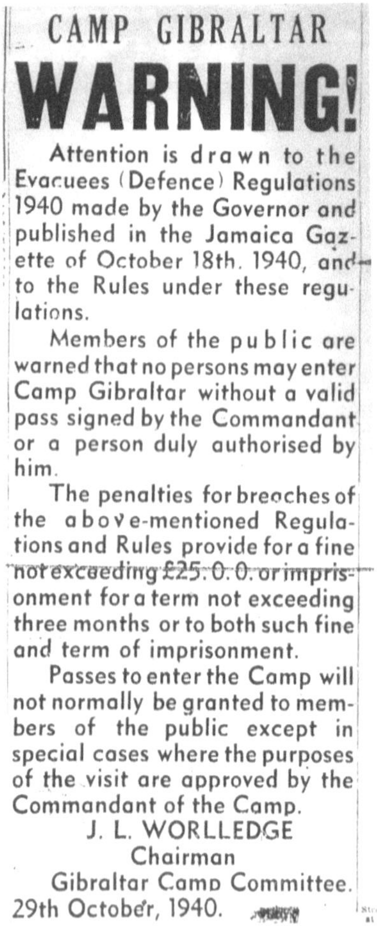

> **CAMP GIBRALTAR**
>
> # WARNING!
>
> Attention is drawn to the Evacuees (Defence) Regulations 1940 made by the Governor and published in the Jamaica Gazette of October 18th. 1940, and to the Rules under these regulations.
>
> Members of the public are warned that no persons may enter Camp Gibraltar without a valid pass signed by the Commandant or a person duly authorised by him.
>
> The penalties for breaches of the above-mentioned Regulations and Rules provide for a fine not exceeding £25.0.0. or imprisonment for a term not exceeding three months or to both such fine and term of imprisonment.
>
> Passes to enter the Camp will not normally be granted to members of the public except in special cases where the purposes of the visit are approved by the Commandant of the Camp.
>
> J. L. WORLLEDGE
> Chairman
> Gibraltar Camp Committee.
> 29th October, 1940.

Figure 11 Gibraltar Camp warning notice in *Gleaner* newspaper.

in for entertainment – teams for sporting competition, the military band which played regularly at the camp, other entertainers on occasion and Jamaican invitees for concerts. Penalties for Jamaicans breaching the regulations were a fine of up to £25 or up to three months imprisonment, or both.[156] For context, the average daily wage for a working-class Jamaican was around 3/9 sterling. One determined vendor who had been "warned off" after trying to sell goods at the camp but still returned to try again was fined 30/-. Another, who sold rum at a provision stall he had been allowed to set up in the camp, was fined £10 or one month in prison.[157] Of the dozens prosecuted and fined for breaching the regulations that forbade access to the camp, most were produce vendors seeking to sell their goods to this new clientele; some were camp employees who were caught on site without their passes, or who remained on the camp after work hours. Analysis of *Gleaner* reports suggested that efforts to circumvent the regulations – or prosecution of such efforts – had virtually ceased by March 1941, some five months after the camp opened.

Living in Gibraltar Camp

Especially for the Gibraltarians, who were in the camp for the long haul, knowing that they would eventually be repatriated home, life in Gibraltar Camp would have settled into a new normal, once the regulations were accepted. One aspect to be negotiated, especially for the adults, related to the use of their time. This was recognized in a welcoming *Gleaner* editorial of 26 October, which commented that while these were "a free people who for their own safety's sake have been removed from a zone of danger" and there was no question of compulsion, they might wish to "do some cultivation and other work for their own benefit". The newspaper commented that "no one likes complete idleness . . . the absence of all exertion becomes a terrific burden after a while".[158] Idleness was not an option for many of the women in the camp, especially coming from a conservative community. On a daily basis, they were occupied with childcare and with household tasks including laundry – sheds with washtubs and corrugated concrete washboards were provided and laundry was hung in the fresh air to dry. However, many of the women and men also took up other tasks in the camp, first on a voluntary and later on a paid basis. Indeed, recognizing the need for occupation and for resources, as well as to balance the regulation preventing residents from seeking employment outside the camp, the camp administration sought to employ Gibraltarians where possible. A December 1940 Memorandum on the Administration of Gibraltar Camp said that the evacuees were occupied doing their own washing and laundry, and at least one hundred and fifty were employed in the kitchens, store and canteen, on field work and as special district constables – initially as volunteers but by then on a wage-earning basis. The memorandum said that this was "proving highly satisfactory and economical. . .our aim is always to employ an evacuee in preference to a local applicant where possible".[159] A year later, paid staff, including the commandant and heads of departments, numbered 647, of whom 194 were Jamaicans and 453 were evacuees – more than one-quarter of the camp population.[160] The camp paid annual wages of about £45,000, about £15,000 of which was paid to the evacuees, many of whom were without other resources. Justifying a staff of nearly 650 to serve a community of 1,540 persons, the report said that it was "naturally, better for their self-respect that they should be placed in a position to earn something, however small, rather than be provided with a dole". Rates of pay offered to residents were stated to be half the local rates for similar services – on the basis that the residents were already receiving accommodation and food.[161]

Estimates of Expenditure for 1943 showed the number of camp employees remaining stable, with 446 camp residents among the 632 employees, though the number increased to 550 in 1944. The camp commandant said that there was "no uniform single rate for all forms of employment, but the minimum pay to any person doing menial work or relatively unimportant work is 10/- weekly". This was in keeping with or more than the earnings of many working-class Jamaicans at the time. Clerical work earned £1 to £2 per week, "depending upon the importance of the position filled". Cobblers, barbers and so on were employed and paid a wage, while persons with professional qualifications were, if possible, employed in their own vocational area but were not paid more than clerical help, "the whole intention being to occupy their time rather than to compensate them fully for services rendered". He said that as much of the camp population was without significant means, it would otherwise have been necessary to give doles of money and free issues of clothes. However, persons employed in the camp were not allowed free issues; they were given limited credit for periods of three months, repaid by instalments from their wages. He said that "a considerable saving has been effected when we offset the amount paid annually for wages against the amount which we would have had to pay out in doles". The employed persons were mainly evacuees, but also included refugees, most of whom the commandant characterized as "people of private means and also craftsmen", as well as shoemakers, tailors and labourers. He said that "wherever possible we have given them employment on the same basis as British evacuees".[162]

Young Gibraltarian women were strictly chaperoned, especially if they were leaving the camp for any reason. However, for some of this group, Gibraltar Camp would prove a somewhat revolutionary environment, providing the preliminary training for the first significant cohort of Gibraltarian nurses. A *History of the Catholic Church in Jamaica* noted that "young ladies of the camp who went into training for the nursing profession" assisted the Dominican Sisters in the camp infirmary.[163] And camp photographs show up to ten young Gibraltarian women with one of the nuns near the camp hospital.[164] When the Gibraltarian community was being prepared for repatriation, a camp record of hospital staff listed four third-year probationers, two second-year probationers and eight first-year probationers, which indicates that the training programme was ongoing.[165] In an interview with Gibraltarian Dr Margaret Williams, two of the trainees said that they had no prior interest in nursing but volunteered in response to an appeal from the camp's medical officer and the nuns who ran the camp hospital. They received some practical training from the Matron and three Jamaican staff nurses who did sessions at the hospital and subsequently received training at the Kingston Public Hospital (KPH) – travelling there by coach. The young women were paid a monthly stipend and the older ones were able to sit preliminary nursing examinations at the KPH.[166] One of the trainees, speaking in Gibraltar in 2015, said that in normal circumstances her strict Catholic father would never have allowed her to pursue such training with a view to working in the field.[167]

As it was, the experience helped shift attitudes to Gibraltarian women working outside the home and contributed significantly to nursing in Gibraltar. A Gibraltarian interviewee from the camp recalled the group members and said that the one who ended the training as top nurse was so inspired by her work in Jamaica that she continued with that career on her return to Gibraltar.[168] An article in the *Gibraltar Chronicle* in December 1944 said that eight out of nine student nurses who were training at the Colonial Hospital in Gibraltar, with a view to going on to study in England, had done initial training in Jamaica.

When the Gibraltarians arrived in Jamaica, the males among them were either considered past their prime or under age. Several of the middle-aged men worked as special district constables, and the postman, firemen and other such functionaries were Gibraltarian. Eventually, a group of some twenty youths, who passed eighteen years while living in the camp, were allowed to join the Pioneer Corps of the British Army, in Jamaica, moving to live at Up Park Camp and remaining behind when the Gibraltarian community was repatriated in October 1944.[169] The sister of one of the recruits recalled that the men were sent to live in barracks on the same road as the Alpha Academy where she went to school.[170] That was the location of the Military Headquarters, Up Park Camp. Eric Canessa's history of Gibraltarians who served in the British forces in World War II said that the young men joined the Pioneer Corps to escape the boredom of the evacuee camp and to make some contribution to the war effort, but also for the pay and because their uniforms attracted girls. A side benefit was that they received free clothing and footwear.[171] The men, who served from July 1943 until 1947, were among those who would have guarded the prisoners of war and internment camps.[172]

The camp's infants, children and young people attended school, following the Gibraltarian national curriculum – overseen by two nuns with other teachers brought in as needed. Only a few of the youths, those preparing for external examinations, were enrolled in Jamaican high schools – unlike an apparent majority of refugee children who lived in the camp between 1942 and 1943.

Adelaide Azzopardi was one of the exceptions. She was nearly eight when she travelled to Jamaica from Gibraltar with her sisters Carmen and Anita, brother Frank and mother Maria. Starting school in Gibraltar Camp, she passed examinations that led to her being sent to Alpha Academy, a Catholic girls' school in Kingston, along with two or three older Gibraltarian students. She remembered that all the students were transported to Papine in a horse-drawn wagon, from where they travelled on the bus and tram to their schools. Because she had motion sickness, it was arranged for her to stay at the school's boarding facility for a time, going back to the camp on weekends.[173] For some months, her schoolmates at Alpha would have included young Polish refugees such as Manne Eckstein, who arrived in Jamaica with her family in 1942. Eckstein later wrote that she attended classes with the Gibraltarians to gain exposure to the English language, before going to Alpha. She recalled that the nuns excused Jewish and Protestant students from weekly chapel, and she classed her education there as "wonderful":

> sewing, cooking, taking care of babies etc. They taught us the three R's also. But we did not have all work and no play! Every afternoon for an hour, we went out of doors to play softball or basketball.[174]

David Cohen, one of the Dutch Jewish boys, also attended a Catholic school in Kingston, presumably St Georges College which was the only Catholic high school for boys in the city. He recalled that at school:

> All of us were wearing a uniform. In the camp as well as outside of it, British traditions ruled. Every day I would go by bus, together with nine other boys of my age, to the school. And every afternoon we were taken from the school back to the camp. My little brother did not go to school outside the camp; he stayed at a nursery school inside of the camp.

Cohen recalled that one of the teachers was Father Knight, who "wore priest's clothes" and who paid special attention to the Jewish boys attending the Catholic school: "He knew we were Jewish and war refugees. The school was in touch with the camp leaders who had arranged for the children to get involved in education."[175]

Another Dutch refugee recalled that the younger children in her group, including her brother, attended lessons at the camp – held in the bar or an adjacent barracks building, with a teacher who was also a refugee. This correspondent's cohort, which arrived in December 1942, started school in January 1943 after six weeks of private lessons with another refugee, Louis Pool. "The Dutch adults knew English and their children learned very quickly", she said.[176] She said that virtually all the older Dutch children attended school outside of the camp – her brother would become a student at nearby Jamaica College – and that learning and practising English was as important for the young Dutch refugees as academics and extra-curricular activities.

Many of the Gibraltarian children were active in clubs – including guiding and scouting groups affiliated to the national movements – and there were several church groups. Popular sports included softball, baseball, tennis and basketball, and teams competed in some schools' leagues, while the men also played football competitively. There was an effort at cricket, but most of these working-class Gibraltarians did not play.

Meals for hundreds of residents were served communally. For the evacuees, there were originally two sittings for each meal – breakfast at 7.00 a.m. and 8.00 a.m., lunch at 12.00 noon and 1.00 p.m., and supper at 5.00 p.m. and 6.00 p.m. – though this was eventually changed to a simpler cafeteria-style system. Dining room C was dedicated to mothers with children under five years, dining room B to mothers and children under fourteen years and dining room A to all others.[177] There was a degree of regimentation – tables and seats were numbered, and instructions and information were provided during meals, over a combined radio/public address unit. Inevitably, cultural differences in styles of food preparation sparked criticism with each new resident population, and both evacuees and refugees came to have a say in the menus prepared by the Jamaican chefs working in their respective kitchens.

For residents of the camp, food was plentiful, with the servings of fresh fruit and milk being especially popular. Commissary provisions as well as frequent large-scale food tendering and some purchases from local contractors ensured that even foods that became scarce for Jamaicans remained available. Jamaican interviewees who lived on the camp recalled that they were never without ham, steak or butter for instance; though they said that they were reduced to powdered egg for some time.[178] Many of the camp residents bought additional fresh fruit and vegetables and the occasional chicken, from vendors who sold near the camp gate and at the Papine market. A Dutch correspondent remembered that her family did not particularly enjoy the food served in the refugees' dining hall and that each week, her mother bought a chicken from a vendor at Papine:

> The chicken would be cooked over a coal fire that my mother would fan the flames of. That is how we might have a Friday night traditional dinner on the veranda outside our barracks rooms. We also always had a basket with fruit outside the door, and a branch [sic] of bananas, and we would let the basket and bananas down and then haul it up again on a pulley, so that it was about six feet or more off the floor.[179]

Snacks and drinks – but not alcohol – were available for sale at a canteen on the camp. And, for a while, four Dutchmen in the lower camp set up a little business squeezing oranges and selling orange juice drinks.[180] The camp itself also became involved in producing some of its own food, a point of pride especially as shortages increased, and there were some media comments on the way scarce foods were divided. In July 1942, the *Gleaner* reported that the camp was producing about one-sixth of its milk requirement – originally all purchased from a local contractor – and rearing pigs.[181] The camp's vegetable gardens were also yielding some produce, though it is not known how much of the demand this supplied on a regular basis.[182]

The health of the community was the responsibility of a camp hospital, with difficult cases referred to the Kingston Public Hospital. Maternity cases were referred to the Victoria Jubilee Lying-In Hospital. Two of the camp nuns, who were trained nurses, assisted the hospital Matron, and a group of nurse trainees was recruited from among the evacuees. The camp also had its own doctor, dentist and dispenser, while public health officials were responsible for public hygiene and mosquito control.

Polish refugee Miriam Stanton, who published a memoir on her family's escape from Europe described Gibraltar Camp as a "bustling and lively little town":

> We were completely self-sufficient. We had schools, a hospital, shops, offices, a police station, even a lock-up. There was always something happening – concerts, weddings, fights, scandals and unfortunately, funerals as well. We had beautiful gardens; everyone tended his own little patch.[183]

Stanton, then Sandzer, was one of the many families which suffered loss during their time on the camp, when her grandmother "Babciu" died. She chronicled the outpouring of support, especially from the local Jewish community where she had made friends through worshipping at the local synagogue.[184] One tragic death, following an accident within the camp, was that of a four-year-old Polish girl, Yvonne Krakowiak, who died in June

1942.[185] That death and two births were recorded among the Poles up to March 1943. A member of the first group of Dutch refugees said that there were no deaths among her group but that there were at least four births.[186] Among the Gibraltarians, there were more than ninety babies born during the period of camp residence, most of them during the last months of 1940 and the first half of 1941, as baptismal records in the camp's church diary indicated. The diary also recorded the deaths and burials, most of which took place at the Catholic Calvary Cemetery in Kingston, though a few also went to the Anglican cemetery at St Andrew Parish Church, the Jewish Cemetery on Orange Street, and the May Pen Cemetery – all in Kingston.[187]

The first wedding on the camp, headlined by the *Gleaner* newspaper as a "Rock" Romance which ripened on Jamaican soil, took place in July 1941 between two Gibraltarians. Subsequently, there were three in 1942, and others in 1943. One of these marriages recorded in the Catholic register was between two Dutch refugees, who later moved to Surinam. At least two other camp marriages were celebrated at the Jewish synagogue in Downtown Kingston, including one between a Dutch woman and a Polish man.[188] In December 1943, two young adults from the Gibraltarian camp population, Frederick Barratt, a soldier attached to the Pioneer Corps and Lourdes McGillivray, married at the Camp. There were also several marriages between Jamaicans and Gibraltarian camp residents, despite the efforts to maintain separation.

Responses to Camp Conditions

Amid the disfunction and displacement of World War II, Gibraltar Camp was a well-run haven for both the evacuee and refugee populations that were its main and most consistent residents. Nonetheless, it was a regulated, even a regimented, environment – described by a Colonial Office source as a "semi-internment facility", despite being designed to accommodate free people.[189] These approaches and conditions that one local newspaper described as "benevolent discipline" proved to be irritants on occasion.[190]

Early criticisms related to the closed nature of the camp and to the regimentation through which the administrators sought to ensure that it ran smoothly. Residents, unused to being confined, chaffed at the initial refusal to allow them out into the local community. Within days of arrival, local newspaper reports focused on the evacuees settling down under strict camp rules. One such story referred to unspecified, occasional "unhappy incidents" which were dealt with "promptly and effectively" by the Gibraltar police officers serving as special constables under Jamaican laws, and the regular local police. The report said that many evacuees did not immediately appreciate the necessity for the action taken but subsided when "firmly assured of the justice of the disciplinary measures adopted".[191] Subsequently, the Camp Committee chairman explained an initial two-week confinement as being "for purposes of quarantine".[192] A Catholic Archives file said that a "strict pass system" was then instituted, based on a "prudent reluctance on the part of the administration to allow the evacuees to leave the camp at will".[193] Each evacuee was given a registration number, which they had to give the security on leaving and entering the camp and permits to leave were initially required. Gibraltarian liaison official B.D. Austin-Cathie, who travelled with the evacuees and remained during their first weeks in Jamaica, said that the Camp Committee wished the people to settle down thoroughly before they went roaming and that passes were initially difficult to obtain, "principally for the protection of our people themselves".[194]

By 9 December, a Memorandum on the Administration of Gibraltar Camp stated that passes to leave camp "are freely given to the Evacuees, the only stipulation being that they must return by 5.00 p.m., unless there is special permission for them to remain later".[195] Perhaps this was not clearly communicated to the evacuees. Nearly a month later, on 6 January 1941, the *Gleaner* newspaper published a letter from Angel P Carreras, an evacuee living in Hut 29, Gibraltar Camp, thanking camp authorities "for having achieved the liberty we so much coveted and which we will enjoy henceforth – the passes to leave the Camp".[196] Two days later, another letter from "One of the Evacuees" charged bad catering and unfair treatment by officials.[197] This may have encouraged *Gleaner* columnist, Englishman G. St.C. Scotter to visit the camp without an appointment – an effort denied by the camp's manager, Ernest Rae. The *Gleaner* of 17 January then carried a salvo titled "Dictatoritis", which included a description of Rae as a "2 x 4 Dictator" and Gibraltar camp as his "sports model concentration camp".[198] Among the responses was a 27 January 1941 report from the camp administration which assured that everything compatible with discipline was being done to make the evacuees feel at home; that their liberty was not curtailed; indeed, that they could leave the camp from 8.00 a.m. and stay out until 10.00 p.m. Later, this would be extended to 11 p.m., and they could stay out for seventy-two continuous hours, once a month.[199] However, the commandant apparently faced criticism from members of the Jamaican legislature for allowing too many three-day breaks, the argument being that this was "against the letter and the spirit of the agreement which said that these people would live in the Camp and not in Kingston".[200]

New York investigators from the Gibraltarian Evacuees Fund visited the camp early in 1941 and filed a positive report, which was carried by the local media including the *Gleaner*. Headlines during May and July 1941 assured the reading public, near and far: "Evacuees Kin Get Favourable Reports on Camp Gibraltar" (27 May) and "Gibraltar Camp. New York Investigators Praise Running of the Establishment. No Fault is Found. Correspondence Which Should Go Far to Silence All Critics of Establishment" (22 July). Concerns about conditions in the camp would re-emerge, fed by wartime anxieties among men far from their families. On at least one well-documented occasion, men in Gibraltar read threats into reports received in letters – some of which would prove to mainly reflect clashes of personality and culture. The most disruptive event, causing exchanges of telegrams between officials in Gibraltar, Britain and Jamaica, involved what T.G. Finlayson described in some detail as the "dining room incident" of May 1942. It was sparked by the camp administration's insistence that meals must be eaten in the dining room, which was enforced by closing or locking the dining room exit door for twenty minutes after meal service started. Objecting, some men and women broke open one of the doors. Further disorder led to the involvement of the camp police, after which one man was sentenced to seven days of detention and several others, mainly women, were fined. In the aftermath, the chief censor in Gibraltar was aware of letters from evacuees in Jamaica containing lurid details, including one urging the receiver to "let the families hear about this!" Several included racial slurs and one compared the camp to a concentration camp. By 3 June, a flyer was being circulated in Gibraltar charging that "for a simple protest brought about by the bad food provided, they order the black force of Jamaica to charge pistol in hand against our families, undefended women; they beat them and take them to prison making them undergo dishonourable humiliations in prison".[201] A petition, signed by about five hundred citizens would be handed to the colonial secretary in Gibraltar, urging amelioration of the situation and the removal of the camp commandant for "their unmerited sufferings and constant ill-treatment".[202]

Resulting investigations saw the dismissal of all the charges. A report to the colonial secretary in Gibraltar from the chairman of the Gibraltar Camp Committee said that the evacuees "had no real ground for complaint" over the quantity or quality of the food they received, or their treatment by the camp commandant and the special constables. He said that the commandant sought to give fullest consideration to the residents but "at times it is very necessary to maintain discipline and that any disciplinary action will probably bring forth exaggerated reports in correspondence to Gibraltar".[203] One interesting aspect of the story is that the police officers involved in the incident were apparently special constables from Gibraltar. The local police force had been withdrawn from the camp in April 1942, leaving the Gibraltarian special constables in charge of the camp policing.[204]

The second half of 1942 found the camp being criticized by its newest residents – a group of Polish refugees coming from Lisbon, Portugal. They complained that they had not been made aware, before embarking from Portugal, that Jamaica had placed conditions of their acceptance as refugees – these being, a requirement to live in the camp and a ban on employment.[205] Official correspondence clearly indicates that the Colonial Office had made the British Foreign Office aware of the conditions under which space was being made available at Gibraltar Camp.[206] However, given the documented British desire to get this group out of the refugee pipeline, the pressure from the Portuguese, and their own desperation to have a place to go, there are multiple possible sources for the breakdown in communication. What is certain is that the belated communication of the conditions, on board ship, perhaps even in Kingston Harbour, meant that many arrived in a negative frame. Bussed to the camp, some later said that they were afraid at the sight of the barbed wire fence, a black man with a machete on guard, and the title of commandant for the man in charge. In subsequent months, they rumoured that the facility was a concentration camp and charged a lack of interest among the local Jewish community – despite documented acts of kindness and welcome by individual members of that community.[207] The JOINT, which underwrote the maintenance of the Polish refugees in Jamaica, recognized a strain in relations with their clients and acknowledged that the refugees "swiftly alienated the local Jewish community of Kingston, which finally refused its help altogether, with the exception of a local resident, Samuel Cohen".[208] The group's efforts to gain attention by describing Gibraltar Camp as a kind of concentration camp also solidified the position of the governor of Jamaica who made it clear that he would not re-think the conditions on which they had been accepted but that they were free to go once they had onward visas.[209]

For these refugees, especially the many men of working age, some with families, the worst suffering stemmed from the ban on finding jobs or starting businesses outside of the camp – especially when they lacked significant resources. Those who could afford to maintain themselves were especially frustrated with the residence requirement. In a recorded interview, former refugee Helene Krakowiak Arnay recalled that some of the Polish refugees "played cards from morning til night" and that there was a lot of fighting "everybody nervous and every little thing sparked argument".[210] In August 1942, a petition to British prime minister Winston Churchill, signed by a group of Polish Refugees at Gibraltar Camp, asked for assistance in getting visas to go to Canada where they could do useful work:

> While a world war rages and hecatombs of victims fall, we young people, wanting to fight and to work and able to be useful through our technical and branch knowledges [sic] are here in complete spirit and health-killing inactivity in Gibraltar Camp.

The group said that they would consider themselves as "parasitical individuals" but for the fact that their inactivity was against their will.[211] The Polish Jews were also discontented at the lack of involvement by the Polish government-in-exile, in their arrangements at Gibraltar Camp, and at the fact that their stay was being underwritten instead by the New York - based JOINT, which helped finance various groups of Jews from Europe to the Caribbean. This exasperation would be further aggravated when they lived beside the Dutch refugees, in whose interest a Dutch Consul had been sent to Jamaica. These issues were clarified in a report by Charles H Jordan, the JOINT Representative in Cuba, who visited Jamaica in December 1942. Jordan's assessment was that, objectively speaking, and given the possibilities in Jamaica at that time, the living conditions of the Polish group were satisfactory, but that their mood was poor, mainly due to prolonged inactivity.[212]

Manne Eckstein, who made friends with her Gibraltarian English teacher and happily attended a Catholic girls' school in Kingston, nonetheless, reflected some of the negative sentiment of her Polish community when she retrospectively wrote about the camp. She said that they "slept in a wooden house built like an apartment, ate in a general kitchen with food made in a kind of fat that we could not stomach; and went to a home-made synagogue to pray". Positively, however, she recalled that most Sundays, her family went for a picnic "in a nearby wood", taking their own lunch and getting refreshment and having fun there.[213] This "wood" may have been the nearby Hope Botanical Gardens. Manne, whose father was a diamond worker, estimated that they lived in Jamaica for two years before moving to more enjoyable surroundings in Havana, Cuba, and then on to the United States where the family settled.

Figure 12 Gibraltar Camp cultural group (Photo courtesy of Priscilla Harris).

Figure 12A Dutch refugee family Schpektor in Gibraltar Camp refugee section (Photo courtesy of Regina Inez Schpektor Baker).

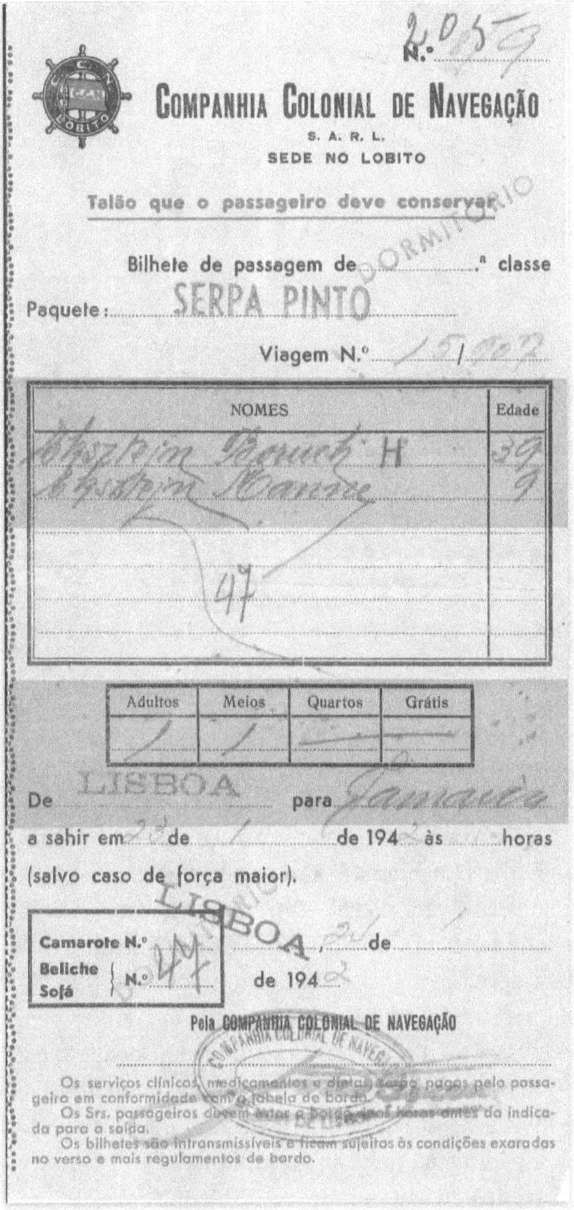
N.º 2059

COMPANHIA COLONIAL DE NAVEGAÇÃO

S. A. R. L.

SEDE NO LOBITO

Talão que o passageiro deve conservar

Bilhete de passagem de .... .ª classe

Paquete: SERPA PINTO

Viagem N.º 15/007

NOMES	Edade
Eksztejn Rauch H	39
Eksztejn Manne	9

Adultos	Meios	Quartos	Grátis
1	1	—	—

De LISBOA para Jamaica

a sahir em 23 de 1 de 1942 às .... horas

(salvo caso de força maior).

Camarote N.º	
Beliche / Sofá N.º	47

LISBOA, 21 de .... de 1942

Pela COMPANHIA COLONIAL DE NAVEGAÇÃO

Os serviços clínicos, medicamentos e dietas serão pagos pelo passageiro em conformidade com a tabela de bordo.

Os Srs. passageiros devem estar a bordo duas horas antes da indicada para a saída.

Os bilhetes são intransmissíveis e ficam sujeitos às condições exaradas no verso e mais regulamentos de bordo.

Figure 12B Ticket aboard SS Serpa Pinto for Polish refugee Manne Eckstein (Photo courtesy of family of Manne Eckstein Aronovsky).

Figure 12C Dutch refugee children in Gibraltar Camp 1943 (Photo courtesy of Jenny Weinshel).

The Dutch refugees were the responsibility of their government-in-exile and most appear to have been reasonably well off. One later wrote a memoir titled *Eén Rembrandt voor vijfentwintig levens* – chronicling how fifteen persons were able to escape the Netherlands at the cost of a Rembrandt painting. While the Dutch adults also baulked at the restrictions imposed on them, they were aware of being in transit to other destinations, with the assistance of a Dutch Consul sent to Jamaica from London. Many of these refugees developed social connections outside the camp and took advantage of opportunities for entertainment. One remembered going into Downtown Kingston to a restaurant called Dixie Doodle to eat "wonderful fried chicken and orange jello (new to me) or sometimes got to go for lunch at the Myrtle Bank Hotel where we also went swimming". She also remembered a trip to the new, air-conditioned Carib Theatre to see Judy Garland in "For Me and My Gal".[214]

Chapter 3

Internment Camps

Three of the four World War II camps located in Jamaica were under military or police control. The first and largest of the three, the Male Internment Centre, established in 1939 adjacent to the British garrison, held civilian internees as well as German and Italian merchant mariners captured in the Caribbean or nearby. The Women's Internment Camp at Hanover Street in Downtown Kingston was established in 1940 to hold women and children, most of them connected to the male civilian internees. The Mona Family Camp or Married Families Camp was a facility belatedly established in the third quarter of 1943 to reunite interned families who had lived separated since December 1940. Additionally, after the Armistice of 1943, some Italian internees were billeted at the Newcastle Military Hill Station and later at Gibraltar Camp after it had become a military facility. For a visual of all camp locations, see Figure 4 on page 16.

Many of the details relating to the living conditions of the populations of all the internment camps in Jamaica, between 1942 and 1946, emerge from regular reports made by the Swiss Vice-Consulate as the *Protecting Power*, as well as in reports by visitors from the Red Cross and YMCA. Swiss consul Rudolph J. Waeckerlin, who was already working in Jamaica before the start of the war, later became increasingly busy with internee affairs, as a *Gleaner* report of October 1943 acknowledged.[1]

There were no documented protests related to the presence of these camps in the local space, even when large numbers of persons identified as enemy aliens were brought in for safekeeping. The local population seemed to accept that these facilities existed for reasons of local and imperial security and even that this meant the sharing of scarce supplies. Legislative Council records and media reports did, from time to time, reflect concerns by some local actors, usually related to prejudice and privilege, especially in the broad context of Nazi racism. Beyond those issues which reached the public media, Colonial Office files from 1940 contain references to possible and actual German objections to coloured soldiers guarding German prisoners and internees. There was also concern for the potential political implications of such objections becoming known locally – precisely at a time when objection to racial discrimination was beginning to be voiced and reported in the local media. The issue would arise, in correspondence, at various points in the war, but the essential policy was established in March 1941:

> The guards on the Male Internment Camp are furnished by the Winnipeg Grenadiers and it will only be in an emergency that the Local Forces will be required to furnish guards for this Camp.[2]

The authorities refused to extend this policy to the Female Internment Camp, where the guards were furnished by local special constables, "all of whom are coloured men, and these men also perform any escort duty which may be required". The Officer Commanding Troops was "strongly averse to employing active service United Kingdom or Dominion Troops to guard interned women".[3] In 1943, when a Married Families Camp was being established at Mona to reunite families separated since their arrival in Jamaica in 1940, the issue again arose and was resolved as follows:

> Local force, coloured troops will be used for external guard duties only and will be stationed outside the Camp perimeter. All internal duties will be performed by specially enlisted European personnel.[4]

The concern by the authorities was an acknowledgement of the attitudes of some prisoners, especially German merchant seamen who had been interned for years and who reportedly became increasingly difficult to control. British Lt Col N.J. Darling, after a visit to facilities in Trinidad, Jamaica and Bermuda, noted a racial aspect to this intractability, reporting that they "resent Jamaicans, coloured and black, but [would] do anything for British Officers and N.C.O.s".[5] These discussions related to the internment camps exemplified some of the complexities in the colonial situation as related to colour and class.

Issues related to the exercise of power and to civil liberties were highlighted when Jamaicans were detained within the same facilities, for political reasons, and when the detainees included Germans and Italians, many of them Jews, who had become naturalized British citizens. Indeed, especially as knowledge of Nazi concentration camps became widely known, the issue of German Jews being interned alongside non-Jews – even confirmed Nazi sympathizers – became an issue at both the Male and Female Internment Camps. Conditions within the women's camp – the only one of the camps not purpose-built – sparked an international situation across enemy lines which belatedly forced the establishment of the Married Family Camp at Mona.

3.1 Male Internment Camp

At the start of World War II, as had been the case in World War I, a detention centre was established, adjacent to the military headquarters at Up Park Camp in Kingston.[6] Indeed, the Local Defence Committee, meeting in July 1939, as war became increasingly likely, discussed the creation of a prisoners of war and alien internment camp at a site close to the Up Park Camp rifle range, which was a low-density area of the city. The proposed design was for 96 persons, at an estimated cost of £3,600, with the possibility of expansion within its barbed wire perimeter to take 192 detainees.[7] Construction appears to have awaited the declaration of war, as the first internees were held in the Detention Barracks of Up Park Camp, and a mid-September newspaper report said that it was estimated that it would take six weeks to move them into new quarters.[8] By 30 October, the men were reported to have been moved to the new internment barracks "from which it is almost impossible to escape". The new facility on the north side of the garrison was reported to be surrounded by "the most elaborate and secure arrangements [sic] of barbed wire fences, around which, day and night, pace relays of armed sentries".[9]

Through the course of the war, the camp population would grow exponentially. Its first residents were some twenty-six German and Austrian civilians living and working in Jamaica, most of them interned as enemy aliens on 3 September 1939, the very day war was declared. They would be joined, in short order, by the first of hundreds of German and Italian merchant seamen captured by Allied vessels in or near the Caribbean Sea, as well as enemy aliens and merchant seamen brought to Kingston from other regional colonies. In December 1940, the camp would receive its largest single intake – some four hundred and thirty German and Italian civilians interned in British West Africa and sent to Jamaica due to logistical and security considerations. The camp numbers would climb over eleven hundred men in late 1943, after which the numbers would begin to stabilize with hundreds of men spending more than five years behind the camp's barbed wire fences.

The changing numbers in the camp are shown in table 1.[10]

The designation of the camp and its mixed population would cause some confusion across several years, in part reflecting varied understandings of the status of German and Italian merchant mariners in context of the 1929 Geneva Convention – officially, the Convention Relative to the

Table 1 Population of Male Internment Camp 1939–1947

Date	Camp Capacity	Camp Population				Comments
		German/Austrian	Italian	Other	Total	
October 1939	96 – expandable to 192	29 German & Austrian – reduced to 18 by end November			29	
March–June 1940		18 internees Merchant seamen			140	
May/June 1940			Italy entered war – June 1940			Note German & Austrian civilians including Naturalized British citizens interned or re-interned
July 1940		220 German merchant seamen from Curacao			360 (estimate)	
August 1940	450 – being expanded for internees from West Africa	13 captains 26 officers 360 merchant seamen 19 civilians			418 (estimate)	
March 1941		19 + 217 civilians from West Africa 360 + 13 + 26 + 91 merchant seamen from Idarwald & Rhein = 726	223 civilians from West Africa	3 Norwegians 1 Dutch 1 Swede, all from Sierra Leone Internees from Jamaica	966	Note total men from West Africa 476 of a total of 592 persons. Breakout from CO968/35/13

Date						Notes
July 1941	Space added for 180	84 merchant seamen from Bermuda				Note released: July – 2 German refugees interned in Sierra Leone Aug/September – 4 Naturalized British October – 2 local internees February 1942 – 1 ditto
September 1942	1,050 (Swiss Vice-Consul Report)	541 merchant seamen 221 civilians	31 merchant seamen 221 civilians	29	1043	Note released: 10 locally interned enemy aliens
July 1943	1,200 (Swiss Vice-Consul)	530 merchant seamen 200 civilians	31 merchant seamen 221 civilians	22		Note released: March 1943 – 6 Jamaicans
September 1943		-56 civilians (to Married Family Camp)	-3?		948 (estimate)	Source: Hoffman Report
November 1943		541 merchant seamen 166 civilians	8 merchant seamen 67 civilians		804 (estimate)	After Armistice, 177 Italian co-operators moved to Newcastle Camp
March 1944	Swiss Consul report	538 Seamen 113 Civilians	8 merchant seamen 67 civilians	22		177 Italian co-operators at Newcastle
May 1944		705 Germans exclusive of Mona Family Camp	8 merchant seamen 70 civilians	4 Romanians 12 Jews, Communists, Other Nationalities		Note to colonial secretary in 1B/5/77/233

(Continued)

Table 1 (Continued) Population of Male Internment Camp 1939–1947

Date	Camp Capacity	Camp Population				Comments
		German/Austrian	Italian	Other	Total	
August 1944		529 merchant seamen 125 civilians	8 merchant seamen 70 civilians	4 Romanians 12 Jews Communists, Other Nationalities		Swiss Vice-Consul report
December 1944		535 merchant seamen 162 Civilians	8 merchant seamen 70 civilians	4 Romanians 12 Jews, Communists, Other Nationalities		Swiss Vice-Consul report
April 1945		538 merchant seamen 144 civilians	8 merchant seamen 70 civilians	4 Romanians 12 Jews Communists, Other Nationalities		Swiss Vice-Consul report
May 1946		-120	-180			Departures on SS *Bergensfjord*
November 1946		-465 mostly merchant seamen [-25 married civilians]	-30		220	Departures on SS *Esperance Bay*. Balance at male camp: 70 merchant seamen; 150 civilians (20 priests)
February 1947						Departures of remaining internees aboard the HMS *Carthage*

Treatment of Prisoners of War. In March 1940, a report to Jamaica's Legislative Council identified, as inmates at the camp: sixty-five prisoners of war, sixteen locally interned civilian enemy aliens, one enemy alien who had been interned in British Honduras, one internee in the mental hospital and one female internee being held at the Young Women's Christian Association (YWCA) hostel in Kingston.[11] The status of these persons already held in the camp in Kingston had been the subject of correspondence between the Swiss vice-consul and colonial secretary Alexander Grantham, head of the colonial civil service in Jamaica, during February and March. In April, Grantham advised the Swiss consul:

> interned merchant seamen are to be regarded as POWs, but as non-combatants they are not covered by the Geneva Convention of 1929 which is therefore only applicable to them in principle, and they may be treated as interned civilians.[12]

The colonial secretary said that there was no convention relating to interned civilians and that, as such, they were subject to the rules and regulations of the camp where they were interned. In August 1940, a telegram to the War Office in London from the Officer Commanding Troops (OCT) in Jamaica distinguished between the 429 detainees then in the camp, noting that they included 45 persons interned as enemy aliens and 384 merchant seamen, of whom three were claiming prisoners of war status.[13] By mid-December, the arrival of the civilian internees from West Africa raised the number in the Male Internment Camp to 972. In response to queries on the categories of internees in the camp, the War Office asked that the term prisoners of war not be applied to enemy merchant seamen or civilian internees.[14]

The ambivalence over the categorization of captured seamen may have rested in part on perception of their status vis-a-vis the military establishment. In *The British Empire and Its Italian Prisoners of War*, Bob Moore and Kent Fedorowich commented that the Germans treated British merchant seamen as prisoners of war and imprisoned them as naval prisoners, because their own merchant mariners "were considered to be state servants and an arm of the military" – while, in fact, British merchant mariners were categorized as civilians.[15] They said that initially, the British differentiated between seamen captured on the high seas and those interned in British ports and that those captured within the British Empire were generally treated as civilian internees. However, this changed in February 1942, "when the British government decided on grounds of reciprocity and administrative convenience to reclassify merchant seamen as POWs".[16]

In 1942, the Swiss Consulate in Jamaica, acting as Protecting Power, formalized provision of regular camp reports for the internees, responding to a template supplied for this purpose. Fifty questions were grouped under camp (accommodation), property of the prisoners of war, postal traffic, food, clothing, sanitary arrangements, church services, wages, work, complaints, how is free time spent, discipline and sundries – many of these referencing articles of the Geneva Convention, which was on exhibit at all the internment camps. In Camp Report of September 1942 on the Male Internment Camp, responding to a question on wages for prisoners of war, the Swiss vice-consul noted that the question did not apply as "there are no prisoners of war in this camp".[17] He stated that the Male Internment Camp served solely for the internment of civil prisoners, housing Germans as well as Italians, and segregated persons such as Jews and other nationalities, all living in different compounds. The foreign internees were able to request that information regarding their internment be conveyed to their governments and to the International Red Cross, and forms were made available for this purpose. However, the notice offering this service also made clear that this decision was one that individual detainees could make voluntarily and that the British government would not convey information about internees to enemy governments, without being requested to do so.[18] Despite this understanding of the camp's status, postal evidence analysed by A.P.D. Sutcliffe indicates that a designation as "Internment & P. of W. Camp, Jamaica" remained in place as late as November 1944.[19]

A table from the Directorate of Prisoners of War: "Return of Enemy Prisoners of War detained in United Kingdom and Dominions as of 15 September 1943" listed thirty-one Italian "Other Ranks" in Jamaica, noting that the classifications for officers and other ranks included army, navy, air force, merchant seamen and merchant navy.[20] While no document has been located which identifies the situation in which these Italians were captured, it is noteworthy that nine Italians who died and were buried in the military cemetery between 1941 and 1945 were identified as *soldato* in the Italian Army.[21] Another table, sourced by Moore and Fedorowich among Cabinet Office documents relating to the Disposal of Prisoners of War Captured in North-West Europe, as of 10 February 1945, listed five hundred Germans in camp in Jamaica.[22]

A War Office document issued in 1945 offered this explanation:

> The position of the German Merchant Seamen is that on landing in JAMAICA they were told they were P/Ws. This was amended later, and they were installed in the Camp with Civil Internees and treated in all respects as internees. In 1944 the Commandant raised the question of their status, but it was considered that after nearly

four years it was not possible to set up a separate Camp for them, or advisable to treat them other than as internees.[23]

Locally Interned Enemy Aliens

Once Britain declared war on Germany, on 3 September 1939, the local authorities moved into action to intern men of German and Austrian extraction who had been living and working in Jamaica. In many instances, ironically, these were Jews who had fled growing threats in Europe – however, these persons had never been officially acknowledged as refugees from the Nazi threat.

By 1939, German nationals were taken to include Austrians – whose country was incorporated into Germany by the Anschluss of March 1938. However, some local reports still distinguished between them. A *Gleaner* front-page report of 4 September stated that twenty-four Germans and two Austrians – including several engaged in commercial and industrial activity in Jamaica – had been apprehended by the police around Kingston and St Andrew and were being held in a compound encircled by barbed wire and under continuous military guard, at the military headquarters. This location was the Military Detention Barracks which remains in use eighty years later. The newspaper report named the twenty-four Germans: Theo A. Deters – the putative German consul, U.L.C. Norman – a brewer working in Jamaica and his son Harold Norman, John Huber, Alfred Huth, William Stretcher, Rudolph Raitz, Rudolph Witte, Gerhard Paul Von der Porten, Arnold Paul Von der Porten, Ludwig Bumister, Richard Khan, Richard Kaiser, Ludwig Klein, Julius Hersch, Fritz Lackenbach, Fritz Lobbenberg, Max Ebersohn, Ulric Hild – a director of the African Fruit Company visiting Jamaica on business when war was declared, Alfred Loffler, dentist Dr Ernest Lobbenberg, Paul Schoenbeck, Mr Gertig and Mr Hans Winkler. The Von der Porten brothers were said to have worked with the Jamaica Public Service Company. The two Austrians were named as swimming coach Walter Lowi and Jose Frayman. An additional Austrian native dry goods peddler Leser Rapaport who held a Polish passport was also reported to have been held in Montego Bay and to be scheduled for transport to camp in Kingston.[24]

In a memoir, German internee Arnold Von Porten wrote that at least half of the Germans swept up by the police on 3 September were Jewish refugees who had recently arrived in Jamaica, along with wives and children, in an effort to escape the Nazis.[25] While subsequent reports suggest that his estimate was exaggerated, the first internees did include Jews and others whose politics or cultural values were reviled by the Nazis, and who had sought to flee Germany and other Eastern European countries since the rise of the National Socialist government in Germany in 1933.[26]

They received little encouragement from targeted countries, including Britain and the United States, though the United States would take considerably more than Britain and did push for more refugee entries later in the war. John P. Fox, looking at "German and European Jewish Refugees 1933–1945", said that great power response to Jewish immigration was based on the policies of the time, the legal and social position of the Jews as well as political and military factors.[27] Louise London in *Whitehall and the Jews* specified that Britain was not interested in the humanitarian aspect of the Jewish plight and looked at refugees based on identity and profession, availability of resources and ultimate destination.[28] There were also conflicting priorities among Britain's various government departments. In looking at the movement of persons fleeing Eastern Europe from the early 1930s, Joanna Newman's *Nearly the New World* said that the Colonial Office sought "to guard native populations against undesired large-scale migration", while the Home Office resisted any relaxation in domestic regulations discouraging immigration, and the Foreign Office was concerned to prevent large-scale Jewish migration to Palestine.[29]

Nonetheless, up to 4 September 1939, when the British government imposed a standstill on the entry of aliens from Reich territories into any part of the British Empire, asylum seekers had managed to find their ways into British colonies. Christian Cwik and Verena Muth indicated that lower immigration thresholds in much of the British West Indies allowed many German and Eastern European citizens fleeing Nazi policies to enter British West Indian territories between the early 1930s and the outbreak of war.[30] Indeed, while terming the British West Indies a way station while other destinations were closed, Newman's *Nearly the New World* nonetheless documented the settlement of several hundred Eastern European immigrants, many of them Jewish, especially in Barbados, Jamaica and Trinidad.

Public recognition of the challenges being faced by Jews fleeing Germany was made clear in an article titled "Unfortunate Victims of Hitler", published in the *Gleaner* on 11 September 1939. It stated:

> "Two fleeing German Jew refugees saw Jamaica from the deck of their ship on Saturday, while police officers kept a watchful eye on them. Sixty-three-year-old Richard Kerb and his fifty-five-year-old wife were aboard a Dutch vessel, fleeing Germany and not knowing whether they would be allowed to land at their ultimate destination of Los Angeles, USA, given that Germany was now at war".

The story said that officials had originally planned to intern them but settled for allowing them to remain on board under guard until the ship departed.

In Jamaica, several German immigrants had applied to become naturalized British citizens. Martin H. Heise, former head of Shell Company in Jamaica, received his papers under the British Nationality and Status of Aliens Act of 1914, shortly before the war started.[31] Von der Porten's brother Gerhard and his wife Dorrie were so advanced in the process of becoming British subjects that their papers had been sent to London for final signature when war was declared. Gerhard's release from internment upon the receipt of his naturalization papers was reported in the *Gleaner* – though he and his wife would be re-interned in 1940, as would other British citizens of German and Italian origin.[32]

On 7 September 1939, the *Gleaner* published a reassuring report on the internees: "Prisoners of War cheerful at camp" and on 14 September 1939 another story headlined, "All is well with Interned Germans", confirmed that the internees – both Aryan and Jewish – were being held at Up Park Camp while a new detention camp was being built and that they were making the best of the restrictions.[33] It suggested a degree of informal separation between the two groups, but also a lack of tension.

Within a few weeks, a procedure was implemented where interned persons could appeal their detention to a special Enemy Aliens Advisory Board, and the locally interned Germans and Austrians did so, some asking permission to be freed to leave the island and others asking to be released so that they could resume their occupations locally.[34] Hearings during October resulted in the mid-November release of at least eight persons, at least three of them German Jews. Those persons were dentist Dr Ernest Lobbenberg, his brother Fritz Lobbenberg and Fritz Lackenbach. The other Germans were Arnold Von der Porten, Max Ebersohn, Alfred Loffler, Willy Gertig who had recently joined the staff of the Friends School in Highgate St Mary and Austrian swimming coach Walter Lowi. Subsequent reports indicated that Wolfgang Kahn and Edward Paul Schonbeck, a chemist at the West Indies Sugar Company, had also been released. However, from this time, the government's adjustment of the evidentiary requirements for internees would affect these and other local detainees. Committees hearing cases could consider information not legally admissible as evidence and could refuse to consider documents or evidence if it thought this was inexpedient in the public interest.[35]

Germans and Austrians who had been released from initial internment in 1939 were re-arrested and sent back into the Male Internment Camp – ten of them on Saturday 18 May, "in keeping with measures which have been taken by the British Home Office to prevent any Fifth Column activities".[36] Louise London made the point that while identifying most asylum seekers in the United Kingdom as enemy aliens, the imperial government in London had not immediately initiated mass internment in 1939. This came after Winston Churchill became prime minister in May 1940 at a point in the war when the Germans were overrunning the Netherlands, Belgium, Luxemburg and France – with that general internment order extended to the colonies.[37] And while the British government would suspend this wholesale internment within months and begin to release various categories of internees, it would take a year or more for many of those interned in Jamaica to be released, despite pleas that they were refugees and anti-Nazi.

On 29 May, the *Jamaica Gleaner* reported that a recently naturalized British citizen of German birth had been interned after he was heard speaking in German on the telephone at his workplace – having first been reported to his boss and compelled to resign.[38] A sentiment in favour of interning naturalized citizens was visible in more than one letter published in the media around the end of May – one writer expressing concern that not only had these persons been left free since the start of the year but also allowed to hold responsible positions. Other naturalized British subjects who would be interned included Dr Hans Stamm, whose wife and mother were sent to the women's camp, Bernard Koth, Joseph Stevens and Italian Salvatore Doro. The total number of naturalized British subjects of German origin, interned in the summer of 1940 under Jamaica's Defence Regulations, would reach twelve, including six Jews – three men and three women. Enemy aliens who had been resident in Jamaica before the outbreak of war and who were interned or re-interned in 1940 would reach twenty-five men – including thirteen Jews, and nine women – seven of them Jewish.[39]

When those defined as enemy aliens were originally interned, their wives and children had been allowed to remain in their homes, with some restrictions on movement, especially at night. Indeed, the government made no provision for interning "female aliens" and the matter was kept under consideration until the change of British policy in May and the concurrent action of one woman.[40] Mrs Beta Czarnecki, a stewardess on the German ship SS *Dusseldorf*, which had been captured and brought to Kingston in December 1939, was subject to an Alien Restriction Regulation that allowed her to live at the YWCA in Downtown Kingston. Forbidden to leave her residence between 5.00 p.m. and 7.00 a.m., she nonetheless went to meet a sailor friend who was in port. Prosecuted, within the context of empire-wide concern about fifth-column activities, she was imprisoned for six months – there then being no Women's Internment Camp in operation.

The judge stated that she could thereafter be interned.[41] A few days later, a letter to the editor of the *Gleaner* suggested that women as much as men could be "Hitler's agents" and urged the authorities to "round up the whole lot of them and put them in safekeeping".[42] A women's facility would in fact be established in June.

Following Italy's entry into the war on 10 June 1940, on the side of Germany, Italians were added to the list of aliens required to register their presence, and gradually Italians who were resident in Jamaica, including some who had become naturalized British citizens, were also interned. Both the *Gleaner* and the *Jamaica Times* newspaper reported the internment of four Italians, following Italy's declaration of war against the allies. The *Gleaner* named them as Rinaldo Doro, Salvatore Doro, Antonio Montigani and Giovanni Paracchini. Subsequently, some information on the members of this group could be glimpsed from notices appealing detention orders, other classified advertisements and occasional correspondence. In 1941, the Catholic bishop in Jamaica appointed Father Gladstone Willson to be the official representative for the Italians in Jamaica – most of them among a large group of civilians brought from West Africa in December 1940. This was in the absence of a duly appointed representative and would have pre-dated the Swiss vice-consul taking up this responsibility. The Catholic Chancery received a list of Italian internees at the Men's Internment Camp, including four with Jamaican addresses among those not wanting their names sent to Italian consular representatives; these were Montigani, a mechanic in Kingston; Rinaldo Doro who gave Salvatore Doro as his next of kin; Giovanni Paracchini, manager of the Llanrumney banana and coconut estate in the north-eastern parish of Port Maria; and a trader, Levi Arrigo who worked with an agency called George & Vendryes.

In Jamaica, in keeping with British policy, persons of Polish and Czech origin were not interned or were released once they appealed. Nonetheless, there were tensions in some cases, such as arose when Czech subject Carol Richter was asked to leave the island in 1941, under the local Alien Restriction Regulation. Richter had arrived in Jamaica in 1938, looking at a possible investment in a local chemical factory, which apparently proved a failure. Richter wrote the Czech Minister in London for assistance in gaining permission to stay and work until arrangements to go to Canada could be finalized. His letter was not forwarded to London for nine months, at which point it was discovered that

> although colonial governments had been informed on the 24 September 1940, that the Secretary of State considered it desirable that persons of former Czech

nationality should not be treated . . . as enemy aliens, the Jamaica Government took no steps to amend the appropriate section of the Aliens Restrictions (Defence) Regulations 1940.[43]

The long-standing detention of many of the Germans and Austrians who had been living in Jamaica prior to the war and whose anti-Nazi position was not in question became an increasing political embarrassment for the Colonial Office – once the British had dialled back the hard-line policy of mid-1940. Personal correspondence reaching the Colonial Office questioned some of the long-standing internments, and questions were raised in Parliament in June 1941, leading the Colonial Office to press Governor Arthur Richards for a review. In August 1941, after more than a year in detention, based on lobbying as well as applications for review of their situation, five internees were released – all of them naturalized British citizens. They were Dr Hans Stamm, Bernard Koth and Salvatore Doro who had been held at the Male Internment Camp and Dr Stamm's wife and mother, who had been interned at Hanover Street.[44]

In March 1942, more than a year after Britain had moderated its own May 1940 mass internment policy, the secretary of state for the colonies wrote to Governor Richards protesting the continued internment in Jamaica of enemy aliens "whose anti-Nazi sympathies there are no specific reasons to doubt". In this, he included a small number of persons – some of them Jews – who had been deported from Sierra Leone in West Africa under special order. Richards had already told the Colonial Office that cases related to Jewish refugees, among the interned enemy aliens, had been reviewed but that he would only release them from the camps if they had either employment or guaranteed maintenance, or a guarantee of a visa to leave the island. The secretary of state said that he had "considerable difficulty" defending the continued detention of people who had been interned on one basis and now were in continued detention for another.[45] In response, the governor insisted that while he was prepared to have a tribunal review cases of internees who professed anti-Nazi and anti-Fascist sympathies, recommendations for release would be accepted on the basis that arrangements were made to remove those released from Jamaica. He said that the security officer and police could not provide adequate arrangements to supervise those released and that there was "a definite danger of pressure being brought to bear on released internees by ill-treatment or threats of ill-treatment to relations still in enemy or enemy occupied territory". [46]

Responding on 13 June 1942, the secretary of state carefully recognized that Jamaica's internment policy had followed the adoption of general internment in the United Kingdom on 29 May 1940, but this policy had been substantially modified from as early as 29 January 1941. He said:

> while I realise local difficulties and security doubts to which you have referred in your telegram on this problem, I have reached [the] conclusion that maintenance in Jamaica of what amounts to a policy of interning individuals of enemy nationality or origin merely as such although there is no basis for individually suspecting their bona fides, is not in accord with the general policy of H.M.O. and cannot be satisfactorily defended

He said that this also applied to the suggestion that released enemy aliens were subject to pressure. He requested an early review of cases of those professing anti-Nazi or anti-Fascist sympathies and a report on the numbers involved.[47] A resultant review in August 1942 saw the release of six internees – four of them in the male camp and two wives in the women's camp. In September, a further review led to the release of seven more internees who had been residing in Jamaica – six of them from the men's camp. These included Richard, Julia and Wolf Kahn, Ludwig Klein, Willie Gertig, J. Paracchini and Giovanni Paracchini.[48] The petitions of four more men and one woman – William Stecher, Rinaldo Doro, Joanna Schoene, Antonio Montigani and Martin H. Heise – were refused.[49] With respect to special cases transferred to Jamaica from West Africa, including German Jew Dr Rudolph Aub, the release was refused "in the absence of any information from the Governments concerned, documents having apparently been lost at sea through enemy action". But Aub was one of five internees brought from Sierra Leone and two from the Gold Coast who were permitted to enlist in the auxiliary military Pioneer Corps. This gave them duties and allowances and substantially increased their freedoms. The review board also allowed this privilege to four captured enemy seamen.[50] The governor said that cases related to German nationals transferred to Jamaica from British Guiana (Henrich Tuxhorn, Stefan Weissmann and Emil Schweitzer), Trinidad (Heinrich Wilhelm Busch), British Honduras (Anton Smith) and Bermuda (Alfred Stocks) had not been reviewed.[51] It is interesting to note that a report on Smith's arrival in Jamaica stated that he was British Honduras's only resident German enemy alien, though there was "a fairly large population of German and Austrian Jewish refugees", several of them doctors practising in the colony, who had not been detained.[52]

Several of those released had restrictions on their movement, which were not removed until March 1944, as reflected in a published notice. These persons, including naturalized British citizens, were: Amadeo Salvatore

Doro, Caroline Ebersohn, Max Ebersohn, Willie Werner, Paul Gertig, Julia Kahn, Richard Kahn, Wolf Kahn, Bernard Koth, Louis Kroneker, Mathilde Kroneker, Alfred Loeffler, Walter Lowi, Dorothea Von der Porten, Gerhard Von der Porten, Emma Maud Stamm, Hans Stamm, Joseph Stevens, Arrigo Levi, Ernst Lobbenberg, Fritz Lobbenberg, J. Parachini, Arnold Paul Von der Porten, Edward Paul Theodore Schonbeck, Emelie Sara Stamm, Fritz Lackenbach and Rosa Lackenbach. It is notable that several of the internees, including the Kahns, Lackenbachs, Lobbenbergs and Ebersohns, went on to apply for naturalization within months of this relief from restriction.

Jamaican Detainees

The other group of persons held at the Male Internment Camp, over whom questions would be raised in Jamaica and beyond, were detained over civil or political statements or actions or the threat of such actions. The context was Jamaica's active labour and political agitation, which had resurged after a brief lull following the outbreak of war, and their detention sparked local debate on issues of individual liberties, within the context of the local Defence Regulations.

The first and most sensational detention was that of labour leader Alexander Bustamante, who would later lead the first local government elected under universal adult suffrage in 1944 and become Jamaica's first prime minister after independence in 1962.[53] Bustamante was interned in September 1940 by order of Governor Sir Arthur Richards, under Regulation 18 (i) of the Jamaica Defence Regulations, "with a view to preventing him acting in any fashion prejudicial to public order". The order, which was eventually rescinded in February 1942, followed a fiery speech in which Bustamante reportedly said: "We want revolution...before the whites destroy us, we will destroy them. I am going to paralyse all industrial works".[54] Bustamante's internment became the stuff of local lore – even finding its way into Ralph Thompson's poem novel, *View from Mount Diablo*, in which the protagonist refers to meeting him in the internment camp when he went there to see his German uncle Johann.[55]

Bustamante would be joined within a few months by longshoreman and vice president of the Maritime arm of the Bustamante Industrial Trade Union (BITU), Wilfred A. Williams. Also detained in March 1941, for making speeches considered to contain matter prejudicial to the war effort, was PNP Propaganda Secretary Samuel C Marquis. His offence apparently included statements relating to the colour composition of the police force.[56] In May 1941, these political internees were joined by George St. C. Scotter, an English sports columnist working at the *Gleaner* newspaper, who wrote the regular "Today" column. He was the columnist who, in January, had termed Gibraltar Camp a "sports model concentration camp" and its commandant "a 2 × 4 dictator", and he was apparently interned for remarks he made in a Kingston bar. Lady Gladys Bustamante, in a memoir, wrote that Scotter, a former police inspector, "stated his objection to the increasing number of American service men in this British colony, and since such remarks were considered offensive by the authorities, he was taken into custody".[57] Lady Bustamante, then Miss Gladys Longbridge, was a stalwart at the BITU and a frequent visitor to the camp while Bustamante was interned. Scotter and Williams would be released in October 1941.[58]

In June 1941, Wilfred A. Domingo, a New York–based activist with the Jamaica Progressive League, was detained on his arrival in Jamaica to help raise the organizational levels of the People's National Party. Domingo's detention would spark concerns in many quarters and would be seen as a prime example of the governor's authoritarianism. Protests over this case would be raised on both sides of the Atlantic, led by Jamaica Progressive League President W. Adolphe Roberts in New York. At that time, prominent local attorney Ansell Hart complained in the press that the governor's emergency powers were being used to sidestep the functions of the court of justice, observing that "the advisory council on internment was mere window-dressing".[59] Domingo would remain in detention until March 1943 on the order of the governor, when he was released without restriction.[60]

Hart's son, Richard, would be one of four more activists interned in November 1942 for labour and political activism considered inimical to the British war effort. The others were brothers, Ken and Frank Hill, and Arthur Henry.[61] The "Four H's", as they became known, were communist members of the PNP, who were working to unionize the government railway and post offices – services considered critical especially during a war.[62] The four would be released unconditionally on 18 March 1943. Samuel Marquis was released on the previous day, with conditions requiring him to remain in the city and preventing him from attending or addressing large political gatherings.[63]

Richard Hart recalled that the Jamaicans were billeted together in the same hut or barracks building and that there were several huts in the compound, which also accommodated an assortment of internees including German Jews, other anti-Nazi German internees including one declared communist, a Slovene priest, Norwegians interned in Sierra Leone and an Italian.[64]

Merchant Seamen

Chronologically, German merchant seamen from ships "taken prize" in the Caribbean and nearby waters were the second group of persons detained in the Male Internment Camp. The first of them, in October 1939, were the officers and crew of the German tanker SS *Emmy Friedrich*, which the crew scuppered when intercepted by British light cruiser *HMS Caradoc*.[65] A 1939 *British Pathe* film on German ships trapped in continental American ports by a British Blockade included the *Emmy Friedrich* in Vera Cruz, Mexico, as well as the *Orinoco*, *SS Rhein* and *SS Idarwald*. Crews from the latter two would also end up interned in Jamaica.[66] When it captured the *Emmy Friedrich*, *The HMS Caradoc* was part of the eighth Cruiser Squadron in Bermuda which ran interception patrols to catch the German and Italian vessels trying to get through. The *Emmy Friedrich* was reportedly *en route* from Tampico, Mexico, when intercepted.

By March 1940, the *Gleaner* reported that nearly one hundred and forty men were in the new internment camp, some of them being the enemy aliens detained while resident in Jamaica or other West Indian colonies, while most were "prisoners of war" from captured German ships.[67] These included the twenty-four men and nine officers who were crew of the seven thousand-ton freighter SS *Dusseldorf*, which had been intercepted and captured by the British cruiser *Despatch* on 15 December 1939 and brought into Kingston Harbour. Unusually, the freighter was captured in the Pacific, off the coast of Chile and brought through the Panama Canal and then to Kingston by a Prize Crew of three British officers and twenty men, despite protest by the German consul in Panama. The case of legal ownership of the captured vessel as a prize of war was determined in Prize Court in Kingston in April 1940.[68]

At the beginning of March, the *Gleaner* reported internment of the thirty-nine-member crew of the German freighter *Troja*, which had been set on fire to avoid capture by the British.[69] Also in March, the crew of the German passenger liner turned freighter, SS *Hannover* was intercepted by a British cruiser between the Dominican Republic and Puerto Rico. Despite the crew's effort to scupper the ship, it was brought to Jamaica where, after a Prize Court hearing, the damaged cargo was advertised for sale in May 1940. The repaired vessel, renamed the *Empire Audacity*, was subsequently attacked by the German Navy near northern Scotland.[70]

The second half of 1940 saw a steady flow of prisoners: In July 1940, the *Jamaica Producer* – a British steam, merchant vessel whose home port was Kingston, Jamaica – sailed to Curacao, escorted by a warship and a guard of three officers and fifty other ranks from the Winnipeg Grenadiers to transport some 230 German internees to Jamaica.⁷¹ By August, there were 418 men in a camp then designed for 450 occupants, and further expansion was imminent to accommodate a large group that would be accepted from West Africa.⁷²

One of the best documented naval capture cases near Jamaica involved the German merchant vessel SS *Idarwald*, which was intercepted by the HMS *Diomede* south of Cuba. The *Idarwald* and the *Rhein* were among a dozen German and Italian vessels, many of them freighters, which spent months in Tampico harbour, Mexico, seeking an opportunity to get their cargoes through the British Blockade. Newspaper coverage out of Mexico, carried in the *Jamaica Gleaner*, said that some, including the *Idarwald*, had been there from the start of the war. In mid-November 1940, they were in a group of four German vessels that left port, but three raced back when they saw a ship that they thought was an enemy warship and one, the SS *Phrygia* was scuppered by its crew. On 26 November, the *Gleaner* carried a story headlined "12 Axis Ships at Tampico Prepare for Early Dash". At least two, the *Idarwald* and the SS *Rhein*, left Tampico on 29 November. The *Idarwald* was intercepted by the British cruiser *Diomede* on 8 December, having been spotted and reported by other vessels. The crew set the ship on fire before the vessel could be boarded by a British Prize Crew, and it continued to burn fiercely until the next day. Photographs of the burning ship, sourced, like these reports, from the Canadian Press wire service via Cable & Wireless, were featured on the front page of the Jamaican *Gleaner* newspaper. Within a few more days, the *Rhein* was captured off the coast of Cuba by the Dutch warship *Van Kinsbergen* which was serving with the British Atlantic Squadron. The crew set fire to their vessel on the approach of the Dutch cruiser and launched lifeboats, but forty-three sailors were captured and taken to Kingston, arriving in camp on 12 December.⁷³

Arnold Von Der Porten, who was in the internment camp, wrote that from his compound, he could see captured German ships in the harbour: "The interior of one of them had been burnt out by the crew before it abandoned ship. It was being refitted to serve the British . . . the crew was in the internment camp with us."⁷⁴ Other groups of prisoners brought to Kingston in 1941 included eighty-four enemy merchant seamen sent from the United Kingdom's Northern Caribbean headquarters, Bermuda. A list of vessels from which men in the camp had been taken, compiled by the Swiss consul in a 1942 report, named: T/S *Vancouver, Henry Horn, Wagogo, Antilla*, SS *Idarwald, Emmy Friedrich*, SS *Rhein*, m/s *Patricia, Norderney*, m/s *Slemdal, Seattle*, m/s *Ino, Adolf Leonard, Wesermuende, Wameru, Norawind*, s/s *El Liberatador, Lottica*, m/s *Pericles, Nero*, m/s *Karibia, Alemania*, m/s

Frisia, Este, m/s *Heidelberg, Hannover*.[75] By September, the number also included the *Saint Gobin*.[76] The report did not break out the number of internees from the various vessels.

Barring repatriations which were limited, and escapes which were short-lived, these merchant mariners would remain within the camp boundaries for several years – many as late as 1947, as this chapter will show. After the end of the war, the colonial government refused appeals for their release until they could be removed from the island, invoking security concerns and anticipated competition for scarce local employment.[77]

German and Italian Internees from West Africa

In August 1940, a decision to significantly increase the camp capacity, then at 450, resulted from Jamaica's agreement to accept 568 German and Italian civilians, then interned in British West Africa as enemy aliens. The governor of Jamaica responded positively to a Colonial Office request, agreeing to accept the internees as an imperial liability, accommodating 456 men in the Military Internment Camp which would be expanded and upgraded for the purpose.[78] The women and children would be sent to the Women's Internment Camp, recently established in repurposed buildings at Hanover Street in Downtown Kingston. Two Caribbean islands, St Lucia and Jamaica, had been considered as possible sites of internment for the group, with Jamaica preferred due to having more accommodation and guards. The Colonial Office dismissed any objection to the Caribbean climate: "The Foreign Office objection to sending Germans to tropical climates may be reasonable as regards Germans from Europe, but Jamaica would certainly be more healthy for them than West Africa."[79]

A large percentage of the Germans in the group had been interned in Nigeria and Cameroon and held for several months at the Umuahia Camp in Ibadan, Nigeria.[80] Nigeria served as the headquarters for the British Empire in West Africa. Importantly, in the context of the war, the governor there also oversaw the British mandate in the Cameroons – a German colony from the late nineteenth century which was split at the end of World War I and placed under respective British and French mandates. German companies had been allowed to return to the British side and continued to operate some fifteen plantations producing bananas, rubber and palm oil. While key German representatives were interned early in the war, most of the German managers, many with their families, continued running the plantations. Indeed, when he acted to intern the Germans in Cameroon, the British Governor of Nigeria recognized the likely impact on the maintenance of the colony's banana plantations and the livelihood of the local labourers.[81] This mid-1940 decision followed soon after Germany invaded France, Belgium, Luxembourg and the Netherlands in May–June 1940 and was rooted in indications that some Germans in the Cameroons were working on behalf of the German war effort. A telegram from the British Colonial Office to the governor in Nigeria flagged "recent indications of subversive activities and sabotage by Germans and possibility of attempt at concerted effort with assistance from Fernando Po" – then an island colony of Spain only about 20 miles west.[82] Spain's ambivalent position in the war was a concern. The British also believed that subversive activity might have extended into the area under a French Mandate. Indeed, the list of Germans interned in Jamaica included individuals and families from the French Mandate.[83]

In addition to the planters and managers, the internment order extended to missionaries from the Basel Mission and German Baptist Mission. A telegram from the governor of Nigeria raised suspicions over the use of German-controlled missions by Nazi authorities, especially in the Cameroons where they had greater autonomy, and underscored the undesirability of having:

> suspected persons at large, in educational or other capacity, providing opportunities for influencing native opinion susceptible of defeatist propaganda; nor are there means available of providing adequate supervision.[84]

Postwar correspondence would again address the activities of enemy missionaries in British Cameroons and Nigeria, and the governor of Nigeria would strongly object to German missionaries returning there.[85]

The Germans from the Cameroons joined at least sixty-five compatriots already in camp in Nigeria – seemingly from as early as December 1939, when the German government representative in Cameroon, Herr Luppe, described the camp in a letter to the German consul in Fernando Po:

> The climate is somewhat better than in the Cameroons and the accommodation is good; the catering is most adequate, but at times somewhat monotonous. The sanitary arrangements and so forth are highly satisfactory. We have four tennis courts, a library in which the books of the internees have been placed, a communal restaurant and a lounge with a bar. Each Thursday a social evening takes place. There are many sports played and, also, a course in foreign language has been started. The feeling amongst the internees is generally good, although some especially the young people are unhappy because they have nothing to do.[86]

A correspondent whose father was an engineer on a banana plantation in Cameroon and whose family was interned said that they arrived in Nigeria around the end of May and remained there for six months before being shipped to Jamaica.[87] He said that the men and women were kept in separate sections of the camp, separated by a road and barbed wire fences but could see and wave to each other.

Also joining the group were three German internees from the Gold Coast – today's Ghana – and a large group of Italian internees: 192 from the Gold Coast and 27 from Nigeria, interned after Italy entered the war on the German side, on 10 June 1940. Some of these internees were attached to the Italian construction group Cappa D'Alberto, which operated in Nigeria from the early 1930s.[88] Most of the Italians were construction workers, and their group included only a few women. The Colonial Office assessed that all the Italian citizens in British West Africa were interned and sent to Jamaica.[89]

The Sierra Leone group consisted of twenty-five Germans, four Italians and a number of special cases and persons removed from ships – including three Norwegians, one Swede, one Dutchman and a German Jew, Dr Rudolph Aub who had fled Germany to escape the Nazis, only to be interned along with many of his Aryan countrymen, both Nazi and non-political.[90] The non-enemy aliens in this group had been detained under a local defence regulation, and the Colonial Office requested that the necessary special order be made by the governor in Jamaica to facilitate their internment there.[91]

As Colonial Office documents indicate, the transfer of the West African internees to Jamaica was mainly undertaken "to help Sierra Leone, Nigeria and Gold Coast to get rid of some of their more dangerous internees" by moving them further from the fighting. Though few of the internees were assessed as ardent Nazis, Sutcliffe referenced a camp officer who believed that some might have been Nazi agents "sent to West Africa in preparation for the outbreak of war".[92] For the War Office, the main concern was to appropriately secure these white internees and prisoners, taking both climate and available guards into account.[93] Other African colonies had been dismissed as possible internment sites: the Union of South Africa due to concern that there was serious fifth-column activity as well as the fact that the government had already taken custody of some five hundred internees from the East African governments of Tanganika, Kenya and Uganda. It was considered inadvisable to concentrate large numbers of internees into Rhodesia, in the event of trouble in nearby Portuguese East Africa. The island of St Helena was also considered as a site of internment but dismissed due to the lack of camp facilities or expertise to erect such facilities, on the island.[94]

The Up Park Camp War Diary entry for 3 December 1940 stated: "Five hundred and ninety-two internees arrived from Freetown, West Africa, aboard the SS *Pennland*. The internees were escorted by a detachment of the 1/4th Essex Regiment."⁹⁵ The *Pennland* was a passenger vessel that had been converted to serve as a British troop transport ship. It boarded those persons interned in Nigeria then collected other groups, finally sailing from Freetown in Sierra Leone. The Diary entry continued: "One hundred and sixteen of these internees were women and children who are now domiciled in Kingston, the remaining four hundred and seventy-six were placed in the Internment Camp, Up Park Camp." Roughly half of the men were German – plantation managers, engineers and other professionals, as well as missionaries – while most of the others were Italian, a large number from the construction trades. A newspaper article headlined "More Enemy Aliens Arrive", noted that "large, interested, but completely undemonstrative crowds gathered on every street corner along their route to watch them pass".⁹⁶

In Britain, the thinking behind the wholesale transfer of skilled civilians from West Africa would be questioned within a few months, when Italian prisoners were being sought to do "heavy works" in West Africa. A minuted note expressed bewilderment, given that Britain had recently sent away,

> principally from the Gold Coast, some two or three hundred Italian civil employees previously employed there by Italian contractors. These people are at present interned at public expense in Jamaica, where they were sent mainly on the grounds that their continued presence in West Africa might prove an embarrassment from an operational point of view.⁹⁷

This group would dissipate in various ways. The special cases sent from Sierra Leone would eventually be allowed to leave the island or have their conditions ameliorated. A newspaper report in July 1941 said that lawyers had taken the case of two German refugees, interned in Sierra Leone while en route from Switzerland to Brazil, and who had been sent to Jamaica for detention. The men were to leave Jamaica on their release.⁹⁸ In 1942, German Jew, Dr Rudolph Aub, who was also interned in Sierra Leone, was eventually allowed to join the Pioneer Corps. In mid-1943, a belated decision to establish a camp for married families and single women saw the reassignment of some fifty-six Germans and three Italians from the Male Internment Camp. It is arguable that these reassigned men could have been among the most stable in the camp, with a mature focus on the well-being of their families as well as themselves. These were also all professional men most of whom had been working in the banana industry in the British Cameroons. In September 1943, in consequence of the Armistice agreed by Italy, the Italian civilians were given the opportunity to move into a less restrictive situation, based on the signature of a cooperation agreement. Some, one hundred and fifty took up the offer and were sent under a relaxed military oversight to the Newcastle Military Hill Station and eventually to Gibraltar Camp.[99] The other German and Italian internees remained in the Male Internment Camp until they were repatriated in 1946 and 1947.

Finns

A group of thirty-two Finns were held at the Male Internment Camp, during the period when Finland was at war with the Soviet Union, which had become a British ally. Most were recorded as having been interned aboard the merchant ship SS *Yiloum*, though no reference to the event has been located. The group also included a cabin boy, Leo Fabritius, who was seized aboard a Norwegian ship, mv *Palbeck*, when it called at Kingston Harbour in December 1941.[100] In a March 1942 report on a visit to the Male Internment Camp, the YMCA's Conrad Hoffmann Jr said of the small group that they:

> seem lost and out of place. What irony that they should be interned with Axis folk by the British. They have adjusted themselves admirably and manifest splendid spirit. They keep up intensive gymnastics to keep in good physical condition.[101]

In July 1942, changes in the progress of wartime alliances led to these internees being moved to Gibraltar Camp where they were essentially given the same freedoms as the refugees, though there was technically a limit on how far from the camp they could wander.[102]

Inter-Group Relationships and Divisions

Tensions within the Male Internment Camp emerged from the interplay of various distinct groups detained together – though with differentiated compounds to try and create a degree of separation and control. The tensions between the groups had many causes, the most evident and damaging being rooted in ethnic, social and political factors. Response to the news of war developments, the sense of inability to contribute as well as the mental impact of long-term incarceration were other factors. There were also differences in approach and ethos between the German merchant seamen, who had been connected to the war effort and who were accustomed to a hierarchical command structure, and the civilians, many of whom were professionals. Among the German civilians from West Africa, the group from British Cameroon had several commonalities – not only because they had lived and worked in a common geographical area, but they would have socialized together as Europeans within the British

West African colonies. The men from the British Cameroon were also largely family men – their wives and children forming by far the largest group of women and children in the women's camp. Among the men's camp population, the Swiss consul's reports frequently noted an overall lack of complaints among the Italian group, most of whom were also quite homogenous. A majority of the construction workers interned in West Africa came from two specific towns in northern Italy: Vercelli, a small city and commune in the Piedmont region, and Bergamo, north-east of Milan in the region of Lombardy.

In February 1941, several months after the camp population had extended beyond the original group of local enemy aliens, concerns about mixing potentially conflicting groups reached the British Parliament, through a question laid by British parliamentarians Samuel Silverman and Philip Noel-Baker. Silverman questioned the internment of people whose anti-Nazi sympathies were not in question and Noel-Baker called on Under-Secretary of State for the Colonies George Hall to urge the governor of Jamaica that if German Jews must be interned, there must at least be effective separation, given "the very grave injustice of interning Nazis and anti-Nazis together". Mr Hall, in response, said that the matter was under discussion with Governor Arthur Richards, then in London for consultation, but underlined "the difficulty of discriminating, particularly among enemy seamen and others, because you must have some corroboration with regard to their political views, before you can take action".[103] In March 1941 another parliamentary question noted that twelve British subjects of German origin who had been detained under Defence Regulations in Jamaica included three men and three women of Jewish extraction.[104] The Colonial Office also received numerous letters relating to this issue in general or specific cases – some of which eventually sparked reviews.[105]

It does, however, appear that some degree of separation was in place at the Male Internment Camp from mid- or late 1940. Arnold Van der Porten, who was re-interned in May 1940, referred to the arrival of the West African internees in December 1940 and wrote that Jewish members of the group joined the compound where the locals were held.[106] This was confirmed by an unpublished memoir written by one of their number, who said that three members of the group:

> were assigned to a special group. We found a group of about thirty, a motley lot, most of them Jewish immigrants. They had been resident in Jamaica for varying lengths of time. Two of them were waiting for the naturalisation for which they had applied. Others, Austrians, had found asylum in Jamaica the year before,

after months of wandering. For political reasons, the non-Jewish internees had been separated from the Germans and Italians. In addition, we found a few Jamaican politicians who for some reason had made themselves unpopular with the government.[107]

By July 1942, a Red Cross report identified the following sections within the Male Internment Camp: two for Germans, one for Italians, one for Jews, one for British subjects, one for the hospital, one for administration and one for provisions, the canteen and workshops.[108] From 1 September 1942, the compounds were reorganized by order of the British camp authorities: All of the German merchant seamen were placed in the "A" Compound, with officers and men roomed together, by ship – though captains had special quarters. The ranking officer thereby became Hut Leader, with responsibility for the behaviour of his crew, as well as for the hut – the term "hut" refers to the wooden barracks. The German civilian internees all fell within the "B" Compound. Each compound had its own kitchen and work gangs.[109] The Italians, including the few merchant seamen as well as the majority of civilians, remained in their own "C" Compound and the other groups were in what was termed the Segregated Compound.

The changes were rooted in concerns about corruption in at least two aspects of camp life among some of the German internees. One related to bullying by gangs, based around one of the two kitchens, with some internees receiving "meagre and perhaps shortened rations", compared to what was served to captains, ships officers and others. The Swiss vice-consul report on this issue said that internees who complained about the poor meals received threats of a severe "licking" by the cook, who had a reputation for violence, and his "kitchen gang". When the kitchen staff was forcibly changed, there was an immediate improvement in the food, but continued unrest and friction engendered by the old gangs involved some of the boys and young men. Another concern, raised in reports between 1942 and 1943, was evidence of homosexuality among some German internees: "With [a] few exceptions one can only talk of homosexual inclination, but this is dangerous enough to lead young men astray."[110]

In November 1943, a further special compound, the "N" Compound, was created to house prisoners who had, in some instances, proved threatening to some fellow residents as well as those who had proved troublesome in other disruptive ways. Camp authorities requested an emergency visit by Vice-Consul R.J. Waeckerlin who was advised that fourteen German seamen and civilian internees had been confined in a separate compound for being involved in "corruption". The authorities told the Swiss representative that "these men were trouble-makers and bad Germans and lowered the morale of the camp, having particularly a bad influence on the weaker members of the Camp".[111] The Swiss report noted an impression that the German and Italian camp supervisors agreed with the confinements, "but for obvious reasons could not say so". To avoid any dissonance between the camp leaders and the general camp population, camp adjutant and quartermaster, Captain H. McCabe, subsequently met with all twenty-eight hut leaders in the detention camp, to explain the decision to segregate the men and make it clear that the separation had been solely a decision of the British authorities.[112]

Three of the original fourteen men confined to "N" Compound, two of them seamen and one a civilian, were returned to the main camp population within a few weeks. However, by March 1943, five more Germans were segregated based on political disturbances that related to some other internees who expressed communist or Jewish sympathies.[113] Another two were added in June 1943 after serving twenty-eight days in solitary confinement for an escape from the camp. They had been recaptured after one day.[114]

In November 1943, there were twelve Germans segregated in "N" Compound, the preceding three months having seen the release of eight men and the addition of two more. The commandant was reported to be satisfied that this segregation improved the discipline and happiness of the camp.[115] By March 1944, it was reported that all occupants of "N" Compound had been returned to the main camp, based on representations and assurances from the German camp leader, who was sure that he could maintain order.[116] Subsequently, two former "N" Compound internees were arrested for assault against two other persons but otherwise calm seems to have reigned and the "N" Compound remained empty but was retained as a cautionary reminder.

Location and Layout

Purpose-built just after the outbreak of World War II, the Male Internment Camp was situated to the north-eastern side of the British garrison at Up Park Camp, then on the edge of Kingston. While only about five kilometres from Kingston Harbour, the site elevation of three hundred feet above sea level, the sheltering Long Mountain to the east and the fact that the area around was sparsely settled, made the location ideal for the residents.[117] Indeed the Swiss vice-consul, whose regular reports provide fine detail on the camp conditions, observed that it was situated "in one of the best parts of the residential areas of St Andrew".

No layout has been located, but the approximately 15 acre or 650,000 square foot site was delineated as stretching from the Up Park Camp military headquarters, along South Camp Road to the south, east and north-east to Mountain View Road, west and south along Old Hope Road, and back to South Camp Road.[118] These were lands under the control of the military, close to the garrison's rifle range. Oral testimony indicated that it was approached from a gate near the Garrison Church in the military camp, along a small road next to the Briggs Park Military Cemetery and that "at that time the POW camp, which has disappeared, was a rectangle divided in the middle so there were two diamond shapes, one for the Italians, one for the Germans. Between was an area that an armoured carrier could go down in case of trouble".[119] Figure 13 highlights the area believed to have been covered by the internment camp, overlaying a late twentieth-century map of Up Park Camp and its surroundings.

Roughly square, the camp was described by an inmate as being surrounded by "two sets of ten-foot-high barbed wire", guarded by several towers in which were soldiers "carrying rifles and manning machine guns".[120] There was a large recreation ground and four – later five – compounds housing various groups. Political detainee Richard Hart said that the adjoining compounds were separated by wire fences, each with military guards at their exits.[121] The "A" and "B" Compounds, housing German seamen and German civilians respectively, were estimated as covering about two hundred thousand square feet each, with the "C" Compound housing the Italian population estimated to cover about one hundred thousand square feet. The smallest section was the "Segregated Compound" housing Jews, naturalized British subjects, Jamaican internees and other nationalities. While the Germans and Italians in the "A", "B" and "C" compounds could access each other's spaces between reveille and lights out, no access or communication was allowed between those compounds and the "Segregated Compound" – as a protective measure.[122] Residents of all compounds had access to the same facilities and services, with the exception of the "N" compound which, while it existed, was denied access to the recreation ground. Rare photographs of the camp perimeter and recreation ground were taken by Canadian serviceman Lloyd Henry McHugh of the Brockville Rifles, which did garrison duty at the camp from 1944–1946 (See Figures 14, 14A, 14B, 14C).

The details made available through the Swiss vice-consul's regular reports indicate that the authorities took seriously their responsibilities of caring for the internees. The men lived in twenty-eight well-spaced wooden barracks buildings, built on pillars about three feet high, with a mix of sizes to accommodate either twenty men (60'×20'), forty men (120'×19')

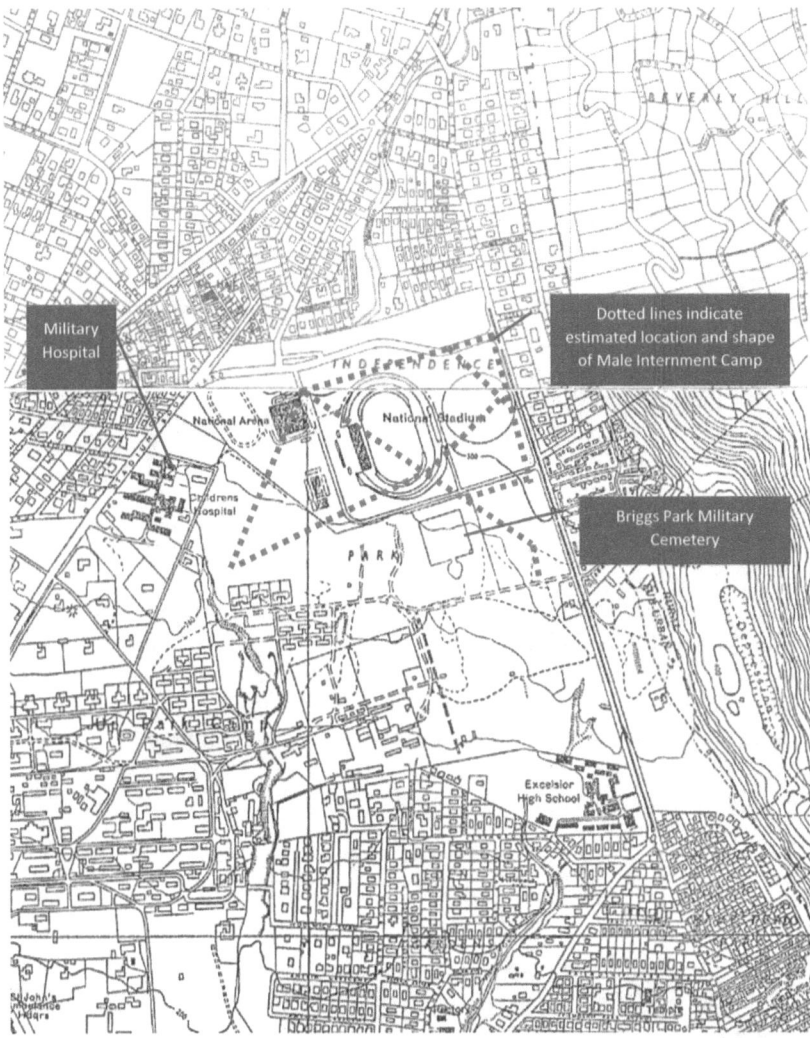

Figure 13 Annotated map of Up Park Camp Kingston showing estimated location of Male Internment Camp (Pattern observed on 1:50000 topographical map of Kingston, Sheet L (1973) is overlaid on Kingston & Environs 1:0000 showing greater detail of Up Park Camp area. Source: Map & Image Library, UWI Mona).

or eighty men (140'×38').[123] More than one hundred younger Germans were billeted in two separate barracks, each under the supervision of senior men.[124] Richard Hart, who lived for several months in the Segregated Compound said that all internees were responsible for keeping their huts tidy and the toilets clean and that these were inspected from time to time. They also had the job of chopping wood for the stove and hoeing out weeds

Figure 14 Internee walking around the outer edge of the recreation field, close to the barbed wire perimeter fence, while others play a match in the distance. Caption on back of photo, presumably written by photographer, Lloyd McHugh of the Brockville Rifles, which was on garrison duty from 1944–1946 states: German walking around inside the prison camp (Courtesy Legion Magazine).

Figure 14A Recreation area adjacent to the barracks buildings which accommodated the male internees. Lloyd McHugh photo (Courtesy Legion Magazine).

Figure 14B Fencing between two segregated areas of the male internment camp. Lloyd McHugh photo (Courtesy Legion Magazine).

Figure 14C Guard on duty at one of the guardposts along the perimeter of the male internment camp. Lloyd McHugh photo (Courtesy Legion Magazine).

in the compounds.[125] The Swiss vice-consul detailed the actual sleeping facilities in a 1942 Report, as follows:

> Bed-planks with supports are provided, most of them with straw mattresses, some with coir; each with a straw pillow, two bedsheets which are changed weekly, two woollen blankets, one mosquito net and one locker. Twenty men have one table at their disposal.[126]

He said that space for flower and vegetable beds was allowed between the buildings and compounds and that some internees were assiduous gardeners. Indeed, a further report in July 1943 noted:

> One is impressed on each visit by the spaciousness of this Internment Camp. At present, especially, the flowers are in full bloom and the enlarged gardens around and between the dormitory huts create a very nice atmosphere. The internees have planted a great many pawpaw trees which are very beautiful and are now bearing fruit.[127]

The camp had regular access to water and electricity, with electric lighting provided in the huts until 10.00 p.m., though it was not sufficient for reading – a condition in common with a general insufficiency of power across the island. Contextualizing camp conditions, the Swiss vice-consul commented that in some towns around the island, the lights were turned off from a main switch before midnight. "Everyone is on a quota based on their former consumption and in many cases, this has forced luxury trades, such as ice-cream making, out of business."[128] Daylight saving had been introduced from April to August, procuring an extra hour of daylight in the evening. The conservation of water was also being encouraged, especially important in view of a persistent drought which affected many people across the island during the mid-1940s.

Administration and Oversight

The Men's Internment Camp fell under the military authority. Camp commandant was Major (later Lt Col) A.R. Moxy of the Royal Inniskilling Fusiliers, until late 1944 when he was replaced by Lt Col R.A.B.P. Watts. The adjutant and quartermaster was Lt (later Capt) H. McCabe. However, the camp authorities quickly encouraged internees to administer their own areas, with little daily interference. This was done through the appointment of German and Italian supervisors, also known as camp leaders or trustees and sometimes designated as *hommes de confiance*, literally men of trust. Instructions were relayed in English from the commandant to these supervisors, who conveyed them to their contingents in German and Italian. Orders and regulations were typed and posted in English, German and Italian.[129] Where there were issues, hut leaders in charge of each barrack building reported to their German or Italian camp supervisor, who took it up with the authorities. These supervisors were "permitted unrestrained correspondence facilities with the military authorities, the government and the protecting powers, though letters for government or protecting power were subject to military censorship".[130] The Swiss vice-consul found the camp authorities receptive to fixing whatever they could and therefore urged camp leaders to take up issues related to camp facilities with the camp authorities, utilizing the channels in place, before bringing them up with external forces including the protecting power.[131]

Reports indicated that in July 1942, Capt. Enno Ulffers and Mr Felix Roerden represented the German seamen and civilian internees in the "A" and "B" compounds respectively, while contractor Ercole F. Selva represented the Italians in the "C" compound.[132] In July 1943, Dr J.L. Robitzsch was listed as trustee for the German groups while Mr Selva continued for the Italians. After the Armistice of September 1943, Selva moved to the Newcastle Hill Station with other Italian co-operators, and Fulvio Casperoni acted as camp leader for the Italians. When dissension in 1944 led him to resign, the other Italians remaining at the Male Internment Camp decided to accept representation by the German camp leader.[133]

With the internal management of the camp mainly undertaken by the internees themselves, the British garrison was responsible for regular inspection and intervention as necessary, for ensuring that the regulations were kept and for guarding the facility. Roll Call was taken at 6.30 a.m. and 6.15 p.m. daily. Garrison duty was taken up by Canadian infantry battalion the Winnipeg Grenadiers in May 1940, relieving the Kings Own Shropshire Light Infantry which had been in camp at the start of the war. Their duties were noted as providing the external guard at the internment camp, a garrison of one company at the Newcastle Hill Station and a mobile reserve.[134] The number of "Other Ranks" detailed for permanent duty at the internment camp was increased from forty to sixty-three in November 1940, when the camp size was being increased in preparation for accepting more than four hundred and fifty male internees from West Africa. The overall unit strength of the garrison was then around six hundred and eighty-five.[135] In October 1941, the Argyll & Sutherland Highlanders of Canada replaced the Winnipeg Grenadiers when that regiment was posted to Hong Kong – where it would be decimated in the fighting for Hong Kong in December. In 1943, the Grenadiers were replaced on garrison duty by the Irish Fusiliers of Canada, followed in 1944 by the Brockville Rifles.[136] While white troops were assigned within the internment camp, local soldiers from the Jamaica Infantry Volunteers – which became the foundation of the Jamaica Battalion – were deployed on external guard duty.

Conditions of Daily Life

The daily life of the camp revolved around sleeping, eating and recreation. Each compound had its own kitchen and cooks and camp reports reflected different approaches to their facilities between the German and Italian groups:

> The Italian supervisor stated that the Italian kitchen was in good condition and had no complaints, and the authorities stated that the equipment in the Italian kitchen was in perfect condition and was well taken care of. They deprecated the rough handling by the Germans, particularly the seamen, which they stated, explained the difference between the kitchens of the two nationalities.[137]

It was generally acknowledged that the food provided for the internees was sufficient and of good quality.[138] Indeed, one report deplored a waste of bread by the German internees.[139] There was some initial resistance to local foods such as sweet potatoes and chochos[140] and some complaints about monotony, especially from the Italians who also expressed a desire for more green vegetables. These, the Swiss vice-consul reported, grew in relatively small quantities in the Jamaican hill country and, with limited transportation, were difficult for even Jamaican residents to access. The internees therefore started their own vegetable garden in October 1942, with around three acres of land made available in the military camp – a plot that had grown to seven acres by 1944. Local interviewees, then children, recalled seeing "little red men" working in vegetable beds in the distance, while out on walks.[141]

Shortages of meat in Jamaica led to arrangements to have the camp provisioned with imported beef by 1943. The Swiss consul noted that families of Kingston and St Andrew had a ration of four pounds of meat a week, no matter how many persons were in the family – if this could be obtained. "Individuals get two pounds each only, if they can get it, which is seldom. Therefore, the internees getting meat twice a day are much better off than the people of the island".[142] To add diversity to the menu, the internees raised rabbits in hutches along the edge of the recreation ground and established a piggery, as well as cultivated significant vegetable gardens – all of them a long-term success. In 1944, the Swiss vice-consul commented that the raising of pigs and rabbits had "provided a welcome addition to the diet although the pig raising is concerned mainly with the making of bacon".[143]

Menus reflected small differences in preparation styles as well as external purchases which the kitchens could and did make. These included seasonings, vegetables, eggs and in the case of "B" Kitchen, pork, outside of what was supplied. The Italian internees also made pasta themselves with flour and eggs, at their own expense. Similarly, during the time when

Jamaican detainees were in the Segregated Compound along with German Jews and other non-Nazi groups, the food there was supplemented through weekly supplies from a grocer named Saultau at Cross Roads in Kingston, paid for privately out of a detainees fund arranged for the Jamaican detainees by Norman Manley, Ansel Hart and others, and shared with the Norwegians, "with whom we were on good terms".[144] Three Norwegians sailors were among the internees from Sierra Leone in West Africa, having been detained when the vessels they were working on docked there.

The German seamen from "A" compound ate in "one large and lofty dining room with adjoining stage which is also used as a concert-hall and theatre".[145] Sixteen German ships' captains had their own dining space and there were two dining rooms for the German civilian internees from "B" compound – spaces also used for music rehearsals. The Italian group, from compound "C", including civilians brought from West Africa and thirty-one seamen of whom two were officers and two wireless operators, had their own dining room with a stage that was used as a theatre, concert hall and recreation room.[146]

A canteen was also in place where camp residents could purchase a wide range of items: from various brands of cigarettes, cigars and tobacco through jam, syrup and honey to tinned meats and fish, seasonings and cooking basics, toiletries, writing essentials and basic items of clothing.[147] Run by an elected committee and a staff of German and Italian internees under strict supervision of the camp authorities, the canteen sold items at the same prices and with the same ration restrictions as were in place in Kingston.[148] A fruit store next to the canteen sold fruit and fresh milk to internees and the Swiss vice-consul noted "that the prices paid for fruit for my own household are even above those paid by the internees in their canteen". He said that these included limes, 4 for 1d; oranges, 4 for 3d; grapefruit, one for 1d; mangoes, five for 6d; bananas, one bunch for 1/-; as well as fresh milk, half-pint for 4d.[149]

Purchases could be made through three systems of financial transaction: British and Jamaican coins up to 1/-, which "completely disappeared from circulation"; token money printed in Jamaica and accepted for amounts up to 1/-; canteen cards which internees would sign when making a large purchase. Persons who had private accounts could draw specified amounts monthly.[150] However there were complaints by some of the internees from West Africa on discrepancies in accounts received and an allegation that the books of the Umuahia Camp Office, where they had been held in Nigeria, were missing.[151] Most of the internees received monthly pocket money from their governments.

Goods were sold with a net profit of 10 per cent, one-quarter of which was held back by the authorities and credited to a General-Purpose Fund used in favour of the internees, including to insure any loss of stock as well as to underwrite the workshop on the recreation ground, football boots for the many internees playing the game and prizes for various competitions.[152] Any profits went into a fund for the benefit of the camp as a whole.

While there were no restrictions on smoking, there were some restrictions on alcohol. In 1942, the commissioned seamen could drink what they wished but others were restricted to beer, which was sometimes scarce. By mid-1943, there was a rum allowance available for the internees generally. At the end of 1944, there was some indication that access to rum might have become a means of transaction, with individuals who did not drink nonetheless purchasing their share and passing it to others.[153]

Internees were in control of personal belongings, except for telescopes and binoculars, cameras, wireless sets and flashlights. Beyond the most basic needs, an important source of items in possession of the individual internees was parcels from family or from organizations like the Red Cross. The German Red Cross frequently sent packages that included tobacco products, sweets, games, books, plays and music as well as toothpaste and other hygiene products. But increasingly, the war on shipping caused transit delays that affected the arrival of parcels and letters at the camp as well as for people across the island. In a report of September 1942, the Swiss vice-consul noted:

> Due to sinking of ships many parcels were lost, damaged or arrived incomplete, but they generally arrive in good condition. Many of the missing parcels may still be in U.S.A. waiting to be shipped. I know that there are thousands of bags of mail and a tremendous amount of goods with the destination of Jamaica accumulated to be shipped whenever a possibility arises.[154]

The Swiss reports reflect the worsening of the mail situation as the war progressed. In September 1942, it was estimated that ordinary mail from Germany was taking one to six months and airmail three weeks to six months, though noting that insufficient postage might be a further factor. From Italy, it was noted that ordinary and transatlantic mail was taking two to three months. The Swiss report detailed the route of two letters sent by airmail, by the postmarks on the envelopes – one via Chiasso, Switzerland, Sofia, Bulgaria and Jerusalem in the Middle East; another via Lisbon and New York. In July 1943, a report noted that mail from Germany was taking one to nine months either by airmail or ordinary mail, while Italian mail was coming through in two months to a year.[155] Not surprisingly, camp reports later in the war reflected continuing delays and a decrease in receipt of packages: "Letters from Germany are being received very irregularly. During March 1944, letters which arrived had been despatched from Germany from August 1943 to January 1944."[156] This continued to be the case as 1944 progressed. Similarly, the Italian internees had received no mail from Italy since August 1943.[157] In December 1944, mail from Germany was still irregular and taking two to three months to arrive.[158] It was also noted that the Swiss were handling an increasing number of Red Cross messages from internees seeking to find family members who may have been evacuated from their homes. Concurrently, they were passing along, to internees, personal radio messages broadcast by families in Germany that were trying to find family members who might have been interned. These were messages picked up by listeners in the United States.

Work and Play

Work prohibited under the Geneva Convention was not required in the camp. Indeed, none of the internees was forced to work, except for keeping their compounds clean and assisting with work in the kitchen, huts and conveniences – from which the captains, hut leaders and men over fifty-five years were exempted. However, opportunities for work were provided within the camp:

> In all Compounds there are many internees employed in jobs like: shoemakers, kitchen, tailor, Camp Supervisor's Office, Librarian, Canteen Staff, Hospital-Dresser, Helper and Cleaning group. The average internee works one week per month.

A few internees volunteered to work in the British military workshops, as carpenters, shoemakers and tailors, working weekdays for 1.5 pence/hour.[159] Internees also took up jobs to build or refurbish buildings within the military and internment camps and worked on the recreation ground within the detention camp. A website hosted by the Jamaica Defence Force (JDF) states that German prisoners of war during World War II built the present Officers Club, replacing a previous structure.[160]

The vegetable gardening scheme, started on land within the military camp in October 1942, became a major source of work and distraction for the internees. While the work was voluntary, those involved earned 1/- per day and received an extra food ration as well as extra clothing and shoes. They also gained a regular opportunity to exit the internment camp and walk across to the military camp where the garden was located. Initially some twenty to twenty-five German and Italian internees worked to break and prepare the land and bring in the first crop. More than ninety-five thousand pounds of produce was grown within the first eight months.[161] By mid-1943, the garden had been divided into plots, each worked by two to fourteen men, and an average of thirty Italians and twenty Germans each day were working from 7.30 a.m. to 11.00 a.m. and then from 1.30 p.m. to 6.00 p.m. Within another year, the now seven-acre farm was run by an internee manager who determined what should be planted in the various plots, overseeing the correct sowing of seed, and maintaining contact with the commandant with regard to the farm and its needs. Seed was purchased and implements supplied by the camp authorities, which recouped the cost once the vegetables were sold. The military camp purchased the crop at current market rates and used most of the produce to supply the internment camp kitchens.[162] The crops included tomatoes, beetroot, carrots, cabbage, turnip, spinach and beans.

Irrigation, once done by hand, progressed to include pipelines and twenty cement tanks each holding three hundred to five hundred gallons of water – a system designed and built by the internees themselves. The 1944 report said that around thirty internees worked regularly on the farm, with more going to work on an occasional basis.[163]

The scheme to raise rabbits had reached about one hundred animals by July 1943, rising to one hundred and fifty and then two hundred rabbits in March 1944 – all fed with leaves and waste produce from the farm. This project was overseen by a German internee who reported to the head of the farm, and meat was sold to the various kitchens, and to individuals in both the internment camp and the adjacent military garrison. The pig-raising scheme, started in 1943 with eight or ten animals purchased by the authorities, also did well – the animals eating kitchen waste cooked in purpose-built stone kilns. Pigs were sold to individuals or groups in the Male Internment Camp but most of the meat was used to cure bacon, an enterprise led by three or four internees with this expertise.[164] By August 1944, arrangements were being made for sausage making to be added, with a special building to be erected in the camp.[165] By April 1945, around 2000 lbs of pork was being butchered weekly.[166] The farm even acquired a small truck which was used for a range of related purposes including moving swill from the kitchens to the pig sties, moving materials and delivering vegetables within the camps.

The link between work and the maintenance of health and morale was acknowledged by various authorities involved with the camp. This was especially the case as the number of years in internment stretched out and as the direction of the war shifted towards an Allied victory. Indeed, the

German camp leader suggested that work in the garden should become a condition for the payment of pocket money – to ensure that internees did a certain amount of work and to promote health, discipline and morale. He told the Swiss vice-consul of his concern that without goals or a requirement to work or to complete an educational programme, many internees had lost all desire to do anything.[167]

The perspective of the men, detained for years, was reflected in a fragment of a diary written in March 1945, around the time the Americans crossed the River Rhine in the push to end the war. The author commented that the war "doesn't look so well". He wrote the details of his day, which included unsolicited work in the "Garrison Garden" pig sty – a one-kilometre walk at 6.45 a.m. after a breakfast of four slices of wheat bread with margarine, cornmeal porridge and coffee and then three hours of work – and commented: "I'm happy that I have my work in the outside in the garden." He also commented that despite being reasonably treated, the internees felt like "trapped animals".[168]

For the interned men, more so than other groups in Jamaica's wartime camps, the recreational facilities within the camp were an important focus – providing a space for shared interest and a site for competition and the expending of physical and mental energy. Laid out on around 4 acres of land, the space included a football field and a 340-metre racetrack, as well as a sandpit for long jump and high jump and a boxing ring and gymnastic facility at one corner. There was also a tennis court and a shed with equipment for boxing and table tennis, as well as a small workshop to repair sports items and where carpenters and others did private work and handicraft.[169] Work on the sports ground was done by the internees, with a significant upgrading in mid-1943.[170] The Italian internees also added a tennis court and three boccia-courts within their compound.

Recreation facilities were open each day from 7.00 a.m to 6.00 p.m, and walking around the field could continue until 10.00 p.m. Reports indicate that hundreds of internees were involved in organized sports and games, including football (soccer), fistball, handball, hockey, gymnastics, acrobatic wrestling, weightlifting, boxing, tennis, table tennis and athletics – with regular tournaments organized for several of the sports. Fistball – a game similar to volleyball but where the ball is hit with the fist rather than the palm – was the most popular sport in the camp, especially for the older men, with thirty teams playing in 1942. Around one hundred and forty men played football (soccer), which had the greatest number of spectators.[171] A year later, in November 1943, the Swiss vice-consul noted that sport occupied a fair

Figure 14D Football team coached by Gerhard Zitzow at the Male Internment Camp gives a rare glimpse into camp life (Photo courtesy of Uwe Zitzow).

proportion of the life of the internees. He said that around one hundred and eighty men played football, with an average of forty-five games each week; the ever popular, fistball engaged some one hundred and ninety internees, with an ongoing competition involving thirty-three teams of six men each; about sixty-five men played hockey each week. Some eighty men were doing four hours of gymnastics training daily.[172] Figure 14D shows one of the teams of footballers within the camp. The rise in numbers playing football between September 1942 and November 1943 is interesting as it coincided with a significant reduction in camp numbers – the married German civilians leaving for a family camp where they re-joined their wives and children, and about one-half of the Italian group signifying their willingness to cooperate with the authorities and moving out to the Newcastle Military Hill Station. Relative as well as actual participant numbers would fall as the years passed and internees were released or repatriated. Nonetheless, a Swiss consul report of April 1945 indicated that about 75 per cent of the camp's 776 men participated in sports.[173]

Musical instruments were available to the internees, and both the German and Italian groups had functioning orchestras as well as theatre groups which performed regularly both within the male camp and for the internees in the women's camp and subsequently for the family camp. Figure 14E shows one of the bands. At one time or another, the Germans

Figure 14E Band from Male Internment Camp, which would also visit and play at Mona Family Camp (Photo courtesy of Uwe Zitzow).

were reported to have a chamber orchestra, a saloon orchestra, a mandolin orchestra and a small orchestra that played during the intermission at various shows organized by the internees. In November 1943, the Swiss consul report referred to a camp orchestra of sixteen members, all amateurs that performed fortnightly and played in intervals at theatre performances. The report said that the internees' Amateur Theatre Movement which had been in existence since August 1940 had given cabaret performances, concerts and stage plays for the male internees and in some instances for internees in the other internment camps in Kingston. The report stated that the thirty-five members – twenty-three amateur actors and twelve technicians – had been able to become self-supporting through a mix of admission fees and contributions.[174]

The internees also had access to libraries of books that had been received from national Red Cross groups, the YMCA and other sources – including educational and professional books as well as works of fiction and sets of music. Books with political content were proscribed.[175] The Swiss report noted that the German group was far better provisioned, with more than two thousand five hundred books out of the total of some four thousand five hundred books in various languages. Only two hundred of these were in Italian.[176] Internees also arranged and offered courses in a wide range of languages as well as professional courses, and regular lectures. By November 1943, small groups were studying English, Spanish, French, Italian, Portuguese, Norwegian, Russian, Japanese, "and various African dialects".[177] Efforts were also in place to establish a programme to educate all 106 young men aged up to 21 years in the camp – only about half of whom were voluntarily making use of educational opportunities.[178]

Weekly church services were provided for both Protestants and Catholics, with several led by ministers among the internees themselves.[179] In 1943, a YMCA visitor recorded "some thirty-four German Protestant and Roman Catholic missionaries interned in the camp". However, he said that since the Protestant missionaries had largely isolated themselves from their compatriots, their influence was less than might be desired.[180]

The cultural life of the camp was impacted by the social, political and ethnic perspectives held by various internees, especially the most vocal. One example related to an offer by the authorities, to arrange regular film shows within the camp. Reports indicated that German internees refused to attend if Jews were also allowed, even though the Jews were segregated from the rest of the camp community.[181] The Italians never made such objections. In the face of the objection, no films were offered during 1942. Based on a subsequent indication that the internees had changed their perspective, efforts were again made to put arrangements in place, though it was noted that the head of the local Cinema Association was Jewish and might have resented the attitude of the German internees.[182] By November 1943, arrangements had finally been completed for the showing of moving pictures twice monthly. Rental was paid from the canteen profits and the audience was charged 3d per man per movie. However, difficulties remained in selecting films which could be generally agreed. In one instance, the German camp leader would not agree to the showing of the film *Rebecca*, because it had a Jewish name "although it is not concerned with the war or nationalities".[183] In August 1944 it was noted that the internees were tired of Western cowboy films, but it was difficult to obtain films that did not deal with the war, especially as most films coming to Jamaica were from Hollywood.[184]

The camp residents' capacity to listen to radio was also negatively affected when some internees objected unless Allied war propaganda was excluded – something difficult to guarantee, especially with programmes emanating from the United States. By July 1943, the internees were asking for music and entertainment programmes even if they included propaganda and the matter was again raised with the authorities – within a context that the authorities would control a large radio unit with loudspeakers throughout the camp. The request was denied "as the only practical programme, that of the local station, is too short and not suitable".[185] However, by March 1944, a loudspeaker system had been installed, fed from a radio controlled by an officer, and a range of programmes were aired especially in the afternoon and evening.[186]

As the war moved towards an end, the camp authorities, through the protecting power, were faced with various externally generated issues affecting the internees and raising anxiety levels. One was a decision by the German government to require that persons receiving pocket money, *reischgelder*, sign a new receipt, indicating that the internee was a true citizen of the Reich and willing to return to Germany when the opportunity arose. This caused some discussion in the camp with the Swiss consul reporting:

> We do not know the exact interpretation the German Government wished to have placed on this clause, but three men and one woman have refused to sign and have not received the last issue of pocket money, because they do not wish to return to Germany.[187]

Visiting the men's camp in August 1944, the Swiss vice-consul also noticed the emergence of "shades of political opinion" which were "not being encouraged by the Camp Authorities as they consider any serious political divisions or fractions [sic] within the camp may have serious repercussions and make it impossible to handle the running of the camp". He said that there was an expectation of some breakdown in discipline, "should internees have continual quarrels, arguments and squabbles with a political basis amongst themselves".[188]

Health

There was universal recognition that the general conditions at the Male Internment Camp were healthy and commodious. The regular reports indicated that internees were tanned from "continuous sunshine and a continuous open-air life in an ideal climate. There is little illness on the whole".[189] In July 1943, with over one thousand internees in camp, about two hundred and fifty of them Italian, records showed that around 2 per cent annually required medical attention, "of which most were minor ailments and slight fever".[190] Most of these cases were treated in the camp's sick bay, where a medical officer Captain S. Ward was assigned in March 1942. The

Swiss consul reported that German doctors interned within the camp had previously seen cases there but that this had to be suspended. The camp authorities said that some of these doctors had "taken advantage of their medical profession by doing all kinds of political underground work and that some of them had a very bad influence on the internees" – allegations that the doctors denied.[191]

Serious cases of illness were referred to the adjacent Camp Military Hospital, where internees were treated in the same wards as the British troops. Indeed, internees were reported to be "impressed with their comradeship" which often included a few words and the offer of cigarettes, and also praised "excellent treatment and kind attention" by the doctors and staff.[192] Several of the internees had arrived in Jamaica with chronic diseases affecting the liver, kidney, digestive system and heart, among other organs, especially the Italian group that was said to include some one hundred and fifty miners from the Gold Coast "who for many years worked under unfavourable conditions and are therefore susceptible to all kinds of diseases. There is also a lot of malaria brought from West Africa".[193]

Up to 1943, internees could also visit a weekly dental clinic at the Military Hospital, where a British military dentist performed extractions, fillings or other work considered necessary for their health. If they required more complex procedures, internees could opt to visit a city dentist, under security scrutiny, if they could afford to do so.[194] Some changes in these arrangements were recorded over the period that the camp was in operation.

Deaths in the camp were mainly related to clear medical conditions with four Italians and six Germans reported to have died in the camp by September 1942 and a further German by July 1943. There was one German suicide, a doctor who killed himself by heroin poisoning – a diagnosis confirmed through a post-mortem examination and coroner's hearing.[195] Between September and December 1944, three Italians and one German died. In 1945, deaths stood at four Germans – including a female German internee – and two Italians. Three more Germans would die in 1947 and be buried at Briggs Park Cemetery.[196] Internee Arnold Van Der Porten wrote in his memoir of watching a funeral procession to Briggs Park, from within the adjacent internment camp.[197]

Despite the general indicators of physical health, there was increasing concern over mental deterioration and, in some cases, out-and-out mental illness – much of it linked to the long period of internment. Conrad Hoffmann Jr of the YMCA's War Prisoners' Aid office, who visited the island's internment camps in March 1942 and September 1943, recognized the pending challenge in a detailed 1943 report:

All the folk interned seem to have settled down to what is to them, permanent internment. A few, as in all camps, have deteriorated, mentally and spiritually, under the combined impact of nothing to do, lack of liberty and lack of privacy. The vast majority, fortunately, are making the most of their leisure time by participation in one or more of the many camp activities than have been organized.[198]

The following year, the Swiss vice-consul's regular reports identified concerns raised by the camp authorities as well as those personally witnessed:

The Commandant stated that he was satisfied with the behaviour and discipline, but he described their mental condition as desperate. He has permitted various changes of barracks among the civilian internees to allow them a change of society and surroundings and he feels this will do something towards easing the strain, especially in the cases where men have been living in the same barracks for some years. To maintain discipline, he does not consider it advisable to separate the merchant seamen. They are, as before, grouped in the various ships' companies. Cases of mental breakdown will inevitably increase and at the present time three or four show signs of complete breakdown. The Commandant stated he was doing everything possible to assist such cases and prevent insanity and possible removal to the mental hospital.[199]

A few months later, the consul noted that long-term confinement behind barbed wire, in an unchanging community, living in a monotonous fashion without access to the outside world, was taking its toll on individuals: "causing ragged nerves and more and more petty squabbling which may or may not have a political basis".[200] Several internees were placed in the local mental hospital: five German seamen were there in March 1944.[201] By the end of April 1945, physical health was counterpoised with mental depression, including acceptance of war news with apparent unconcern: "The lack of desire to work or keep themselves occupied is very noticeable in the younger men."[202] However, the imminent end of the war also seemed to have relieved some of the building mental tension mentioned in previous reports.

There were efforts, at various times during the war, to have internees repatriated, in some instances on medical grounds. Petitions of Repatriation were referred to a Medical Commission; however, many requests were refused on security and logistical grounds. An October 1943 memorandum from the Defence Security Office to the colonial secretary underlined that repatriation could be refused to anyone considered suspicious on security grounds. Specifically, the memo indicated that "some, at any rate, of the members of the Nazi party in the internment camp here intend to make an attempt to have themselves repatriated on medical grounds".[203]

In the end, many of the German and Italian internees spent five to seven years in the camp before being repatriated in 1946 or 1947, as the local government refused to release them ahead of their repatriation, citing security concerns – even after the end of the war.

Some prisoners also sought to take things into their own hands by seeking to escape the camp, beginning very early in the war. In December 1939, a sentry belonging to the local Jamaica Infantry Volunteers, patrolling the camp during the Christmas season, discovered a prisoner working on a narrow tunnel, which already stretched nearly thirty feet from one of the buildings towards the nearest double layer of barbed wire fencing. The prisoner captured was reported to be a sailor from a German ship seized in the Caribbean soon after the outbreak of war. It was estimated that several more prisoners were involved in the escape effort, based on the amount of earth that had been moved out of the tunnel and was awaiting disposal – apparently in a camp garden.[204]

After a long lapse in reports, two escapes were noted in June 1943, with the German prisoners recaptured the next day and sentenced to twenty-eight days solitary confinement before being sent into segregation in the "N" compound.[205] Two more escapes were reported in the first quarter of 1944 – again they were recaptured quickly, within forty-eight hours, and also sentenced to two weeks of solitary confinement, with the same diet as the rest of the camp.[206] Later that year, a group escape plan reportedly "became known before it had reached any serious proportions or a break from the Camp had been effected". The report said that those identified as engaged in the attempt had been "conducting private trading" through an old fence at one end of the recreation ground, as a result of which a new barbed wire fence was being erected.[207] In April 1945, two internees cut through the wire fences and left the camp but were recaptured a few hours later.[208] In September 1946, an internee escaped the internment camp during the night and was recaptured a few days later in Montego Bay, while another escaped from the Barbican Military Farm in St Andrew and was recaptured a couple of days later near Folly, in Portland.[209] In February 1947, virtually on the eve of repatriation, a young internee escaped but was recaptured a day later. In all instances, the white escapees were very visible in the local landscape, with its mainly black and brown population, facilitating their sighting and re-capture.

Interviewee Peter McCauley, a former soldier, said that many of the Germans in the male internment facility were ardent Nazi supporters and that many escape attempts were in keeping with a "Prisoner of War Code". Under this code, he said, the only way in which you could assist your country's war effort was to cause as much trouble as possible, so that soldiers had to be diverted to guarding you instead of fighting.[210]

Changes to the Camp Population

The second half of 1943 saw significant changes to the population within the Male Internment Camp. Fifty-five German civilians and up to three Italians whose wives and children had been separated in the Women's Internment Camp were reunited with them in a new camp. Additionally, some 154 Italian civilians from among those who had been interned in West Africa and sent to Jamaica accepted a new status and were moved to the Newcastle Military Hill Station. In just a few months, the population of the Male Internment Camp moved from 1,043 to 808. One might speculate that those 235 men may also have been a noticeably stable element in the population.

The need to address the status of the Italian internees followed the fall of Mussolini in Italy and the signing of an Armistice with the Allies. Discussions on how to avoid serious incidents in the Male Internment Camp, where Italians were interned alongside a majority German population, were being held from as early as July, especially given that the local authorities considered it impractical to officially set them free in the island:

> Consider urgent they should in that event be moved out of internment camp which also accommodates 750 Nazis. Propose releasing on parole to carry out work on W.D. [War Department] property Newcastle and Port Royal.[211]

The secretary of state for the colonies acknowledged that unlike the United Kingdom,

> the release of Italian civil internees in the colonial dependencies particularly those interned in Africa, in order to assist the war effort, involves a number of questions of some complexity, e.g. the reaction on local labour conditions and the difficulty of employing white persons in labour gangs.

He requested the development of local policy taking account of local conditions.[212] In December 1943, the new Governor of Jamaica Sir John Huggins told the Colonial Office that while a review of the situation of Italian internees was in progress and many were likely to be recommended for release from the internment camp, difficulties were anticipated as there was "no (repeat no) possibility of providing employment in Jamaica".[213]

The Italian internees and prisoners would be offered the option to sign a cooperation agreement printed in English and Italian and sent from England where it was also being utilized. The declaration stated:

> As a result of the Armistice concluded between the United Nations and the Kingdom of Italy and the state of war which now exists between Italy and Germany, I declare that I am willing to work as directed on behalf of the British Commonwealth of Nations and to assist them to the best of my ability in the prosecution of the war.
>
> I undertake not to abuse the confidence and trust placed in me, by the violation of any of the conditions governing any special privileges extended to me, as a result of making this Declaration.
>
> I undertake to obey all orders or regulations issued by the British Military Authorities and I understand that if I do not do so, my privileges may be withdrawn.[214]

Those who agreed to cooperate with the authorities were allowed to move to the Newcastle Military Hill Station, where some 154 were "practically free and only under protective custody".[215] Figure 14F is an image of the Newcastle facility. The seventy-eight Italians who refused to sign remained in the Male Internment Camp. As late as March 1944, the Swiss consul acknowledged the complexities of the situation, rooted in the local colonial conditions:

Figure 14F Image of Newcastle Hill Station from 1940s postcard.

The ones who are not financially able to support themselves could not be absorbed by any industry or work here. The situation is not the same as in other countries where perhaps they have been employed on the land. White farm labour is not used in this country and in addition the unemployment question here is a serious one. The local Authorities do not feel that they should be asked to handle the problem of having a large number of Italians in the community without any means of support or the opportunity of providing their own by work.[216]

The UK government was not willing to accept any of the internees, especially given that these were not considered to offer high-value occupations. Nor was transport available to remove them from Jamaica – leaving the Italian ex-internees and the local authorities in a kind of limbo.[217] Despite efforts to keep them in a kind of semi-internment at Newcastle and public statements that they were not to enter the local employment market, the Italians gradually settled into a new normal in which they were billeted in the Newcastle Military Hill Station under military oversight but had considerable freedom, and efforts were made to find them employment without directly confronting the local labour unions. The Swiss consul reported in August 1944 that:

Seven have already been placed in one of the leading hotels on the north coast. A man and his wife have gone as barman and sewing maid, one as a pastry cook, one as chef and three as masons. They have been given accommodation, food and a salary.[218]

Arrangements were also made for two Italians to go to the Public Works Department as draughtsmen. It was further reported that some £4,000 to £5,000 had been spent by the local government authorities to employ the Italians accommodated at the Newcastle camp, many of whom had been employed in construction in West Africa, on road and reservoir work. By August 1944, this task-based work had included the construction of 1.5 miles of road, a reservoir and various retaining walls at an average earning of around £6 per person per month. A small group under a gardener had also done work laying out and improving gardens in the vicinity of Newcastle, though the governor was unwilling for the Italians to be employed on work that Jamaican labourers could do.[219]

These men were reported to be in excellent health, with complete freedom of movement in the vicinity of the Newcastle facility.[220] They also had access to passes for visits to Kingston – issued ten each day and valid until 11.00 p.m. – the main drawback to which was limited transport, especially returning from Kingston – a distance of some seventeen miles (twenty-seven kilometres). The last public vehicle returned around 5.00 p.m. or 6.00 p.m., after which there were only private taxis. These severe, war-related transportation issues affected the island as a whole: "Not only is petrol severely rationed but it is anticipated that all private cars may have to be taken off the road in view of the tyre situation."[221] In the face of these transport-related constraints, some Italians identified as "responsible men in good standing" were allowed one to three days passes in Kingston, staying at a hotel. However, the Swiss Consul said that the authorities were concerned "as to the possible reaction amongst the local population should the Italians be given unrestricted liberty in the city at night." By late December 1944, some thirty of the Italians from Newcastle were already staying in Gibraltar Camp, which was now a military camp. They were doing construction work for the Royal Engineers, with "complete freedom of movement" and easy access to Kingston.[222] Another six were working with the military "at a summer camp about fifty miles from Kingston".[223] On 27 December, the number of Italians at Newcastle was 113, of whom some 50 were reported to be destitute and being supported out of previous canteen profits.[224]

The Swiss report indicated that consideration was being given to permitting the Italians to be housed in barracks, at Gibraltar Camp, with a certain amount of freedom, and being allowed to bid on various projects presented by the authorities, on a task work basis:

> The suggestion is that they be placed in groups such as carpenters, masons, roadmakers etc. and then each group would undertake any particular job offered them. This would probably be work under the military under whose protection they would remain.[225]

The report also noted a suggestion to put an unused, government-owned tile factory into operation, worked by Italians with local labour, but said that this involved various adverse political issues. This was the Clay & Tile Factory in Cockburn Pen, western Kingston, where several Italians would in fact be employed.

Some of the cooperating Italians expressed their willingness to volunteer to go to the United Kingdom to do any suitable work. Names were taken, though transportation remained a barrier.[226] A group of some twenty-six Italians also submitted a request to be returned to Nigeria, not Italy, when transport was available – seven even expressed willingness to pay their own transportation by air. However, the Government of Nigeria – by then, Sir Arthur Richards, former Governor of Jamaica – only agreed to accept five Italians when circumstances permitted.[227] Reports from mid-1945 would indicate that some of these Italians had already left the island.

In respect of those remaining in the Male Internment Camp, the Swiss vice-consul suggested in December 1944 that their unwillingness to sign the cooperation agreement might have partly related to the formulation of the declaration, which some might have read as putting them in danger of forced service in the British military. He also expressed concern that some of the remaining Italians were being "influenced and almost terrorised" by other camp occupants and that special arrangements were needed to effect their removal. These men were completely without funds since the payment of pocket money from the Italian government came to an end with the Armistice.[228] In a subsequent report, the vice-consul said that some of these Italians had explained their initial refusal as concern about possible repercussions for their families who were still in the north of Italy. By the end of 1944, the state of the war in Italy "presented the situation to them in a different light".[229]

Long-Term Detainees

It took nearly two years after the end of the war to repatriate the last of the male internees from Up Park Camp, as well as the Germans in the Family Camp and those Italians who had been allowed to live outside the camp and who had not been able to arrange visas to other destinations.

Some three hundred German and Italian internees sailed aboard the SS *Bergensfjord* on 26 May 1946 – including one hundred and eighty Italian men.[230] Married couples and women, who could not sail on the troopship because of lack of facilities, would leave six months later along with most of the German civilians, aboard the SS *Esperance* Bay, a passenger ship used for troop transport during the war. A page-one *Gleaner* newspaper report of 23 November 1946 said that 505 German and Italian internees were sailing that day for Europe from Kingston Harbour. The report said that most were merchant seamen captured by British warships from vessels running the Allied Blockade in African and US waters. The group comprised of 465 single Germans, 25 married German men, 35 married German women, twenty-six German children, thirty Italian single men and 4 hospital cases.[231]

A few days later, on 26 November, the *Gleaner* reported that seventy German and Italian "prisoners of war (merchant seamen)" and one hundred and fifty German internees were left at the Male Internment Camp – including twenty priests. It was expected that a vessel scheduled to bring a new garrison, the Second Battalion of the Gloucestershire Regiment in mid-January, would take these detainees away.[232]

A Colonial Office minute on 27 November 1946 discussed the vexed issue of the interned German missionaries from the Cameroons and Nigeria, though it mentioned twenty-nine not twenty persons:

> Earlier arrangements to remove them from Jamaica to the United States broke down because the United States authorities were unwilling to admit internees unless they had previously been unconditionally released and the Governor of Jamaica was not prepared to do this as there were security objections against twenty-six of the twenty-nine . . . When the question of repatriating them to Germany arose in May this year we had to tell the Governor to defer this as the question of the future of German and Italian missionaries was then under discussion with Archbishop Matthew . . . we have now heard that the United States authorities are prepared to admit nineteen out of the twenty-nine to the United States straight away and arrangements are in train to send them there. This leaves a balance of ten who are presumably those to whom there are the strongest security objections, and it is probable I think that it is for this reason that the United States authorities are not prepared to admit them. The Governor now asks for authority to repatriate these ten Germans at the next opportunity which is likely to be a ship leaving Jamaica at about the end of the year. As it has been accepted that they will not be allowed to go back to West Africa and the United States authorities won't admit them, then I think that in the circumstances we must agree.[233]

A newspaper report in January 1947 stated that German internee Dr Robert Lassig, a missionary in Cameroons who was interned in Nigeria before being sent to Jamaica in 1940, left Jamaica for the United States in January 1947 along with his wife and three children.[234] In February 1947, the remaining German and Italian prisoners/internees from the Men's Internment Camp were repatriated aboard the HMT *Carthage*, alongside the departing British garrison – the Eighteenth Battalion of the Suffolk Regiment.[235] A postscript on the experience was a letter to the editor, published in the *Manchester Guardian*, United Kingdom, stating that German war prisoners had been satisfied with their treatment in Jamaica. The letter, from one of the German officers who had spent years in the camp, F. Von Witte, stated:

> Generally speaking, I can say life in an internment camp is no pleasure but considering that a war was on, the authorities did much to lighten the heavy burden of captivity by providing us with good accommodation, good food, practical sanitary conveniences, etc., and by encouraging and assisting the large and helpful actions done by the many organisations which in the most generous way provided us with thousands of articles – and finally by encouraging our own endeavours to keep mentally and physically fit.[236]

Figure 14G Military Detention Barracks at Up Park Camp.

The intertwined references to internees and German war prisoners recalled the shifting nomenclature of the camp which was at one time termed a Male Internment & POW Camp but subsequently – to square away issues related to the prisoner status of the German merchant seamen – was considered simply an internment camp.

Some German internees were allowed to remain in Jamaica for a while longer, while they awaited the outcome of job applications elsewhere and to facilitate the issue of visas already in process. Certainly, the *Gleaner* reported in September 1947 that a group of Germans, Leo Poltjans, George Gigpenbacher, Frank Winkler and Heinz Koentje, had left Jamaica for the United States.[237] While not covered in the newspaper, the family of Gerhard Zitzow, a technician who had worked in the banana industry in British Cameroons, also left in 1947, on a visa for the Dominican Republic.[238]

3.2 Women's Camp, Hanover Street

Women and children classified as enemy aliens were held at an internment camp repurposed in early 1940 from an old Anglican Deaconess Home and school between 91 and 93 Hanover Street in Downtown Kingston. The location lay within the city limits, just one kilometre from the centre of

Kingston but away from the main commercial area, alongside several large, older structures, including the YWCA headquarters which was adjacent to the camp while the YMCA headquarters was down the road at 76 Hanover Street.[239]

The building at 93 Hanover Street was officially opened on 14 November 1890 to house deaconesses, an order established by Anglican Archbishop Enos Nuttall, who also advocated for the education of Black West Indians.[240] Bishop Nuttall urged the head of the order, Sister Madeline to start the Deaconess Home School which opened in 1899 as an experiment in the education of young women, on premises beside the Deaconess Home, at 91 1/2 Hanover Street. Boarders, some of them the daughters of people working in the Panama Canal Zone, lived in the Home and later at a house at the corner of Hanover and Charles Streets.[241] The growing facility became the Deaconess High School in 1925 and changed its name in 1928 to St Hugh's High School for girls. In 1939, the expanded school moved to a new location in Cross Roads, on the edge of the Downtown Core,[242] and in 1940 the Home was closed. The colonial government had acquired the site for a proposed new Legislative Council building which was not a priority in wartime and one building was being used for offices. Hence the property was available when the need arose.

It was the only one of Jamaica's wartime camps whose physical structures had a history, though it was in no way celebrated. Instead, use of Deaconess House reflected a swift and somewhat second-rate approach to confining female enemy aliens. When the men were first interned in September 1939, the news reports indicated that no decision had yet been taken on the internment of German-born women. In May 1940, when a German stewardess who had been allowed to live at the YWCA was jailed for flouting restrictions on her movements, the judge noted that no women's camp was yet operating.[243] This was at the same time when Britain had decided on mass internment of enemy aliens – a short-lived British policy that would have a long life in Jamaica. By mid-June, the Women's Camp was opened in the former Deaconess House and school. And it would continue to be stretched way beyond capacity.

The first residents of the repurposed site, "including the wives and families of thirteen prominent local Germans", arrived in June 1940 with an escort of police cars. They had originally been allowed to remain at large, under curfew conditions, when their husbands were interned. Now, they were being locked up, one newspaper reported, "by reason of Government's relentless drive to suppress possible 'trojan horses' or blustering 'fifth columnists'".[244] Less poetically, another newspaper said that the camp for enemy alien women had been opened with ten, named occupants, enclosed by a big, strong and high barbed wire fence and with an armed guard on constant patrol around it.[245] The women were listed as Kathe Norman, Julia Kahn, Rosa Lackenbach, Dorothy Von der Porten, Hugette Heise, Matilda Kroneker, E. Stamm, N.E. Stammn, Johanna Ana Schone and Karaline Ebersohn. Various newspaper reports on the internees suggest that seven of these locally detained women were naturalized British citizens and three were Jews. The two Mrs Stamm's, the wife and mother-in-law of a male internee, would be released in 1941 but most would remain in detention for at least another year.

Three months after the camp opened, several changes occurred, preparatory to accepting more than one hundred additional women and children from West Africa. The entire property was assigned to the camp. Officials who had been working in one building on the edge of the site were reassigned to another location and those quarters were repurposed for domestics supporting the Matron.[246] The Matron herself was changed, raising questions of racial bias among some local Members of the Legislative Council. Ms Sterling, a Jamaican-born nurse, was replaced by the English-born Ms Middleton, former head nurse at the Kingston Public Hospital. The Matron reported to the director of medical services for the colony who was camp commander and there was a Visiting Committee composed of three Englishwomen.

Six months after the first detentions, in December 1940, the camp population was swollen by seventy-eight German and Italian women and thirty-nine children. They arrived in Jamaica from West Africa where they, along with their husbands and fathers, had been among hundreds interned in Nigeria, British Cameroons, Gold Coast and Sierra Leone. Despite hopes that the families would be interned together, the groups were separated into gender-specific facilities and would remain so for more than two years – though there were arrangements to facilitate letters and visits between residents in the male and female facilities.[247]

These arrivals brought the total residents at the Women's Detention Camp to eighty-nine women and forty-three children – which appears to reflect the arrival of another woman and four children between June and December. There would also be six births at the camp.[248] Indeed, in March 1941, the camp population had already increased by three children.

A report on the facility made in February 1941 by M.M. Mills for the YWCA described

> a fairly large compound with a church in the centre – now emptied and used as the main dining room – with several separate buildings, each with several rooms, but none of them very big: an open space, green at this time of year, the usual

outhouses etc . . . There are guards at the gate and high fences with barbed wire around the property.

Life is always busy, and with so many small babies and small children around, there were endless lines of laundry in every direction. . . . A number of the women have sewing machines, and dressmaking, laundering, and tidying up their own rooms seemed to occupy a good deal of their time.[249]

Some expansion of the camp did take place at the end of 1941, according to correspondence between the colonial governor and the Colonial Office.[250] Consistent reporting on the camp was put in place as part of the Swiss role as protecting powers for interned Germans and Italians, and Mrs Helen Waeckerlin, wife of Swiss consular agent in Jamaica, R.J. Waeckerlin, visited on several occasions. The Swiss reported that by February 1942, some additional land had been made available for recreational purposes and accommodation had increased with six extra bedrooms and a sickroom with its own bath and lavatory.[251] In March, there was a little more room following the release of eleven women and the transfer of eight women and five children refugees to Gibraltar Camp.[252] Ten of the women released would have been original residents, with the other being a Swede married to a German held in the men's camp, whose departure was handled by the Swedish consul with the financial support of relatives in Sweden.[253] It is unclear who the refugees were. By mid-1942, a Red Cross visitor recorded that there were four houses for the internees, one of them just for Jewish residents, another for women without children and single women, while a fifth building housed the administration, and there was a small four-bed hospital. Though still "a bit constrained", the report noted that the camp was located in an agreeable area[254] (see Figure 15: Outline drawing of the Women's Internment Camp).

A report of September 1942 described the layout of the camp as follows:

> There are three big, two storey living facilities, one barrack, one large chapel, that is also serving as dining facility, and various other buildings for kitchen, pantry, office of Mother Superior, dressing room, sick bay, pharmacy and doctor's office, ironing room, and Catholic chapel.[255]

The sleeping quarters had high ceilings, were lofty and were being kept clean. Three dormitory rooms held, respectively: twelve women, seven women and five women/six children. The other women and children were accommodated in thirty-nine rooms – many of them, single rooms. The five Italian women had been allocated single rooms to make up for the fact that they had long had to share one common room. There were thirteen bathrooms with single bathtubs, two shower rooms and nineteen toilets. Hot water was limited but in a tropical country, this was not an issue.

Internment Camps | 171

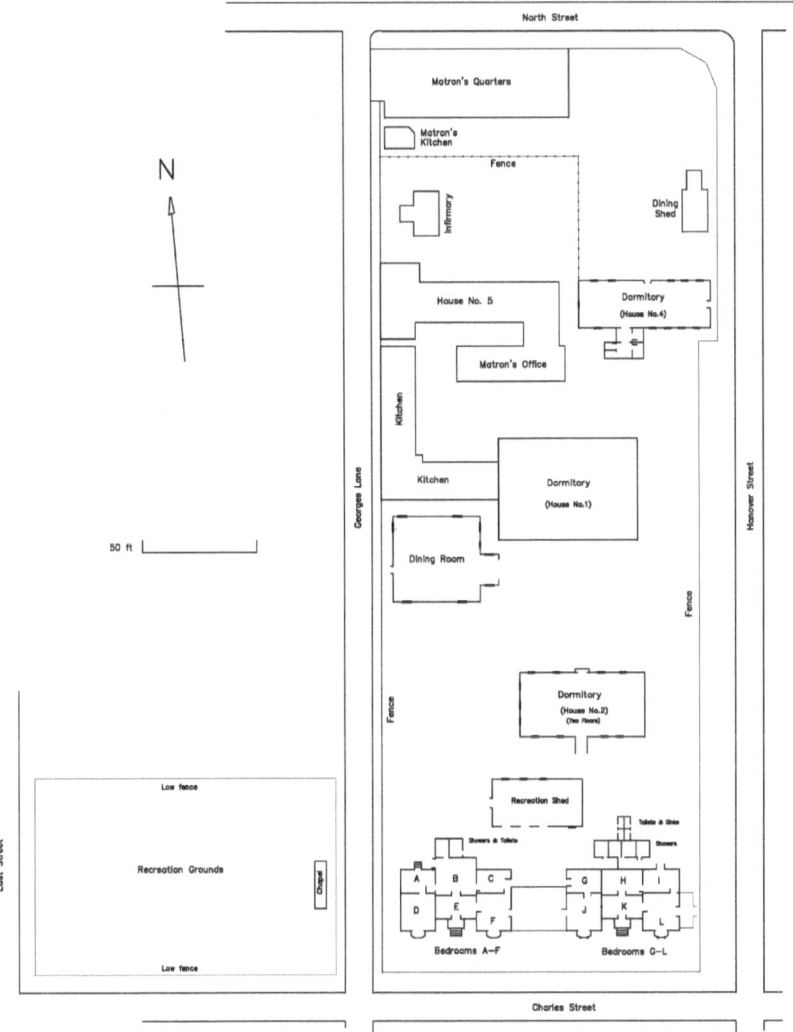

Figure 15 Outline Drawing of Women's Internment Camp (Drawn by Uwe Zitzow based on rough plan in microfilm records of Swiss Federal Archives).

Electric lighting was good and floodlighting outside was still adequate to see, even after lights were turned out in the rooms. The women were allowed to stay outside until 10.30 p.m.

> Between all these building there is free space with a few large trees. A large part of this free space hangs mostly full of freshly washed children's clothes. Wherever it was possible, there now were lawn areas and flower beds. A little in the distance but still within the same fenced area there is a play- and sports-

Figure 15A Zitzow family on visiting day at the Women's Internment Camp (Courtesy of Uwe Zitzow).

area. Unfortunately, this area is without any trees and therefore can only be used during early morning or late evening hours due to the heat in the sun. The whole facility is surrounded by barbed wire and a 2.5-metre-high corrugated metal fence. Even though the corrugated metal fence is really not necessary, but prevents nosy passersby from looking in, at the same time it emphasises the prison-like appearance.[256]

A correspondent indicated that before the corrugated metal sheets were installed, some of the women enjoyed looking outside at the activity on the street.[257]

Once the locally interned women were released, the camp population would remain fairly stable. By September 1942, the Swiss reported that the Hanover Street Camp had a population of eighty-three Reichs-German women with forty-five children, four non-Aryan [Jewish] women and five Italian women.[258] In July, a Red Cross report had differentiated the camp population – then reported as eighty-four women – into eighteen single and sixty-six married, sixty of those having husbands in the men's camp. Of the forty-four children, all but two were German and only one was over ten years. Six were aged six to ten years; fifteen were aged three to six years; twenty-two aged one to three years; and two were under a year.[259] A year later, just before the camp was closed, the report was that the internees numbered seventy-two Reich-German women and forty-five ditto children. The number of Italian women was unspecified but presumably remained as before. There were also two female German Jews and one Italian Jew who were separated from the rest.[260] The capacity of the camp was noted as one hundred and fifty persons and the Swiss representative admitted that the facility was "rather tight" and added that this was felt, more so, because of the constant unavoidable noise due to the presence of forty-five small children, ranging in ages from one to eight years, setting the nerves of all the inmates on edge.[261]

Living Conditions

Like the other internees and evacuees in Jamaica, the women were neither allowed to take employment nor were they required to work, except for keeping their areas tidy and looking after their children. However, they benefitted significantly from the work done by the Matron, her Jamaican assistants and staff of Jamaican servants who did the cooking – using four wood stoves – as well as the heavy housework and the laundry. In 1943, a Swiss report said that personnel within the camp included three cooks, two servers, five laundry women, two cleaning ladies and one "girl for special services". In the office were two in-house civil servants and a Matron's assistant.

The main point of communication between the authorities and the residents – as in the male camp – was a camp leader appointed from among the residents. In case of the women's camp, the camp leader was Mrs Jacobi, a member of the group interned in British Cameroon. Mrs Jacobi was recorded as conveying a request that led, in 1941, to the guards' patrols being shifted from inside the camp to the outside of the corrugated metal fence – with the exception of one sentry at the gate.[262] Security at the women's camp was always in the hands of the local forces, with local, coloured police officers generally deployed there as guards.[263] These guards were also assigned to accompany women who were given special permission to leave the camp, for reasons such as a medical or dental appointment or to make needed purchases.[264] The imperial authorities dismissed the idea of using white, active service personnel to guard female internees.[265]

There were some efforts to allow the interned women recreational opportunities, especially given the limited space and facilities within the camp, and the hot and crowded city location of the camp itself. However, this generated some publicly expressed opposition. In 1941, the *Gleaner* newspaper reported on an effort to reserve a weekly time slot during which the popular Rockfort Mineral Bath, east of Kingston, could be secured for use by the female internees and their children. The page-one story, headlined: "Can This Be True? Reported Move to Reserve Mineral Bath for Exclusive Use of German Internees", reported that the women would have exclusive use of the popular facility for two hours on a Wednesday morning. If the intent of the headline was to generate negative feedback, it succeeded, as the newspaper subsequently reported that the privilege had been disallowed.[266] Similarly, in early 1942, *Public Opinion* published adverse comments related to the extension of privileges to the internees, suggesting that the claims of non-Jamaican internees were more readily met than those of Jamaicans: "The humanitarian instincts of our masters fail entirely when the matter involved is the welfare of Jamaicans."[267]

There were also efforts to facilitate the women getting an occasional opportunity to walk outside the cramped quarters of the camp. An initiative to take the internees and their children on a visit to the Hope Botanical Gardens near Papine, outside the city, was derailed after many of the women scattered in all directions, causing some alarm to their guard, and some complaints from other persons using the gardens. Mrs Waeckerlin, representing the Swiss vice-consul, reported that this had led to a temporary restriction of such outings, though trips to the beach as well as the gardens continued to be arranged for the interned children.[268]

Within the camp, schooling was organized, with some two dozen small children in a kindergarten group, held in a thatched-roof shed in the play area, while six children at primary levels had classes in a room at the adjacent YWCA. The classes were taught in German by one of the internees. The adults had access to a keep-fit class, but there were few opportunities for sports. There were also language classes, especially in English, though it was reported that most persons already had a good understanding of the language.

Amenities within the camp included an occasional "canteen" where residents could purchase small accessories. In May 1941, the Swiss reported:

> Fruits can be bought from a vendor who comes regularly with a handcart. Issa's Department Store sends a salesman with samples of dress material, woollens, shoes etc, who takes orders. All other items that may be required are bought for the internees in town.[269]

Resources were limited. Only four women had access to their own money. Most depended solely on a regular allowance distributed to internees from the German government. Parcels through the Red Cross were a welcome distraction, and it was reported that the internees often shared what they received. Particularly welcome were visits from or to the male internees, when transport and security permitted. A February 1941 YWCA Report indicated that visits were frequent in the early months, with buses constantly outside the camp, as various groups of men took their turns to visit their families. A rota worked out to about one visit, each fortnight.[270] Figure 15A shows a family at the Women's Internment Camp during a visit.

In February 1942, two weddings cemented more links between the camps. For each ceremony, held at the women's camp on 14 February and 28 February respectively, the groom and two best men were conveyed from the men's camp along with a priest. After a civil ceremony in the Matron's office:

> the wedding party with flower adorned children up front followed by the adults moved to the nicely decorated Chapel. Each time Pastor Ittmann conducted a festive wedding with piano music, solo and group songs. Following the ceremony, closest friends of bride and groom still sat together for another hour, but then the men had to return to their camp. Preparations for these wedding celebrations occupied all women and children for many days and were a big happening. [271]

However, as the war progressed and especially when gasolene was rationed, visits became rarer. Early in 1943, the Swiss reported that they had arranged with the authorities:

> that the single ladies in the camp could accompany the married ones when they visited the Male Camp, so that they could see their men friends. We further arranged for male internees to be allowed to send flowers to their wives.[272]

As with the men's camp, church services were consistently offered. As Swiss reports reflected, a German Mission Priest from the men's camp visited monthly to conduct a German service for the Lutherans, while services were also occasionally offered by an English priest. For Catholics, a service was held every Sunday and every Wednesday by an American Jesuit, with a German priest saying mass monthly.

Food and health care were assured, though the women played no part in the cooking and serving. Reports on the camp indicated that the women and children were well provided for. The 1942 Swiss report stated that ration levels were equivalent to that used in public hospitals. This had been the case from March 1941 and rations per person per day were: "Meat 6oz or fresh fish 8oz; green veg 4oz; butter 1oz; lard 0.5oz; cow's milk 0.5 pint; coffee, tea or cocoa 3 drams; sugar 3oz; 0.25 of an egg; potato 4oz; rice 3oz; bread 1lb;

fruit ½; 1lb ice".²⁷³ Fruit provided for the camp per month was listed, in May 1941, as: 1,800 bananas, 600 tangerines, 1,000 oranges. While adequate, the women consistently sought to purchase additional butter, cheese and fruits, using whatever pocket money they had available. There were initially some complaints over local foods such as sweet potatoes, over the thin, light local bread which was of a different texture from bread to which the internees were accustomed and over the small ration of butter.²⁷⁴

Complaints about shortages did emerge in mid-1943, with the Swiss reporting that during June and July, "food was in very short supply and people did not get enough to eat".²⁷⁵ This was blamed on the fact that the camp was not managed by the military, as was the Male Internment Camp, and that hence it was more difficult to ensure consistent supplies: "For instance the men's camp receives meat every day, while the women's camp only receives thirty pounds per week, including bones."²⁷⁶ Availability of some popular items – specifically butter, cheese, tea and bacon – was reported to be affected by restrictions on food availability and distribution on the island.²⁷⁷ The food situation for the women and children did improve after complaints were made to the Matron and commandant. By this stage, also, a long-deferred decision had been taken to open a new Family Camp for married internees as well as single women, under military control. It was anticipated that food supplies at the new camp would be an improvement.²⁷⁸

The health of the residents was overseen by a local physician, and it was reported that there were German doctors and nurses among the residents.²⁷⁹ For serious illnesses and for the six obstetric deliveries throughout the life of the camp, the women were taken to the Kingston Public Hospital and Victoria Jubilee Hospital respectively – Mrs Waeckerlin reporting that "the same ward reserved for refugees [sic] from Gibraltar is open to them".²⁸⁰ Typical physical illnesses affecting residents included dengue fever, influenza, eczema and boils. Fifteen women who had come from Cameroon all suffered from an illness called filaria, contracted there, with symptoms being itching and sleeplessness.²⁸¹ In 1943, the health of the internees was assessed as good, overall, but it was observed that many suffered from nervousness and depression. Aside from the care of individual residents, the Kingston & St Andrew Corporation did a monthly inspection of the camp premises "to ensure necessary precautions to safeguard health and hygiene".²⁸²

Dental health was also taken care of, two groups per week walking some ten minutes to the Kingston Public Hospital, accompanied by a guard, to see the official dentist, Dr H. Lopez. The Swiss reported that "the teeth of almost all the women are in a poor condition, due to years of neglect in Africa" and that long treatments were necessary, "and therefore it takes a long time until everybody is taken care of".[283] While necessary treatments were free, internees were also allowed to visit private dentists for elective work, though most found these treatments too expensive.

Challenges

Complaints about conditions within the Women's Camp surfaced at various points during its existence. A male, German internee whose sister-in-law was at Hanover Street wrote that the women described conditions in the camp as inhumane and that his sister-in-law "suffered both mentally from the degrading situation and physically from the constant heat".[284]

With the introduction of some seventy-two more German women, some of them with strong political sentiments supportive of the German Reich, there was consistent tension between various sub-groups in the small, contained camp. The resultant discomfort especially affected the small group of Jewish internees forced to share space with those who had Nazi sympathies – mirroring a problem in the men's camp. M.M. Mills of the YWCA, who visited the camp in February 1941 and spoke with various women, also noted the frustration of some who had lost possessions, the limited space for the large numbers and the concern that it would be very hot in warm weather. Nonetheless she:

> found the small Italian group the most happy and contented. There seemed to me to be such different points of view among the German groups as to make for some conflict, although Miss Middleton (the English Matron) has done her best to divide them in the most helpful way.[285]

February also heard a parliamentary question in the House of Commons, London, highlighting the "grave injustice of interning Nazis and anti-Nazis together", in internment camps in Jamaica.[286] By August, Member of Parliament Eleanor Rathbone of the Parliamentary Committee on Refugees was writing to the Colonial Office raising complaints from a German Jew, married to an Italian interned in the Male Internment Camp, and relayed through her sister:

> Unfortunately, in this camp, by far the majority of the women are Nazis, and life is being made extremely difficult for the Jewish internees . . . The camp itself seems to consist of a block of houses surrounded by barbed wire, and so the hostile parties, Nazis and Anti-Nazis, are thrown on each other in a very small space. Everybody who knows the Nazis will understand what that means.

It means that, having escaped from their torturers in Germany, the poor refugees are handed over to them again in the internment camp. They cannot even go for walks, the camp being so small, and so in order to avoid the Nazis, they hardly ever leave their rooms.

The correspondent appealed for separation of the groups and for space for exercise.[287] Responding on 31 October 1941, nearly three months later, Governor Sir Arthur Richards indicated that he had "now authorised the construction of the additions at the Women's Internment Camp which are required to separate the Nazis from the non-Nazis and have given instructions for the work to be put in hand at once".[288] This small extension, which allowed the Jewish women to room together, apart from Aryan internees, eased that situation somewhat. Efforts were also made to allow single women and the Italian women some separation – which was considered especially important in view of the large number of young children on the camp.

Complaints regarding conditions in the camp were also reflected in petitions for repatriation between 1941 and 1943. The first of these was made by a group of fourteen single women, including doctors, nurses and missionaries, expressing their anxiety to be exchanged and returned to Germany on a neutral vessel. They said they had remained at their posts in West Africa at the start of the war, in part based on assurances that they would not be interned.[289] Forwarding the letter to the Colonial Office, Governor Sir Arthur Richards said the local government had no objection to an exchange. However, Foreign Secretary Eden, while acknowledging that the women were eligible for repatriation if a route was available, did not consider it advisable to allow them to leave. A letter from the Foreign Office stated:

> The German government have shown no disposition to attempt to facilitate in any way the return of the large number of British women and children, natives of the United Kingdom, whom they hold. The number of German women in the UK who would be willing to return to Germany is believed to be inconsiderable and it would weaken efforts to attempt to obtain the release of British women held by the German authorities if German women held in the British colonies were despite the attitude of the German government, repatriated. Mr Eden therefore trusts that the German women in Jamaica will for the present be kept there.[290]

In June 1943, twenty-three single and married German women with children submitted a request for speedy repatriation. They wrote that there were cases of illness among some of the women and charged that some of the children are permanently ailing and are the cause of great anxiety to their mothers. Presumable [sic] they would thrive better in a cooler climate. . . .During three years of life in thickly crowded internment camps in a tropical climate, we were all subjected to great psychical [sic] stress, some of us had a nervous breakdown. Some of the mothers have small children at home under the care of strangers whom they would like to join.[291]

In August, one of the same internees again wrote to the colonial secretary, petitioning the repatriation of her son, Horst Reibnegger, born in British Cameroon in February 1940, on grounds of ongoing ill-health. None of these petitions would succeed, but by the time of the second petition, the local authorities had finally acquiesced to the establishment of a new camp where married families in the male and female camps could be reunited. It was determined that overcrowding at the women's camp would thereby be resolved.[292] The broad sentiment was expressed by Commandant of the Male Internment Camp, Lt Col A.R. Moxy in 1944. He disagreed with "overburdening United Kingdom with internees who are well housed, well fed and cared for, here". He noted that most of them had spent a good part of their life in tropical climates and that most were in good health; he also suggested that transfer of the particular internees who had made petitions would encourage mass requests from all interned married families.[293]

The demise of the Female Internment Camp in the third quarter of 1943, and its rebirth as the Married Family Camp, had a long gestation and was eventually forced upon the authorities – in London and locally. The issue had been brought before local colonial officials as early as January 1941, when a letter from some of the internees at the male camp asked to be reunited with their wives and families. The letter, signed by Dr Pauli Magnus, Dr R. Lassig, P. Woehr and fifty-one others, said that authorities in Nigeria had assured them that the families would be interned together in Jamaica.[294] The Home Office logged correspondence on the possibility of a family camp in Jamaica in May 1941 and subsequent correspondence involving the Colonial Office explored the extension, throughout the empire, of a practice adopted in Britain where the Home Office had primary responsibility for civilian internees.[295] Neither the governor nor the officer commanding troops was in favour of creating a separate internment camp for married persons, nor did they favour the Home Office practice of segregating a small area of the main internment camp. The practice of allowing visits between the separated camps at "reasonable intervals" was therefore continued. However, in the face of complaints in Britain about Jewish women having to share space with women of Nazi views, as well as complaints about general overcrowding and discomfort, the colonial government did make some efforts to improve the physical conditions at the women's camp, as Swiss correspondence noted in February 1942.[296]

The Colonial Office recognized that the situation in Jamaica could cause difficulties. It said that "handing over of male civilian internees to the military and the segregation of the sexes in separate camps" had doubtless proved a cheaper alternative to establishing a family camp:

> But it does not follow the policy adopted by this country, by most other colonies and partially even by Germany herself. It also entails the danger of anomalies which may give a handle for complaint and reprisal.[297]

Time would prove them correct. The tipping point may have been the temporary suspension of visits to the women's camp, by husbands at the male camp from mid-1942, due to a local petrol shortage. Concerns were expressed by the Swiss consular representative, who suggested that the internees be allowed to walk the manageable distance from camp to camp under guard. This was refused, in part, as the officials said, "for internees' own sake to avoid molesting and likely attacks".[298] In July 1942, after a visit to the men's camp, the Swiss consul again raised the matter of creating married quarters "with highest authorities but was refused".[299] Though it does appear, from later correspondence, that the authorities may have begun considering possible options for a family camp from that point. From August, the military authorities did put arrangements in place to expedite mail between the camps, removing the requirement that mail be censored by the police as well as the chief censor and thereby reducing the minimum transit time to four days. In September 1942, the Swiss vice-consul noted that animal-drawn vehicles were being arranged so that visits could re-start after being halted until vehicles were adjusted to accept animal power.[300]

However, by this time, Germany appears to have decided to take action of its own. Reports began to emerge of worsening conditions affecting British women held at the Liebenau Camp in southern Germany and at Vittel Camp in north-eastern France.[301] In a report of 6 October 1942, the British Legation in Berne told authorities that there was no ground for complaint in Jamaica and asked for an end to reprisals against British women at Liebenau.

Later correspondence suggested that one spark may have been an unspecified "mendacious description of the camp" by Dr Conrad Hoffmann Jr of the YMCA Prisoners Aid office, quoting Women's Camp Leader Mrs Jacobi. Hoffmann Jr had visited Jamaica in March 1942, when he wrote a report on the Men's Internment Camp and visited the Women's Camp.

Correspondence involving the British Embassy in Washington DC and the POW Department of the Foreign Office proposed trying to "damp Dr Hoffmann Jr. down". It also quoted a letter from Harry Edwards, the secretary of the YMCA in Jamaica suggesting that Mrs Jacobi had "exaggerated" but that two cases of nervous breakdowns, removed from the Women's Camp to St Joseph's Sanatorium, might have served to drive reconsideration of "the whole question of a family camp".[302]

In January 1943, a telegram from the colonial authorities to the Colonial Office said that they were considering two proposals for a new family camp. One involved the building of a new camp at Mona using material from unoccupied Gibraltar Camp buildings, at a cost of some £36,000, while the other would convert the northern end of the lower level of Gibraltar Camp, at an estimated cost of £5,000. It said that the Gibraltar Camp oversight committee was opposed to the second, and far cheaper, option, "feeling that the psychological effect on Gibraltar of the establishment of an internment camp within the precincts of the camp, would be serious".[303]

The situation had continued to deteriorate for the British women in the targeted camps in Germany. A telegram to the Foreign Office, dated 19 February, reported on a January visit to "Ilag Liebenau" by representatives of the Swiss Legation in Berlin:

> Camp containing 603 internees is greatly overcrowded, number of beds insufficient and some latest arrivals sleep on straw mattresses on floor. Seventy women still sleeping in theatre room and accompanying German official stated they were to remain there owing to conditions under which German women were interned at camps in British Empire.
>
> Swiss representatives state that since their last visit conditions have considerably deteriorated, chiefly owing to overcrowding and lack of heating.[304]

A further telegram the following day indicated that although German authorities would not admit that the deterioration of conditions in Liebenau was "an actual reprisal measure", they had "allowed it to be understood that conditions in Liebenau have been adjusted to those of German internees camp in Jamaica by a process of equalisation".[305] It was conveyed that the contrast between Liebenau and Vittel on the one hand and the Female Internment Camp, Hanover Street, Kingston on the other was too marked to be any longer tolerated by Germany.[306] And it was clear that no improvement at Liebenau could be expected until things improved for the German women in Jamaica – about whom it appeared that the German authorities had previously complained. The Foreign Office expressed concern that not only would conditions at Liebenau not improve but that the provision of family camp facilities at Liebenau and Vittel would be cancelled as a result of bad conditions of internment in Jamaica. It said that the International Red Cross had also approached the Foreign Office urging "the reuniting of such interned families as are still separated" and noting that wives in Jamaica were now "almost the only women in colonial territory who are interned separately from their interned husbands".[307]

In April 1943, Governor Richards drew Colonial Office attention to enhanced social conditions for the married internees, especially those at the women's camp. He sent the secretary of state for the colonies an excerpt of the Swiss consul's February 1943 report, which acknowledged the resumption and enhancement of excursions for the women and children, which had been suspended in the last quarter of 1942:[308]

> Wives visit the men's camp in small groups monthly and husbands vice versa. In addition, weekly trips are made to the sea, and every woman can take part in a weekly excursion. These excursions take place in the mornings from 7:30 to 11:30 in groups of seventeen persons. The wagon is first driven through the city and its surroundings. There are often short walks in addition. Every morning from 6.00 to 8.00 there are two tennis courts of the Y.W.C.A. at their disposal, which are much appreciated and used. The children are allowed to go on the excursions with their mothers once or twice per week in the afternoons. In addition to this there are school excursions twice a month. All excursions, as well as the use of the tennis courts, are now free to all internees. Since these excursions have become regular, the atmosphere of the camp has considerably improved.

On 21 April 1943, the secretary of state for the colonies telegraphed Governor Richards:

> In view of the high-cost construction new camp and desirability of avoiding delay which might have prejudicial effect on treatment of British internees in Liebenau Camp I approve adoption of proposal 2 in your telegram.[309]

In May 1943, a telegram to the War Office from the Commander of the North Caribbean Area regarding the new internment camp for married families said it was proposed that the camp be under military control with European civilian internal staff. He asked approval for local forces to carry out external guard duties only, stating that the "Governor has no (repeat no) objection".[310] By then, Governor Arthur Richards was on the point of reassignment.

There was an interesting footnote to the closure of the Women's Camp and the establishment of a Family Camp under military control. The Jamaica Security Report of 31 May 1943 welcomed the change on the basis that enforcing adequate security measures "through the female Jamaican staff of the Women's Internment Camp has been almost impossible".[311] Nine female and two male employees of the Women's Camp were laid off when the camp closed, with just three female and one male orderly later re-employed at the new Mona Family Camp.[312] A different perspective on the Jamaican orderlies was offered by interviewee Uwe Zitzow who was a child during World War II and whose family was separated for nearly three years by the camp policy:

> During the time when husbands and wives were separated, native Jamaicans guarded the camps. While correspondence was officially forbidden, these guards would sneak notes from the men and women between camps. They were much endeared not only for doing so, but also for their wonderful, good nature.[313]

3.3 Mona Family Camp/Married Families Camp

The new Mona Family Camp was a far cry from the Women's Camp on Hanover Street in Downtown Kingston – immediately praised for "a cool, healthy climate in most beautiful surroundings". Located on a plateau in the foothills of the Blue Mountains, about nine miles from the city, it was also spacious, set in about ten acres of open country, with "ample space for moving around and walking".[314] It was still a military camp: rectangular in form and surrounded by two rows of barbed wire fencing, about four or five metres high, with a raised sentry post and armed guard at each corner, and closed to visitors without permission from the camp commander. Yet the Swiss consul captured something of a nuanced approach to this camp when he described it as:

> excellent . . . ably administered with tact and discipline. It has and it has been arranged and furnished with an eye to attractiveness as well as usefulness.[315]

The barracks structures and communal facilities would not have been dissimilar to infrastructure of the Male Internment Camp. In relation to regulations, it appears logical that there would be adjustments to take account of the internal dynamics and demands of families, compared with dealing with individuals. But one might argue that there was a difference in approach and tone, which may have sought to somewhat make amends for the debacle over inadequate conditions at the Women's Camp – which precipitated an international incident and forced the overdue creation of the facility. At the family camp, this was reflected in a more relaxed attitude to food service and more so, in an empathetic approach to division and use of the barracks accommodation, even compared to arrangements in the civilian evacuee and refugee camp at the other end of the same property.

The administration was also something of a hybrid – a blend of military on the outside, with an internal staff composed of European civilians. Miss Middleton, Matron at the Hanover Street Camp, was transferred to Mona with a staff of four. The military operation fell to Assistant Commandant J. Edwards, with the adjutant and quartermaster being Lt W.V.G.S. Ewen – creating a subsidiary operation under the overall control of the Male Internment Camp, located about four miles away by road.[316]

The issue of the camp guard had taken some time to resolve. Following a May 1943 proposal that the camp would be under military control with European civilian internal staff and external guard duties only to be carried out by local forces, the discussion moved to London. The next two months saw a flurry of correspondence rooted not so much in legal requirements as in cultural and diplomatic considerations – with an eye also to the way in which decisions would be perceived in Jamaica. The Colonial Office underlined that: "The use of non-European troops for the purpose of guarding internees does NOT constitute a breach of any international conventions."[317] However, a 15 July 1943 note to the Colonial Office, from the Prisoner of War Department in the Foreign Office, opined that it would be "most unfortunate" if coloured troops were used to guard the new family camp given Germany's attitude to the conditions of Germans interned in Jamaica. It added that Germans in Jamaica should not be guarded by coloured troops, whatever was the case in the other West Indian islands.[318] In parallel, on 16 July, the War Office advised the Colonial Office that the outside guards at Jamaica's internment camps were from the Canadian battalion while the inside staff was two-thirds white and one-third coloured.[319] It stated: "Can find white personnel for new camp. Agree with GOC [General Officer Commanding] proposal to use coloured troops outside".[320] And on 31 July, a telegram to the secretary of state for the colonies from the officer administering the government, Jamaica noted: "Local force, coloured troops will be used for external guard duties only and will be stationed outside the Camp perimeter. All internal duties will be performed by specially enlisted European personnel."[321]

As in the male and female internment camps, communication between the authorities and the camp population was carried out through a Camp Leader agreed by the internees. At Mona he was German medical doctor Max Diederich, a Roman Catholic who had been interned in Nigeria, West Africa.

Internment Camps | 185

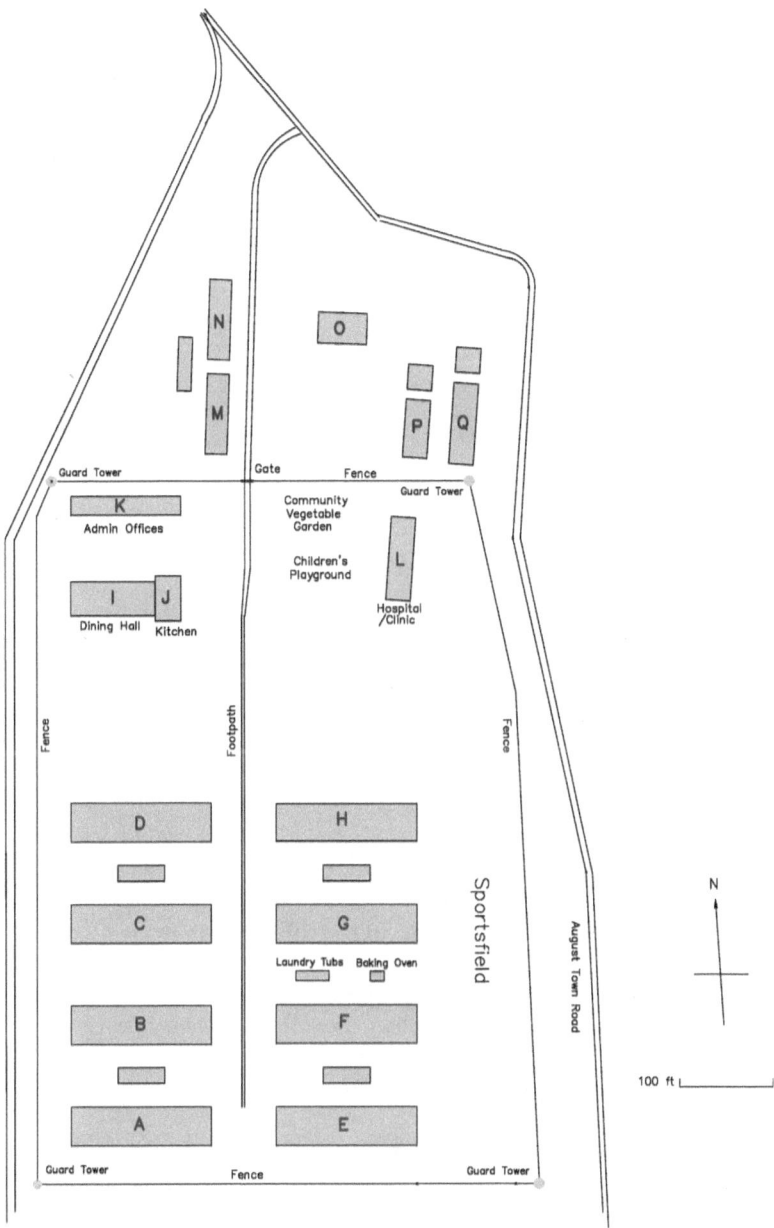

Figure 16 Plan of Mona Family Camp (Plan created by Uwe Zitzow from his family archive as well as a hand-drawn layout – Figure 16B – by another internee, Frau Berger).

> MONA FAMILY CAMP INDEX:
>
> A-G: Wooden barracks buildings, most of them divided for living quarters, each pair attached to a sanitation block. Barrack D, which accommodated single women and widows, was surrounded by a fence
>
> H: Barrack used for sewing, school and church
>
> I: Dining Hall and recreation facility with stage at one end
>
> J: Kitchen
>
> K: Military Administrative Offices
>
> L: Sick Bay
>
> M-N: Military Personnel
>
> O: Commandant
>
> P-Q: Military Barracks – believed unoccupied

Figure 16A Index to Plan of Mona Family Camp.

The camp was first populated in August 1943 by the male internees who would be moving there and who were involved in making initial preparations to welcome the women and children. One of the choices that they made to speed the transition was acceptance of Primus pressure gas lamps in the accommodation barracks as electric wiring was then in short supply.[322] Hence, only the hospital and dining room had electric lights. A September 1943 report from Conrad Hoffmann Jr, of the YMCA's War Prisoners Aid fund, captured the excitement prevailing among the dozens of men, women and children who would be affected:

> Families separated some three years, and more are to be reunited. The men as the women are full of keen anticipation, though the women seem anxious for they wonder how the fathers will take to the children, their noise and romping, after three years of separation.[323]

When the Swiss vice-consul first visited in mid-October, he found the entire camp population working to arrange and finish their personal spaces as well as the outside areas and to manage the available facilities:

> The women have made the living quarters very attractive with curtains, covers and personal possessions etc. Many of the men are already engaged in gardening work, and in many cases, flower gardens in front and at the back of living quarters have been started. Food is cooked by native cooks, but serving, clearing of tables and washing-up is done by the male internees as well as the everyday

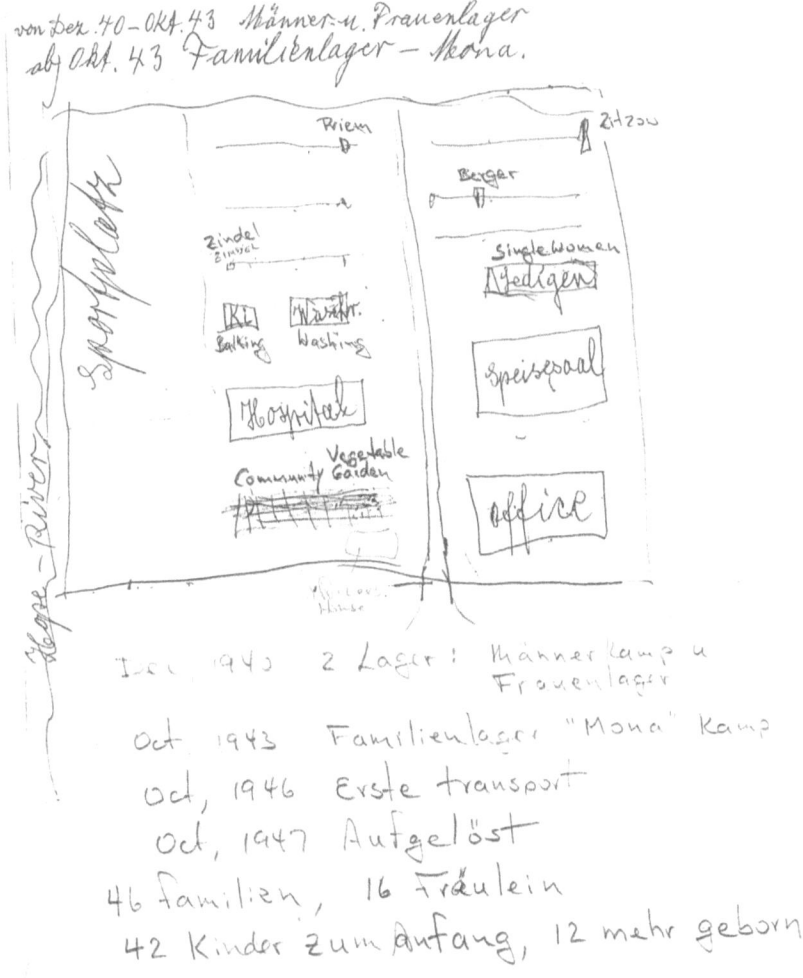

Figure 16B Frau Berger layout of the Mona Family Camp (Courtesy Uwe Zitzow).

    maintenance of the camp. Everyone works in turn, and one or two suffering from rheumatism have been given inside office work by the authorities. Three internees run the canteen, and such work as the making of paths between the barracks will be done by all.

    No wages are paid for voluntary work in the camp at the present time.
    There are no working Commandos.
    There is no prohibited or unhealthy work.[324]

The initial population of the camp was recorded as 171, when the Swiss vice-consul visited on 18 October 1943, though the numbers given did not quite add up. The breakdown was fifty-three German married couples with forty-three German children and seventeen other German women, whether single or widowed. There were also an Italian couple and an Italian widow.[325] This would total 169 persons, not 171. However, it appears that there was some fluidity in the early days of the camp. When the Catholic priest from Gibraltar Camp visited on 9 October, he said that there were three Italian families, all couples.[326] By early 1944, at least one Italian couple had decided to become co-operators and were moved over to Gibraltar Camp, joining couples already there. The Swiss would also later report that an initial total of eighty-seven women moved to the family camp but that fourteen were released leaving seventy-three women, seventy-one of them German and two Italian.[327] The make-up of the fourteen was not explained.

The camp soon had its own tally of babies. A mid-1944 YWCA Report on Women Internees in Jamaica, which praised arrangements at the camp, noted that four babies had already been born in July and understood that fifteen more were expected by Christmas.[328] In December 1944, the Swiss vice-consul reported eight, named, newborns.[329] One death was reported among the female internees: Sister Frieda Maier committed suicide by drinking Lysol on 8 June 1944, after a long history of illness and talk of suicide. She had been in and out of facilities but had been discharged to the Family Camp. After taking the poison, she asked to be transferred to mental hospital, where she stayed calm until she died the following day. She was buried at Briggs Park Military Cemetery, Up Park Camp.[330]

In February 1945, as the war neared its end, the population of the Mona Family Camp or Married Families Camp was given as 186 German and Italian civilian internees, men, women and children, including fifty-six men, and one stewardess in the category: Merchant Seamen (P/W). The report stated: "The married families give no trouble at all."[331]

Layout and Conditions

The new camp consisted of eight wooden barracks with adjacent sanitation blocks, one of which was used for recreation, including library, church, sewing room and school. There was also a large dining hall with stage, canteen and kitchen attached and an administration building where a young internee recalled that "some eight or more men and women dressed in military clothes pounded typewriters and filed papers".[332] A small infirmary was located away from the other buildings and a laundering facility consisting of washtubs and ironing boards was sheltered by a galvanized iron roof. Seven of the barracks were subdivided for accommodation. Each of these structures was one hundred and fifty feet long and twenty-five feet wide, with an additional seven-foot wide, covered verandah running the length of each side. See Figures 16 and 16A for a plan of the camp, created from varied sources including 16 B, a contemporaneous hand-drawn sketch.

There may have been a special effort to make the wooden barracks buildings work optimally for the interned families. Correspondent Uwe Zitzow recalled that each family's "apartment" ran the width of the barracks building, opening on to a private covered verandah on either side. This meant that the walls between the individual apartments ran the entire width of the building including the verandahs, so that each apartment included its own indoor and covered outdoor space. This description largely agreed with that provided in a Swiss consul report of a visit in October 1943. Zitzow said that each room was therefore twenty-five feet wide and approximately ten feet deep. A family with two children, like his family, had two such rooms. There was an internal partition between the two rooms, thereby separating the living area from the bedroom area, with blankets further subdividing one room to create separate sleeping spaces for the parents and children.

Zitzow said that in the barracks building, which housed the seventeen single German women and widows, the entire structure was divided longitudinally, and then horizontal partitions created single rooms, each with access to a verandah. The Swiss consul's report suggested that the longitudinal wall was more of a partition. This barrack was set within a fenced area whose gate was closed at 9.30 each night. During the day the women participated freely in camp life.

The Swiss described the design of the camp accommodation as generally "admirable", adding that each room had its own patio area with chairs, while the apartments were furnished with built-in furniture including single beds for each internee, each with sheets, pillows and blankets. Mosquito nets were available though it was considered that they were unnecessary in such a salubrious area. Each barracks building also included a room that could be used for storage or any other purpose.[333]

The physical divisions used in the family camp barracks suggest an evolution in the approach to space use, compared with the division of the same barracks structures for the Gibraltarian evacuees and the groups of refugees. Their barracks had corridors running the length of each building, with rooms for individuals and families assigned on either side of the corridor and joined as necessary by the cutting of internal openings. Given the far-reaching issues over space and overall conditions within the Women's Internment Camp, which preceded the establishment of the Family Camp, these enhanced spatial arrangements may have been an effort at conciliation.

The dining room was an airy building, around seventy feet by thirty-five feet, with tables seating six to eight persons and with a stage at one end. In the kitchen attached to the dining room, Jamaican cooks employed by the camp prepared meals for the internees, who were receiving the same rations as British military personnel, though it was proposed that extra butter and milk be available for the children. Zitzow recalled: "The families were provided three meals a day in the mess hall. You could eat there (which most everybody did for the main noontime meal) or take the food to your room." This also appeared to mark an amelioration in conditions compared to any of the other wartime camps for evacuees, refugees or internees – where taking food from the common areas was generally discouraged.

Zitzow said that a German volunteer from among the camp residents was involved with cooking duty.[334] This would have been one of the two Germans noted as part of the kitchen staff. The Swiss Consular reports noted that the internees "look well and healthy, and many are stout". There was a canteen built into one corner of the dining room, which sold a range of canned foods, sanitary items and other conveniences, as well as tobacco and rum without restriction. And the authorities apparently turned a blind eye to a private arrangement between the internees and the kitchen, whereby coffee was served between 10.00 and 11.00 each morning.

The camp's sick bay or infirmary was divided into wards for men, women and children, and there were nurses always on duty. The camp also had a bi-weekly clinic with the Army Doctor; more frequent visits had been found unnecessary. He was, however, always on call. There was also a female physician among the residents in the Married Families Camp.[335] Male internees requiring dental attention were taken to the military camp and women to the Kingston Public Hospital. As before, necessary procedures and appliances were provided free but internees wanting elective procedures or better-quality appliances would have to meet the costs themselves.

All instructions were given in German, through the camp leader, and a copy of the Geneva Convention was posted.[336] There were two roll calls per day, at 7.30 a.m. and 5.00 p.m., but no other scheduled checks on the internees. And the authorities had been asked to continue the outings, excursions and sea-bathing permitted to the women and children at the old camp in Downtown Kingston.[337] Arrangements were even made to allow ten children from the Mona Family Camp to spend two weeks' holiday at the seaside, with the children going in successive groups of two and the military assuring transport – though some challenges were reported in finalizing the transport arrangements.[338]

The Swiss vice-consul played the role of facilitation. Reports indicated that some women in the Mona Family Camp approached Mr or Mrs Waeckerlin for assistance in petitioning the authorities to allow visits by relatives or friends in the Male Internment Camp. As a result, it was agreed for adult sons and brothers to be allowed to visit whenever the opportunity arose. With respect to male friends from the men's camp being allowed to visit single ladies at the family camp, it was stated that the commandant, who had discretion in the matter, was prepared to allow such visits "from time to time, subject to the over-riding considerations of transport and security".[339] Uwe Zitzow recalled that some friends of his father, from the Male Internment Camp, were occasionally allowed to visit. One of these may have been the artist, recalled only as being a male internee, who painted a scene looking out from the Zitzow apartment (see Figure 17).

Figure 17 Painting by German internee from Zitzow verandah at Mona Family Camp (Courtesy of Uwe Zitzow).

Figure 17A Photograph of residents of Mona Family Camp (Courtesy of Uwe Zitzow).

Figure 17B Photograph of young children at Mona Family Camp (Courtesy of Uwe Zitzow).

Schooling was in place for the children within the camp. The library from the Women's Camp had been transferred and residents had daily access to the island's newspapers, which were delivered to the camp and passed to the internees uncensored – giving them a window on the progress of the war. Regular entertainment was also put in place, with a monthly concert by a band from the men's camp and a twice monthly theatre offering by another group from the same camp. Films – mainly American comedies and sometimes a war drama – were shown twice monthly and Zitzow recalled being allowed to watch cartoons which were sometimes offered at the start of a film. There was a concert of recorded music on Sunday afternoons – mostly classical pieces from long-playing records played on a phonograph.[340] Occasionally, live concerts were arranged among the internees, and Zitzow recalled his mother playing the piano at such events. In addition, some sporting equipment was installed in the new camp, mostly for gymnastics, and residents taught others and led classes. Fistball was also popular, as it was in the men's camp. Figures 17A and 17B portray the population of the Mona Family Camp.

Church services were provided in German and English. The weekly German language service was led by a married Protestant Minister among the internees, while Catholic services were held by priests from the Male Internment Camp and Gibraltar Camp on alternate Sundays.[341] The Church Diary for the Sacred Heart Church on Gibraltar Camp recorded that the Family Camp was visited on 6 October 1943, by Catholic Superior Fr Thomas Feeney, who advised that the priests from Gibraltar Camp should provide Mass in the Lower (Prisoners) Camp, two Sundays each month.[342]

On a daily basis, household activities, childcare and gardening were the major activities. Space between buildings allowed for the cultivation of flowers as well as vegetable gardens. But as with the residents of the Male Internment Camp, the men at Mona soon had land under cultivation and were rearing rabbits to benefit the camp population. Eventually, some of the lettuce, carrots and other vegetables grown in the community garden were:

> sold or traded to women who came to the camp for the produce they would then take to the market. The exchange provided not only other goods or money for greater food variety but also a means to buy such niceties as chocolate and cigarettes.[343]

A 1944 report confirmed that there was a big community garden as well as a personal section for each family;[344] and in 1945, a Swiss Consular report stated that the men had "excellent allotments in full production" and that proceeds from sales during 1944 had realized about £3,000.[345] Uwe Zitzow, who augmented his own, juvenile recollections by interviewing his parents, said that his father also built a community cooking oven that was used by all to bake bread and cake.[346]

Most of the camp residents left Jamaica in November 1946 aboard the SS *Esperance Bay*, a passenger ship being used for troop transport, which had facilities to accommodate women as well as men. Newspaper reports said that the passengers included twenty-five married men and thirty-five married women, twenty-six children as well as more than four hundred single Germans and some thirty Italians.[347] Several other persons and families made other arrangements, if they were able to source visas. Zitzow, who was aged seven when his family left Jamaica, said that most Germans had to return to Germany and that his family was one of around three that were allowed to remain in Jamaica while they waited for responses to job enquiries elsewhere:

> We were the last to leave the Mona Family Camp in 1947, living at that time just outside the camp gate in what used to be the officers' quarters . . . Initially we tried to stay in Jamaica, but the rules were that no foreigners could take on a job that could be offered to a Jamaican or British citizen anywhere . . . My dad got a job at chocolate factory in Dominican Republic and eventually, in 1952, we immigrated to the United States.[348]

Interestingly, his recollections extended to the refugee community of Sosúa, a Jewish community in the Dominican Republic, established during the war with permission of the then dictator, Rafael Trujillo. Zitzow said that Sosúa was about an hour's drive east of Puerto Plata where his family was living:

> There was a man in a pickup truck, Mr Kirchheimer, who would come to Puerto Plata laden with all kinds of wonderful German foods made in Sosúa to sell from door to door all around the area. These goods included delicious sausages of all kinds, cheeses, cakes and other good stuff. It makes my mouth water just to think about it. He introduced us to Sosúa and the people there and soon we found ourselves going over there some Sundays to go to their beach. The beach was a large sandy cove with nice clear water. And, of course, in the late afternoon we would go to their beer-garden-style restaurant to have something to eat and socialise. It was a completely German community. Both German and Spanish were spoken there. Occasionally an afternoon movie matinee would be available, and I would join the children there to go watch an American cowboy movie.[349]

In this instance, the common cultural connection appears to have overcome very present wartime and post-war tensions between Jewish and non-Jewish Germans.

Chapter 4

Isolation and Interaction in Colonial Jamaica

Jamaica's wartime camps were a response by colonial officials to an imperial need. It is important to distinguish a response by colonial officials from a colonial response which might imply a degree of engagement of the colonized, even if their status did not require their concurrence. There was no such effort. After the decisions on the camps and their residents were made, the communication between officials and the public largely related to the regulatory context and to preferred behaviour in response to those regulations.

Indeed, the lack of engagement by the colonial authority extended to the local elected representatives in the Legislature. As was noted earlier in relation to the establishment of Gibraltar Camp, elected members complained during the 1941 sitting of the Legislative Council that they had not been advised of the advent of the Gibraltarians – as, subsequently, did the mayor of Kingston. In the same sitting, "the matter of the Gibraltar Evacuees coming to Jamaica" and the leasing of land to the United States were among the issues on which Elected Member J.A.G. Smith sought to censure the government. His complaints related to the way government monies were spent, as well as "the system of withholding information relating to public business of the island and not consulting with Elected Members on questions of importance affecting the island".[1] While the motion failed to attract necessary support, it did draw attention to these issues at a time when concerns over self-government were simmering in Jamaica.

The government agreed to accept nine thousand evacuees – though some sixteen hundred arrived and resided on the island in a civilian camp. Subsequently, it accepted several hundreds of refugees into the same camp. In parallel, hundreds of persons categorized as enemy aliens were accepted for safekeeping in internment camps. As previous chapters have shown and as this chapter will discuss, conditions were in place to buffer the free as well as the un-free incomers from the local population. It is arguable that this was to try and support the imperial cause while avoiding further disruption to the colonial condition which was already being challenged by local labour and political activism as well as unwelcome attention to racial and civil discrimination. Nonetheless, there was interface and interaction between the camps and their residents and the communities in which they operated, some of it suggestive of a certain amount of agency on the part of elements of the local population. The terms interface and interaction are deliberately used to suggest levels of connection between Jamaican residents and incomers in the face of official efforts to buffer and isolate.

Isolating Friends

The decisions to accept thousands of Gibraltarian evacuees having been made in June 1940, the buzz of employment in the Mona area during August and September, advertisements for temporary professional staff in mid-September and the late September engagement of Deputy Mayor Ernest Rae as camp manager sparked a series of detailed news reports on the camp. On 21 September 1940, an extensive report was headlined, "Evacuees Need Haven and Township is Born. Mona springs to life as home of 9,000" with a follow-up feature on 7 October. The level of activity was also reflected in a complaining letter to the editor from one user of public transport, who had faced competition from hundreds of workmen over the previous weeks, and published notices from Camp Commandant H. Simms urging a halt to thousands of unsolicited job applications "for every conceivable sort of jobs".[2] He said that twelve hundred applications had been received in response to the initial advertisements.[3] On 17 October, the *Gleaner* carried a notice that the speculation of recent weeks would be assuaged that afternoon by a broadcast on ZQI by the Deputy Director of the Public Works Department (PWD) Mr P. Martin-Cooper.[4] While the prior reports included information that must have come from some official sources, these had not been identified. A report on 21 October addressed public queries regarding the possible impact on food supplies and said that the food controller was giving the assurance that there would be no dislocation.[5] Despite these reported concerns the local population was generally welcoming, perhaps following the lead set in the media. Seemingly without organization, crowds greeted the first Gibraltarian evacuees as they arrived on 25 October, suggesting empathy as well as possible opportunity. The *Gleaner* reported that thousands lined the waterfront and the sidewalks to cheer as several thirty-five-seater buses drove the first arrivals to camp, followed by lorries for their luggage.

Fr William Feeney said that local Catholics had been asked for voluntary assistance in getting the evacuees into their barracks. Catholic students had made their beds and volunteer priests and nuns, assisted by "a host of Catholic lay-folks from Kingston", allotted rooms to the evacuees and showed them their quarters.[6] These locals were on hand when bus after bus drove down August Town Road, unloaded its occupants at the camp gate and returned to the dock for another busload.[7]

A *Gleaner* editorial on 26 October 1940, the day after the first Gibraltarians arrived, commented: "Jamaica will be their home while the war endures. We have heard no murmuring against this amongst the Jamaica [sic] people." It said that the only speculation had been over food sufficiency and suggested that extra, steady demand for local foodstuff should stimulate local production. The well-wishing extended to small gestures – on 30 October the *Gleaner* reported that ZQI, the local radio station, would that afternoon present the first performance of a composition titled "Welcome Gibraltar", composed by Earl Levy and performed by Archie Lindo.[8] The newspaper later reported on a gift to the Gibraltarians, of a large-scale model of a ship, the HMS *Nelson*, which was well-known in their country.[9]

Positive reading of the local response, recorded in the newspaper, extended beyond the island to the West India Committee – the merchants' lobby in London – which had been consulted during the preparation phase and which commented that "Jamaicans have extended to their fellow Colonials from Gibraltar a welcome worthy of the best traditions of West Indian hospitality". The committee described the arrangement as:

> a remarkable instance of co-operation between two widely separated Colonies and gives one more proof of the loyalty of the people of the Empire not only to the Mother Country but also to one another.[10]

Despite the excitement and positivity, it has to be recognized that no government announcement advised Jamaicans of the decision to accept what was expected to be up to nine thousand persons – albeit fellow colonials – from the Mediterranean area or urged Jamaicans to engage with this contribution to the war effort. Nonetheless, a *Gleaner* editorial on 26 October was outspoken: "By this island furnishing a temporary home for some thousands of the evacuees", it said, "it proves distinctly useful to the Mother Country in this war. This is precisely what Jamaica should wish. It is precisely what Jamaica does wish". The *Gleaner* said that this would be one of the ways in which Jamaica was contributing to the war.[11] However, the extent of the government's expectation of Jamaicans was made plain in advertisements published in the newspapers from 30 October. The advertisements gave notice that Evacuees (Defence) Regulations 1940 had been gazetted on 18 October and that they forbade local access to the Gibraltar Camp without permission from the commandant, on pain of prosecution, and stated that permission would not normally be granted.[12] The media, like the public, was denied access except with special permission – though it would be the main source of information throughout the camp's existence.

From the start, the government was determined to create a secure enclave for the Gibraltarians – mainly southern European, mainly female, middle and lower socio-economic level, white and overwhelmingly Catholic. Gibraltar's governor asked for the involvement of the Catholic Church in the running of the camp, and Jamaica's governor followed up with alacrity. Additionally, the Colonial Office facility was given a military flavour with a commandant, deputy commandant and commissary officer – the first commandant, a retired British military officer. The camp would have a location close enough to the capital to be supplied with infrastructure and services, but away from most passersby – except persons in two nearby rural communities. It was surrounded with barbed wire fencing; ominous sign boards warning away non-residents; a dedicated police post as well as Gibraltarians sworn in as special constables for the duration – all to create a secure shell. Inside, while egress could not be forbidden – though for a time it was discouraged – everything was provided to make it unnecessary. Getting to town also involved effort and cost – a walk or ride the mile to the tramline's Papine terminus, and then a tram or bus fare to Kingston, and back. Security concerns on the outside were implied or stated, though there were no reports of any residents being or feeling threatened during their years there.

However, the government efforts to regulate the camp and discipline the population were not without pushback. There were camp residents who objected to the constraints, both regarding regulations on lifestyle including the matter of eating meals where they were served and also regarding freedom of movement into the community. The same camp conditions applied when various groups of mainly Jewish refugees were added to the camp in 1942 and 1943, including the requirement to live in the camp and the ban on employment outside the camp without special permission. There were some differences rooted in religion and ethnicity and, especially once the Dutch refugees arrived, in social class. Nonetheless, requests to live outside the camp were refused as were requests for opportunities to contribute in practical ways. Residents could only move out of the camp to leave the island, once they had acquired visas to go elsewhere.

The ban on employment reflected a government concern over the huge unmet demand for jobs at every level – which was partly addressed by large construction projects and programmes for overseas employment. The ban on Gibraltar Camp residents applying for local jobs was partly resolved by offering them many of the jobs within the camp for which Jamaicans had rushed to apply, even before specific advertisements were published. This lessened the job opportunities for local people but proved an economic benefit to the camp administration as lower wages were paid to residents. Additionally, fewer non-residents had to be granted even limited access to the camp. What of the threat posed to the local job market by the camp residents? In the case of the Gibraltarians, most were female with dependent children, or elderly and had not previously worked outside their homes as this was not encouraged in Gibraltar. Female or male, their preferred language was Spanish, though most also spoke English and they could only leave the camp between 8 a.m. and 11.00 p.m. – factors that raise the question of what and how many jobs they would have been qualified or preferred for. In the case of the Polish and other Eastern European refugees, male and female, there may have been a greater range of job skills, but language was an issue. It appears likely that the replacement of local jobs, especially at the level covered by the labour unions, would have been quite limited. But the government would have been concerned with the optics as well as the numbers.

The potential impact of large numbers of additional people on scarce resources was another factor – one especially evident on an island where all manufactured and many basic commodities had to be imported and where shipping was already diverted or at major threat from enemy action. This was, in part, addressed by stockpiling some supplies for the camps. Imports of others, like meat, were planned to avoid disrupting local supplies. And there were programmes, across Jamaica and within the camps, to grow food and rear livestock. Having the incomers living within secured camps made it easier to provision in bulk, to protect stocks and to ensure that these groups had access to common resources.

The government and the camp administration also had to take into consideration potential health issues that might affect both the incoming camp populations and the local residents with whom they might come into contact – more so where there was actual interface. In relation to the local geographic environment, there was a concern to ensure that mosquito breeding sites in the vicinity were eliminated – a procedure that provided an unplanned benefit for the adjacent communities, as well as for camp residents. Other "special medical and sanitary measures in the interests both of the evacuees and the public" included the compulsory inoculation of the evacuees against typhoid, a process accomplished "without any appreciable opposition".[13] With the arrival of the first Polish refugees in 1942, a suspected case of typhus on board ship led to the group being quarantined in their section of the camp. When one person developed fever and a rash, Polish refugee Miriam Sandzer Stanton wrote that the commandant "took good care that the news should not be spread outside the camp. Nobody could leave or enter . . . Isolation was imposed". She said that tests eventually showed that the illness was dengue fever.[14]

The decision to accommodate the free incomers in a restricted enclave offered a benefit to the empire and potentially some economic benefit for the colony through building work, employment and maintenance charges, while controlling the local impact of this new group variable. Despite the local demands for greater involvement in local governance, there be little action suggestive of engagement with the local population on these concerns and decisions. Official communication generally related to ensuring that rules and regulations were followed, and public challenges to government decisions were frowned on, especially when they were well formulated by members of the upper classes. A July 1941 letter to the editor of the *Gleaner* newspaper criticized a previous writer who had challenged government actions on civil liberties, stating that such sentiments were "entirely above the heads of the common herd and are for the most part misunderstood by them".[15]

Securing Enemies

Limiting access to Gibraltar Camp and discouraging interaction with its residents were inevitably a greater challenge than was the case with the internment camps – which were secured camps for persons detained by the authorities. Hence, the public had no expectations of engagement. Interviewees who were children during the 1940s recalled male Europeans, seen through a fence, from a distance, only as curiosities.[16] The government intended that they would be detained for the course of the war and then shipped home. Indeed, even after the war's end, the colonial government insisted that for security reasons and to preserve local employment opportunities, internees must remain in camp until they could be marched onto ships for repatriation. This took more than a year. Nonetheless, a handful managed to stay on by marrying Jamaican women or leveraging other connections.

In the interim, a challenge did arise as war fortunes and alliances shifted. In 1942, a small group of interned Finns were moved to Gibraltar Camp with a degree of free movement. And the Armistice in September 1943 precipitated a change in status for a large group of Italians – most of them from the construction trades – who agreed to cooperate with the authorities and thereby gained greater freedom of movement, economic opportunities and opportunities for social interaction. The situation not only challenged the government edict on incomers working, it also evoked a potential disruption of the colonial status quo by white, working-class persons being seen undertaking manual jobs normally done by black people.

One area where there was an effort to engage the public in respect of potential enemy aliens was through encouragement to report them to the police. A front-page news story headlined, "If You Suspect He Is German, Tell C.I.D" said that with Britain now at war with Germany, it was the duty of citizens to report any Germans of whom they were aware, though not to accost or accuse them indiscriminately.[17] The article did not quote a government source, hence it may equally have represented editorial support for the government's effort to round up all aliens in the country, especially enemy aliens.

Media Interface

The Jamaican public was introduced to the wartime camps through the media – at the time, mainly the newspapers of which the *Gleaner* was the most consistent and far reaching. There was also coverage in the weekly *Jamaica Times*, the PNP's influential *Public Opinion* and the newsmagazine *Spotlight* as well as the *Catholic Opinion* magazine. Although the government initiated short daily local broadcasts on ZQI in June 1940, the scripts are not in the archived files, and what remains of them are advertisements for broadcasts, some of which were later reprinted in the media.

In relation to the internment camps, the *Gleaner* provided consistent coverage of the first internments – those of German and Austrian men who had been living in Jamaica. This included details of the initial detention site and some description of conditions in the new camp built near the Briggs Park military cemetery. The friendly tone and level of detail were reduced as the war continued, and while this would have reflected a negative perception of Germany and its policies, it may also have reflected efforts to reduce the length of reports in the face of material shortages including limited newsprint supplies. Most reports on the Male Internment Camp dealt with new inmates, escapes and eventually with repatriations. The *Gleaner* reported on the opening of the Female Internment Camp and subsequently that of the Married Families Camp at Mona, as well as on the release of naturalized British citizens and a few other locally interned aliens from detention. Additionally, consistent and detailed coverage of the Legislative Council sittings included criticism by elected members, when white or light-skinned officials or troops were given preference over coloured or black Jamaicans, or if special arrangements were made to lighten the conditions of detention for German women – given the racist perspective of that country and its leaders. The detention of local political and labour activists in 1940–1942, debates on civil liberties and the release of these activists in 1942 and 1943 were also extensively covered.

A review of the media coverage of Gibraltar Camp over the wartime years suggests that the local media in broad terms, and the *Gleaner* in particular, provided a distanced and sanctioned interface between the camp and the local population. There is no evidence, in correspondence or reports, that this was an intentional strategy. Indeed, in the early months, the *Gleaner* coverage was not overwhelmingly positive though the tone was generally supportive. *Gleaner* reports focused on the evacuees settling down under strict camp rules and included a detailed report on the rules for the evacuees and the public as well as advertisements warning the public to stay away. There were also rousing reports on separate visits to the camp by Governor Sir Arthur Richards and Lady Richards.[18] One report noted that there had been occasional "unhappy incidents" which were dealt with "promptly and effectively" by the Gibraltar police officers serving as special constables under Jamaican laws, and the regular local police. After one such incident, the newspaper said, many evacuees did not immediately appreciate the necessity for the action taken but subsided when "firmly assured of the justice of the disciplinary measures adopted".[19]

Support for the administration's hard line on discipline and a degree of prescriptiveness in terms of the Jamaican public were expressed by the weekly *Jamaica Times*:

> the evacuees are decent, self-respecting persons who are in no sense of the word under any kind of stigma; yet it is clear that hundreds of persons, moved bodily into a new country, under strange conditions and in what is really a foreign environment, must for their own protection be subjected to a certain amount of benevolent discipline . . . If the public understand the problem, we feel sure that they will extend that co-operation which is so necessary if the right spirit is to be created.[20]

Development of the relationship between camp officials and media houses was uneven, and the camp sometimes adopted a carrot and stick approach. A *Gleaner* reporter seeking to visit the camp without an appointment was refused entry – resulting in a blistering commentary that described the camp as a "sports model concentration camp" and Commandant Rae as a "2 x 4 dictator".[21] A few days later, the *Gleaner* published a letter from an evacuee that described the camp gates as "gloomy portals" and complained about restraints on the residents' freedom and the quality of the food.[22] Following up, *Spotlight* newsmagazine was invited to tour the camp, publishing an extensive report, including a comment from the commandant that "we are all very happy. This interference annoys me very intensely".[23] Refutations of the charges in the "Gloomy Portals" letter were released to the media, including positive reports from investigators who had visited the camp. These were fully carried by the local media, including the *Gleaner*, helping to smooth any negative consequences that bad publicity might have caused, locally and abroad. The newspaper also carried stories of many Jamaicans prosecuted for breaching the camp regulations and barriers, some of whom received salutary warnings from judges as to harsher penalties for any subsequent offences.

News reports on the camp gave an insight into the newcomers, tempering some of the inevitable curiosity, and provided an assurance that harsh discipline applied to the camp and its residents and to outsiders trying to get inside. The latter message appears to have been received. Several Jamaican interviewees asserted their impression that they should not become involved with the persons at Gibraltar Camp. They said that these persons were the concern of Commandant Ernest Rae and under the protection of Governor Arthur Richards. As one interviewee noted, most colonial people did as they were told, and Governor Richards was "a hard man".[24]

Within a few months, media coverage of the camp settled into consistent, mainly bland titbits related to groups and events on the camp – presumably supplied to the media by camp officials. These included brief reports on concerts, guide and scout troops, marriages and participation in church activities. A large number related to camp sporting teams that participated in local competition – especially the pugnacious and for a time successful "Gibraltar (Rock) Scorpions" football team. This media coverage aside, the only official public output on the camp was a film featurette on the daily life of the residents, aimed at managing interest and providing propaganda footage for use in the United Kingdom and Gibraltar. "Gates of Gibraltar" was shown at the popular Carib Theatre in Kingston, in June 1941, ahead of feature film "Kitty Foyle". The *Gleaner* said that the film gave:

> intimate details of the Mona Camp for refugees from which the public is barred. Thus for the first time the public will be given the opportunity of seeing the sort of life our guests from Gibraltar live and how they are looked after... Those who have never been within its portals will see it turned inside out.[25]

The British Ministry of Information, which viewed the film in September 1941, commended the photography – work of local photographer Duncan Corinaldi – but considered the production "unbelievably naïve and very uninteresting", especially lacking an interesting commentary. Dismissed for general viewing, the master negative and only print were sent to Gibraltar.[26]

The *Gleaner*, whose reportage introduced most Jamaicans to the camp in mid-1940, the arrival of its first residents in October and November and various glimpses of its residents, would also report the departure of the Gibraltarians in October 1944. Beyond Gibraltar Camp, it also provided the public with the most consistent information on the residents of the various internment camps, including their eventual departures from the island.

Physical Interface: Impact of Gibraltar Camp on the Immediate Community

The insertion of a large, modern urban enclave into a populated, semi-rural location had the incidental impact of shedding unaccustomed light on adjacent communities and provoking responses from citizens – especially in August Town, close to the camp's south-eastern boundary. Specific points of interface related to infrastructure, as well as the health status of the wider community – with health and sanitation being the main areas where government efforts extended beyond the camp itself. For very practical reasons, these included government mosquito control efforts put in place ahead of the arrival of the first evacuees. In mid-September 1940, health officials embarked on an extensive anti-malaria campaign east of Mona, throughout the valley to August Town and beyond. It was reported that a senior sanitary inspector was surveying the area and a medical officer of health and sanitary staff member would also be involved in a programme to fight mosquito breeding in rivulets running into the Hope River, where watercress was cultivated.[27] A year later, the camp's regular public health programme included mosquito control, extending "outside of Camp limits to a radius of about two miles".[28]

In mid-November 1940, a monthly meeting of the Kingston & St Andrew Corporation heard a report on health conditions in August Town, based on which it was recommended that a committee visit the area and ascertain which areas should be declared as slum areas. Sanitation Committee Chairman Dr E.A. Anderson described this plan as a "hullabaloo . . . raised by the Government with regard to the sanitary conditions of these people", because of the evacuees being near August Town. However, the mayor of Kingston considered the matter to be urgent, citing "responsibility for the protection of their people's health" and "conditions which might develop at the Gibraltar Evacuees Camp, which might jeopardise the health of the people of August Town who were just nearby".[29] At the following meeting, the council took a report of the assistant medical officer of health, with regard to sanitary arrangements at various premises in August Town and agreed that the Sanitation Committee should be empowered to make such temporary alleviation as was necessary, not exceeding £200. Councillor Noel Nethersole suggested that instead of requiring each house owner to construct a lavatory, certain areas in the district be zoned and suitable conveniences be erected there for the people, "many of whom could not afford elaborate constructions, however inexpensive they might appear to be".[30] A subsequent meeting received a letter giving the council the government's approval to spend up to £150 for providing sanitary conveniences on properties in August Town owned by indigent people, "the expenditure to become a charge against the property". The matter was to be dealt with by the senior sanitary inspector of the Board of Health and medical officer to health.[31]

That same meeting noted that engineers were preparing a scheme to fill in a pool – some twenty feet deep – under the Hope River Bridge, above Papine, where "for many years several persons have lost their lives by drowning". The scheme involved blasting adjacent rocks to fill the pool and widening the channel. It may be coincidental that this came soon after the opening of the camp, and that camp residents had been swimming in the river – as later reports, raising concern about pollution of drinking water, would note.

The uneven approach to camp and adjacent community was plain on matters of infrastructure. Construction of the camp had brought modern utility lines to the area. These included a new ten-inch water main from the Hope Road to the 181,000-gallon tank supplying Gibraltar Camp. In December 1940, it was announced that the central government had directed the PWD to extend a pipeline to supply a standpipe in August Town. The report noted that "heretofore, residents of August Town obtained water either from springs, or by carting containers to Papine from which centre many obtained supplies for household use".[32] However, months would pass without a standpipe, due to a *contretemps* between the Water Commission and the Kingston and St. Andrew Corporation (KSAC) over responsibility for water distribution by means of standpipes.[33] At the May 1941 meeting of the KSAC, the mayor read a letter from the Commission which stated that the Gibraltar Camp water supply was temporary, for the use of the camp, and that since these water mains had been laid down by the Imperial Government, it was possible that they would have to be taken up at the end of the war. The Water Commission "could not bind itself to undertake the management of a standpipe for August Town at the present moment". It also refused to take responsibility for what would normally be a function of the municipal council. This position was described by Alderman W.M. Seivwright as "a reprehensible policy in a government department"; one that showed "callousness, indifference, and a desire to shift responsibility". He also noted, inaccurately even by estimate, that "August Town contained as many people as Gibraltar Camp".[34] The matter of the August Town water supply would be taken up by the Federation of Citizens' Associations at the request of the August Town Citizens Association, whose President Mr F.A. Francis said that August Town residents had been agitating for a proper water supply since 1932.[35]

The KSAC's May 1941 meeting also heard a repeated complaint about Gibraltar Camp residents bathing in the Hope River, above Gordon Town – a protected area that supplied water to people further down the river. Councillor T. Duval, who said he had spoken on this matter at the previous meeting of the council, noted that "the people of the area had been agitating for a considerable time for pure water to drink". He commented that it appeared that August Town residents "would have to remain inconvenienced until the war was over" and questioned whether this was "the way the people were to be treated in their own country?"[36] There was no official denial, but a letter to the editor a few days later commented that any bathing in the River by Gibraltar Camp "people" must surely be taking place below the intake tank, or the water supply of the entire corporate area would be affected.[37]

Another, equally inconclusive initiative towards improving a situation in a community neighbouring the camp came in mid-1944, after the typhoid outbreak on the Mona Commons, between Papine and the camp. The medical officer of health urged the provision of standpipes for people in the community, noting that the cause of the outbreak, which was still in existence, was believed to be the water supply running in an earthen gutter which led from a conduit down to Gibraltar Camp and August Town. The *Gleaner* report noted another apparent dispute between the Water Commission and the KSAC over which agency was responsible for supplying the Mona Commons' residents with water.[38] This issue also predated the camp but came into focus due to the provision of enhanced supplies in the vicinity. Neither was resolved during the time the camp existed.

These instances aside, the local communities appear to have had their infrastructural concerns considered only when they took the initiative – making use of opportunities created by the camp's presence in the landscape. There had already been a move to revive citizens' associations at the local and national level, and a delegation from August Town was one of several at a June 1940 meeting of the revived Federation of Citizen's Associations (FCA).[39] The delegation was reported to have expressed interest in affiliating with a strong Federation.[40] A few months later, the Federation supported a complaint by the local Citizen's Association, related to an access road between August Town and Papine that was blocked by the eastern boundary fence of Gibraltar Camp.[41] FCA Secretary Sam A. McFarlane wrote to the colonial secretary complaining that August Town residents had been informed "that the roads which they have used all these years will be blocked and that they will not be permitted to use the roads again". He said that one of these roads passed between the upper and lower levels of the camp and the other on the outside edge along the side of the Hope River.

> The Residents of August Town will be glad if the Government will intervene and make arrangements so that they will have the continued use of the road which passes on the outside edge of the Evacuees Camp. Such arrangement will enable the people to have an outlet from their district to take them to their Market place and to the point of embarkation which is the tram and omnibus terminal.[42]

The acting director of public works had also written to the colonial secretary that "the residents of August Town should be very grateful" for the improvement of the roads in the area, including the application of asphalt surfaces – a benefit to the general population from the building of the camp.[43] The official response, at the end of December, was to plan construction of a bridle path, "so that pedestrians and pack mule traffic may still have a short route to Papine".[44] However, further concerns were raised over the planned path which was steep and prone to flooding during the rainy season. Another letter to the colonial secretary argued:

> If the protection of or interference with the Evacuees of Gibraltar Camp is the prime consideration of the Government, then, if the wire fence mentioned be

moved in a distance of 7 or 8 feet and the bridle path constructed along it, then for the further protection of the Evacuees what has been done on another side of the Camp, namely: the erection of another wire fence inside and parallel with the first to avoid interference with the Evacuees, will certainly meet the case.[45]

On 17 February 1941, a letter from the acting colonial secretary to the president of the Citizen's Association advised that a new road on the lower, outer boundary of the camp, nearest the river valley, was being fenced off from the camp and would be available as a driving road between August Town and Papine. In April 1941, a *Gleaner* report on a sitting of the Legislative Council made it clear that the road was still inaccessible to the people of August Town adding: "Arrangements were made to open it at once".[46] This eventual opening of the road was one of the achievements listed by the August Town Citizen's Association at its fourth-anniversary church service in October 1943. The report of activities also listed success in getting the district listed as a rural area, and the association's efforts to get a water supply for the district which came to fruition in 1941.[47]

Such issues of interface with a local community did not arise in respect of the internment camps. The Male Internment Camp was within the extensive Up Park Camp property, while the Women's Camp was on the edge of a commercial district. Any issues relating to interface with neighbours were unreported, except for a decision to surround the Women's Camp with corrugated sheeting so as to prevent outsiders from looking in. The Mona Family Camp would be within the Gibraltar Camp boundaries but would not exist until mid-1943.

Economic Interface

Despite efforts to separate the acquisition of goods for the camps from regular local sources of supply, including by special importation, there was overlap and interface with local suppliers which impacted Jamaican consumers to some degree, especially during the period when German submarines were targeting vessels in the Caribbean and Atlantic. "Extensive purchases have been made and will be made abroad and in the case of things such as fish, they have already bought up a considerable reserve, which is kept in cold storage", the *Gleaner* reported in October 1940, with respect to nine thousand evacuees expected at Gibraltar Camp. "In regard to fresh vegetables, many people have been specially contracted to plant for the camp alone and these plantings would not have taken place otherwise."[48] A similar approach would have been taken to the Men's Internment Camp, which was provisioned by the military. Indeed, separation from military control would be blamed for mid-war shortages at the Women's Camp.

Reports in 1940 said that farmers were being encouraged to produce for the camp at Mona, which would provide a sure market for their products, but also "guaranteed prices for practically every agricultural crop grown".[49] Distributors also benefited from frequently advertised tenders to supply food items, usually to cover a six-month period – sometimes for individual items such as dried salted cod fish and sometimes for a range of foodstuffs or supplies. In November 1940, the camp advertised for "moderate quantities only" of canned salmon, evaporated fruit of all kinds, jelly crystals, pork and beans, canned vegetables, dried green marrow fat peas, haricot beans, golden syrup in gallon tins, tomato sauce or ketchup, tomato puree and canned tomatoes. By mid-February 1941, tenders for the six months ending 30 September 1941 included fresh milk (daily) as well as other foodstuffs: ice, rolled oats, Jamaican vinegar, beef to be purchased in whole sides, pork by the carcass without heads and feet, lard, margarine, granulated and brown sugar, evaporated milk, macaroni, vermicelli, imported spaghetti, tomato catsup in six-pound tins, brown bread, coffee, curry powder, firewood and coal.[50] The amount of beef being required for Gibraltar Camp only, in the tender of 15 February 1941 was 16,000–20,000 pounds of beef and 800–1,000 pounds of pork monthly.

As imports were affected by naval warfare, local supplies were increasingly stretched, with discussion given to the issue of rationing in 1942 – though it was decided then that a quota system would be more suited to the local situation.[51] Governor Arthur Richards noted that methods of price stabilization originally instituted in the United Kingdom were being applied throughout the empire "to prevent inflation and the hardships which would arise from further excessive or rapid increases in the cost of living to the working classes".[52] As local scarcities increased, there were some negative news reports suggesting or raising suspicions that Gibraltar Camp and, to a lesser degree other camps, were getting more than their fair share of items like meat and rice which became scarce in 1942. Between September 1941 and August 1943, at least thirteen news reports in the *Gleaner* newspaper and others in *Public Opinion*, focused on the shortage of beef and made a connection between perceived scarcity and supplies reserved for Gibraltar Camp, Up Park Camp and, at one point, the US Base in Clarendon.[53] Shortages of fish, flour, rice and kerosene, which also significantly affected the local population, were less frequently connected in media reports, to the presence of Gibraltar Camp and other large imperial facilities. Not pulling any punches, *Public Opinion* commented in May 1942:

> If you suddenly increase the meat consumption of a small island by the influx of five or six thousand heavy meat consuming newcomers, using meat every day and having priority of supply, and if you keep increasing the number and have a government that refuses to ration the supply, it naturally follows that the general public will be starved out.[54]

Gibraltar Camp, at least, appears to have had some sensitivity of this, releasing positive news stories during mid-to-late 1942 on its own efforts regarding transportation and food supply needs. These focused on a new type of flour developed by a Czech refugee, which might be of interest given local shortages; on the development of the camp's own dairy herd and drove of pigs; and efforts to slash gas consumption in the face of local gasoline rationing, by de-mechanizing its transport.[55]

Within the Male Internment Camp and later the Married Families Camp at Mona, efforts were made to establish vegetable gardens on a significant scale, starting in 1942 and 1943, respectively. Rabbits were also reared for meat, and the Men's Camp had a significant drove of pigs. Whereas all of the output of the Men's Camp farm was purchased internally, the excess vegetables from the Mona Family Camp's garden were sold to higglers, who sold in the local market.[56] Local shopkeepers and vendors also sold to camp residents and though this economic connection cannot be quantified, its contribution to the level of interface, transaction and interaction is reflected in oral testimony – even going beyond the economic into the social realm.

The efforts by local vendors to connect with possible new customers predated the first residents. A *Gleaner* reporter noted, with, some amusement, neat signs left on newly constructed structures on the camp worksite: "For loans, see me first!"; "Shop at __, where a dime is worth a quarter!"; and "Fi Refugee Herb, si mi a mi aufice!" (For marijuana, see me at my office.)[57] Once the first residents were in the camp, vendors rushed to offer their wares, but the residents were confined to camp for the first weeks and, also, had everything they needed within the fence. Vendors also found themselves faced with the strict camp regulations and several were prosecuted for getting too close or trying to breach the fence. Nonetheless, some vendors, especially from the nearby communities, established a regular mini market on a small piece of land at the side of the road just outside the camp gate. Oral testimony suggests that many of those selling at that site, over the long term, were East Indians who tenanted and farmed small plots in the Papine area. Reports suggest that at various points, approved vendors may also have been allowed onto the camp. One newspaper article reported on the prosecution of such a vendor after he was discovered to be selling rum at a provision stall that he had been allowed to have inside the camp.[58] Many of the camp residents also got in the habit of walking up to the Papine market to buy extra local fruit including bananas, pineapples, watermelons and oranges. A Dutch refugee said that her mother would buy a weekly chicken from a vendor who would wring its neck and pluck it on the spot. Though food was provided by the camp kitchen, the preparation of a family meal in familiar ways, though on an outside fire near the barracks, was a fond memory.

Besides the vendors, bars and dance halls in the Papine area also benefited from regular patronage by camp residents. An interviewee from the area said that camp residents would come out in the evenings and drink at the local bars in Papine.[59] In the case of the Gibraltarians, given the cultural and religious norms of the group, these would have been the men, not the women. A young Gibraltarian male evacuee, given special permission to work outside the camp, also recalled patronizing local nightclubs farther afield. The cultural and gender norms were evidently less strict among some of the camp's refugee residents, such as the Dutch couple that regularly visited Papine to watch the dancing on a Friday night. However, their pre-teen daughter was not allowed to accompany them, as she recalled with a twinge of remembered jealousy.[60] The presence of a social dimension to this economic activity can be found in literary sources. Louise Bennett's poem "Jamaica Patois" refers to people in Papine learning Spanish words and phrases in their interactions with people from Gibraltar Camp, who lived there for four years. And *Gleaner* columnist, Hartley Neita, recalled and retrospectively recorded the hugs and the tears shed between Jamaican market women at Papine and their regular Gibraltarian customers, when the day of repatriation arrived.[61] In some situations, economic or professional exchange led to prolonged social encounters. One interviewee offered two distinct but connected instances. One was a long-standing friendship that developed between the owners of a local clothing/sewing store in Kingston and an internee from the Women's Camp who sometimes shopped there, escorted by a guard. He said that local acquaintances were also developed by some civilian internees in the Mona Family Camp, who gained relative freedoms, at the end of the war, that were out of reach of fellow civilian internees remaining in the Male Internment Camp. One of these, an engineer was sometimes asked to assist with hydraulic and civil engineering projects and developed acquaintances that led to invitations for himself and his family after the war had ended.[62]

Aside from the significant economic connection between the camp and the local and wider economies, through tenders and purchases, Gibraltar Camp also contributed to the local economy through receipt of payments for maintaining the evacuees and later, the refugees also, as well as through the employment of Jamaican staff at various levels.

Interface and Interaction – Employment

Employment of Jamaicans at Gibraltar Camp was significantly more limited than was initially anticipated – in part because the camp was never populated to capacity but also because officials decided to employ camp residents where possible, to temper restrictions on their employment in the wider community. This proved an administrative benefit, as camp residents were paid at local rates – less accommodation, food and services. It also lessened the extent to which the administration had to provide a dole for indigent residents and provided many residents with some occupation. And it lessened the number of Jamaicans with access to the camp. Those Jamaicans who did find employment within Gibraltar Camp were policed, to limit opportunities for socializing between the local and visiting populations. Local employees were required to strictly adhere to arrival and departure times, with staff passes checked through security. For a time, to guarantee compliance, the camp bus was used to transport some of the employees in and out. Guards sought out persons not recorded as having left and those found breaking the rules could be prosecuted.

Nonetheless, interviewees shared small recollections of connections between residents and Jamaicans on the camp. One local interviewee, employed to the camp's grounds staff, said that there were sometimes gatherings near the kitchen, when "they might say 'what you do over there?' We would say 'we do cultivation . . . items like tobacco, peas, all different things' ". He said that camp officials would come and listen to what was being said.[63] And there were Gibraltarian memories of helpful Jamaican employees: the storemen who "never refused in giving extra food to the ones in need" or the cooks who "spent time in teaching them how to make bread".[64] There is little information on the identity of these working-class Jamaicans who helped to keep the camp running. Harold Ramdeen, who worked on the grounds staff, recalled that his colleagues were both black and East Indian, including some retired soldiers and that most of them were employed in the camp kitchen. A *Spotlight* newsmagazine feature identified one of the employees as "big, brown-skinned Master Chef, David Thomas".[65] A few visual images from collections on the camp also record

Figure 18 Staff at the Gibraltar Camp hospital (Courtesy of Anthony Lara).

a few obvious black and coloured Jamaicans among the white residents of Gibraltar Camp, including one young black woman on a cleaning crew, and black men working in the kitchen.[66] It is more challenging to positively state that light-skinned or white individuals, not known otherwise, are Jamaicans, though clothing and style of hair can help to give clues. In both the evacuee and refugee kitchens and later in the kitchen at the Mona Family Camp, most of the line staff were Jamaicans. However, persons from the camp population were sometimes involved in menu supervision and oversight, to cater for the individual tastes of the relevant populations. A Polish woman was remembered as being in charge of the refugee kitchen and two German internees as chefs at the Mona Family Camp. Figures 18, 18A, 18B and 18C show some of the staff contingents at Gibraltar Camp.

That employment on the camp offered a route to friendships, despite the regulatory frame, was clear from comments by Gibraltarian, Frank Tucker, then a young man living on the camp: "Friendly Jamaicans working in the camp struck up friendships with some of the families and entertained us outside the Camp". He remembered a party at Ballater Avenue, near Half Way Tree, where the guests included a local judge. He also recalled a trip to Morant Bay, in the east of the island, to the home of the local clerk of the courts, where he climbed his first coconut tree and threw a coconut down to another guest, a young woman from the camp who had also been invited.[67]

Figure 18A Staff in the refugee camp kitchen (Courtesy of Inez Baker).

Figure 18B Office staff at Gibraltar Camp (Catholic Archdiocese Archives, Jamaica).

Tucker was one of just two Gibraltarians given permission to work outside the camp – with the officials underlining that this did not constitute a change in policy. The other Gibraltarian exception was Elsie Lillian May who worked at the Imperial Censorship Office. A few refugees may also have been given permission to work. Polish refugee, Ignas Krakowiak, was employed as a gymnastic instructor at Jamaica College, about two miles from the camp. His daughter said that he acquired a bicycle which he rode to work.[68]

The limitation on Jamaicans working in the camp, so that the bulk of jobs could go to residents, was a trade-off for the ban on residents seeking employment in Jamaica, which the governor made a condition of all free arrivals. Nonetheless, oral testimony indicated that at least a few residents operated as micro-vendors to the local economy, selling items that they had made, in camp workshops or in their personal spaces. Interviewee Harold Ramdeen, who continued to live in the camp vicinity, recalled that Gibraltarians would sometimes bring sewn items – specifically, shirts and "ganzees" – out of the camp in their shopping bags and baskets, and discreetly offer them for sale in Papine. If the person approached was interested, the size was right and the price could be agreed, a sale would be effected. He said that the items were well made and cheaper than those sold in "Town" – Downtown Kingston, the main shopping district – with a "ganzee" that cost 3/- in Kingston selling for 1/6.[69] Similarly, some refugees did handwork for sale, with bags or embroidered items being sold through friends and contacts developed outside the camp.[70] The Finns, who lived in Gibraltar Camp between 1942 and 1943, were also known for woodcarving, including decorative boxes and models of ships – items given as gifts to the wives of camp officials, among others.[71] Toys, made by Czech refugees, were remembered as being available for sale at Christmas Grand Market in Downtown Kingston, through Jamaican handcart men, though this may have been after rather than during the war.[72] There was a concern that, if allowed, the Eastern European refugees would seek to engage in trade in Kingston which, it was felt "would create difficulties and lead to bad feeling towards refugees".[73]

Manne Eckstein (later Aronovsky), who lived in the camp with her parents and sister from 1942 to 1944, recalled that the Polish men were not allowed to work, which made life difficult. Nonetheless, her father, an accomplished jeweller who had his tools with him, would frequently be asked to go to the homes of wealthy Syrian families in Kingston, to fix jewellery in need to repair: "all he needed was a table and good sunlight. He would leave early in the morning, take a shuttle bus into Kingston, and be back in the evening before curfew". She said that he sometimes brought things home to work on them.[74]

Within the Men's Internment Camp, internees also made craft items that were sold to employees at Up Park Camp and beyond. Jamaican Auxiliary Territorial Service (ATS) volunteer Connie Mark recalled purchasing high-quality leathercraft and wooden miniatures from internees while working as a medical secretary at the British Military Hospital, Up Park Camp, during the war.[75]

There were also residents within Gibraltar Camp who worked informally in contravention of the regulations. Finnish residents reportedly did some discreet construction work for pay, both in the refugee section of the camp and outside.[76] And at least one classified advertisement indicated that other residents in the camp in 1943 may have worked outside too, despite the ban. The ad asked for a "Reliable man (Foreigner) at Gibraltar Camp to reply to POB 373. First class opportunity for the right man".[77]

This ban on employment was extended to persons wishing to engage in business – a policy which may have reflected a desire to avoid camp residents putting down roots, and perhaps creating possible postwar competition for British firms, but which also evidences a lack of interest in the generation of new skilled workers and jobs, and the establishment of a self-sufficient local economy.

In his report on a September 1943 trip to Jamaica, the YMCA's Conrad Hoffmann Jr wrote of an Italian internee with "considerable funds" who was eager to invest them in an agricultural enterprise in Jamaica which would provide fifty of his compatriots the opportunity for farm work. He said that while he had written to the authorities in this regard, he had no response – though he noted the possible impact of changes consequent on the Italian surrender. In 1945, it was reported "with regret" that Jamaica Welfare Limited had been unable to get government approval "to take advantage of the services of Italian internees for the instruction of Jamaicans in the skilled arts and crafts in which the internees are well versed". This surprise was greater, said the report, because the secretary of state for the colonies, then Col. Stanley, had indicated that "as far as the Imperial Government was concerned there was no objection to such use being made of enemy internees". The criticism was repeated the following year by the Jamaica Imperial Association.[78] Proposals by refugees to establish businesses were not entertained. In 1944, the commandant reported to the local colonial secretary that there were, among the refugees, "craftsmen in industries such as diamond working, etc, for whom there is no scope in Jamaica".[79] There were several diamond industry experts among the Dutch refugees and at least one among the Polish group.

The case of the Italian co-operators who were accommodated, under light supervision, at Newcastle Military Hill Station and then at Gibraltar Camp, reflected a complex interaction with the local economy, after 1943. Despite stated government determination to prevent the incomers from competing for local employment, means had to be found whereby the Italian co-operators could earn a basic living. The Swiss vice-consul acknowledged the difficulty of assigning them to some types of jobs, such as farm work, which was not traditionally done by white persons. Reports indicate that local government funding was used to employ them on road and reservoir projects while they were billeted at the Newcastle Military Hill Station. They were also able to find landscaping and gardening work in the area – work that would have brought them into contact with householders. A few of the Italians, including a married couple, were found employment in hotels on the island's north coast. A group with construction expertise also were allowed to undertake contract work with the army engineers. In 1945, after the Newcastle area was impacted by a prolonged drought, the Italians there were moved into empty barracks at Gibraltar Camp. The former evacuee and refugee camp had shrunk – most of it taken over by the military following the departure of the Gibraltarians in early October 1944.[80] At Gibraltar Camp, the Italians were allowed to have a workshop where they produced ceramic pipes, basins and other items for homes and gardens, which they sold to people from outside the camp. One correspondent recalled coming to the workshop with her father, to purchase such items.

A correspondent who worked at the United States Consulate in Kingston during the war said that she got to know some of the Italians who came in seeking visas. She recalled artist Umberto Cattaneo and lunchroom operator Osvaldo Ricci as two of the many who would move to North or Latin America. She recalled that some got independent work as tilers and that it was the Italians who first produced benches and fences made of concrete shaped to look like tree branches – a style still popular locally. Some worked for local businessmen and others set up businesses of their own – a few of which lasted for many years.[81]

More than a dozen Italians were also employed at the government's Clay, Tile & Brick Factory at Cockburn Pen, on the western outskirts of Kingston. The PWD took over the factory in May 1945, and a lack of expert management and trained labour among local employees was the initial basis for the involvement of the Italians. In May 1946, when most Italians – those remaining within the camp as well as those living outside – were being repatriated, permission was granted to retain a works manager, carpenter, wood fitter, two other specialists and ten or twelve other employees. In June 1946, it was stated that they would not be granted permanent residence if they should request it, though they could stay in Jamaica for a time if it was felt that they could teach Jamaicans new skills or trades.[82] However, a September 1946 debate in the Legislative Council heard complaints that no training was taking place at the Clay, Tile & Brick Factory and that some forty-five Jamaicans employed at the plant were only utilized as labourers.[83] Subsequently, it was reported that all these jobs would be terminated as the factory was being sold.

The multi-faceted experience of these Italians reflected several factors. There was the government's awareness of the growing strength of the labour and linked political movements in Jamaica, explaining consistent statements that free incomers – the evacuees and refugees – would not be allowed to seek employment. It was a policy that was stated for the cooperating Italians, conditionally freed from the internment camp in 1943, who at the same time had to be found means to earn a living while they remained in Jamaica. The local government and military were involved in finding work for these skilled persons, while the central government continued to insist that they would not be allowed to compete with local labour or to remain in Jamaica after the war. Reports stating that the Italians would not be allowed to work were carried by the *Gleaner* on several occasions.

Despite the rhetoric, there were Italians who managed to stay in Jamaica after the war. Among those who made a long-standing impact on the building industry in Jamaica was Domenico Vaccino, who was among the group living at Gibraltar Camp and who set up a workshop employing Jamaicans in construction jobs after the war.[84] His name is still linked to various structures, from tombstones and benches to chapels and schools, especially within the local Roman Catholic community.[85] Italians Antonio Filisetti and Andrea Maffessanti, who had also been among the internees, established the construction firm Filisetti & Maffessanti after the war and became well-known for building "fine tourist homes" on Jamaica's north coast.[86] The firm later changed its name to Maffessanti Brothers Limited.

As the war moved towards an end, concern grew about the protection of job opportunities for Britishers who had been fighting the war. In a July 1944 letter, the British commander-in-chief Jamaica expressed concern about the employment of Germans and Italians in Jamaica:

> When war broke out between ourselves, Germany and Italy, a number of Germans and Italians resident in Jamaica were interned. A small number of German citizens, mostly Jews, whom the Security authorities passed as firmly anti-Nazi, have been released. All the Italians have been released now that Italy is our co-belligerent.
>
> All these Germans and Italians were employed – and those released are now re-employed – in jobs in Jamaica which could equally well be done by Englishmen

and Jamaicans. When we make peace with Germany, is it proposed to release the admittedly pro-Nazi Germans now interned and permit them to re-occupy the positions they held at the expense of British subjects?

Some local feeling has already been aroused at the release of the Italians and the allegedly anti-Nazi Germans who remain as much German as they were originally.[87]

Author and former military man Ian Fleming pointed to Jamaica as a possible destination for English citizens "to seek fortune and freedom" postwar in the empire. In "Dear John", a series of published essays, shortly after the war, he argued that "if you are at all competent in your trades and professions (outside the middleman professions) you should be able to find a niche". He expressed certainty that "many new industries will come to Jamaica and much foreign capital and, if you are on the spot, you may get into one of the new enterprises".[88] Fleming visited Jamaica for four days in July 1943 – including a stop at Gibraltar Camp where at least two refugees recalled their families meeting him – and returned postwar to purchase a holiday home where he invented super-spy, James Bond.

In October 1944, a *Gleaner* columnist acknowledged and addressed some local resentment over a declared Colonial Office policy of enlisting British subjects who had served in the forces for jobs in Jamaica. Pragmatically, he accepted that even with the constitutional change of 1944, Jamaica was still a British colony:

> It is perfectly fair and just that the Colonial Service, as at present conceived and administered, shall offer some of its vacancies, expected to be greatly increased after the war, to those fighting men who have helped to maintain and to preserve the Empire.

He said that Jamaicans would have most of the positions in the Local Government service, while Britain, which footed bills for the colony, would continue to assist in its administration.[89]

Social Interaction

Occasions for free social interaction, with no link to job function or presence, or to economic transaction, were limited by camp regulations and circumstances. In consequence, many social activities involving persons outside the camp were limited to competitive or performative aspects where the level of interface could be significantly controlled.

For Gibraltarian evacuees, the camp environment had been designed by government officials in Gibraltar and Jamaica, to incorporate Catholic religious oversight as well as administrative regulation. This applied to most of the evacuee population, though there were a small number of Jewish and Anglican Gibraltarians, and perhaps others also who would have been less constrained by religious norms. The Catholic Church oversaw the education, health and social aspects of the camp and played a significant role in organizing groups and activities especially for the young Gibraltarians – including active Wolf Cub, Rover Scout and Guide packs as well as church-related sodalities. Nuns also chaperoned excursions, both outings to local attractions and attendance at cultural and religious events. These included the participation of seventy-five choristers and guides in a golden jubilee celebration for Bishop Thomas A. Emmet at the Holy Trinity Cathedral in Kingston, in 1943.[90] A troupe of Gibraltarians performed Spanish songs and dances at a variety of events and venues in Kingston, including Catholic schools and the Catholic Church headquarters at Winchester Park, and presented a Spanish-themed cultural package at the Ward Theatre. Some forty-eight *Gleaner* newspaper items cover these sanctioned cultural activities involving evacuees from Gibraltar Camp. Jamaican entertainment scheduled within the camp, such as regular performances by the Jamaica Military Band and occasional vaudeville shows involving local artists, was also at arm's length.

Many more reports mentioned the sporting contacts between teams from the camp and local leagues, often schools' competitions, in softball, baseball, tennis, basketball and football. An effort to introduce cricket was undersubscribed. The active but short-lived participation of the Gibraltar or Rock Scorpions football team in the local leagues may have provided some opportunities for interaction with Jamaican players – though the Gibraltar team would have been transported to and from the games and supervised by the camp chaplain. Visiting teams were also supervised, and not encouraged to stray or to stay past the end of the encounters. Indeed, there was no indication that participation in any of these games or events was intended or allowed to initiate wider social contacts between locals and visitors.

The official opening of the camp's new football field and sports complex in August 1941 provided a "rare occasion" on which the general public was admitted to any part of the camp. However, a newspaper report made it clear that an entrance fee set some limits on attendance and activities, and access was limited to the field, located at the south-easterly end of the camp, on the lower level, closest to August Town. There may have occasionally been unsanctioned interaction between camp footballers and local football enthusiasts from August Town, who would go to watch the Gibraltarians practice. One interviewee, who concurred with the general observation that the Gibraltarians were strong footballers, recalled the local people watching and, sometimes, playing football, informally, with them.[91]

While there were many religious observances within the camp, there are no entries in the camp's Sacred Heart Church diaries to suggest that visits were organized to church communities outside the camp, nor that they hosted any such groups. Neither of two local Catholics from nearby Gordon Town recalled Gibraltarians visiting the church there. *Catholic Opinion* newsletter, which carried a regular "Evacuee Evangel" report on the Gibraltar Camp group, was similarly silent on this point. The local community was certainly willing. Reports record the "generous involvement" of local Catholic nuns, priests and laypeople who volunteered to help the first group of Gibraltarians settle into their new quarters. And an interviewee said that local Catholic churches encouraged members to offer hospitality to people from the camp. But the examples of such local hospitality which are recalled, by Catholics and others, all involved persons from the refugee groups rather than evacuees.[92]

Even though camp residents could go out between 8.00 a.m. and 11.00 p.m., and occasionally on weekend passes, there were still cultural limitations that would have restricted even the adults; and disproportionately restricted the women, who were the larger percentage of the camp population. The gender norms of the time and especially of the Catholic culture meant that the small proportion of adult men in the camp would have had the greatest freedom, though several of them also had some level of employment within the camp. The adult women, many of whom were mothers and grandmothers and some of whom also undertook some level of camp employment were shown in images visiting the city in groups. However, the distance and cost of transportation would have limited such outings, as they reportedly did the outings of some refugees.[93] Trips up the road to the shops and market in Papine may have been far more frequent. Photographs of Gibraltarians on outings to the beach or pool – possibly Bournemouth Bath and the Constant Spring Hotel pool in Kingston – appear to show homogenous groups of evacuees, often accompanied by one or other of the nuns from the camp.

Camp culture would have limited unsanctioned excursions for youths from the camp though these standards, again, applied more to the young women than the young men. A Jamaican nun who often visited the camp, with permission, recalled that the young women were not allowed out without a chaperone.[94] A Gibraltarian interviewee, who was a senior schoolboy, went on to teach at the camp and then had special permission to work outside, explained that young Jamaican men would try to strike up conversations with the girls. "In the hut where I lived, we had a very large number of very nice girls indeed", he said, adding that he got invited to parties, where his presence would make it appear safer for the girls to come too.[95] Another young male Gibraltarian recalled meeting friends in nearby Hope Gardens and, also, romping with two young Jamaicans who lived nearby and who rode their horse across unused portions of the camp without permission.[96]

In *The Fortress Came First*, Gibraltarian historian Thomas Finlayson recorded claims that officials wanted "to prevent the evacuees and the workers from getting too sociable with each other".[97] Former Kingston Alderman and political commentator John Soulette, writing in the *Gleaner*, criticized elected members for not raising more questions about efforts to prevent or at least discourage interaction between the camp and the local population. Describing Gibraltar Camp as a "semi-internment" camp, Soulette asked: "What is behind all this? Is it that the authorities don't want them to mix with the natives?" He suggested that the authorities did not understand real English principles and that, "our freedom is assailed on all sides."[98] Some interviewees agreed: In one case, a Gibraltarian recalled generational family stories that the authorities "actively limited interaction between the two groups."[99] However, another Gibraltarian who was a teenager in the camp explained the "great stress put on keeping us apart".[100]

> It was the intention of the Camp Commandant that these women and children would be returned to their husbands and fathers and that the young women would go back to those they loved and had to leave on the Rock. It was for that reason that it was made difficult for Jamaican people to have access to the camp.[101]

Asked whether people in the camp had any concerns over their inability to entertain Jamaicans in their homes on the camp, the evacuee responded that they "did not regard this as a significant matter . . . we had so little to offer under the conditions in which we lived . . . Privacy went out of the window . . . it was particularly difficult when you wanted to have a visitor".[102] He noted that this was a more conservative time, that many of the women had left husbands behind, that most of the evacuees were working class with little money to spend and that the customs and language were mainly Spanish.

Differences in accent and language were apparent and, along with culture, could have created some barriers. An interviewee, then a teenager living on the camp, suggested that barriers to connection included culture, language and class. She remembered the Gibraltarians as Spanish-speaking and strictly Roman Catholic whereas, at age fifteen, even in wartime, her interests were in "boyfriends and parties and outings".[103] Most of the residents spoke Spanish for preference, though they also spoke English. Louise Bennett's wartime poem "Jamaica Patois" indicated a willingness among working-class Jamaicans, to connect with the visitors by learning a little Spanish.[104]

There are only a few references to specific, identifiable linkages between Gibraltarians and Jamaicans, beyond the oral testimony of slight connections to employees within the camp. Evidence of relationships and marriage is explored in a subsequent section. Two other instances are reflected in non-work-related photographs shared by interviewees, which show white Gibraltarians with evidently black acquaintances (See Figures 19 and 19A). For one of them, the circumstances were recorded in an unpublished family chronicle by a Gibraltarian correspondent, born in Kingston in 1942:

> My Aunt Vicky's little son, Fernando, had a friend, a little coloured boy called Orville. They used to play together, and there is a photo of them both, with me as a one-year-old, sitting together on the grass. I have no idea who Orville's parents were or why he played in the camp.
>
> I was given a black baby doll, which came to be called Orville as well, and which I adored and brought back to Gibraltar. It had a rag body and a head

Figure 19 Photograph of Aileen Mansfield her cousin Fernando and his friend Orville around 1944 (Photo courtesy of Aileen Mansfield Gordon).

Figure 19A Lara family at Gibraltar Camp (Photo courtesy of Anthony Lara).

that was made of a kind of ceramic which seemed indestructible. I had it for years, until another child maliciously broke its head. I have never forgotten that moment or that child![105]

Despite any restrictions, the Gibraltarians involved themselves in the local society in various small ways. There were numerous cases where Gibraltar Camp residents were listed among the winners of small prizes in various local competitions as well as instances where camp residents wrote letters of complaint or thanks to the local daily newspaper.[106] Acknowledgement that the Gibraltarians had made friends in Jamaica was made by Commandant Rae when he advised them to pack up and say goodbye as they would be leaving soon – an announcement made over microphone in the camp and reported in the *Gleaner* newspaper on 23 September 1944.[107]

Fewer social restrictions applied to the groups who would occupy the lower level of the camp, where the formal religious oversight was not in place, though all other camp regulations remained the same. Age, class and religiosity may still have played a part in connections made between various refugees and Jamaicans on and off the camp, as well as with the local Jewish community. Young Jamaicans living in the camp with parents or spouses employed there recalled forming friendships with some of the younger and livelier among the refugees accommodated on the lower level of the camp from February 1942 onward. It was intimated that some of the more cosmopolitan European Jews were invited to middle and upper-class Jamaican homes – capacity with the English language and facility with related cultural norms being among the attributes of these guests.[108]

Polish Jewish refugee Miriam Sandzer Stanton wrote in a memoir how she was welcomed into the home of Jamaica's well-off Matalon family and enjoyed hospitality of the DeLeon, Delgado and other local Jewish families.[109] A family history interview with Polish refugee Helene Krakowiak Arnay also mentioned the Matalons as an example of "charitable people" who facilitated breaks from the camp. Another Polish refugee, Manne Eckstein, who later wrote down events of her life as a school project, recalled that her family made social connection with Jewish families in the city, including the large and rich group of Syrian Jews in the fabric business, through her father's unofficial work as a jeweller:

> These families were so glad to finally see some more Jews in their city that they opened up their homes to us very frequently. During Purim and Hanukah, they would have all the children over, and we played games on their huge lawns, and we all received toys.[110]

These connections reported by Polish Jews were quite different from the negative tone of some others in that refugee group, who suggested that they experienced disinterest from the local Jews. Polish composer and violinist Dr Arthur Steigler experienced a different kind of involvement, in a community of interest, outside of faith, when he wrote *Quo Vadis Domine – In Poloniam* – a composition related to the genocide being perpetrated by the Nazis in Poland. In 1943, the Poetry League of Jamaica became involved in translating the words into English, an effort led by poet C.A. Escoffery and poet-musician Astley Clerk, with violinist Jack Lewis assisting with the music and Granville Campbell arranging the music for quartet. Poet and writer Roger Mais congratulated the League on extending valuable assistance "to a guest, an ally, who from this remote corner of the world addresses his appeal to Christianity everywhere". Steigler, who later discovered that his wife and daughter had been sent to concentration camps, finally left Jamaica in 1946. Leslie Ashenheim, later Chairman of the *Gleaner*, wrote that Steigler "desired fervently to place his talents at the disposal of the war effort, particularly along the lines of Anti-Hitler Propaganda. For reasons best known to the Defence Regulation Authorities his offers were refused and, in spite of vigorous representations on his behalf he was not even permitted to publish his patriotic, Anti-Hitler Song".[111]

One of the Dutch refugees recalled that her parents became friends with a Dutch Jewish family that had been living in Jamaica for some years, as well as two Jamaican families with Jewish links. Both had children with whom she became somewhat acquainted.[112] Dutch Jews from the camp were active participants in an Intercessional Service for Persecuted Jews held at the Jewish Synagogue in Kingston, May 1943. It was reported that Mr Van Den Bergh opened the Ark the first time and Dr Plotz took out the Scroll of the Law. Local awareness of the plight of the Jews was also reflected in the organization of a fundraising ball, held at the popular and upscale Glass Bucket Club in April 1943, in aid of Jewish War Refugees in Palestine, who had escaped there from Axis-occupied countries.

Those of the refugees with the means enjoyed whatever facilities were available in Jamaica and remained in the camp only because it was required until they had an onward visa. While subject to the same rules as their evacuee fellows, their willingness to push the envelope with the authorities was out of step with the general approach of the colonials both within and outside the camp. An interesting footnote with respect to the refugees is an advertisement published in the newspaper in February 1942, around the time of the first arrivals, publicizing a song titled "I'm just a refugee". The notice said that the "beautiful local composition", a waltz, was available in local music stores or from Mr A.V. Armond. However, no copy of the song or its lyrics was discovered.

The capacity of the Germans and Italians detained within the internment camps, to interact with the local population was significantly limited. However, some groups grasped or even created opportunities. Some newspaper reports of escape attempts from the Male Internment Camp include details that suggest some degree of local social connection. A November 1946 report when a group of German men were being repatriated, quoted a young German merchant seaman, Albrecht Kohler, who had escaped from the camp two months before and was caught hiding in bushes near Montego Bay. He told the reporter that he once tried to marry a Jamaican girl.[113] Another escapee, just prior to repatriation in February 1947, was a twenty-three-year-old internee who was described in the media as having been dressed in a grey suit and red tie when he escaped. He was recaptured late the following night at a home in Delacree Lane, off Spanish Town Road in lower St Andrew. His connection with the residents was not explained.

The group which had the most connection with Jamaicans at several levels were the Italian ex-internee co-operators, who operated within the Jamaican space much more freely than their status officially allowed. Many of them rode the buses, talking with Jamaicans, some of whom invited them home. One interviewee recalled: "A cousin of my Pa's and her daughter were on the Hope bus one day and Domenico (Vaccino) started a conversation with them – that's how our acquaintance began. Domenico would join in bridge evenings at home while some time later, Gino (Falzone) would play chess with my Pa."[114]

School created a particular opportunity for the young camp residents who were sent to Jamaican schools. This affected only a small number of Gibraltarians, who attended Catholic schools outside the camp but appears to have been the preferred option for the children of refugee families who attended a range of traditional high schools run by various religious denominations.[115] Specific refugee students are known or believed to have attended the Anglican-run St Andrew and St Hugh's girls' schools and Jamaica College for the boys; the Catholic-run Immaculate Conception High School and Alpha Academy for the girls and St Georges College for the boys, and perhaps others. Churches or Trusts ran most secondary schools, with government oversight, and allowance was made for children of other faiths, as some of these persons recalled. While some interviewees recalled meeting and being aware of camp residents or Jamaicans respectively, at school, just a few made abiding connections. One young Gibraltarian attending St George's College struck up a friendship that extended to his friend's girlfriend – later wife. They were still in touch decades later. Factors in their favour may have included a common interest in sports – specifically hockey which they all played.[116] Additionally, this young Gibraltarian had English parents, which may have given him an advantage in negotiating the local, middle-class school environment, compared to other Gibraltarians who had more Mediterranean cultural perspectives.

Gibraltarian Adelaide Azzopardi who attended Alpha Academy, along with two or three older Gibraltarian students, actually stayed at the school's boarding facility for a time, going back to the camp on weekends.[117] While friendships are not recorded, it appears likely that she may have developed some relationships with other boarders. Young refugee, Manne Eckstein also attended Alpha, along with friends from the Polish group during 1942 and 1943. Her autograph book included greetings, written in Spanish, from at least one school contemporary with a Kingston address and at least one Gibraltarian, who wrote her greeting in French.[118] One Dutch refugee, whose school may have been St Hugh's High from her description of the uniform, recalled befriending Jamaican girls, but not their names, nor home visits.[119] At least two Dutch refugees attended St Andrew High School. One said that other students were aware that they lived at Gibraltar Camp. She was the only interviewee among the refugees who recalled visiting the home of a schoolmate.[120] Coincidentally, a Jamaican interviewee who also attended St Andrew High School recalled taking the tram north, towards Papine, with schoolmates going to the camp. However, while acknowledging them, she said she knew that they lived at the camp and "you couldn't go there".[121]

Interface and Interaction: Birth, Death and Marriage

Birth and death were some of the important experiences connected to the experience of the wartime camps. In Gibraltar Camp, evacuee women gave birth to nearly one hundred babies. Dozens of mostly older persons died, seemingly from age-related debilities, one tragically falling from a bridge, for which foul play was not considered.

Correspondence with persons who had connections to Gibraltar Camp includes stories related to life events, including births and deaths. One Gibraltarian recalled her mother telling her that her own mother had died shortly after arriving in Jamaica. The young woman was assigned to share accommodation with another Gibraltarian in a similar circumstance. The correspondent said that her mother had found comfort in visiting the grave every day, and she was especially moved to hear Jamaicans enter the cemetery singing, not crying and wailing, when they brought someone to be buried.[122] From the range of reference numbers in the Calvary Cemetery register, the Gibraltarian graves appear to have been scattered across that Catholic graveyard. Many, if not most, were not tombed with a concrete or stone slab and headstone, and a cemetery official said that some might no longer be identifiable, especially as the cemetery had become run down and insecure.[123]

In March 1944, when repatriation of the evacuees in Gibraltar Camp was being discussed, there was official correspondence regarding the possible exhumation and removal of the remains of Gibraltarians who had died in Jamaica. There were then fifty-three evacuees buried in the Calvary Roman Catholic Cemetery. The Gibraltar Camp commandant wrote to the Gibraltar authorities noting that it would be "hard for the families who have lost one or more of their kin to think of them buried in far off Jamaica", and asking consideration of "undertaking the removal of all the dead evacuees". The letter was passed from the Chamber of Commerce to the Resettlement

Board and on to the colonial secretariat, which sympathized with the desire of the families, but declined on the basis of "acute restrictions on cemetery space here". [124]

Among the refugees, there were fewer such milestones. The Jewish Community in Jamaica recorded four deaths, one birth and one marriage among the refugees at the camp, though these may have been only the most religious.[125] A member of the first group of Dutch refugees said that there were no deaths among her group but that there were at least four births.[126] Among the Polish refugees, one death and two births were recorded between the first quarter of 1942 and the same time the following year.[127]

With no evidence to the contrary, the births recorded to camp residents must be presumed to have all resulted from relationships within families on the camp. Additionally, beyond marriages referenced below, there is no evidence of babies resulting from local relations with residents at Gibraltar Camp. However, it would be hard to ignore the possibility, which was the subject of postwar comment, including a poem by Louise Bennett "White Pickney". The preface to the poem notes that by 1949, war babies had excited comments in the press everywhere. Briton R.W. Thompson, who was stationed in Jamaica for about a year during the war, also recalled the relationships between local women and soldiers stationed in Jamaica, with a seeming desire for lighter-skinned children being one part of the equation. Thompson's memoir, and the recollections of interviewees, made it clear that relations with British, Canadian and American soldiers, and with German and Italian internees, existed across the class spectrum.[128] Only a few of these relationships – notably those documented with the mainly Roman Catholic Gibraltarian evacuees and a few with German internees – included marriage.

Several births were also recorded within the Women's and Family internment camps – at least six and eight respectively were mentioned in reports. Internees – both civilian and merchant seaman/prisoners of war – who died in detention were buried in the Briggs Park Military Cemetery at Up Park Camp. A list on the site of the Commonwealth Graves Commission, related to World War II, includes four German civilians – one a woman – as well as twelve members of the German merchant marine and nine Italians listed as soldiers.

Within the camp populations, several marriages were recorded – some ten among the Gibraltar Camp populations, and at least two between Germans at the male and female internment camps. Some, between camp residents, included celebrations that extended beyond the camp population. One, between a Dutch woman and a Polish man took place at the Jewish synagogue in downtown Kingston and was followed by a reception attended by the Dutch and Polish groups and Jamaican acquaintances at the Victory Club in Kingston, followed by a dinner party "at the residence of Mr Melhado of Seymour Avenue in Kingston".[129] Several marriages also took place between camp residents and Jamaicans, despite all the barriers to interaction.

Among the Gibraltarians, there were at least two documented cases where women in the camp community married Jamaicans. One was a Spanish refugee among the Gibraltarians who married a Spanish-speaking Jamaican jeweller who had been volunteering at the camp. Another was a young Gibraltarian woman who met her young Jamaican husband while she was confined to the "TB Sanatorium", now the National Chest Hospital, where he had a part-time job. It was a case of love at first sight, according to an article written decades later in the *Gibraltar Magazine*.[130] The two, with their two children, would later migrate from Jamaica to Canada. A Jamaican nun, who became principal of Alpha Academy for Girls in Kingston, recalled in an interview that "a couple of Gibraltarians fell in love and stayed . . . it wasn't an isolated case". She theorized that the young people met at events, an idea supported by the son of a Gibraltarian/Jamaican couple, who said that the Gibraltarians "invited locals to their shows".[131] A *Gleaner* newspaper correspondent, looking back nearly half a century, wrote that the evacuees and refugees gradually made friends with Jamaicans. "I know of several Gibraltarian girls who married Jamaican boys", she said.[132] Unfortunately no further details were provided.

Records were located for five marriages between Jamaican women and Gibraltarian men – most of them taking place at the Holy Trinity Roman Catholic Cathedral in Kingston. Marriage records indicate that at least one other Gibraltarian man married a Jamaican woman in Kingston during that time. Anecdotes suggest that there may have been more.[133] Four of the bridegrooms were young men who had joined the military auxiliary Pioneer Corps and stayed in Jamaica until the end of the war, after repatriation of the other evacuees. At least one Gibraltarian woman also stayed in Jamaica with her Pioneer Corps husband during that period. At least three of these Jamaican wives accompanied their husbands back to Gibraltar when they were repatriated, via the United Kingdom, in 1947. At least one bride was daunted by the prospect of such distance from her homeland and decided to remain in Jamaica when her husband was repatriated. Their daughter later went to Gibraltar to meet her father and married a Gibraltarian.[134]

Connie Mark, a Jamaican who joined the ATS during the war and subsequently migrated to England, mentioned these Gibraltarians in an interview for a book on *The Caribbean at War*. She said that the Gibraltarians knew they were returning home at the end of the war, but:

> as is expected, some married Jamaicans and they integrated quite a bit. It was usually Jamaican women marrying men from Gibraltar. After the war was over, they mostly went to Gibraltar with their husbands.[135]

Mark was deployed in the Military Hospital at Up Park Camp where she also met some of the internees who were hospitalized there when they became ill. In at least two verified instances, German internees at the Male Camp met Jamaican women at the camp hospital, whom they married and with whom they remained in Jamaica when their compatriots were repatriated in 1946 and 1947. They found jobs in Jamaica and in some cases became involved in the Jamaica-German society that formed in the 1950s, supporting cultural exchanges and events such as a local Oktoberfest celebration. The child of one of those marriages said that she knew of several similar stories among her father's friends.[136]

There were other references to marriages between German men and Jamaican women. A correspondent whose family was in the Married Family Camp at Mona confirmed that several bachelors in the Men's Camp married Jamaican women – relationships that he testified to having lasted as the families would sometimes visit his own parents in the United States. He also said that a German "who was chief cook in the family camp married a Jamaican woman who worked with him in the kitchen".[137]

Chapter 5

Traces in Heritage

World War II camps in Jamaica were created to serve an imperial need by securing various target populations – whether through a burden of care as with the evacuees and refugees or through a concern for local and imperial security as with the internees and prisoners of war. As such, the island's contribution to the Allied cause was more multifaceted than is often acknowledged – beyond the more recognized participation in fund raising for aircraft, canteens and various comforts, and personnel in the air force, army, factories and trades, mostly recruited late in the war.

Creation, administration and supply of the camps made little reference to the local colonized population. Those in elected positions in the legislature complained of being bypassed in the original decision-making, though they were required to support necessary allocations of funds. Indeed, the colonial government set out to buffer the population from the imperial decisions and, to the extent possible, from the incomers themselves. In so doing, as far as possible, the camps were prevented from generating any change to the colonial status quo. The main concession to the local context was with respect to the labour front, which had seen strikes and riots in recent years, and which was connected to growing political organization. The prohibition of free incomers from seeking employment was therefore a major precondition for haven in Jamaica, though this prohibition also reflected a desire to protect local jobs for Britishers fighting in the war. The other precondition was residence within a camp, specifically Gibraltar Camp where the Gibraltarian evacuees and mainly Jewish evacuees were accommodated. Given the numbers of persons expected, and the range of socio-economic conditions from which they came, the government would have had to ensure that residential space was available. However, the decision to make the camp an enclave – heavily regulated within and closed to local engagement from without – went a step further into social management of colonized populations on both sides of the fence.

The residential requirement, the efforts to discourage local interaction with the camps and the initiatives to lessen or moderate forays by camp residents into the Jamaican community clearly sought to restrict interaction between the incomer groups and the local population. An assumption expressed by the West India Committee in London, that the Jamaican community would be engaged in hosting their fellow colonials, was wrong from conception, though the population at all levels was welcoming.[1] With respect to the Gibraltarian evacuees in Jamaica – a white, mainly Catholic community, overwhelmingly female and mostly without husbands and fathers present – gender and race were both in play. The concern was to avoid local entanglement and to return Gibraltarian womenfolk to their normal environment, as they were sent. The restrictions on residence and employment, and the connected regulations, also applied to the refugees. However, these were independent Europeans without an immediate colonial perspective, despite the limitations of their refugee status. Additionally, some had resources that diminished their dependence on their host's goodwill, so that they were not "amenable to camp discipline and have continually sought permission to live outside".[2] Though these requests were denied, the refugees were given some weekend passes and many of the Dutch refugees were treated, by their government, to a holiday in Montego Bay Jamaica. Many of the wealthier refugees also took advantage of the local entertainment and hospitality that was available. The Dutch refugees moved on, either to Dutch West Indian colonies through Dutch government arrangement or to other destinations where family contacts or business opportunities facilitated the issue of visas. The same was true for most of the Eastern European, mainly Polish refugees, though a small group filtered into the local community when Gibraltar Camp closed in 1947.

The government did also seek to manage the logistical aspects of the camps, particularly as regards provisioning. Reports make clear that local access to scarce foodstuff, especially meat but also fish and rice, was nonetheless impacted by the camps. This was admitted by the Colonial Office and might have been anticipated on an island far from many of its suppliers, in conditions of war. It is interesting to speculate on the far greater scale of that impact if the nine thousand evacuees for whom the camp was designed had actually arrived.

For the German, Austrian and Italian civilian internees and merchant seamen, detention within a closed camp was a given and was generally expected and accepted – though this did change somewhat for some groups as the war progressed.

Beyond the regulated environments, there was a determination to prevent any of the incomers, even fellow colonials, from becoming permanent residents. In March 1944, seven months before the Gibraltarians were repatriated but shortly after this plan was mooted, camp chaplain Father Feeny advised the Camp Committee "that several Gibraltar evacuees had expressed the desire to remain in Jamaica either permanently or for the duration of the war".[3] Official consternation ensued, with a flurry of consultation including an opinion from Attorney General Henry Mayers that the existing law generally entitled the Gibraltarians to remain in Jamaica after the war:

> But as they came here under an evacuation scheme it would, in my view, be perfectly proper for action to be taken under the Emergency Powers requiring them to return to Gibraltar at the expiration of the Emergency which was the occasion of their evacuation. Apart from the foregoing, this matter seems to depend entirely upon considerations of political and economic expediency rather than of law.[4]

At the end, Governor John Huggins wrote to Secretary of State for the Colonies Oliver Stanley that, with his agreement, "when arrangements for the removal of evacuees from Jamaica are made, to provide by Defence Regulations that they should be required to return to Gibraltar".[5] On 6 October 1944, when the ss *Duchess of Richmond* left Kingston Harbour, all the evacuees were on board with the exception of a troop of young men who had signed up for duty in the Pioneer Corps, and the few young women who were remaining with Jamaican or Gibraltarian husbands.

The desire to prevent any of the incomers from remaining in Jamaica extended to those who brought skills or professional qualifications or even those proposing investment in the local economy. Suggestions, during the war, that some of the refugees might start businesses in Jamaica were refused by the local authorities, out of hand. Similarly, in 1945 and 1946, the Jamaica Welfare Limited and the local Imperial Association respectively would bewail the failure to upgrade local construction skills by involving some of the Italian internees with specialized skills, in training local workers. Many of these Italians, who had been working in West Africa before the war, did work in Jamaica for a time between the 1943 Armistice and their repatriation in 1946 or 1947. A few were able to remain longer, and a very few became long-term residents. A number of structures, especially within Catholic institutions, would be designed and constructed by some of these ex-internees. Some of the construction techniques they used were also acquired or copied and became part of the local landscape, without any general recollection of their provenance – such as the concrete benches discussed below, within the context of material heritage.

The Germans, Austrians and Italians, who had been interned as enemy aliens while living and working in Jamaica, had a range of outcomes. Some returned to previous occupations for a time. A number of those who had not become naturalized British citizens before the war made applications for this change of status soon after release from internment. They would have been aware that naturalized British citizens of enemy origin had also been interned, though as a recognized category and generally for shorter times and would have made the calculation that this was still a step in the right direction. Newman in *Nearly the New World* noted that the Caribbean was rarely seen as a permanent destination for these persons who had fled growing danger in Europe, and it appears that most ended up moving on in the postwar period. In the case of the larger groups within the Male Internment Camp – both merchant seamen and civilians interned in West Africa – most remained behind camp fences until they were marched onto troopships for repatriation in 1946 and 1947. Two sub-groups were somewhat more fortunate. These were the group of Italian co-operators whose conditions were significantly eased after the Armistice of 1943 and the mainly German families who moved into a specialized and less rigid camp in 1943 – some of whom were able to arrange onward visas to jobs elsewhere and avoid repatriation to a war-torn Germany. A few male internees – only German examples have been identified – married Jamaican women and stayed in the island after the war. The Italians, most of who lived for three years under mild military oversight, also had a range of outcomes. While the majority eventually returned home, a few were given permission to return to British West Africa, some arranged visas to move elsewhere and a few stayed and set up businesses in Jamaica.

Material and Cultural Remains

In Jamaica and for Jamaicans, little remains in the material or cultural heritage of World War II camps in which thousands of Europeans, in several groups, were maintained as a contribution to the war effort. Assessed in terms of size and numbers, the camps were significant facilities. Gibraltar Camp was acknowledged as "the biggest construction effort of its kind ever attempted in so short a time in Jamaica".[6] Indeed, for its time, it was probably the biggest with no caveats. Originally conceived for four thousand persons, it was scaled up to meet a demand for nine thousand persons at its highest projection. The fact that far fewer of these evacuees actually arrived in 1940 – with refugees adding to the camp population in 1942 and beyond – does not take away from the scale of the effort. Additionally, there were hundreds of merchant seamen and civilian internees who were held in camps from 1939. And, official correspondence in 1940 and 1941 records that Governor Arthur Richards had offered to accept ten thousand Italian prisoners of war – though they were eventually imprisoned elsewhere. So, the scale of what the colonial government conceived was truly ambitious for a country with a population of just over one million people and even the most scaled-down version was not insignificant.

The fact that these camps were designed to be separated if not isolated from the local community led to them leaving a light footprint. The determination to repatriate the groups completely, which was substantially achieved despite the few examples to the contrary, made this footprint still lighter. Little thereby remained by way of a community connected to any, or all, of the various camp experiences. Those Jamaicans who worked in the camps, some at a managerial or supervisory level, the majority as kitchen staff, watchmen and cleaning crews, would have quickly moved on to other jobs. Jamaica also largely moved on. The years 1943–1944 saw thousands of mostly young Jamaicans finally getting the long-awaited opportunity to volunteer for war service, and thousands also applied to go abroad for farm work in North America. The year 1944 saw the granting of a new Constitution and Universal Adult Suffrage, with the two major political parties active in seeking popular support for their participation in early national representational politics. In 1949, the new University College of the West Indies began building its teaching hospital on the Papine Common, adjacent to Gibraltar Camp, sparking an exodus of the mainly East Indian tenants who had lived and farmed there – some moving south-east to the Hermitage area, some to nearby Elletson Flats, many out to western Kingston communities like Cockburn Pen.[7]

Memories of Gibraltar Camp, and more so of the secured internment camps with which communities around Up Park Camp and Hanover Street had little or no interaction, would have easily submerged, with little to reinforce them. Those memories that were retained have been a rapidly wasting resource as that generation passes away, and have long become subject to flaws, including loss of detail and conflation. Nonetheless, elements remained which could be interrogated within the context of contemporaneous textual records and which could reinforce and illustrate documentary and media records. Archival records of the time include the imperial and colonial wartime documents, maps and photographs, some sieved through the net of repatriation to Britain, upon independence, but nonetheless accessible at the National Archives in London. Their partial counterparts, reflecting records of the Colonial Secretariat in Jamaica, remain in the Jamaica Archives and Records Department at Spanish Town. There is also local as well as international media coverage during a feisty time in local national development, some – like the *Gleaner* newspaper – accessible online.

In terms of the material heritage, little remains, especially of the closed camps. The Male Internment Camp largely disappeared under Jamaica's National Stadium, which was built to host the 1962 Central American and Caribbean Games, and has since been extended. The government had purchased a little over seventy-eight acres of the site, described as part of Briggs Park, from the War Department in 1960 to build the facility.[8] At that point, the internment camp buildings had already largely disappeared. Ahead of the sale, in August 1959, the War Department advertised for demolition and removal of a single internment camp building 144 feet long, 36 feet wide and 10 feet high at the eaves, built of timber with a boarded and felted roof, the building supported on 3-foot concrete piers.[9] Such details help with the visualization of a military facility that apparently – and perhaps unsurprisingly – generated few photographs.

While the built camp has been erased under the Stadium sports complex, a part of the fifteen-acre campsite may remain within the Up Park Camp military compound, in sight of the tall stadium lights. This is suggested by a little-known monument within Up Park Camp, which commemorates the site where labour leader Alexander Bustamante spent some eighteen months in internment between 1940 and 1942 (see Figure 20). Bustamante, who became prime minister and later National Hero, was present when the monument was unveiled in 1969, by his wife who as his trusted assistant had frequently visited him in camp. It may identify the front of the Male Internment Camp, where Bustamante and other Jamaicans were detained in a compound with Jewish and other internees, segregated from the main population of Germans and Italians. Or it may identify that segregated compound itself. Without formal plans for the camp, it is hard to tell. However, the monument is some 450 yards or 415 metres as the crow flies from Statue Road on the Stadium site, which would make it possible that both Richard Hart who said that the camp had been subsumed by the stadium and Alexander Bustamante who confirmed the site of the monument were correct. This hypothesis informed Figure 13, which proposes an outline layout for the Male Internment Camp in relation to current boundaries, based on maps of the area and comments by persons related to the camp. Archaeological investigation of the monument site

Figure 20 Bustamante monument inside Up Park Camp (Photo by Suzanne Francis-Brown).

itself and of such space between the monument and the stadium wall as remains relatively undisturbed, could provide some answers.

The Women's Internment Camp on Hanover Street in Kingston is also largely unidentifiable – the site is occupied by the National Land Agency, much of it now under a modern concrete structure. The Mona Family Camp – repurposed in 1943 from the northern end of Gibraltar Camp's lower level – has completely disappeared, as have all the buildings on that lower level. A University of the West Indies (UWI) heritage sign does indicate the existence of that camp.

Several similar signs and an obelisk in the area of the upper camp, sometimes termed Camp I, recognize Gibraltar Camp as the previous incarnation of the UWI's Mona Campus. Since 2007, rooted in the research that spawned this work, the UWI has undertaken some memorialization of the historical heritage on the site of its Mona Campus.[10] An obelisk, developed through collaboration between a Gibraltarian camp descendant and a UWI Mona Campus Heritage Committee, commemorates the population that lived and died at Gibraltar Camp[11] (see Figure 21: Gibraltar Camp obelisk). Heritage signs mark the few low-profile wooden structures

Figure 21 Gibraltarian Anthony Lara and UWI Mona Campus Principal Elsa Leo-Rhynie with the Gibraltar Camp monument in 2007.

Figure 21A Gibraltar mayor Kaiane Aldorino Lopez in 2019 beside a heritage sign marking the entrance to Gibraltar Camp (Photo by Suzanne Francis-Brown).

Figure 21B UWI heritage sign marking site of Mona Family Camp (Photo by Suzanne Francis-Brown).

which survive from the camp – now a bare handful – as well as remaining features. See Figures 21A, B and C as well as Figure 24E: Gibraltar Camp Church Bell and Figure 24F: Metal Water tank. The structures initially played an important role in the commissioning of the then University College of the West Indies. Indeed, its site was in part chosen for the camp buildings which could be repurposed as lecture rooms and laboratories, offices, dormitories, common rooms, dining rooms and faculty housing. Public Works Department official R.G. Medwen inspected the site, and in April 1944, early University College of the West Indies council member Raymond Priestley visited "the camp where several thousand refugees

Figure 21C Gibraltar Camp building remaining on UWI Mona site (Photo by Suzanne Francis-Brown).

[sic] from Gibraltar have been settled" and concluded: "The place where they were appeared to me to be quite a possible site for a university."[12] Postwar, the colonial government gave the camp a scrap value of £12,000, and a swift programme of refurbishment allowed the University College of the West Indies to take its first students in October 1948.[13] On the first Sunday in that month, the *Gleaner* which had written about the emergence of Gibraltar evacuee camp almost exactly eight years before, wrote:

> You go in through the main iron gates and there is the asphalted road leading through an avenue of trees, the buildings in use by the University College are right and left of this road.
>
> Right, are huts 19 and 24, now the men's halls. Hut 44 at the left has been turned over to the ladies. Largish, with a through air passage, the rooms are furnished with pieces of polished yacca and mahogany.[14]

Road signs, for Gibraltar Camp Way and Gibraltar Hall Road, continue to mark the area where the camp once lay. In 2017, an archaeological impact survey of a planned building site along Gibraltar Camp Way found a few artefacts of the period, which are housed in the UWI's Archaeology Lab on the campus:

finds were identified detailing the built environment and daily life of people who lived in Gibraltar Camp 1. Notable artefacts from this 2017 assessment include a British coin dating to 1933, a Vicks Va-tro-nol bottle of nose drops dating to 1931, and a variety of tableware ceramics imported from Europe.[15]

The campus archaeologist indicated an intention to continue investigation of those sections of the campus that fell within the old camp footprint, which remain relatively untouched by modern construction.

Buildings aside, the main material remains of World War II camps are graves in multiple Kingston cemeteries. The Catholic's Calvary Cemetery, the public May Pen Cemetery, the Jewish Cemetery on Orange Street in Downtown Kingston and the St Andrew Parish Church Cemetery in Half Way Tree, all hold remains of evacuees and refugees who died during their time in Jamaica. Close to one hundred persons were reported to have died during their residence at Gibraltar Camp, most of them elderly Gibraltarians.[16] A confirmed sixty-four are named on the Gibraltar Camp obelisk at Mona and the plaque notes that there were others. At least fifty-three were interred in Calvary Cemetery, based on a cemetery burial record at the Catholic Archdiocese Archives in Kingston.[17] However, many of these graves were untombed and some may have been buried over – with no commemorative marker extant. Dozens of internees lie buried in the Briggs Park Military Cemetery, alongside the remains of soldiers from many decades – some of whom might have helped to guard them. These and other graves from the time are a permanent, even if sometimes crumbling and largely unacknowledged connection.[18] See Figure 22: Briggs Park military cemetery.

A few artefacts of the camps also remain – most of them within the UWI Mona Campus which has grown out of the Gibraltar campsite and which acknowledges this site as part of its own physical heritage. The collection of the UWI Mona Library, the university's original repository, includes a model ship made by a Finnish ex-internee and presented to the wife of Camp Commandant Ernest Rae in the 1940s,[19] as well as a commemorative stone presented to the university in 1978 in recognition of the haven Gibraltarians found on that site. The UWI Museum, established in 2012, has also collected a painting of the Mona landscape by Italian internee Umberto Cattaneo (see Figure 23B) and a British military helmet found amid the old camp buildings by Martin Aub – a UWI lecturer whose father Rudolph came to Jamaica among the German and Italian internees from West Africa in December 1940. Additionally, there are unrecognized traces in material culture. It is said that in their workshop at Gibraltar Camp,

Traces in Heritage | 243

Figure 22 Briggs Park Military Cemetery adjacent to the National Stadium whose lights can be seen above the graves (Photo courtesy of Uwe Zitzow).

Figure 22A Joan Arnay Halperin places a stone on the grave of her sister Polish refugee Yvonne Krakowiak at Orange Street Jewish Cemetery (Courtesy of Joan Arnay Halperin).

Figure 22B Grave of Elizabeth Epsworth Lara at St Andrew Parish Church cemetery in Kingston (Photo by Suzanne Francis-Brown).

around the end of the war, Italian co-operators developed many of the sculpted pineapples, lions' heads and other concrete forms that adorned many gateposts of middle- and upper-class homes throughout Kingston – a style which still has adherents today. The Italians also made garden furniture from concrete, including two styles mentioned by respondents.

One of these has a curved concrete slab atop two curved and decorated uprights. Most ubiquitous, though, is a concrete form made to look like tree branches – said to have been used as fencing at the Alpha School in Kingston, but most often as benches. Steadman Bloomfield, in Gordon Town, St Andrew, recalled meeting various former internees while a youth in Papine, where his grandmother sold in the market. In 2007, he still had a concrete plaque, long mounted by his front door, resembling tree bark, which he said that he had got from these internees. Correspondent Rose Sharpley, whose family befriended several of the Italians, received one of the original benches, which she left in her brother's garden in Kingston when she migrated abroad some years later. She remarked that

Figure 23 Concrete benches originally made by Italian ex-internees and now an unquestioned part of the local landscape (Photo by Suzanne Francis-Brown).

Figure 23A Modern versions of the concrete benches (Photo by Suzanne Francis-Brown).

in copies by various local manufacturers over the subsequent years, the resemblance of the concrete forms to tree branches had gradually become less distinct. Sturdier versions of these wartime manufactures continue to adorn many outdoor spaces in Kingston, including educational institutions and the Hope Botanical Gardens – a continuing, though unrecognized, construction-related legacy of these World War II internees.

Figure 23B Painting of Mona landscape by Italian internee Umberto Cattaneo (Collection, UWI Museum).

Lived Heritage

Little experience of the camps or their residents remains in Jamaica's lived heritage. Many people had slight exposure to the camps and their residents whether through media stories – for the literate and the many who received information at second-hand – or as employees, vendors and unknown numbers of others who formed various relationships. These memories, already slight at the end of World War II, have had little to sustain them. A few poems by popular folklorist Louise Bennett mention the wartime experience, including the Spanish-speaking Gibraltarians and the refugees; but without an understood context these have little resonance and are rarely performed. Similarly, there is little acknowledgement of old texts such as the wartime commentary of A.E.T. Henry and little understanding of the context for St Lucian Nobel Laureate Derrick Walcott's postwar musings on:

> those raft-planked bunkhouses christened "Gibraltar"
> By World War II D.Ps, as if they knew
> We'd drift like displaced persons too, even further
> From Europe than the homeless Homesick Jew.[20]

The only aspect of World War II contribution given any official recognition in Jamaica has been the loss of life in military service. Hence any social or cultural connection to the wartime camps and their residents – initially weak due to relative isolation and discouraged interaction – has lacked reinforcement over decades. One might argue that this experience is common to many elements of colonial history where colonized citizens were not engaged in events affecting them. Albert Memmi of Algeria, writing about that French colonial experience, argued that colonial people were condemned to lose their memories because of loss of past history, loss of confidence and separation from participation in decisions taken about their own lives.[21]

However, while the colonial context may have thinned the level of local engagement and underappreciated its real connection and contribution to the war, there are some social and cultural – as well as material – traces of those interactions that did take place. Beyond diminishing personal recollections and thinned connections, there is the objective fact that some Jamaican families have links through marriages and children to Gibraltar, to Germany and perhaps to Italy. And though rarely recognized, there are some tenuous ties remaining among some of the former evacuees and internees who married Jamaicans during or immediately after the war.

Counter-intuitively then, it is not the Jamaicans, whose space was impacted by the incomers, who retain or foster the memories of this time. The strongest ongoing connections reside with the evacuees, refugees and internees who more robustly recall the period of disruption, the different environment as well as the safe haven in wartime. They and their descendants who have nurtured their stories have a link of interest to Jamaica and perhaps to Jamaicans. Many individual stories remain, some of them recorded; some of them published and thereby saved and shared. Some persons from all the groups have returned to the island to visit the sites where they – or their parents and grandparents – spent the war and have contributed memories to various projects; though the extent has varied by group.

Among the groups of refugees, only a few developed connections to Jamaica that were rooted in birth, marriage or death. Nonetheless, several refugees who were children or teenagers during the war have recalled the experience in Jamaica as a youthful adventure, undoubtedly removed from the adult responsibilities that would have impacted their parents. The experience of haven in Jamaica – though limited to only a few hundred people – also became part of the story of the Jewish experience of World War II. This has not generally extended to fixed physical commemoration. Though they faced similar threats and shared common experiences, the refugee groups in the camps in Jamaica were made up of individuals and families who had made singular or small group decisions to flee their invaded or increasingly insecure homes. Drawn together temporarily under national or other aegis to access scarce haven in a camp in Jamaica, they regained their prior individual or family focus as they sought after longer-term destinations and new lives. The Dutch refugees who spent months in Jamaica did have the assurance of support from their government-in-exile, which arranged the temporary stay through an appeal to the British government. The mainly Polish group received a financial guarantee from the American Jewish Joint Distribution Committee after an appeal from the Polish government-in-exile; however, the lack of active involvement by this government was a source of anger and disappointment among the refugees. There is no known record of any official commemoration of the connection to Jamaica by either the Dutch or the Polish governments, both of which had contingents of citizens in the camp. However, in 2020, a tree-planting event on the UWI Mona campus site, organized through the local Jewish community, specifically recognized the refugees who found haven in Gibraltar Camp.[22]

Among the persons who lived in the internment camps, there were also births and marriages recorded in both the Women's Camp and the Mona Family Camp – at least two marriages between residents of the Women's and Men's Camps. As with the evacuees and refugees, there are – albeit few – recorded instances of persons expressing a continuing connection to Jamaica as well as to the specific aspect of the camps.[23] These include the German and Italian internees brought to Jamaica from West Africa, the Germans and Austrians who had sought a new start and who were living in Jamaica when war broke out, the recently naturalized British citizens who were still penalized for being born in the German Reich, Italians in similar situations, the Finnish sailors also interned, and captured merchant seamen from German and Italian vessels. Of the civilian German men who married Jamaican women at the end of the war and who stayed in Jamaica for some time after, some later migrated. A Jamaican interviewee whose father was German recalled other similar families, some active in local celebrations of German events such as Oktoberfest.

Among the evacuees at Gibraltar Camp, there were births, marriages and deaths. The population of this camp was overwhelmingly made up of older and young Gibraltarians and young adult women. As well as the elders who died during the four years in Jamaica, some one hundred babies were born there between 1940 and 1944, some of whom proudly point out the birthplace recorded on their Gibraltar identity cards. And unlike the refugees who only married among themselves, a few Gibraltarians married Jamaicans – though most of these were young men from the Pioneer Corps group who stayed in Jamaica after the main group of Gibraltarians left.

Three stories from the lives of a range of interviewees with direct connections to the period help to show how wartime experiences created long-standing connections to Jamaica.[24] Aileen Mansfield was born at the Victoria Jubilee Lying-In Hospital in Kingston in July 1943, one of the youngest of Gibraltar's Jamaican babies as her parents were married in the camp in 1941.[25] In 2015, Aileen Mansfield Gordon travelled to Jamaica with her daughter and two young granddaughters, to visit the place where she was born and hear more about the places and events. She was able to take photographs with a Gibraltar Camp heritage sign in the old camp location on the UWI Mona Campus, to see the building – now an examination hall – where her parents were married, and to see old laundry cisterns where her mother and other Gibraltarian women would have regularly washed their clothes. She said that visiting the site had been always in her mind and was something she would not forget. "It was very enlightening to walk where my parents and my family had lived for four years," she said, "and to feel the wonderful vibes that the place gave me".

Two other stories related to death. In 2005, Gibraltarian Anthony Lara visited Jamaica, seeking to fulfil a family commitment that his father had been unable to complete during his life. His father was eighteen years old at the time of the evacuation and hence did not go to Jamaica with his mother Elizabeth Epsworth Lara and other relatives. Four years later, on the wharf to welcome her home, he discovered that she had died a couple of weeks earlier, just before the Gibraltarians embarked for home, and had been buried in Jamaica. Lara said that his father never recovered and always wanted to go and find her grave and, if necessary, arrange to take her home. Luckily for the search, as many Gibraltarian graves in Kingston's Catholic graveyard were not well marked, Epsworth Lara was Anglican. With the involvement of several Jamaicans, Lara eventually located his grandmother's grave in the old, formal graveyard of St Andrew Parish Church in Kingston. He was so pleased with the assistance he had received in his search that he was content to re-tomb the grave as it lay and has remained interested in and connected to events in Jamaica.[26] Figure 22B shows the tomb of Elizabeth Epsworth Lara. Her grandson is pictured in Figure 21, which records the unveiling of the Gibraltar Camp obelisk.

A similar connection was made by Joan Arnay Halperin, who searched for information about a sister she belatedly discovered: Yvonne Krakowiak, aged four, who was injured in an accident when her parents were refugees in Gibraltar Camp and who died at the Kingston Public Hospital. She was buried in the Jewish Cemetery on Orange Street in Downtown Kingston in 1942. Arnay Halperin, who wrote a family history titled *My Sister's Eyes*, visited Jamaica in 2014 to renew and rededicate her sister's grave (see Figure 22A).[27]

A written recollection from the period of the war related to the outpouring of good wishes received by Polish refugee Miriam Sandzer when her grandmother, her beloved "Babciu", died in 1945. She was buried at the Jewish Cemetery in Kingston. "Her funeral was something incredible," Stanton wrote later. "Most of the Jewish community from Kingston came, and those still in the camp were present also."[28] Stanton was one of the few camp residents known to have retained relationships with Jamaican-Jewish connections developed during her wartime sojourn on the island. There were reports of visits by some of these persons, to her London home, over the years.[29]

These emotionally charged experiences occurred in Jamaica and their accomplishment, in the twenty-first century significantly involved a range of Jamaicans; though the events and people that they commemorate were rarely recorded to have included Jamaicans. Stanton's deep engagement with the local Jewish community, recorded in her *Escape from the Inferno of Europe*, was unusual for camp residents and especially for the Polish group of which she was a part. However, Diana Cooper-Clark's *Dreams of Re-Creation in Jamaica* suggests that there were a few other examples where such wartime connections stretched on.

Beyond individual experience, the key factor in retention of this wartime connection over time appears to be rooted in community – enabling the ongoing refreshing and even memorialization of the shared experience.

While such community may be cultural – such as that shared strongly among the Jewish refugees – infusion of such experience into heritage appears strongest where there is a physical community and where there is memorialization and active commemoration. Among the Gibraltarian residents of Gibraltar Camp, who were members of one community and whose evacuation had been mandated by their (colonial) government, the experience of camp life in Jamaica – while a significant disruption – was closer to being a continuation of home life than was the case for any of the other incomer groups. A religious community ran that section of the camp at the request of the Gibraltarian government; the school system was on the Gibraltarian curriculum. After four years in Jamaica, they were returned en masse to the Rock in 1944 where many remained, in small communities, periodically refreshing their memories through stories shared with neighbours, friends and family as well as a national narrative of the civilian evacuation. Memories of Jamaican fruit and food, especially mangoes and breadfruit, remained with the Gibraltar evacuees who were children in the camp, and memories of having lived in Jamaica have passed down to younger generations and sometimes translated into an interest in Jamaican music and events in Jamaica.[30] Their family histories include the experience of the evacuation but also contain civil records marked with the faraway places where they found haven – Jamaica as well as the United Kingdom and Madiera. Up to the second decade of the twenty-first century, eighty-plus years after the evacuation, there were persons whose identity cards recorded not only their Gibraltarian citizenship but also the unique factor of their Jamaican birth. Here are families whose grandparents not only lived in a camp in Jamaica during the war but whose remains still lie there. Secondary sources, including museum exhibitions and historical texts as well as media articles, have contributed to the firm rooting of these connections.

This communal recall has also translated into formal commemoration of the connection to Jamaica and to the other locations where Gibraltarian evacuees lived. Memorials in Gibraltar mark the evacuation in 1940, with specific reference to the United Kingdom, Jamaica and Madiera (Figure 24: Evacuation monument in Gibraltar). The seventy-fifth anniversary of the evacuation was marked by civic ceremonies and an exhibition and included a lecture on the evacuation to Jamaica[31] (Figure 24D: Lecture in Gibraltar). In 2019, the rector of the Shrine to the Patron of Gibraltar, Our Lady of Europe, presented a replica statuette to the UWI Museum, as a formal commemoration of the evacuation – similar replicas having previously been presented to other evacuation locations (Figure 24A: Presentation). Interestingly, that act of commemoration was part of a mutual civic recognition – the twinning of Gibraltar and the City of Kingston, Jamaica, in 2018, with reciprocal visits by the respective mayors.[32] Mayor of Kingston, Delroy Williams, visited the UWI Museum for a historical grounding on Gibraltar Camp prior to his visit to Gibraltar, and he accompanied Gibraltar mayor Kaiane Aldorino Lopez, Culture Minister Steven Linares and rector of the Shrine of Our Lady of Gibraltar, Charles Azzopardi, on a visit to the Museum and the Gibraltar Camp site[33] (Figure 24B: Gibraltar and Jamaican Officials at Mona). Gibraltarians born in Jamaica while their mothers or both parents were living at Gibraltar Camp attended the civic function in Gibraltar, many showing off their Gibraltar identity cards reflecting that they were born in Jamaica (Figure 24C: Gibraltarians born in Jamaica during World War II).

The wartime evacuation experience – including the connection to Jamaica – became part of Gibraltar's national narrative and a part of its heritage. Much more so than was the case in Jamaica where the camps were sited, where any local experience of the camps was individual and where

Figure 24 Gibraltar Evacuation monument (Courtesy Anthony Lara).

Figure 24A Presentation of replica of Our Lady of Europe to the UWI Museum in 2019 (Courtesy UWI Museum).

Figure 24B Gibraltarian and Jamaican officials at the site of Gibraltar Camp on the UWI Mona Campus (Photo courtesy UWI Museum).

Figure 24C Gibraltarians born in Jamaica during World War II at the official twinning of Gibraltar and Kingston Jamaica (Courtesy Aileen Gordon).

Figure 24D 2015 Lecture at the Gibraltar Library (Courtesy Gibraltar Government).

Traces in Heritage | 255

Figure 24E Gibraltar Camp church bell now the centrepiece of a park honouring Caribbean leaders who are graduates of the university (Photo by Suzanne Francis-Brown).

Figure 24F Original Gibraltar Camp tank still serves the UWI Mona Campus (Photo by Suzanne Francis-Brown).

nurture of these and other incomers became a largely unacknowledged contribution to the war effort. The colonial Jamaicans, discouraged from shared "national" engagement with the camps and their residents during the war, then largely left this wartime experience behind with the colonial baggage as they moved to engage with the shared imaginary of political independence and nationhood. Traces nonetheless remain, and the more recent civic engagement may yet spark new interest in this largely faded heritage.

Notes

Preface

1. These various aspects of the site's history are explored in Suzanne Francis Brown, *Mona Past and Present: The History and Heritage of the Mona Campus, University of the West Indies* (Jamaica, Barbados, Trinidad and Tobago: UWI Press and UWI Department of History, 2004).

Introduction

1. "Gibraltar Camp, 1940-1947. Isolation and Interaction in Colonial Jamaica". A thesis in fulfilment of a PhD History degree at the University of the West Indies (UWI) Mona Campus by Suzanne Clare Francis-Brown, 2008.
2. Suzanne Francis-Brown, "Jamaica: Fixed-Time Haven and Holding Tank during World War II", in *World War II and the Caribbean*, ed. Karen E. Eccles and Debbie McCollin (Jamaica, Barbados, Trinidad and Tobago: UWI Press, 2017).
3. "The Defence Regulations in Jamaica", Letter to the Editor, *Gleaner*, from Civil Engineer Braham T. Judah, 14 July 1941.
4. The term "incomers" was used in "Gibraltar Camp 1940-1947. Isolation and Interaction in Colonial Jamaica", PhD UWI Mona, 2008, to subsume all the groups of persons brought to stay in the island but who were never considered as potential immigrants.
5. René Maunier, *The Sociology of Colonies. An Introduction to the Study of Race Contact*, Vol. 1 (London: Routledge and Kegan Paul Limited, 1949), 139–40.
6. Aimé Césaire, *Discourse on Colonialism* (New York and London: MR, 1972), 21–22; Albert Memmi, *The Colonizer and the Colonized* (Boston: Beacon Press, 1965), 87–92.
7. Jürgen Osterhammel, *Colonialism. A Theoretical Overview* (Princeton: Markus Wiener Publishers; Kingston, IRP, 1997), 183.
8. Interview with Frank Gordon, 2007.
9. Gaylord Kelshall, *U-Boat War in the Caribbean* (Annapolis: Naval Institute Press, 1994).
10. Francis-Brown, "Jamaica: Fixed-Time Haven and Holding Tank during World War II", 273–302.

11. Karen Eccles and Debbie McCollin (eds.), *World War II in the Caribbean* (Jamaica, Barbados, Trinidad and Tobago: UWI Press, 2017), 4.

12. Humphrey Metzgen and John Graham, *Caribbean Wars Untold* (Jamaica, Barbados, Trinidad and Tobago: UWI Press, 2007), 126.

13. Joanna Newman's *Nearly the New World, The British West Indies and the Flight from Nazism, 1933-1945* (New York and Oxford: Berghahn Books, 2019).

14. Miriam Stanton, *Escape from the Inferno of Europe* (London: Self-Published, 1996) and Robert Lemm with David Cohen, *één Rembrandt voor vijfentwintig levens* (One Rembrandt for 15 lives) (Amsterdam: Uitgeverij Aspekt, 2013).

15. Diana Cooper-Clark, *Dreams of Re-creation in Jamaica. The Holocaust, Internment, Jewish Refugees in Gibraltar Camp, Jamaican Jews and Sephardim* (Canada: FriesenPress, 2017).

16. Christian Cwik and Verena Muth, "European Refugees in the Wider Caribbean in the Context of World War II", in Eccles and McCollin (eds.), *World War II and the Caribbean*, 247–72.

17. "Exiles and Refugees. The Intellectual Migration from Fascist Italy (1920s-1940s)". https://www.dissgea.unipd.it/exiles-and-refugees-intellectual-migration-fascist-ltaly-1920s-1940s. Accessed June 2021.

18. Peter Hawkins Hall, "The Gleaner and the Russian Revolution", UWI MA Thesis, 1992 and Gloria Neal Bean, "World War 2, 1939-1945. The Daily Gleaner and The Jamaican Response", MA History thesis, UWI, 1994.

19. Spanish Town at 12,028 and Kingston with 108,973 were the only two larger concentrations of people in Jamaica according to the Census Department Bulletin published 23 March 1943 in Legislative Council papers.

20. TNA: WO 216/150 Jamaica General Administration 1940-1942: Jamaica Command Intelligence Summary, 1 April–30 June 1941.

21. TNA: CO 137/852/9 Evacuation of British from Europe 17 May 1941 & 4 June 1941. A memoir of one British evacuee and her family, *An Evacuee in Jamaica 1940 to 1945* by Esmé Brock was published by Titchfield Publishers in 1990.

22. "Evacuees", *Gleaner*, 26 October 1940.

23. <powsincanada.ca/tag/ymca>. Accessed 2021.

24. "Annual Meeting of Manchioneal Community Centre", *Gleaner*, 28 January 1941.

Chapter 1

1. Howard Johnson, "The British Caribbean from Demobilization to Constitutional Decolonization", in *The Oxford History of the British Empire: The Twentieth Century*, ed. Judith M. Brown and Wm. Roger Louis (Oxford and New York: Oxford University Press, 1999), 604.

2. TNA: CO 537/1329 Secret letter referring to Telegram #567 of 29 December 1944 on purported effort by *Trinidad Guardian* to acquire control

of Jamaican newspapers. The *Gleaner*, with its circulation estimated around 40,000, reached many more though being read aloud to the illiterate. The Board included prominent local Jews and representatives of prominent merchant houses.

3. http://www.jamaicaobserver.com/news/jamaica-8217-s-political-journey-to_106279?profile=1373.

4. TNA: CO318/442 Electors in the West Indies, 1939 Return. Gov. To SoS, 9 February 1939.

5. J.M. Lee and Martin Petter (eds.), *The Colonial Office, War & Development Policy: Organisation and Planning of a Metropolitan Initiative, 1939-1945* (London: Institute of Commonwealth Studies, 1982), 18 and Cosmo Parkinson, *The Colonial Office from Within: 1909-1945*, by Sir Cosmo Parkinson (Faber & Faber, 1945), 63.

6. TNA: CO323/1798/1 Internment of Enemy Aliens Jamaica Individual Cases. Council of Aliens FO to Robinson CO, 23 December 1940.

7. Richard Peel, *Old Sinister. A Memoir of Sir Arthur Richards, GCMG, First Baron Milverton of Lagos and Clifton in the City of Bristol, 1885-1978* (Cambridge: Privately published 1986), 71.

8. Ibid., 70–71.

9. Metzgen and Graham, *Caribbean Wars Untold*, 99.

10. Johnson, "The British Caribbean", 606.

11. WM MacMillan, *Warning from the West Indies: A Tract for Africa and the Empire* (London: Faber & Faber, 1936), 196.

12. Alexander Grantham, *Via Ports: From Hong Kong to Hong Kong* (Hong Kong: Hong Kong University Press, 1965), 33. Grantham served in Jamaica from 1938 to 1941.

13. Johnson, "The British Caribbean," 604.

14. Edward Denham (1876-1938) was Governor of Jamaica from 24 October 1935 until his death on 2 June 1938.

15. "Report of the West India Royal Commission: Bad Housing. . .Lack of Social Services", London, 28 January published in *Gleaner*, 24 February 1940, 11.

16. Moyne quoted in Kenneth Blackburne, *Lasting Legacy. A Story of British Colonialism* (London: Johnson Publications, 1976), 76–77.

17. Fernando Henriques, *Family and Colour in Jamaica* (London: Eyre & Spottiswoode, 1953), 42–43. Actual percentages for various racial categories are quoted by Lady Molly Huggins, in a memoir, *Too Much to Tell* (London: William Heinemann, 1967), 109: Black, 77%; Coloured, 17%; Indian, 3%; Chinese, 1%; White, 3% including Creole White. Lady Huggins' husband, Sir John Huggins was Governor of Jamaica for seven years, from 1943.

18. Ken Post, *Arise Ye Starvelings: The Jamaican Labour Rebellion of 1938 and Its Aftermath* (The Hague: Institute of Social Studies, 1978), Chapter 6 passim.

19. Henriques, *Family and Colour*, 169.
20. "Drama Grips Council as Man and Woman 'On a Mission' Halt Session," front page story, and photograph captioned: "Shocked Legislators", *Gleaner*, 7 April 1943.
21. Dudley Thompson with Margaret Cezaire Thompson, *From Kingston to Kenya. The Making of a Pan-Africanist Lawyer* (Dover: The Majority Press, 1993), 16. Thompson was born in Panama in 1917 to a Black schoolmaster and a "high brown" seamstress.
22. *Gleaner*, 21 March 1941.
23. S.R. Ashton and S.E. Stockwell (eds.), *Imperial Policy & Colonial Practice, 1925-1945*. Vol. 2, British Documents on the End of Empire. Series A (London: Institute of Commonwealth Studies in the University of London, 1996), 32–33.
24. Blackburne, *Lasting Legacy*, 85.
25. Relevant files include CO 875/13/16, PR Jamaica 1942, 30 May 1942, Telegram from Gov Jamaica to SoS Colonies re clash between police and Americans in May Pen.
26. "Help Needed, White, Male and Female", *Gleaner*, 8 December 1943; "Sequel to Regrettable Incident", 14 December 1943; "The USO Discriminates", *Public Opinion*, 11 December 1943.
27. "Social & Colour Barriers Operate", *Public Opinion*, 29 November 1941 and Editorial Page.
28. "Can This be True? Reported Move to Reserve Rockfort Mineral Bath for Exclusive Use of German Internees", *Gleaner*, 30 May 1941; "German Women Internees to Use Bath at Rockfort", *Gleaner*, 3 June 1941; "Current Items", *Gleaner*, 19 July 1941.
29. "1943 Newsreel – March", *Spotlight*, December 1943–January 1944.
30. WA Domingo, "Racial Segregation. Sir Arthur Richards' Legacy Found", *Public Opinion*, 28 August 1943.
31. Correspondence quoted in Ken Post, *Strike the Iron: A Colony at War, 1939-1945* (The Hague: Institute of Social Sciences, 1981), 103–04.
32. TNA: CO 137/854/14, Situation in Jamaica, 1 June 1942, Gov Jamaica Arthur Richards to CO.

> TNA: CO 137/854/14, Situation in Jamaica, 20 May 1942, Inspector P Long, Security Department, Criminal Investigation Department, Kingston, Jamaica to Commissioner of Police.

33. Huggins, *Too Much to Tell*, 129.
34. Ibid..
35. Petrine Archer-Straw, "Cultural Nationalism, its development in Jamaica -1944", M. Phil thesis, UWI, 1986.
36. "Estimates of Government Departments", subhead "Internment Camp, The Local Forces", *Gleaner*, 15 March 1941. The KSLI were the King's Shropshire Light Infantry. Also "The Day in Council", *Gleaner*, 27 March 1941.
37. "MLC moves to Censure Govt", *Gleaner*, 5 February 1941.

38. G. St C. Scotter, "Today", *Gleaner*, 1 May 1941.

39. TNA: CO 323/1800/4, Removal of Internees from West Africa to Jamaica, 11 August 1940, Telegram from Gov Jamaica. Return of telegram brought the information that the group could be broken down by Italian men internees of artisan class; Italian men internees of higher class; German men of higher class. Both the German and Italian women were classified as being of the "higher class".

40. TNA: CO 137/852/9, Evacuation of British Subjects from Europe 1941, 17 May 1941 and 4 June 1941, Telegrams from Gov Jamaica to SoS, Colonies.

41. Thompson, *Kingston to Kenya*, 32.

42. Edgar Pereira, "Letter to the Jewish Refugee Society", 15 May 1939, quoted in Joanne Newman, "Nearly the New World: Refugees and the British West Indies, 1933–1945". PhD diss., University of Southampton, 1998, 246.

43. TNA: PRO HO 213/1833, Italian Civil Internees Disposal Due to Lack of Employment in Jamaica 1943–1945, 11 November 1943, Circular from SoS Colonies to OAG re UK Policy on Italian civilians and merchant seamen; formulated for the United Kingdom but circulated to inform colonial governments. The file also included a comment from Governor Richards, recently moved to Nigeria, that "there would be strong local objection, in Jamaica, to leaving these people idle" and that they would not be allowed to work – the official policy but not the reality.

44. Finlayson, *The Fortress Came First* (Gibraltar: Gibraltar Books Ltd, 2000), 2–3, details the decision to evacuate women, children as well as aged and infirm men who constituted "useless mouths" in a fortress colony under siege.

45. TNA: WO106/2842, 30 September 1942, Telegram, Gov. Gibraltar from SOS Colonies.

46. TNA: WO106/2842, 1 October 1942, Telegram from Gov. Gibraltar.

47. TNA: WO106 2842, 5 October 1942, L.N. Mayle, CO to Major C Wynne-Jones, WO.

48. TNA: WO106 2842, 31 October 1942, Telegram from WO to Commander, North Caribbean Area, Jamaica.

49. TNA: WO106 2842, 7 April 1943, Telegram to Gibraltar from SoS Colonies.

50. Francis J. Osborne, *History of the Catholic Church in Jamaica* (Chicago: Loyola University Press, 1988), 379. A conversation with Fr Gerald McLaughlin S.J., then Curator of the Archdiocesan Archives at the Catholic Chancery, Kingston, was also helpful in situating the Catholic community in Jamaica during the mid-twentieth century.

51. *Census of Jamaica*, 1943, Racial Composition stated that there were 723 Jews in Kingston & St Andrew, and 1,259 islandwide. The census data was quoted in Colin Clarke, *Kingston, Jamaica: Urban Development & Social Change, 1692-2002* (Kingston and Miami: Ian Randle Publishers, 2006), 109. A somewhat higher estimate is given in Marilyn Delevante and Anthony

Alberga, *The Island of One People: An Account of the History of the Jews of Jamaica* (Kingston and Miami: Ian Randle Publishers, 2006), 196.

52. JARD: 1B/5/77 Report on the Organization of Gibraltar Camp as at 30 September 1941.

53. Richard Hart, *Towards Decolonisation. Political, Labour & Economic Development in Jamaica. 1938-1945* (Barbados, Jamaica, Trinidad and Tobago: Canoe Press, UWI, 1999), 4.

54. "Voices & Echoes, A Catalogue of Oral holdings of the British Empire & Commonwealth Museum", including interviews with soldiers and others in the UK during the war, includes at least two Jamaicans (Henriques, CS18 and Thompson, CS22) who said that most Jamaicans were happy with the British connection. This is also mentioned by some interviewees in the taped collection of the African Caribbean Institute of Jamaica (ACIJ) in Kingston, Jamaica.

55. Johnson, "The British Caribbean," 617.

56. TNA: CO 137/834, Jamaica Original Correspondence 1939–1940, 24 February 1939, Gov Jamaica to SoS Colonies, quoted in Post, *Strike the Iron*, 47.

57. JARD: Legislative Council Minutes, 10 October 1939, 390.

58. JARD: Legislative Council Minutes 1939, 390.

59. Peel, *Old Sinister*, 73.

60. "The Governor Answered", *Public Opinion*, 21 December 1940. *Public Opinion* consistently challenged the Governor. A 17 January 1942 report deplored the "small circle of bureaucrats who have shut themselves off from "the public mind and agitation" and whose concern appeared to be "to stifle legitimate criticism and foster internal dissension." Also "Plain Facts Give Lie to Governor's Claims in Fireside Interview", *Public Opinion*, 10 October 1942.

61. JARD: Legislative Council Minutes, "Governor's Address", 4 February 1941, 35.

62. JARD: Legislative Council Minutes, "Governor's Address", 16 February 1942, 40.

63. "Codfish Arrives. Acute Shortage Relieved", *Public Opinion*, 10 October 1942.

64. *Public Opinion*, 17 January 1942.

65. "Bustamante Tells All", *Gleaner*, 1 April 1942; "Sensational Charges Against Bustamante", *Gleaner*, 17 February 1942.

66. TNA: CO 137/854/14, Situation in Jamaica, 1 July 1942: Minuted note re 1 June 1942 letter from Gov Jamaica Sir Arthur Richards.

67. Peel, *Old Sinister*, 78.

68. TNA: CO 137/854/14, Situation in Jamaica, 1 June 1942, Gov Jamaica Sir Arthur Richards to HF Downie, CO.

69. Ibid.

70. TNA: CO 137/854/14, Situation in Jamaica, 22 July 1942, Gov Jamaica to SoS Colonies.

71. TNA: CO 137/854/14, Situation in Jamaica, 1942 & 43, Minute re Gov Arthur Richards' letter of 1 June 1942.
72. "Lord Moyne's Despatch Irks Federation of Citizens' Ass'n", and "Constitution Issue: Federation of Citizens' Asscns Claims Flaws", *Gleaner*, 23 February 1942.
73. Ibid.
74. Peel, *Old Sinister*, 81–82; Huggins, *Too Much to Tell*, 131. The paucity of other constitutional advance within the Empire during this period is noted by Jeffery, "The Second World War", in *The Oxford History of the British Empire: The Twentieth Century*, ed. Brown and Louis, 321.
75. W. Adolphe Roberts, "The Future of Colonialism in the Caribbean: The British West Indies", in *The Economic Future of the Caribbean*, ed. Eric Williams (Dover: The Majority Press), 60. Roberts was speaking at a mid-war conference in the United States, chaired by Eric Williams.
76. Roberts, "The Future of Colonialism", 37–38.
77. Ibid., 61.
78. TNA: CO 137/849/42 File 68714, in Hart, *Towards Decolonisation*, 176.
79. "Measures for Island's Safety", *Gleaner*, 26 August 1939.
80. Gordon Lewis, *The Growth of the Modern West Indies* (United Kingdom: M[onthly] R[eview] Press, Modern Reader Paperbacks, 1968), 182.
81. JARD: Legislative Council Minutes, 1939 War Address.
82. "Seditious Literature", *Catholic Opinion*, October 1940.
83. Hart, *Towards Decolonisation*, 88–89. Marquis had pointed to the fact that rank and file police officers were all black; commissioned officers, white or of noticeably light complexion; party leaders concluded that he was detained to silence this criticism of the race line which might undermine discipline in the force.
84. "Report of Conference on Civil Liberty in the Colonial Empire held in London Feb 15 & 16", *Public Opinion*, 3 May 1941.
85. "The Pathway to Detention", Leslie Ashenheim, originally published in the *Gleaner* on 27 May 1941, 3 was discussed in "Detention", *Public Opinion*, 31 May 1941.
86. Ibid.
87. "Stop the Tittle Tattle", *Public Opinion*, 7 June 1941.
88. "Review of the Detention Situation. The Home Secretary Lays Down Principles". By Mr L.E. Ashenheim, *Gleaner*, 29 January 1942.
89. TNA: CO 140/300 Jamaica, Legislative Council Minutes, 26 June 1941, 270.
90. "Govanah", Louise Bennett, *Jamaica Labrish* (Jamaica: Sangsters, 1966), 123.
91. "Detention Powers Branded Tyranical & Arbitrary", *Public Opinion*, 5 July 1941.
92. Roger Mais would be prosecuted for sedition after the publication of scathing article in *Public Opinion* titled "Now We Know".
93. Letter, *Gleaner*, 14 July 1941.

94. "The Defence Regulations in Jamaica: Opinions of Correspondents", Editorial Page, *Gleaner*, 18 July 1941.

95. "Defence Regulations – Mr Ansell Hart & the Exercise of Power & Authority", Letters Page, *Gleaner*, 26 July 1941.

96. "Criticism of Mr Hart's Recent Letter", *Gleaner*, 30 July 1941.

97. PNP 1941 Annual Report quoted in Hart, *Towards Decolonisation*, 125. Hart was then a member of the PNP.

98. *The West India Committee Circular*, 13 November 1941, 274, identified changes to the regulation corresponding to UK regulation 18B which allowed persons suspected of being Nazi sympathisers to be detained without warning or recourse to the courts; and Jamaica regulation 23 which critics had suggested should be brought into line with UK regulation 39B, which made it an offence to publish material prejudicial to the prosecution of the war or defence of the realm. Details on the regulations from *The World War II Reader* by Gordon Martel (New York: Routledge, 2004).

99. Hart, *Towards Decolonisation*, 207.

100. The events relating to this use of the wartime regulatory powers are set out in detail in Hart, *Towards Decolonisation*, Chapter 22, 194–208.

101. "Press Censor Baffled", *Public Opinion*, 19 July 1941.

102. "Classified Advertisement", *Gleaner*, 20 August 1942.

103. "Britain Rechecks Her Enemy Aliens", *Gleaner*, 10 April 1940 detailed the start of tribunals that would lead to a policy change on internment in May as reported in "Yard is Active", London 27 May 1940, reprinted *Gleaner*, 28 May 1940.

104. TNA: CO 968/68/13, Security Arrangements Jamaica: Enemy Aliens (including Enemy Missionaries & Seamen), 14 January 1943, Defence Department Memo.

105. "A Plea for Tradition", *Public Opinion*, 1 March 1941. Soulette was described as one of the older generation who believed implicitly in the greatness of British liberty and who was bewildered at the whittling away of these liberties.

106. Leo Fabritius, Correspondence with author, 13 May 2004.

107. Fred DuQuesnay, Interview by author, Kingston, Jamaica, 14 November 2007.

108. *Public Opinion* stories on crime: "Police Protection", in "This Week" column, 15 February 1941; "Thugs & Thieves of Corporate Area Launch Spring Offensive", 25 April 1942; "Criminal Assaulting of Women on Increase", 30 May 1942; "Violence", 21 August 1943; "Thieves Busy", 14 June 1944.

109. Thanks to Dr Jonathan Dalby, UWI, for access to his on-going research on "Circuit Court Prosecutions in the 1940s", October 2007.

110. JARD: CSO 2505/40, Sutton Street Court, Kingston, Bound Volume of CSO Notices, Letter of 27 February 1942.

111. "Criminal Statistics", *Blue Book (1945-46), Island of Jamaica*, 321.

112. Jamaica was not expected to be at significant risk. A dispatch to Governor Richards from Secretary of State for the Colonies Malcolm McDonald, 17 March 1939 in JARD: CSO 1B/5/31 Jamaica Defence Scheme. However, there was some media comment on the possibility of raids, following the development of the US Base in Clarendon, in south-central Jamaica. There was War Risks Insurance in place in case of submarines destroying stock in Jamaica, according to interviewee Ambassador Don Mills, who worked in the government information office and then the Treasury, during the war. CO 968/72/5, Civil Defence Progress, Jamaica, 1943, noted that the Jamaican government did not expect anything more serious than shelling by a raider or light air attacks without warning, but considered the provision of fire-fighting appliances to be justified because there were large stores of inflammable material, especially rum, on the docks.
113. Fitzroy Baptiste, "The European Possessions in the Caribbean in World War II. Dimensions of Great Power Cooperation and Conflict", PhD thesis, UWI 1983, 69 and 143–45.
114. TNA: CO 968/35/13 Trading with the Enemy Regulations, 1939; Report dated 25 November 1940.
115. "500 German Merchantmen Ordered to Return to Reich", Paris 23 December republished in *Gleaner*, 27 December 1939.
116. TNA: CO 968/68/5, Jamaica 1942–1943, 11 November 1942, Report on the Political Situation in Jamaica by D. Denis Daly, Commander, N. Caribbean Area, 1.
117. Kelshall, *The U-Boat War in the Caribbean*, xi. The Up Park Camp War Diary records the arrival, for internment, of German merchant seamen taken prisoner in engagements in the Caribbean – one of them between Cuba and Jamaica on 10 December 1940.
118. TNA: WO 106/2842, Troop Movements, 9 July 1943, Jamaica Local Intelligence Summary.
119. Baptiste, "The European Possessions in the Caribbean in World War II", 25–26.
120. Kelshall, *The U-Boat War in the Caribbean*, 14.
121. Alma Mock-Yen, Interview with author, 7 April 2005. Mock-Yen, then a youth living in Kingston, juxtaposed that distress with frequent disinterest in the war news.
122. https://memorialgates.org/history/ww2/participants/caribbean/connie-mark.html (accessed 20 September 2020).
123. *Gleaner*, 18 March 1942.
124. Vayden McMorris, Telephone Interview by author, Kingston, 16 January 2006: "There were British convoys in the harbour. So the U-boats used to hang out south of us . . . East Queen Street was quite a place for Germans wanting recreation." McMorris also mentioned the signalling story, which appears to have involved a German named Herr Dikkers who spent

weekends at Flamstead, in the hills above Kingston, was eventually interned and was said to have been exchanged for a high-ranking prisoners of war at Berlin's request (http://www.angelfire.com/stars3/eaglefl/AnUncommonLookoutFlamsteadaHistoricalHeavyweight.htm)(accessed August 2007); Sybil Francis, Interview by author, Kingston, 9 January 2005: "There was some fear, yes, because they knew that the boats were around. I don't know if it was so much invading the country as it was attacking the ships in the harbour." The story re Bournemouth also came from an interview with Francis; Alva Dawkins Telephone Interview 2004: "I remember hearing that German submarines were almost in Kingston Harbour. It was so frightening. We heard that the Germans would come off their submarines and visit the bars, especially in the St Thomas area. I don't know if it was true, but I remember hearing that"; Marjorie Humphreys Telephone Interview 10 January 2007: People talked a lot about the possibility of German warships coming to Jamaica and about German spies. The possibility of submarine landings even became the subject of a Home Guard training exercise, as recorded in papers of S.A.G. Taylor, then a captain in the "Home Guard", the popular name for the Jamaica Volunteer Training Corps under Major Moulton Barrett, M.C. Tactical Exercises in SAG Taylor Papers, Box B, National Library of Jamaica.

125. http://jamaica-gleaner.com/article/news/20170207/flamstead-historical-heavyweight.

126. Attacks within the harbours of Port of Spain, Trinidad and Castries, Saint Lucia are documented in Eccles and McCollin, *World War II and the Caribbean*.

127. The information on Theodore Deters is drawn together from newspaper reports and his own notice of appeal against his internment.

128. Report of the Secretary of State for the Colonies: *The Colonial Empire* (London: HMSO, July 1947), 1.

129. "Jamaica Gazette", 6 November 1942, reported in the *West India Committee Circular*, February 1942, 30–31.

130. TNA: CO 968/68/5, Telegram from DSO, Kingston, 11 July 1942.

131. *The Colonial Empire*, 7.

132. Budgetary details are set out in the Legislative Council Minutes. Figures for 1940 ("Governor's Address", Legislative Council Minutes, 4 February 1941, 9) showed the extent of the problem: domestic exports had dropped to approx. £3m compared to £4.6 for 1938 with significant drop in banana export accounting for most of the decrease. All commodity exports were down except fruit juices, hardwoods, tobacco and rum. Imports for 1940 were estimated at just over £6m, down a half million from 1939 though prices had risen to counterbalance the decrease. The figures would continue to decline and the deficit to rise. Discussion of the economic situation is also available in Post, *Strike the Iron*.

133. TNA: CO 137/854/14, Situation in Jamaica, 1 June 1942, Gov Jamaica to CO.

134. Linda D. Cameron, ed., *The Story of the Gleaner: Memoirs and Reminiscences* (Kingston, Jamaica: The Gleaner Company Limited, 2000), 122.

135. The food production campaign encouraged in the *Gleaner* is discussed in Bean, "World War II, 1939-1945. The Daily Gleaner and the Jamaican Response".

136. Grantham, *Via Ports*, 42.

137. "The Production of High-Grade Motor Spirit", Letters Page, *Gleaner*, 17 September 1940.

138. "Busta ready. . ..", *Gleaner*, 13 September 1946.

139. "Explain Please, Homer", *Public Opinion*, 11 October 1941.

140. Hart, *Towards Decolonisation*, 107–12.

141. TNA: CO 323/1846/6, Polish Jewish Refugees in Jamaica 1942-43, 13 October 1942, Gov Sir Arthur Richards to Lord Cranborne, SoS Colonies.

142. "Final Session of Legislative Council Last Wednesday", subtitle: "Discourage Immigration", *Gleaner*, 15 June 1940.

143. "Unemployment Barometer Shows Danger Ahead", *Public Opinion*, 9 August 1941. A 22 February 1941 edition of the paper had noted that there were nearly 22,000 unemployed in Kingston, and serious unemployment in Montego Bay, Spanish Town in St Catherine, Port Antonio etc. Also, "'Employment' in Legislative Council Report", 4 February 1941.

144. TNA: WO 216/150 (38), (41).

145. Ibid.

146. "Unemployment Barometer Shows Problems Ahead", *Public Opinion*, 9 August 1941.

147. "1943 Newsreel", *Spotlight*, December 1943–January 1944, reported the arrival of US business magnate Sam Zemurray seeking 10,000 labourers. The Farm Work programme is also the subject of a UWI thesis: "The US-Jamaica relations: The Farm Work Programme, 1943-1962" (UWI, Mona, 2000) by Sheryl Andre Reid.

148. "Po' Mufeena", Bennett, *Jamaica Labrish*, 1972, 89.

149. "Can This be So? Americans Pattern Local Employers – Uncle Sam Drives a Hard Bargain. Will Pay Only What He Must", *Public Opinion*, 18 January 1941; "Government Launches Islandwide Unemployment Relief Project", 26 April 1941; "The Minimum Wage", 12 December 1942.

150. For more on the Jamaicans who joined the RAF, see Patrick Bryan, *Jamaica. The Aviation Story* (Kingston, Jamaica: Arawak Publishers and Airport Authority of Jamaica, 2003), 50–55. The stories of some Jamaicans and other Caribbean people who went to war and stayed in Britain are told in *Caribbean at War. 'British West Indians in World War II'* (London: The North Kensington Archive at the Nottingdale Centre, 1992) researched and edited by O. Marshall. These include Ivoran Fairweather who joined the Home Guard as a schoolboy and was one of the thousands who volunteered when recruitment finally began in Jamaica in 1943.

151. Jeffery, "The Second World War", 313.

152. "Report of the Governor (continued)", *Gleaner*, 14 April 1944.

153. Interviews by author with Noel Fraser (2005), Sybil Francis (2005), Daphne Rae Morrison (2006), Allan Rae (2001 & 2002), Kingston.

154. Sir Howard Cooke, Interview by author, 16 January 2004, Kingston, Jamaica. Cooke became Jamaica's 4th Governor General.

155. Allan McDermott, E-mail correspondence with author, 13–14 February 2006. During the war, McDermott worked with the Lands Department in Kingston.

156. Telephone conversation with Kenneth Smith, who was posted in the eastern parish of St Thomas. Others indicating relative disinterest included Vayden McMorris and Fred DuQuesnay, both of whom were in Kingston.

157. Allan McDermott, E-mail correspondence with author, 13–14 February 2006. The term 'backra' implies white boss, singular or group.

158. Peter McCauley, Interview by author, Kingston, Jamaica, 14 September 2007.

159. John Dean in Marshall, *The Caribbean at War: "British West Indians in World War II"* (London: The North Kensington Archive at the Notting Dale Urban Studies Centre, 1992), 22.

160. Bryan, *Jamaica. The Aviation Story*, 50–51.

161. JARD: Legislative Council Minutes, 10 October 1939, 386–7.

162. TNA: CAB 68/1 His Britannic Majesty's Government: "The Colonial Empire at the Outbreak of War", September 1939.

163. Jeffery, "The Second World War", 313.

164. "Poor Response", *Public Opinion*, 21 December 1940.

165. "Through the Looking Glass", *Public Opinion*, 26 April 1941.

166. "Mobilising the Colonies", *The Economist*, 14 March 1941, Reprinted in *Public Opinion*, 4 July 1942.

167. "Whose War?" *Spotlight*, May 1942.

168. Ibid.

169. "Through the Looking Glass", *Public Opinion*, 31 May 1941.

170. "Naval Affairs", *Public Opinion*, 31 May 1941.

171. TNA: CO 137/854/14, Situation in Jamaica, 7 July 1942, Richards' handwritten letter to Downie, Colonial Office.

172. Peel, *Old Sinister*, 90.

173. Ambassador Don Mills, Interview by author, Kingston, Jamaica, 10 December 2004.

174. Noel Walcott, Interview by author, Kingston, Jamaica, 14 January 2005.

175. *Catholic Opinion*, January 1941, 37; *West India Committee Circular*, September 1943, 173.

176. Allan McDermott, E-mail correspondence with author, 13–14 February 2006.

177. The story of the cold supper shop was told by telephone interviewee Frank Gordon and by Richard Hart in *Towards Decolonisation*, 64–65. Hart said that the proprietor of Reid's Cold Supper Shop amplified the broadcasts

to attract customers who did not own their own radios; a practice ended when the Police Commissioner threatened to arrest him. The comment was from Gordon.

178. Hart, *Towards Decolonisation*, 64.
179. *The Colonial Empire*, 5.
180. Jeffery, "The Second World War", 313.
181. John Grinan who started *ZQI*, offered it to the govt at the start of the war as a virtual contribution to the war effort. Dennis Gick and Archie Lindo were its first two employees.
182. The *ZQI* Logbooks, held at the Jamaica Archives & Records Department, indicate the station's programming, including the inauguration of the daily news broadcast on Monday 3 June 1940. The Thursday 28 November 1940 broadcast log notes a seven-minute talk by JL Worlledge, Commandant of the new Gibraltar Camp. The Archives holdings do not include the *ZQI* scripts; however, Mr Worlledge's talk was carried in the press. Legislative Council Minutes for 4 February 1941 indicate that test broadcasting took place between 17 November 1939 and 31 May 1940 for one hour each Friday.
183. Jeffery, "The Second World War", 313.
184. "Info Office in High Gear", *Public Opinion*, 17 July 1943.

Chapter 2

1. Catholic Archives: Fr William Feeney, "Gibraltar Camp", Typewritten article, 29 January 1989. Fr Feeney, an American and Spanish-speaker whose brother Thomas was No. 2 in the local Catholic hierarchy, was priest at Gibraltar Camp from its inception to 1943. Feeney's "Native Sisters" are the Franciscan Missionary Sisters or Blue Sisters.
2. TNA: CO 91/515/12, Public Works Department, Interim Report on the Construction Works Carried Out at Camp Gibraltar, Mona, Jamaica, BWI, 25 July 1940–31 January 1941.
3. TNA: WO 216/149, Jamaica General, 3 August 1940, Telegram from OCT Jamaica to The War Office.
4. "Electives Continue Expression of Views on Island's Budget", subhead: "Gibraltar Camp", *Gleaner*, 12 March 1941.
5. "Councillors Demand Reason for Excess", *Gleaner*, 13 May 1941, 9. Newman, "Nearly the New World", 243, also observed the scant attention to local opinion.
6. Early newspaper reports: "Mona, Haven of the Refugees", *Gleaner*, 7 October 1940 and "The Feeding of the Nine Thousand", *Gleaner*, 21 October 1940. Also, TNA: WO 216/149, Jamaica General, 24 September 1940, Telegram from OCT Jamaica to War Office.
7. Catholic Archives: "Gibraltar Camp", 29 January 1989, Fr William Feeney, S.J., Priest at Gibraltar Camp, 3.

8. TNA: FO 916/71, Internment Camps for Germans and Italians in Jamaica 1941, Various correspondence 1940 and 1941.

9. This reconstruction of the sequence of events is based on newspaper stories and on brief notes in the War Diaries of the time, in TNA: WO 176/24, Jamaica Garrison: War Diary 11 November 1944 and TNA. PRO WO 176/58 Transit Camp Jamaica: War Diary September–November 1944.

10. Interviews by author with Peter McCauley, Luther George Lewis, Noel Walcott.

11. Catholic Archives: Typewritten report, n.d., p3. In box labelled Gibraltar Camp 1940–1945. The camp's population included a small group of Jewish Gibraltarians and a few Anglicans.

12. Months of discussion between Germany and neutral Spain, to clear the way for a backdoor invasion of Gibraltar, came to nothing. An August 1940 news report, datelined Washington, suggested that secret negotiations between the Franco government and a special British Mission had affected Spain's refusal to give the Germans free passage; and that this stalled the Nazi blitzkrieg against Britain as Germany hesitated to invade England "unless and until Gibraltar falls" fearing that the western Mediterranean fleet could race through the Straits of Gibraltar to Britain's relief. Finlayson, *The Fortress Came First* (2 and 62) and "Report Spain's Refusal Has Stalled Blitzkrieg", *Catholic Opinion*, October 1940, quotes an 22 August 1940 story datelined Washington DC.

13. Finlayson, *The Fortress Came First*, 2.

14. Catholic Archives, Kingston: Untitled typewritten document describing the camp, in a Gibraltar Camp file. The second group arrived in on 15 November 1940.

15. "1,100 Evacuees Now at Gibraltar Camp", *Gleaner*, 26 October 1940, 1 and "Nearly 400 More Evacuees Here", 16 November 1940, 1.

16. JARD: CSO 1B/5/77/1, 1944, Camp for Imperial Government at Mona - Payment of Wages to Evacuees, 19 January 1944, Acting Commandant, Gibraltar Camp to CS.

17. JARD: CSO 1B/5/77/220 - 1940, Report on the organisation of Gibraltar Camp as at 30 September 1941. Persons in need applied to the Catholic priests who made relevant recommendations to the administration regarding free issues of shoes, clothing, etc. from the Dry Goods Canteen.

18. Celia Mary Gomez and Josephine Mary Zammitt, "From Gibraltar Rock to Gibraltar Camp", *Catholic Opinion*, December 1940, 25. In addition, a 31 October 1942 Letter from the War Office to the Commander, North Caribbean Area, Jamaica, noted that the Gibraltarian evacuees "were sent to Jamaica much against their wishes" (in WO 106/2842, Troop Movements).

19. Finlayson, *The Fortress Came First*, 67.

20. Ibid., 43.

21. TNA: WO 216/149, Jamaica General, Outside Minute M.O.4/4/41 117.

22. TNA: CO 91/515/4, Evacuation of Civilian Population from Gibraltar [Parts 2 to 4, 1941], W.P.41.96, War Cabinet. Gibraltar: Further Evacuation of Civilians. Memorandum by Secretary of State for the Colonies.

23. TNA: CO 91/515/4, Evacuation of Civilian Population from Gibraltar [Parts 2t-4 1941], 4 June 1941, JP/FH.

24. "Five Gibraltar Evacuees Here", *Gleaner*, 29 July 1941.

25. "Chronicle of My Family", unpublished memoir by Aileen Mansfield Gordon, Gibraltar; shared with Author.

26. Gibraltar Archives: Introduction; "Jamaica;" Bayside School project, 29 June 2000, based on research and interviews with Gibraltarian evacuees; sourced in Gibraltar by Anthony Lara.

27. Finlayson, *The Fortress Came First*, 69, 72.

28. JARD: CSO 1B/5/93/1, 2 and 3, Census of evacuees taken at Gibraltar Camp, 31 December 1943. These three files reflect persons with initials A-C, D-H, and I-P respectively.

29. "From Gibraltar Rock to Gibraltar Camp", *Catholic Opinion*, December 1940.

30. "Nearly 400 More Evacuees Here", *Gleaner*, 13 November 1940. An interview with Amalia Fink, daughter of camp resident Josefa Castro and Jamaican Norman Ennevor who were married in 1943, confirmed that Castro and her family were Spanish refugees.

31. TNA: CO 91/515/4 Parts 2-4, 1941, Further Gib Evacuation, 2 July 1941, Letter from A.B. Acheson.

32. *Gleaner*, 13 November 1943.

33. TNA: FO369/3015, Plans for Returning Evacuees, December 1943, Report of CO meeting on Return of Evacuees.

34. Finlayson, *The Fortress Came First*, 147–48.

35. TNA: CO137/865/2, Refugees 1943-5, 20 September 1944, Gov Jamaica Sir John Huggins to SoS Colonies.

36. Spanish Vice-Consul David Sabio who was born in Spain and worked in Cuba before moving to Jamaica where he worked as a menswear manufacturer [*Who's Who in Jamaica*, West Indies (Kingston: Who's Who (Jamaica), 1957).

37. "Gibraltar Evacuees", *Gleaner*, 12 December 1944, 12. Also, Joe Gingell, *We Thank God and England. A Collection of Memorabilia about the Evacuation of the Gibraltar Civilian Population 1940-1951* (Gibraltar: Joe Gingell, 2011), 378.

38. Stanton, *Escape from the Inferno of Europe*; Robert Lemm with Cohen, *één Rembrandt voor vijfentwintig levens*, Joan Arnay Halperin, *My Sister's Eyes: A Family Chronicle of Rescue and Loss During World War II*, by Joan Arnay Halperin (JMA Press, 2019) Also unpublished memoirs by Manne Eckstein of the Polish group and Jenny Weinshel from the Dutch refugee group.

39. Testimony of Joan Krakowiak Arnay Halperin about her family who were among the Polish refugees. http://www.ajpn.org/personne-Isaak-Krakowiak-8397.html.

40. TNA: CO 137/854/7 Refugees 1941. Letter from P. Rogers, Colonial Office to A.W.G. Randall, Foreign Office, 8 November 1941.

41. David Regev, "The Exodus from Jamaica", *Jewish World*. https://www.ynetnews.com/articles/0,7340,L-4113958,00.html.

42. TNA: CO 137/854/7, Refugees 1941, 8 November 1941, Rogers, CO to Randall, FO. These conditions were stated, in correspondence from the Colonial Office, before the proposal was put to the Governor of Jamaica.

43. TNA: CO 137/854/7, Refugees 1941, 26 December 1941, Telegram from Gov Jamaica to SoS Colonies.

44. TNA: CO 137/854/7, Refugees 1941, 3 January 1942, Randall, FO to Rogers, CO and 15 January 1942, Telegram from FO to Lisbon.

45. Louise London, *Whitehall and The Jews* (Cambridge: Cambridge University Press, 2000), 6–9 and John P. Fox, "German & European Jewish Refugees 1933-45. Reflections on the Jewish Condition under Hitler and the Western World's Response to their Expulsion and Flight", in *Refugees in an age of Total War*, ed. Anna Bramwell (London: Routledge, 1988), 75.

46. TNA: CO137/854/7, Refugees 1941, 26 November 1941, Minuted note.

47. TNA: CO 137/854/7, Refugees 1941, 28 January 1942, Telegram from Lisbon to FO. There were varied numbers given in correspondence related to this group. FO sources list 165 Poles and four Dutch refugees (January 29, 1942, Telegram from Lisbon to the FO); and the Polish Legation counts 163 Polish Jews to whom visas were issued but said that some did not board the ship. These 163 included 68 men, 69 women and 26 children. (7 January 1942, Telegram from Antoni Balinski to Randall); both pieces of correspondence in CO137/854/7.

48. JOINT: S. Bertrand Jacobson, "Saved for the Duration. What is Happening to the 152 Polish Jewish Refugees Who Were Brought to the Island of Jamaica by the J.D.C.", 3 December 1942.

49. TNA: CO137/854/7, Refugees 1941, 14 March 1942, Telegram to Gov Jamaica from SoS Colonies; CO 137/854/8, Refugees 1942, 13 May 1942, Gov Jamaica to SoS Colonies. The correspondence does not appear to support Paul Bartrop (From Lisbon to Jamaica)'s figure of 500 Polish refugees.

50. TNA: CO137/854/8, Refugees 1942, 13 May 1942, Secret Letter to SoS Colonies from Gov Jamaica.

51. TNA: CO 137/854/8, Refugees 1942, 13 May 1942, Letter with enclosures from Jamaica to SoS Colonies. Some references state that the refugees were quarantined for typhoid, a fever spread by bacteria and also characterized by abdominal pain and diarrhea, rather than typhus which is spread by body lice and characterised by high fever, violent headaches and a rash.

52. Stanton, *Escape from the Inferno of Europe*, 200. Stanton stated that the camp administrators took great care that knowledge of illness did not spread outside the camp, but a story in the May 1942 issue of *Spotlight* magazine made reference to the refugees bringing twenty slight cases of typhus.

53. Interview with and unpublished talk by Maurice Tempelsman, UWI, 2008.

54. Tomasz Potworowski, "The Evacuation of Jewish Polish Citizens from Portugal to Jamaica 1941-1943", *Polin* 19, no. 2007 (2007): 155–82", agreed that the refugees seemed not to have been advised of the conditions attached

to their landing permits – that they would have to live in camp and not engage in employment outside it. Potworowski, and Paul R. Bartrop, "From Lisbon to Jamaica. A Study of British Refugee Rescue during the second World War", *Immigrants & Minorities* 13, no. 1 (March 1994): 48–64, both wrote about the Polish refugees; while Newman, "Nearly the New World", published by Berghahn Books in 2019, writes about Jewish refugees and the British West Indies during the war.

55. JOINT: Letter from Committee of the Polish Group, Gibraltar Camp, 25 May 1942.

56. Potworowski, "The Evacuation", 172 noted that there was particular concern relating to information on shipping and air traffic into and out of Kingston.

57. JOINT: File Notes 884–885, Jamaica, 1941–1944.

58. TNA: CO 323/1846/6, Polish Jewish Refugees in Jamaica 1942–43, 13 October 1942, Gov Jamaica Sir Arthur Richards to Lord Cranborne, SoS Colonies. The Governor referred to Lord Moyne's Secret Telegram #957 of 22 December 1941 and Richards Secret Telegram #867 of 26 December 1941. Also, CO323/1846/6, Polish Jewish Refugees in Jamaica 1942–43, 27 November 1942, J.B. Sidebotham, CO to A.W.G. Randall, FO.

59. TNA: FO 371 32654, 28 August 1942 from Polish Embassy to Randall, Foreign Office, London and CO137/864/2, 1943 Feb24-1945 Nov17, Enquiries about Evacuation of Polish Refugees from Gibraltar to Jamaica.

60. TNA: FO 371/32677, Refugees 1942, 6 August 1942, FO to P. Rogers, CO.

61. TNA: CO 980/35(5), WO to CO, 16 July 1943, Trinidad.

62. TNA: FO 371/32677, Refugees 1942, 7 August 1942, CO to Randall, FO.

63. TNA: CO 968/166/4, Jews & Refugees General Policy 1944. There were references to a transfer of over 200 Dutch refugees aboard a *Transatlantica* vessel, however they were not confirmed as arriving.

64. TNA: FO 371/32677, Refugees 1942, 5 November 1942, Telegram to Gov Jamaica from SoS Colonies. These unauthorized valuables included diamonds sewn into the hems and in other ways concealed by wealthy Dutch refugees. A later search of some refugees by local officials created problems which had to be resolved by direction from London. On 26 May 1944, *Public Opinion* carried a page one story, "Refugee Fined £30 for Finance Breach", following the discovery of US$516 in his Gibraltar Camp barracks.

65. TNA: FO 371/32677, Refugees 1942, 16 September 1942, Dutch diplomat Jonkheer Teixeira de Mattos to Foreign Secretary Anthony Eden; 17 October 1942, Randall, FO to Emmens, CO.

66. Correspondence with Inez Baker, family name Schpektor, whose family was among the first group of Dutch refugees arriving in Jamaica, 27 December 2004.

67. *Gleaner*, 19 March 1943.

68. TNA: CO137/864/2, Dutch Refugees 1943, 5 August 1943, Netherlands Embassy, London to Foreign Office.

69. TNA: CO137/864/2, Dutch Refugees, 20 August 1943, Telegram from SoS Colonies to OAG Jamaica. A note dated 11 January 1944 in CO968/66/4 [3] referred to a brief on the reception of Jews into the Colonial Office that had been taken to the Bermuda Conference in April 1943 and stated that Jamaica had undertaken to receive up to 400 refugees from Spain and Portugal as a result of the conference. It added that a number, mainly Dutch, had gone to Jamaica, and that the establishment of a camp in North Africa for refugees from Spain and Portugal would lessen the need to send others to Jamaica.

70. "Dutch Consul Leaving Island Deals with Refugee Problem", *Gleaner*, 30 November 1943.

71. *Gleaner*, 28 December 1943.

72. Regina Inez Baker. E-mail correspondence with author.

73. JARD: 1B/5/77/1 – 1944 Camp for Imperial Government at Mona – Payment of Wages to evacuees.

74. Newman, "Nearly the New World", 265. Newman, and Tomasz Potworowski, both refer to a party of Dutch refugees for Jamaica travelling on the ss *Magellanes*.

75. TNA: FO 371/42826, Political General, Refugees (WR), 20 November 1943, Telegram #362: Apportionment of Expenditure from 5 December 1942–31 March 1943 for Dutch Refugees ex ss *Marques de Comillas*.

76. TNA: FO 371/51165, Maintenance of Refugees in Jamaica (WR608), 24 January 1945, Saving telegram #27. However, a JOINT Report of December 1942 by Charles H. Jordan said that a group of 200 Dutch refugees arrived from Vigo, Spain, during his presence in Kingston.

77. Regina Inez Baker, E-mail correspondence with author, quoted another, older refugee, Felix Levenbach, as recalling that "the first (our) convoy of 172 people left Vigo, 16 Nov. and arrived in Kingston on December 4, 1942. The second convoy consisted of 110 people. Felix is now 88".

78. TNA: CO 91/522/8, Estimates for Gibraltar Evacuee Camp Jamaica, 1944–1945, File Notes to Estimates of Expenditure, 1 April 1944–31 March 1945.

79. *Gleaner*, 18 July 1944.

80. Catholic Archives: Fr William Feeney, "Gibraltar Camp", typewritten article, 29 January 1989; for publication in the *Gleaner*.

81. Claus Stolberg and Katja Füllberg-Stolberg, "Jewish Exile in the British Colonial Empire – Gibraltar Camp Jamaica, 1942-1947", Translation by Alfred Gutmann, *Hannoversche Schriften* 11 (1996): 85–102.

82. Stanton, *Escape from the Inferno of Europe*, 217.

83. TNA: FO371/42826 Details of Numbers in, arrivals, births and departures from Came 2, Polish Group.

84. A list from the Dutch Archive listing persons with Nederlandsche passports was sourced by former Dutch refugee Inez Baker through Thamar Barnett of the London Jewish Museum. Correspondence with Inez Baker 16 October 2017.

85. TNA: DO 35/1331, Asylum for Refugees, 30 October 1944, Report WP (44)608.
86. TNA: FO371/42826 Details of Numbers in, Arrivals, Births and Departures from Camp 2, Polish Group.
87. TNA: CO 91/522/8, Estimate for Gibraltar Evacuation Camp, Jamaica, 1944–1945, File Notes.
88. TNA: FO 371/42426, Polish & Other Refugees in Jamaica 1944, File #4 (WR), 20 November 1943, Saving telegram #362.
89. TNA: FO 371/42826 Political General Refugees 1944 file #4 WR 23 October 1944, Foreign Office to Colonial Office and CO137/864/2 Refugees 1943-45 Colonial Office to Foreign Office 23 October 1944.
90. JARD: CSO 1B/5/77/200, Minute 30, 16, note to CS.
91. Correspondence quoted in Cooper-Clark, *Dreams of Re-creation in Jamaica*, 101.
92. "Work for Refugees", Letter to the Editor by Polish musician and composer Dr Arthur Steigler, *Gleaner*, 21 April 1945. A subsequent news item noted that the writer's daughter had died in a concentration camp while he was in Gibraltar Camp.
93. JARD: CSO 1B/5/77/200, Minute to file 2122/44/S3, 12–13.
94. JARD: CSO 1B/5/77/200, Minute 30, 16, note to CS. The minuted discussion relating to disposition of these refugees noted that some had made friends locally and that the Commandant was investigating "whether these people are of a desirable type and whether they will be willing to take in their refugee friends as paying guests and on what terms". (Notes 3 and 10, 4 October 1947). CSO 1B/5/77/200, Gibraltar Camp Estimates 1947/1948.
95. Suzanne Francis-Brown, "Finnish Sailors among World War II Internees", *Jamaica Journal* 29 (3 December 2005–April 2006): 60–62.
96. TNA: CO 968/66/2, Enemy Alien Seamen, 2 September 1942, Gov Jamaica Sir Arthur Richards to SoS, Colonies. Official Order printed in Supplement, Emergency Powers Defense Act.
97. TNA: CO 91/522/8, Estimate for Gibraltar Evacuation Camp, Jamaica, 1944–1945, File Notes.
98. SFA: Camp Report 24, Male Internment Camp, 14 and 16 August 1944, 3.
99. SFA: Camp Report 33, in Connection with Italians, April 1946, 1.
100. Ibid., 2.
101. Interviews by author with Jean DaCosta and Vayden McMorris.
102. Jean DaCosta, "Memories of World War Two", 11 July 2007; also, follow-up telephone interview.
103. SFA: Swiss Report, April 1946.
104. JARD: CSO 1B/5/77/223, Gibraltar Camp Accounts 1940–1942, 26 January 1944, Gov. Jamaica Sir John Huggins to SoS Colonies Oliver Stanley re camp accounts for the year ending 31 March 1942.
105. Stanton, *Escape from the Inferno of Europe*, 202.

106. Regina Inez Baker, E-mail correspondence with author, 27 December 2004–15 March 2006.

107. Daphne Rae Morrison, Interview by author, Kingston, Jamaica, 11 January 2006. During World War II, Morrison was the teenage daughter of Camp Commandant Ernest Rae.

108. "Former Resident of Gibraltar Camp Leaves for the U.S.A"., *Gleaner*, 19 July 1946.

109. Manne Eckstein, "Events of my childhood", Unpublished, undated memoir written as a school project when she reached the US after spells in Jamaica and Cuba.

110. Jenny Weinshel, E-mail correspondence with author, 15 February–9 March 2006.

111. "Polish-Dutch Bridal at Jewish Synagogue", *Gleaner*, 16 December 1943.

112. "This Day in Our Past", *Gleaner*, 25 February 2005, C9, and "Catholic Church Diary", Gibraltar Camp, Catholic Archives, Kingston.

113. Regina Inez Baker, E-mail correspondence with author, 27 December 2004–15 March 2006. Polish refugee Manne Eckstein also recorded positive impressions of life in Cuba in the mid-1940s.

114. Eckstein, "Events of my Childhood", dated 1946, written as a school project in New York, USA. Shared with the author by her daughters during a visit at the UWI Museum in May 2019.

115. Leo Fabritius, conversation with Kuako Savolainen in Finland on behalf of author, 11 November 2004.

116. "Matters Before Water Commission", *Gleaner*, 9 December 1940, reports the Commission affixing its seal to a sub-lease of 200 acres at Mona, to the Colonial Secretary.

117. "Trams Now Stop at Matilda's Corner", *Gleaner*, 17 January 1944. The report noted that tramcar service to Papine was replaced with buses in January 1944, after 40 years.

118. JOINT: File 884–885, Jamaica 1941–1944, 17 December 1942, JOINT Report by Charles H. Jordan, 4.

119. Ambassador Don Mills, Interview by author, Kingston, Jamaica, 10 December 2004 and Sybil Francis, Interview by author, Kingston, Jamaica, 9 January 2005.

120. Frank Gordon, Telephone Interview by author, 26 January 2006. 'Peeniewallies' are a kind of firefly.

121. Jean DaCosta, Interview by author, Kingston, Jamaica, 2 October 2007.

122. TNA: CO91/515/12 Interim Report on the Construction Works carried out at Camp Gibraltar, Mona, Jamaica, during the period 25 July 1940 to 31 January 1941.

123. Catholic Archives: Fr William Feeney, "Gibraltar Camp", typewritten article, 29 January 1989; for publication in the *Gleaner*. Fr Feeney's labour estimate was higher than the government's estimate that Gibraltar Camp and the Palisadoes Aerodrome together employed about three thousand men.

124. TNA: CO 91/515/12, Construction of Camp in Mona, Jamaica for Gibraltar Evacuees, 1940–1941, PWD interim report on work carried out on the camp from 25 July 1940 to 31 January 1941.

125. "Camp Commandant and Doctor Speak from ZQI Today", *Gleaner*, 28 November 1940. The talk was later published as "The Rock in Jamaica", and reference retained in JARD: CSO 1B/5/77/220.

126. TNA: CO 91/515/13, Construction of Camp in Mona, Jamaica for Gibraltar Evacuees, 1941, 1 December 1941, Revised Estimate.

127. JARD: CSO 1B/5/77/30, 28 January 1941, Sam McFarlane, August Town Citizens Association to OAG Jamaica.

128. TNA: CO 91/515/12 "Gibraltar Camp", *Gleaner*, 17 July 1941, Letters Page. Letter sent to the SOS Colonies by Governor, Gibraltar, 14 October 1941.

129. This intent was stated in a newspaper report: "Evacuee Artist's Work", *Gleaner*, 29 November 1940, [6]7, which also pictured the Gibraltar flag drawn by one of the evacuees.

130. The main gate was close to the present Irvine Hall Gate into the UWI Mona Campus while the subsidiary gates corresponded to the present Post Office and Mona Bowl gates.

131. Allan Rae, Interview by author, Kingston, Jamaica, 15 May 2001.

132. *Gleaner*, 18 December 1940.

133. JARD: CSO 1B/5/77/220, Report on the organisation of Gibraltar Camp as at 30 September 1941, 4.

134. JARD: Legislative Council Minutes, 4 February 1941, 31, "Jamaica Constabulary".

135. "Police Transferred from Evacuee Camp", Gleaner, 24 April 1942.

136. William H. Feeney, "Gibraltar Camp", *Sunday Gleaner*, 30 April 1989 (also typescript in Catholic Archives); Section C; Also, "Here They Are", *Catholic Opinion*, January 1941, 35–37. The nuns included Sister Xavier, Sister Emmanuel, Sister Bede, Sister Divine Heart, Sister Berchman, Sister Francis and Sister Dominic. *A History of the Franciscan Missionary Sisters of our Lady of Perpetual Help, 1929-1995* (Kingston, Jamaica: Franciscan Missionary Sisters, 1996), 27, noted that four Blue Sisters worked at the camp during the period – Sister Maria of the Divine Heart, Sister Ita Maria, Sister Francis Maria and Sister John de la Lande. The cottages were designed to hold small families, but Finlayson, *The Fortress Came First*, said that they were not allocated to evacuees because of concerns about evoking jealousies.

137. Osborne, *The History of the Catholic Church in Jamaica*, 378–79.

138. Descriptions of the improvements to the church are mentioned in issues of *Catholic Opinion* newsletter, especially the April 1941 issue, page 59.

139. Finlayson, *The Fortress Came First*, 72.

140. JARD: CSO 1B/5/77/220, Report on the Organisation of Gibraltar Camp as at 30 September 1941.

141. Archdeacon Maxwell Conversation with author, Kingston, Jamaica, 11 June 2006.

142. JARD: CSO 1B/5/77/220, Report on the Organisation of Gibraltar Camp as at 30 September 1941.
143. Allan Rae, Interview by author, Kingston, Jamaica, 15 May 2001.
144. Finlayson, *The Fortress Came First*, 69.
145. Frank Tucker, Interview by Ruth Francis on behalf of author, London, UK, 26 January 2007.
146. Esther Chapman in *Catholic Opinion*, February 1941, 17, and on *ZQI* Radio, 3 February 1941.
147. Regina Inez Baker, E-mail correspondence, 3 June 2021.
148. Helene Krakowiak, later Arnay, Family History video interview by daughter Joan Arnay Halperin, 1989.
149. Regina Inez Baker, E-mail correspondence, 27 December 2004–16 March 2006.
150. https://archives.jdc.org Interior of the synagogue in the camp for 200 Polish Jewish refugees, NY_06871.
151. Anecdote told by Anthony McFarlane, Jamaican Jew, in conversation with Author, 2010.
152. "Evacuees Settle under Strict Rules at Mona", *Gleaner*, 28 October 1940.
153. JARD: CSO 1B/5/77/264, Camp for Imperial Government at Mona, Miscellaneous (Personal), 14 July 1942, SoS Colonies Lord Cranborne to Gov Jamaica Arthur Richards, enclosing 19 May 1942 letter to British Ministry of Health from Gibraltarian Evuacee to London, Joseph Sanchez.
154. Regulations listed in Finlayson, *The Fortress Came First*, 73–74.
155. "Gibraltar Camp WARNING Notice", *Gleaner*, 31 October 1940.
156. Ibid.
157. Newspaper coverage of this issue identified in the *Gleaner* only: "Five Fined for 'Gate Crashing' Gibraltar Camp. Judge Warns that Next Time Penalty will Increase", 28 November 1940; "Three Fined for Breaking Gibraltar Camp Rules", 5 December 1940; "Gibraltar Breaches Hail Many to Court", 7 December 1940; "Heavy List before Half-Way-Tree Court", 9 December 1940; "Entered Gibraltar Camp Without Pass", 20 February 1941; "Rm Sale Draws Fine", 7 March 1941. Efforts to follow up some of these cases proved fruitless due to the state of the records at Sutton Street Court.
158. "The Evacuees", Editorial Page, *Gleaner*, 26 October 1940.
159. JARD: CSO 1B/5/77/220, Memo on Gibraltar Camp Administration, December 1940.
160. JARD: CSO 1B/5/77/220, Report on the organisation of Gibraltar Camp as at 30 September 1941.
161. TNA: CO 91/515/6, Evacuation of Civil Population from Gibraltar, Financial Arrangements 1941, Minuted note re camp conditions and contributions to the upkeep of residents. This notes that the rate was agreed with the Colonial Office in London.
162. JARD: CSO 1B/5/77/1, 19 January 1944, Gibraltar Camp Commandant's Office to Colonial Secretary.

163. Osborne, *The History of the Catholic Church in Jamaica*, 378.
164. Photographs in Gingell, *We Thank God and England*, 287.
165. Gibraltar Archives: Box MP 0048 S/1 Repatriation from Jamaica, Staff Arrangements. The Nurse Probationers listed are A. Baker, E. McIntosh, M. Orfilla, E. Manser, all 3rd year probationers earning 25/- per week; P. Edwards and A. Cano, 2nd year, earning 20/- weekly; P. Zammitt, M. Brooks, M. Bear, C. Carreras, N. Battem, Y. Conquy, M. Valverde, C. Ferro, all 1st years earning 10/- per week.
166. Dr Margaret Williams unpublished manuscript on nursing in Gibraltar; shared with the author in 2018; also JARD: CSO 1B/5/77/220, Report on the Organization of Gibraltar Camp as at 30 September 1941, 2.
167. Conversations by the Author in Gibraltar following a lecture, From Rock to Rock, at the Gibraltar Library, 75th Anniversary of the Gibraltar Evacuation, May 2015.
168. Frank Tucker, Interview with Ruth Francis on behalf of author, London, UK, 26 January 2007. The JOINT Report by Charles H. Jordan noted that a young Polish man who had previously been training as a doctor, also interned at the Camp hospital and was to be attached to the KPH.
169. *Gleaner*, 27 October 1944, 1.
170. Recollection of Fay Azzopardi relayed in interview with Eddie Power, 2019, UWI Museum.
171. Eric Canessa, *They Went to War, the Story of Gibraltarians Who Served in His Majesty's Forces in World War* (Gibraltar: Eric Canessa, 2004), 228.
172. A.P.D. Sutcliffe, *The Military Mail of Jamaica. A Philatelic History* (Roses Caribbean Handbook No. 5, 1982), 71–72.
173. Information from Eddie & Joanne Power who interviewed Adelaide in Gibraltar; Eddie is Adelaide's grandnephew. His mother, Maria, was born to Adelaide's eldest sister, at Gibraltar Camp in 1941.
174. Epstein, "Events of My Childhood".
175. Cohen, *één Rembrandt voor vijfentwintig levens*, Chapter 15, translated from Dutch by Marjan deBruin Maxwell, Jamaica.
176. Regina Inez Baker, E-mail correspondence with author, 27 December 2004–15 March 2006.
177. "Lady Richards Pay Visit to Evacuee Camp", *Gleaner*, 8 November 1940.
178. Interviews with Allan Rae, Daphne Rae Morrison, Priscilla Harris, Kingston, Jamaica.
179. Regina Inez Baker, E-mail correspondence with author, 27 December 2004–16 March 2006.
180. Ibid.
181. "At Camp Gibraltar", *Gleaner*, 16 July 1942.
182. JARD: CSO 1B/5/77/220, Report on the organisation of Gibraltar Camp as at 30 September 1941.
183. Stanton, *Escape from the Inferno of Europe*, 217.
184. Ibid., 218–19.

185. Krakowiak's story was later told by her sister, Joan Arnay Halperin in *My Sister's Eyes: A Family Chronicle of Rescue and Loss during World War II*.

186. Regina Inez Baker, E-mail correspondence with author, 27 December 2004–15 March 2006.

187. Catholic Archives, Kingston: Church Diary for Gibraltar Camp; also, Osborne, *The History of the Catholic Church in Jamaica*, 379, which noted that the evacuees "wrote into their record" 93 baptisms, 52 confirmations, 9 marriages and 93 burials.

188. "Polish-Dutch Bridal at Jewish Synagogue", *Gleaner*, 16 December 1943.

189. TNA: CO 137/854/7, Refugees 1941, 8 November 1941, Rogers, CO to Randall, FO. "Semi-internment conditions" included confinement at night and not being allowed to engage in any business without special permission.

190. *Jamaica Times*, 23 November 1940 in Finlayson, *The Fortress Came First*, 79.

191. "Life Gets More Orderly at Camp Gibraltar Daily", *Gleaner*, 5 November 1940.

192. JARD: CSO 1B/5/77/264, Camp for Imperial Government at Mona, Miscellaneous (Personal), Correspondence re complaint by Joseph Sanchez.

193. Catholic Archives: File titled "Gibraltar Camp", Untitled typewritten document describing the camp.

194. Austin-Cathie quoted in Finlayson, *The Fortress Came First*, 74.

195. JARD: CSO 1B/5/77/220, 9 December 1940, Commandant's Office, Memorandum on the Administration of Gibraltar Camp.

196. Letters Page, *Gleaner*, 6 January 1941.

197. *Gleaner*, 8 January 1941.

198. "Dictatoritis" in "Today" column by G. St.C. Scotter, *Gleaner*, 17 January 1941.

199. JOINT: File 884–885, Jamaica 1941–1944, 17 December 1942, JOINT Report by Charles H. Jordan, 4.

200. Ibid., 4. The way in which the last point is made raises the question of whether refugees had been working while on their more frequent breaks.

201. Ibid., 88.

202. Finlayson, *The Fortress Came First*, 88–92.

203. The story is related in Finlayson, *The Fortress Came First*, 89–92. It should be noted that Gibraltarian evacuees in London, U.K. also complained of bad conditions, in their case, overcrowding and harsh treatment, as reported in "Evacuees from Gibraltar", *Times of London*, 26 July 1943, 2. For much of its life, the Gibraltar Camp Committee was chaired by Barclays Bank Director P.M. Mortimer.

204. "Police Transferred from Evacuee Camp", *Gleaner*, 24 April 1942.

205. Potworowski, "The Evacuation of Jewish Polish Citizens".

206. TNA: CO 137/854/8 Refugees 1942, 22 May 1942.

207. Polish refugee Miriam Sandzer, later Stanton, *Escape from the Inferno of Europe*.

208. JOINT: JDC File 884–885, Jamaica, 1941–1944. Cohen was a local merchant.

209. TNA: CO 323/1846/6, Polish Jewish Refugees in Jamaica 1942–1943, 13 October 1942, Gov Jamaica Arthur Richards to Lord Cranborne, SoS Colonies re Polish Jews' complaints.

210. Helene Krakowiak, later Arnay in a video recorded family history interview with daughter Joan Arnay Halperin.

211. TNA: CO 323/1846/6, Polish Refugees in Jamaica 1942–1943, 24 August 1942, Letter from Group of Polish Refugees at Gibraltar Camp.

212. JOINT: File 884–885, Jamaica 1941–1944, 17 December 1942, JOINT Report by Charles H. Jordan.

213. Eckstein, "Events of my Childhood".

214. Regina Inez Baker, E-mail correspondence with author, 27 December 2004–15 March 2006.

Chapter 3

1. *Gleaner*, 5 October 1943.

2. TNA: FO 916/73, German Internees & Prisoners of War in the Colonies 1941, 24 March 1941, CS Jamaica to H. Beckett, CO.

3. Ibid.

4. TNA: CO 980/35, Civilian Internees in Jamaica 1943–1944, 31 July 1943, Telegram from OAG Jamaica to SoS Colonies.

5. TNA: WO 106/5124A, Report on visits by Lt Col N.J. Darling to Trinidad, Jamaica & Bermuda, 10.

6. World War I Detention Centre at Up Park Camp held several hundred German sailors taken prisoner during actions by British vessels.

7. TNA: WO 216/149, Jamaica General, 18 July 1939, Jamaica Defence Scheme. Report by Secretary of Local Defence Committee. The site is around the present location of Jamaica's National Stadium.

8. "Interned at Camp", *Gleaner*, 14 September 1939, 5. The detention barracks, colloquially known as Red Fence, are still used by the military at Up Park Camp.

9. "Was a Canard", *Gleaner*, 30 October 1939.

10. Swiss Consul Reports from Jamaica, in SFA: E2200.179 1971/169/4 Lagerberische 1942–1945.

11. JARD: Legislative Council Minutes, 5 March 1940, 79.

12. SFA: E2200.179 1971/169/5 Correspondence, 1942–1947, Grantham CSO to Swiss Vice-Consul, 19 April 1940 re letters of 17 February and 13, 14, 18 March 1940.

13. TNA: WO 216/149, Jamaica General 19 April 1940, from Grantham, Colonial Secretary; 26 August 1940, OCT Jamaica to WO.

14. TNA: WO 216/149, Jamaica General, 21 December 1940, War Office to OCT Jamaica.

15. Bob Moore and Kent Fedorowich, *The British Empire and Its Italian Prisoners of War, 1940-1947* (Basingstoke: Palgrave, 2002), 18.

16. Ibid., 19.

17. SFA: E2200.179 1971/169/4 Lagerberische 1942–1945 Camp Report 12, Male Internment Camp, 21–24 September 1942, 25.

18. TNA: CO 323/1796/6, Prisoner of War Information Bureau, Internment Camp Notice.

19. Sutcliffe, *The Military Mail of Jamaica*, 66. The stamp referenced is Figure 112 on page 75.

20. Moore and Fedorowich, *The British Empire*, 228. The authors also referred (page 220) to 10 Italians, held in Jamaica, who were brought to the UK after the war and taken overland with a police escort, to Milan.

21. The men are listed among the war graves at Briggs Park Military Cemetery, Up Park Camp, Jamaica, by the Commonwealth Graves Commission. While there were Italian merchant vessels and naval vessels operating in the Caribbean, the source of this group of Italians has not been identified.

22. Ibid., 230.

23. TNA: WO 106/5124, Report of Visit by Lt. Col. N.J. Darling to Trinidad, Jamaica & Bermuda, March–May 1945, 10.

24. Some of the spellings have been corrected based on later reports. Note that Theo Deters would be sent home, under an exchange programme in September 1940: "Deters to be sent Home", *Gleaner*, 27 September 1940.

25. Arnold Von Der Porten, *The Nine Lives of Arnold. The Story of My Life: Hamburg Germany 1917 to Leaving Jamaica BWI, 1953* (USA: Author House, 2001, 2007), 192.

26. Newspaper reports on the detentions and releases identified Jews among the men as Dr Lobbenberg, Fritz Lobbenberg, Fritz Lackenbach. News stories referring to the Jewish men include: "Move to Get Aliens Enemies Liberated, Beginning with German Jews", *Gleaner*, 11 September 1939; "Four Interned Enemies Are Released", *Gleaner*, 16 November 1939. There were also Jews among the naturalised British citizens of German origin who would be interned in 1940.

27. Fox, "German & European Jewish Refugees 1933-1945", 75.

28. London, *Whitehall and the Jews*, 1, 8, 9.

29. Newman, *Nearly the New World*.

30. Cwik and Muth, "European Refugees in the Wider Caribbean".

31. "German is Made a Naturalised Citizen", *Gleaner*, 22 May 1939.

32. "Now a Britisher", *Gleaner*, 7 October 1939.

33. "All is Well with Interned Germans", *Gleaner*, 14 September, 5; the friendly headline matched by a story that the inmates were making the best of conditions which would shortly improve.

34. "Date set for Hearing of interned Aliens' Appeals", *Gleaner*, 22 September 1939.

35. "Interned Aliens", *Gleaner*, 7 October 1939.

36. "Ten Enemy Aliens Sent to Camp", *Gleaner*, 20 May 1940.

37. London, *Whitehall and the Jews*, 170.

38. "Recent Incident in Large Concern in Kingston", *Gleaner*, 29 May 1940.

39. Colonial Official George Hall provided these statistics in June 1941, in response to a parliamentary question from Mr Wedgewood.

40. "All Aliens Must be Registered", *Gleaner*, 5 September 1939.
41. "Enemy Alien Is Sent to Prison", *Gleaner*, 21 May 1940.
42. TNA: [CO968 68 13[9] Jamaica: Enemy Aliens; and 'German Women Here', *Gleaner*, 1 June 1940.
43. TNA: CO 968/68/12 1942-1943 Security Arrangements Jamaica, Case of Carol Richter.
44. "Five Internees are Released on Grounds they Are Naturalised British Subjects", *Gleaner*, 25 August 1941, 7.
45. TNA: CO968 64 11 Internment of Enemy Aliens (Policy), SoS Colonies to Gov Richards, 28 March 1942.
46. TNA: CO 968/64/11 Internment of Enemy Aliens [Policy, Telegram #274 from Governor Jamaica to SoS, Colonies, 8 April 1942.
47. TNA: CO968 64 11 Internment of Enemy Aliens [Policy], Telegram #14381/2/42 To Governor (Sir A. Richards) from Secretary of State for the Colonies; 13 June 1942.
48. *The Gleaner* listed these as Paraseel, but a reference in the Catholic Archives's files gives the surname as Paracchini, noting that Giovanni Paracchini was a planter in Port Maria, St Mary.
49. TNA: CO 968/68/9 Security Cases Telegram from Governor Jamaica to SOS Colonies, 7 August 1942; CO 968/68/11 Jamaica Detainees Secret Telegram Governor Jamaica to SOS Colonies, 21 September 1942.
50. Ibid.
51. TNA: CO968 68 13[9] Jamaica: Enemy Aliens.
52. "Br. Honduras Alien Enemy", *Gleaner*, 30 October 1939.
53. There have been references, including Ken Post quoting Sir Arthur Richards, which place Bustamante at Gibraltar Camp; however a letter to the Executive Committee of the Bustamante Industrial Trade Union from Inspector Peter Long of the Criminal Investigation Department, stating that letters to the labour leader at "the internment camp, Up Park Camp, must come through this Office prior to delivery at the Camp" confirms a clear statement from Gib Camp resident Allan Rae, son of Camp Commandant Ernest Rae (Interview with Author 15 May 2001) that Bustamante was never held there. Long's letter quoted in Hart, *Towards Decolonisation*, 87.
54. Hart, *Towards Decolonisation*, 82.
55. Ralph Thompson, *View from Mount Diablo*, An Annotated Edition edited by John Lennard, 51–54.
56. Hart, *Towards Decolonisation*, 88–89.
57. *The Memoirs of Lady Bustamante* (Kingston: Kingston Publishers Limited, 1997) 130.
58. "Mr Scotter and Mr Williams Are Released", *Gleaner*, 13 October 1941.
59. "What History Teaches", *Gleaner*, 21 June 1941.
60. TNA: CO968 68 6, Jamaica Detainees Domingo, Extract of Official Report 10 March 1943.
61. Another writer, Roger Mais, was prosecuted in summer 1944 for breaching Section 23 of the Jamaica Defence Regulations and sentenced to

six months in prison. *Public Opinion*, which published the offending article, "Now We Know", was fined £200.

62. The governor's efforts to quash these unions and disable their personnel were discussed earlier under the use of the Jamaica Defence Regulations. Details would later be given by Richard Hart in *Towards Decolonisation*.

63. *Gleaner* reports 18 and 19 March 1943.

64. Richard Hart, E-mail correspondence with author, 7–11 January 2005.

65. TNA: CO 968/35/13 Trading with the Enemy Regulations, 1939; Report dated 25 November 1940.

66. https://www.britishpathe.com/video/belligerent-ships-in-usa-ports, 1939 (accessed May 2021).

67. "Enemy Aliens at Camp Number Close on 140", *Gleaner*, 5 March 1940, 19.

68. "Nazi Ship held by British was to Come Here", *Gleaner*, 27 December 1939; "Seized German Ship now Lawful Prize", *Gleaner*, 23 April 1940.

69. *Gleaner*, 4 March 1940.

70. *Gleaner*, 24 October 1940.

71. TNA: Letter from OC Troops to War Office, 367 cipher 2 July 1940. Also, "220 More Germans Now at Up Park Camp", *Gleaner*, 9 July 1940, 7. The *Jamaica Producer* was struck by torpedoes in March 1943: https://uboat.net/allies/merchants/ship/2767.html.

72. TNA: CO 323/1800/5 Letter from OC Troops Jamaica to War Office; 496 Cypher 14/8. This expansion at an estimated cost of £15,000, required spending approval and importation of lumber from Canada or America to replace local stock and material depleted by construction of the Gibraltar Camp, which had begun in the summer and was still ongoing.

73. *Gleaner*, 13 December 1940.

74. Von Der Porten, *The Nine Lives of Arnold*, 266.

75. SFA: E2200.179 1971/169/5 Correspondence, 1942–1947, List of German ships from which internees were recorded in the Male Internment Camp, February 1942, in correspondence sent from Swiss Consul to Swiss Legation Special Division, London.

76. TNA: CO 968/68/11 Jamaica Detainees.

77. "No Permanent Residence Here for Internees", *Gleaner*, 4 June 1946, 9; also correspondence.

78. TNA: WO 216/149 Jamaica General, 14 August 1940, OCT Jamaica to War Office. The cost of maintaining the men was calculated at 1/11d per man night in CO 968/36/11(2), 10 June 1941.

79. TNA: CO 323/1798/5[8] Letter to Mr Dawe.

80. The Umuahia Government College was closed down on 4 July 1940 and the facility was repurposed as an internment camp for enemy aliens starting with those detained in the Cameroons: Terri Ochiagha, *Achebe and Friends at Unuahia: The Making of a Literary Elite* (Woodbridge: Boydell & Brewer, 2015), 43.

81. TNA: CO323 1 798 1[4] Officer Administering the Govt of Nigeria to SoS Colonies, 17 June 1940.

82. TNA: CO 323/1798/5 Internment of Enemy Aliens, Cypher Telegram from SoS Colonies to Officer Administering the Govt of Nigeria, 1 June 1940. The telegram was in response to an indication from the Nigerian authorities that internment of Germans on the Cameroons plantations might become necessary.

83. SFA: Several camp reports include lists of German internees at the male and female internment camps. These reports on the various camps visited by the Swiss Consul and his wife are archived in the Swiss Federal Archive under E2200.179 1971/169/4 Lagerberische über deutsche, italienische, jüdische Interessen 1942-1945, alongside correspondence and messages archived in E2200.179, 1971/169/5. Thanks especially to Scientific Advisor Daniel Bourgeois, Swiss Federal Archives for assistance in accessing some of this large trove of information in 2004. In these notes, the Camp Reports are referenced by their numbers and dates.

84. TNA: CO 323/1800/4 Telegram of 31 October 1940 #1491.

85. Especially correspondence in TNA: CO537/1290 Enemy Missionaries.

86. TNA: CO323/1753/12 German Activities, December 1939 (translated from German by Lutz Pershmann).

87. Correspondence with Uwe Zitzow, who was born in Cameroon and interned in Jamaica with his family.

88. A reference to Italians working with the firm of Cappa and D'Alberto in Nigeria having been interned in Jamaica: Imeh Udonkim, "Cappa and D'Alberto, New Realities and New Thinking", *Nigerian Business Review* (1986): 47–50 from Wikipedia article on Cappa & D'Alberto PLC. Most of the Italians were, however interned in Gold Coast, and at least some are described as miners.

89. CO 968/36/10(6) Letter from Camp Leader, Male Camp, Jamaica to Italian Ambassador, USA, 9 January 1941.

90. TNA: CO 323/1800/4 Telegram from Governor Sierra Leone to Governor Jamaica, 6 September 1940; CO 968/36/10 Letter from Govt House Sierra Leone to Lord Lloyd of Dolobran, 31 December 1940 in Trading with the Enemy Regulations, 1939; CO 968/35/13 Report dated 25 November 1940.

91. TNA: CO323 1800 6[4] Removal of internees from West Africa to Jamaica: transfer of non-enemy aliens detained under defence regulations.

92. Sutcliffe, *The Military Mail of Jamaica*, 66.

93. TNA: CO 323/1798/1, Internment of Enemy Aliens Jamaica, Individual Cases, August 1940, Minuted Note #29 as well as CO 968/45/3, 23 May 1941, War Office to Colonial Office. While the continent would see significant action in North Africa, there was concern over security, especially in countries with former German allegiances, such as British Cameroon.

94. TNA: CO 323/1798/1 Report in [6–7].

95. National Archives of Canada: War Diary, Up Park Camp, Jamaica, Entry for 3 December 1940. The number of persons arriving varied in other reports. TNA: WO 216/149 JG 106 Report of Defence Committee on Events 1 October to 31 December 1940 gave numbers of 447 males, 78 females and 39 children.

96. "More Enemy Aliens Arrive", *Gleaner*, 5 December 1940, 1.

97. TNA: CO 968/45/4 Transfer of POWs to West Africa, Minuted note, W Robinson 28 August 1941.

98. "Interned Germans to be Released", *Gleaner*, 21 July 1941.

99. The number of men is differently stated in some reports, and reflects changing circumstances. In the case of the Italians, the Swiss noted that at least one couple was moved to the Mona Family Camp with the German families, but subsequently opted to become co-operators and were moved over to Gibraltar Camp (SFA: Camp Report 34, 1946).

100. Francis-Brown, "Finnish Sailors among World War II Internees", 60–62.

101. YMCA: Conrad Hoffmann Jr., YMCA Report on Visit to Male Internment Camp, 20–28 March 1942.

102. Jamaica Gazette Supplement 239, 17 July 1942.

103. TNA: FO916/71, Internment Camps for Germans & Italians in Jamaica 1941(Part 2 of file), 6 February 1941, Parliamentary Question: Jamaica (Refugees).

104. *UK Parliament Hansard* Vol 370, House of Commons, Jamaica, 26 March 1941.

105. TNA: CO 968/68/9 Letters.

106. Von Der Porten, *The Nine Lives of Arnold*.

107. Rudolph Aub, unpublished memoir, 1988, 8. Collection of St Andrew High School museum, Kingston, Jamaica.

108. AICRC, Geneva: M. Roth, "Report on the Male Internment Camp", 8 July 1942 (original in French). The Jewish internees had been separated from the anti-Semitic Germans after several complaints, as noted in CO968/35/13, 10 January 1941, From OAG Jamaica.

109. SFA: E2200.179 1971/169/4 Lagerberische 1942–1945, Camp Report 12, Male Internment Camp, 12–24 September 1942.

110. Ibid., 38.

111. SFA: Camp Report 16, Male Internment Camp, 26–29 July 1943, 15.

112. Ibid.

113. Ibid., 14–15.

114. Ibid., 16–19.

115. SFA: Camp Report 19, Male Internment Camp, 25 and 29 November 1943.

116. SFA: Camp Report 22, Male Internment Camp, 23 March 1944, 7.

117. SFA: Camp Report 12, Male Internment Camp, 21–24 September 1942, 2.

118. Boundaries from sketch of Up Park Camp Male Internment Camp in Sutcliffe, *The Military Mail of Jamaica*.

119. Peter McCauley, former soldier, interview with author 14 September 2007.

120. Von Der Porten, *The Nine Lives of Arnold*, 245.

121. Richard Hart, E-mail correspondence with author, 2005.

122. SFA: Camp Report 12, Male Internment Camp 21–24 September 1942, 2.

123. The reference to twenty-eight units emerges from a reference to twenty-eight hut leaders, in SFA: Camp Report 16, July 1943.
124. YMCA: Conrad Hoffmann Jr., Report on 20–28 March 1942 visit to the Male Internment Camp.
125. E-mail correspondent with Richard Hart, 2005.
126. SFA: Camp Report 12, Male Internment Camp 21–24 September 1942.
127. SFA: Camp Report 16, 26, 27 and 29 July 1943, 19.
128. Ibid., 2.
129. SFA: Camp Report 12, Male Internment Camp, 21–24 September 1942, 4. Confirmed in mid-1942 Red Cross report.
130. SFA: Camp Report 16, Male Internment Camp, 26, 27 and 29 July 1943, 4.
131. SFA: Camp Report 16, Male Internment Camp, 26, 27 and 29 July 1943.
132. IRDC Archive: Roth; also reports from the Swiss Consul in Jamaica during 1942 and 1943, at the Swiss Federal Archive.
133. SFA: Camp Report 24, Male Internment Camp, 14 and 16 August 1944.
134. TNA: DO35/1694 Canadian Troops in Oct25 file] Particulars of Canadian Troops Employed at Jamaica, Nassau and Bermuda.
135. National Archives of Canada: War Diary, Entries for 4 November and 7 November 1940.
136. Regiments Serving in Jamaica, http://www.jamaicanfamilysearch.com/Members/r/Regiment.htm (accessed September 2020)
137. SFA: Camp Report 16, Male Internment Camp, 26, 27 and 29 July 1943, 7.
138. SFA: Report 16, Male Internment Camp, 26, 27 and 29 July 19943, 4–5 includes kitchen menus.
139. SFA: Camp Report 12, Male Internment Camp, 21–24 September 1942, 11.
140. Ibid.
141. References to seeing internees working in the fields, from a distance, are from Donovan Davis, E-mail correspondence with author, 18 September 2005; Rosie Johnston who was a small child living in the Swallowfield area during the war who recalled seeing them while on walks; and a reference in http://www.jamaicanfamilysearch.com/Samples/milww1-2.htm (accessed 10 February 2008).
142. SFA: Camp Report 16, Male Internment Camp, 26, 27 and 29 July 1943, 6.
143. SFA: Camp Report 22, Male Internment Camp, 23 March 1944, 1.
144. Richard Hart email correspondence.
145. SFA: Camp Report 12, Male Internment Camp, 21–24 September 1942, 16.
146. Ibid., 16–17.
147. Ibid., 7–8.
148. Ibid., 21–24 September 1942, 17.
149. Ibid., 18.
150. Ibid., 25.

151. Ibid., 27.
152. Ibid., 18.
153. SFA: Camp Report 28, Male Internment Camp, 6–7 December 1944, 5.
154. SFA: Camp Report 12, Male Internment Camp, 5.
155. Ibid., 3–5.
156. SFA: Camp Report 22, Male Internment Camp, 23 March 1944, 1.
157. SFA: Camp Report 25 in Connection with Italians, Male Internment Camp & Newcastle Hill Station, 28 and 30 August 1944, 1–2.
158. SFA: Camp Report 28, Male Internment Camp, 6–7 December 1944.
159. SFA: Camp Report 12, Male Internment Camp, 21–24 September 1942, 26.
160. https://web.archive.org/web/20061127110619/http://www.jdfmil.org/overview/bases/bases_home.html (accessed June 2021).
161. SFA: Camp Report 16, Male Internment Camp, 26, 27 and 29 July 1943, 10–11.
162. SFA: Camp Report 22, Male Internment Camp, 23 March 1944.
163. Ibid., 2.
164. Ibid., 3.
165. SFA: Camp Report 23, Male Internment Camp, 14 and 16 August 1944.
166. SFA: Camp Report 31, Male Internment Camp, 23, 25 and 26 April 1945, 1.
167. SFA: Camp Report 23, Male Internment Camp, 14 and 16 August 1944, 4.
168. "Some days from the Internment Camp – Jamaica", Fragment of a handwritten diary, no author named, shared by Rolf Jung in January 2009. A reference in the text indicated that the writer had been interned in Likomba, Cameroon.
169. SFA: Camp Report 12, Male Internment Camp, 21–24 September 1942, 30.
170. SFA: Camp Report 16, Male Internment Camp, 26, 27 and 29 July1943.
171. SFA: Camp Report 12, Male Internment Camp, 21–24 September 1942, 17 and 30.
172. SFA: Camp Report 19, Male Internment Camp, 25 and 29 November 1943.
173. SFA: Camp Report 31, Male Internment Camp, 23, 25 and 26 April 1945, 2.
174. SFA: Camp Report 19, Male Internment Camp, 25 and 29 November1943, 4.
175. Email Correspondence with Richard Hart.
176. SFA: Camp Report 12, Male Internment Camp, 21–24 September 1942.
177. Ibid., 7.
178. Ibid., 33.

179. SFA: Camp Report 16, Male Internment Camp, 3.
180. TNA: FO 916/202 Dr Conrad Hoffmann Jr., YMCA, "Report on Civilian Internment Camps in Jamaica", September 1943.
181. SFA: Camp Report 12, Male Internment Camp, 21–24 September 1942, 35; Red Cross Archive: Roth Report, July 1942, 7.
182. SFA: Camp Report 12, 21–24 September 1942, 35.
183. SFA: Camp Report 22, Male Internment Camp, 23 March 1944, 4.
184. SFA: Camp Report 23, Male Internment Camp, 14 and 16 August 1944, 4.
185. SFA: Camp Report 19, Male Internment Camp, 25 and 29 November 1943.
186. SFA: Camp Report 22, Male Internment Camp, 23 March 1944, 4.
187. SFA: Camp Report 23, Male Internment Camp, 14 and 16 August 1944, 6.
188. Ibid., 7.
189. SFA: Camp Report 16, Male Internment Camp, 26, 27 and 29 July 1943, 9.
190. Ibid., (Version including Sanatorium), 37.
191. SFA: Camp Report 12, Male Internment Camp, 21–24 September 1942, 28.
192. Ibid., 20.
193. Ibid., 22. No details have been found on the prior work assignment of the Italians interned in the Gold Coast.
194. Ibid., 22.
195. Ibid., 23.
196. The Commonwealth Graves Commission lists twenty-six burials related to the internment camp, at the Briggs Park Military Cemetery: four German civilians, one German woman, twelve German merchant mariners and nine Italians listed as belonging to the Italian army.
197. Von Der Porten, *The Nine Lives of Arnold*, 264.
198. TNA: FO 916/202, Conrad Hoffman Jr., YMCA Report, 5–16 September 1943.
199. SFA: Camp Report 23, Male Internment Camp, 14 and 16 August 1944, 5–6.
200. SFA: Camp Report 28, Male Internment Camp, 6–7 December 1944, 2.
201. SFA: Camp Report 22, Male Internment Camp, 23 March 1944, 8.
202. SFA: Camp Report 31, Male Internment Camp, 23, 25, 26 April 1945, 1.
203. JARD, 1B/5/77/27: Defence Security Officer, Ref S/TF/43) ()? 19 October 1943.
204. "Foiled in the Nick of Time", *Gleaner*, 30 December 1939.
205. SFA: Camp Report 16, Male Internment Camp, 26, 27 and 29 July 1943, 16.
206. SFA: Camp Report 22, Male Internment Camp, 23 March 1944, 7.

207. SFA: Camp Report 28, Male Internment Camp, 6–7 December 1944, 5.
208. SFA: Camp Report 31, Male Internment Camp, 23, 25 and 26 April 1945, 3.
209. *Gleaner*, 12 September 1946.
210. Peter McCauley, Interview by author, Kingston, Jamaica, 14 September 2007.
211. TNA: CO968/68/5 Secret Cipher Telegram No. 142092, 26 July 1943 from Commander North American Area to The War Office, London.
212. TNA: HO 213/1833 [Annex 1 From the Secretary of State for the Colonies to the Officer Administering the Government. Circular Telegram Saving. 11 November 1943.
213. TNA: HO 213/1833 (Italian Internees), From Jamaica (Sir J Huggins) to S. of S. Colonies, 17 December 1943. No. 1065.
214. SFA: Camp Report 25, Italians, 28 and 30 August 1944, 2, responding to cables 2028 and 2029.
215. SFA: Camp Report 24, Male Internment Camp, 14 and 16 August 1944, 1.
216. SFA: Camp Report 22, Male Internment Camp, 23 March 1944, 5.
217. TNA: HO 213/1833 Italian Internees, Extract from the Minutes of the 3rd Meeting of the Commonwealth Citizens Committee held on 2 May 1944; C.C.C./P. (44)4.
218. SFA: Camp Report 24, Male Internment Camp, 14–16 August 1944, 2. One of these reports was subsequently sent back as unsuitable.
219. SFA: Report 25 on a visit to the Newcastle Hill Station on 30 August 1944
220. SFA: Camp Report 30, Regarding Italians at Newcastle Hill Station, 27 December 1944.
221. Ibid., 1.
222. Ibid., 5–6. This is in keeping with recollections of interviewee Rose Sharpley who was one of several Kingston residents who became friendly with these Italians.
223. Ibid. The presumption is that these men were working at the military training camp at Moneague in St Ann.
224. Ibid., 2.
225. SFA: Camp Report 30, Regarding Italians at Newcastle Hill Station, 27 December 1944.
226. Ibid., 3.
227. Ibid., 4.
228. SFA: Camp Report 24, Male Internment Camp, 14 and 16 August 1944.
229. SFA: Camp Report 29, Male Internment Camp, Italians, in connection with cable 147, 6 and 7 December 1944, 2–3.
230. SFA: Report 34 of April 1946, 7.
231. *Gleaner*, 23 November 1946, 1.

232. "Twenty Priests among Internees Now Left at Camp", *Gleaner*, 26 November 1946.
233. TNA: CO537 1290[Enemy missionaries 2] Minute, 27 November 1946.
234. "Former Internee Leaves", *Gleaner*, 30 January 1947.
235. "Carthage", *Gleaner*, 10 February 1947.
236. *Manchester Guardian*, UK, republished as "German War Prisoners Were Satisfied With Their Treatment in Jamaica", *Gleaner*, 12 August 1947.
237. 'Current Items", *Gleaner*, 9 September 1947.
238. Email correspondence with Uwe Zitzow.
239. Lower sections of Hanover Street, towards the port, did have a reputation as a haunt of sailors and prostitutes, however there is no indication that this extended to the northern end of the street where the camp was located.
240. National Library of Jamaica: "Anglican Deaconess Order Centenary Magazine, 1890-1990".
241. https://www.shaafl.org/?page_id=30.
242. http://sthughspsa.org/articles/history-of-st-hughs-high-school.html (accessed 19 October 2020). The site further indicates that Rev Enos Nuttall, then Archbishop of the West Indies, was an advocate for educating Black West Indians and also established an Anglican Order of Deaconesses in Jamaica, one of whom, Sister Madeline Thomas, started the Deaconess Home School at the Hanover Street site.
243. "Enemy Alien Is Sent to Prison", *Gleaner*, 21 May 1940.
244. *Jamaica Times*, 15 June 1940.
245. *Gleaner*, 15 June 1940. The report named the ten women.
246. *Gleaner*, 9 and 11 September 1940.
247. TNA: WO 216/149, Jamaica General, Report by Secretary of Local Defence Committee on Events from October 1 December 1940. The group included enemy aliens who had been living and working in British Cameroon, Nigeria, Sierra Leone or Gold Coast, who were transferred to Jamaica for safekeeping.
248. TNA: CO 968/35/13, Treatment of Enemy Aliens, Jamaica 1941 – Enclosures, 25 November 1940, Report from the government department responsible for the Trading with the Enemy Regulations. These women were missionaries or wives and children of planters, engineers etc. detained in West Africa and shipped out with their husbands for security reasons.
249. TNA: CO 968/35/13, Treatment of Enemy Aliens Jamaica 1941, Extract from YWCA Report by M.M. Mills who visited Jamaica from 3–26 February 1941.
250. TNA: CO 968/35/13, Jamaica, 31 October 1941, Gov Jamaica to Lord Moyne, So S Colonies.
251. SFA: E, 2200.179 1971/169/5 Correspondence, 1942–1947, From Swiss Consular Agent to Swiss Legation Special Division, London, 26 February 1942.
252. The provenance of the latter group is unclear.

253. SFA: E2200.179 1971/169/4 Lagerberische 1942–1945, Bericht 4 Frauen-Internierungelager, Kingston, Jamaica, 17 September 1942 (Report 4 on Women's Internment Camp), Translated from German by Lutz Pershmann.

254. AICRC: C SC, Service des camps, Jamaïque, RT, M Roth Camp D'Internes de la Jamaïque, Camp des Femmes, 7 July 1942, 1–2.

255. SFA: Report 4, Women's Internment Camp, 17 September 1942, Item 15. Translated from German by Lutz Pershmann.

256. Ibid.

257. Correspondence with Uwe Zitzow, whose mother related this to him later.

258. The Swiss reports typically used the term *Reisch-German*. While the term is not explained, it is thought to have a political implication during this period, and to exclude the 'non-Aryan', Jewish, Germans.

259. AICRC: C SC, Service des camps, Jamaïque, RT, M Roth Camp D'Internes de la Jamaïque, Camp des Femmes, 7 July 1942, 1–2. (Roth visited both the Female and the Men's camps in July 1942).

260. SFA: Report 6, Women's Internment Camp, 28 September 1943. Translated from German by Lutz Pershmann.

261. Ibid.

262. SFA: Camp Report 4, Women's Internment Camp, 17 September 1942, Translated from German by Lutz Pershmann.

263. TNA: CO980 35[2] [From Commander, North Caribbean Area to War Office; 5417 cipher; 6 May 1943.

264. SFA: Camp Report 4, Women's Internment Camp, 17 September 1942, Item 15. Also, correspondence with former internee Uwe Zitzow.

265. TNA: FO 916/73 (1941) CSO Jamaica to Beckett CO, 24 March 1941.

266. "Can This Be True? Reported Move to Reserve Mineral Bath For Exclusive Use of German Internees", *Gleaner*, 30 May 1941; "Women Internees to Use Bath at Rockfort", *Gleaner*, 3 June 1941; "Current Items", *Gleaner*, 19 July 1941.

267. "Enemy Internees", *Public Opinion*, 31 January 1942; "Amends & Protest", *Public Opinion*, 7 February 1942.

268. SFA: Camp Report 6, Women's Internment Camp, 28 September 1943, Translated from German by Lutz Pershmann.

269. SFA: Report on Women's Internment Camp, 3 May 1941, 3.

270. TNA: CO 968/35/13, M. Mills, YWCA, February 1941.

271. SFA: Camp Report 4, Women's Internment Camp, 17 September 1942, Translated from German by Lutz Pershmann. On 14 February 1942, a wedding ceremony of Sister Marie Louise Fritsch (Red Cross) to Mr Priem was conducted, and on 28 February the wedding of Miss Frida Mauthe to Mr Funk (Basel Mission) was held.

272. SFA: E2001-02/16/17, B.27.A.2 (5) 12 German Interests in Jamaica 1939–1944; Men's Internment Camp Report 16, July 1943, 37.

273. SFA: Camp Report, Women's Internment Camp, 17 September 1942, Translated from German by Lutz Pershmann.
274. Ibid.
275. Menus were recorded for the "lean time" as well as the normal circumstances.
276. SFA: Camp Report 16, Men's Internment Camp, 26, 27 and 29 July 1943.
277. SFA: Camp Report 6, Women's Internment Camp, 28 September 1943, Translated from German by Lutz Pershmann.
278. Ibid.
279. Ibid.
280. Ibid., 4.
281. Ibid.
282. SFA: Swiss Consul Report of Visit, 3 May 1941.
283. SFA: Camp Report 4, Women's Internment Camp, 17 September 1942, Translated from German by Lutz Pershmann.
284. Von Der Porten, *The Nine Lives of Arnold*, 237. Von der Porten also referred to a suicide at the Women's Camp, but no confirming report has been located.
285. TNA: CO 968/35/13: M.M. Mills, YWCA, Report of visit to the Women's Camp during a visit to Jamaica 3-26 February 1941.
286. TNA: FO 916/71 Jamaica (Refugees (Part 2 of file) Parliamentary Question, 6 February 1941.
287. TNA: CO 968/35/13 Rathbone Query Letter from M.P. Eleanor Rathbone, Parliamentary Committee of Refugees, to the Colonial Office, 8 August 1941.
288. TNA: CO968 35 13 Jamaica No.537 31 October 1941 from Governor Jamaica to Lord Moyne, S of S Colonies.
289. TNA: FO916/71 From Gov Richards Jamaica to SoS Colonies, Lord Moyne, 2 September 1941. Letter from women was dated 16 August 1941.
290. TNA: FO 916/ 71 W. Roberts FO to U SoS, CO, 14 November 1941.
291. JARD: CO 1B/5/77/217 Letter to the Colonial Secretary from the Women's Internment Camp; 22 June 1943, #17–18.
292. Ibid., 22 June 1943.
293. JARD: MP 550/43/51 Minuted note to Colonial Secretary from Commandant, Internment Camp, 28 February 1944.
294. TNA: HO 215/368 Letter to Colonial Secretary, Jamaica from Internees, 12 January 1941.
295. TNA: HO 215/368 7 May 1941.
296. SFA: E2200.179 1971/169/5 Correspondence, 1942–1947, Correspondence, 26 February 1942 from Swiss Consular Agent to Swiss Legation Special Division London re Conditions at Female Camp, Jamaica.
297. TNA: CO 980/35 Note on Civilian Internment in Jamaica; undated document No. 9450/8(1).

298. SFA: Nr E.2200.179, 1971/169/5 Correspondence 1942–1947 Swiss Consul to Berne, 7 July 1942.

299. SFA: Ibid., 8 July 1942.

300. SFA: Camp Report 12, Male Internment Camp, 21–24 September 1942, 27.

301. The camp held some 600 Allied/British women as well as children and teenagers. Boys over 14 were sent to a men's camp. https://www.bbc.co.uk/history/ww2peopleswar/stories/70/a8174270.shtml.

302. TNA: CO 980/35, Letter from British Embassy, Washington DC to POW Department, FO, 10 March 1943. Also FO 916/202.

303. TNA: CO 980/35 Civilian Internees in British Territories, Jamaica. Telegram from OAG Jamaica to SoS Colonies, 20 January 1943.

304. TNA: CO 980/35, Civil Internees in British Territories, Jamaica, From Berne to FO, 19 February 1943.

305. TNA: CO 980/35 Civil Internees in British Territories, Jamaica, From Berne to FO, 20 February 1943.

306. TNA: CO 980/35, Civil Internees in British Territories, Jamaica – Family Camp, 20 February 1943, Correspondence re German Camp conditions including undated note on Civilian Internment in Jamaica; and Telegram from Berne to FO.

307. Ibid.

308. TNA: CO 980/35 Telegrams from Governor Arthur Richards, Jamaica to SoS Colonies, #560 Secret, April 1943. Refers to Swiss Consular Report on the Camp dated 28 February 1943.

309. TNA: CO 980/35 Cypher Telegram to Richards from SoS Colonies, 21 April 1943.

310. TNA: CO 980/35 Secret Cipher Telegram from Commander British Caribbean Area to War Office, 6 May 1943.

311. TNA: CO980 35 [3] Extract from Jamaica Security Report, 31 May 1943; SR/38-5/43.

312. JARD: CSO 2761, 1943, Enemy Aliens – Female Internment Camp. Transfer to Gibraltar Camp: Letter of 10 November 1943 to the Colonial Secretary from the Director of Medical Services.

313. Correspondence with Uwe Zitzow, 23 January 2006.

314. SFA: Camp Report 17, Mona Family Camp, 18 October 1943, 8.

315. Ibid., 14.

316. Both these latter officers were noted as "General List".

317. TNA: CO 980 35[2] CO to FO 9 August 1940, para 3 and from Commander, North Caribbean Area to War Office; 5417 cipher, 6 May 1943.

318. TNA: CO980 35 [4] H.E. Satow of the Prisoners of War Department to Lt Col S.J. Cole of the Colonial Office 15 July 1943.

319. As the Women's Camp was guarded by local police, he presumably was referring to the Male Camp; or perhaps was creating an official position on the matter.

320. TNA: CO980 35 [4] Letter from the War Office to Lt Col S.J. Cole, 16 July 1943.
321. Ibid 31 July 1943, #661 secret.
322. SFA: Camp Report 6, Women's Internment Camp, 28 September 1943, Translated from German by Lutz Pershmann.
323. TNA: FO 916/ 202, Jamaica, 5–16 September 1943, KW4/4.
324. SFA: Camp Report 17, Mona Family Camp, 18 October 1943, 8.
325. SFA: Ibid.
326. Catholic Archives, Kingston: Marriage Register & Church Diary, Sacred Heart Church, Gibraltar Camp The numbers of Italians are variously recorded. In the Gibraltar Camp Church Diary, the priest who visited the Catholics at the Family Camp on 9 October 1943 said that there were three Italian families; all couples.
327. SFA: Camp Report, Mona Family Camp, 11 January 1944.
328. YWCA Report on Women Internees in Jamaica, following a visit by Marianne Mills in 16 July–1 August 1944.
329. SFA: Cable to London re visit to Mona Family Camp on 4 December 1944.
330. SFA: Camp Report 9, Women's Internment Camp, 8 October 1944, Translated from German by Lutz Pershmann.
331. TNA: PRO WO 106/5124A 1945, Report of Visit by Lt Col N.J. Darling to Trinidad, Jamaica and Bermuda, 10. Reports of the Swiss Consul in Jamaica, 1943, lodged in the Swiss Federal Archives, corroborate these observations.
332. Email correspondence with Uwe Zitzow, April 2003.
333. SFA: Camp Report 17, Mona Family Camp, 18 October 1943.
334. Email correspondence with Uwe Zitzow, 19 March 2002. This may have been the same internee whom Zitzow recalled as having married a Jamaican woman who worked in the kitchen.
335. TNA: WO 106/5124A 1945, Report of Visit by Lt Col N.J. Darling to Trinidad, Jamaica and Bermuda, 10. Reports of the Swiss Consul in Jamaica, 1943, lodged in the Swiss Federal Archives, corroborate these observations.
336. SFA: Camp Report 17, Mona Family Camp, 18 October 1943.
337. Ibid., 9.
338. SFA: Camp Reports, Mona Family Camp, 18 October 1943 and 8 October 1944.
339. SFA: Camp Report 22, Male Internment Camp, 23 March 1944, 11.
340. SFA: Camp Report, Mona Family Camp, 8 October 1944 and Correspondence with Uwe Zitzow.
341. SFA: Camp Reports, Mona Family Camp.
342. Catholic Archives, Kingston: Marriage Register & Church Diary, Sacred Heart Church, Gibraltar Camp.
343. Email correspondence, Uwe Zitzow.

344. YWCA Report on Women Internees in Jamaica, following a visit by Marianne Mills in 16 July–1 August 1944.

345. SFA: Camp Report, Mona Family Camp, 5 February 1945, Translated from German by Lutz Pershmann.

346. Email correspondence with Uwe Zitzow, 19 March 2002.

347. *Gleaner*, 23 November 1946.

348. Email correspondence with Uwe Zitzow, 19 March 2002.

349. Email correspondence with Uwe Zitzow, 23 April 2021. Also, Simone Gigliotti, "Acapulco in the Atlantic': Revisiting Sosúa, a Jewish Refugee Colony in the Caribbean", https://www.tandfonline.com/doi/abs/10.1080/02619280600590209?journalCode=fimm20.

Chapter 4

1. "MLC moves to Censure Govt", *Gleaner*, 5 February 1941.

2. "The Omnibus Service", Letter, *Gleaner*, 30 October 1940; "Notice, Gibraltar Evacuee Camp", *Gleaner*, 30 September 1940.

3. "Notice, Gibraltar Evacuee Camp", *Gleaner*, 3 October 1940.

4. "Talk on Refugee Camp over ZQI This Afternoon", *Gleaner*, 17 October 1940.

5. "The Feeding of the Nine Thousand", *Gleaner*, 21 October 1940.

6. Ibid. Also interview with Sister Bernadette Little, 15 January 2007.

7. Catholic Archives: Fr William Feeney, "Gibraltar Camp", typewritten article, 29 January 1989.

8. "Local Broadcast", *Gleaner*, 30 October 1940.

9. "HMS Nelson Now at Gibraltar Camp", *Gleaner*, 14 March 1941. A photo of a Gibraltarian evacuee posing beside the model was included in the 2006 Evacuation Photo Exhibition in Gibraltar.

10. "Colonial Co-operation", *Gleaner*, 10 February 1941, reprinted from the West India Committee Circular, London.

11. "The Evacuees", *Gleaner*, 26 October 1940.

12. "Gibraltar Camp Warning", *Gleaner*, 30 October 1940 – signed by Gibraltar Camp Committee, 29 October 1940.

13. JARD: Legislative Council Minutes, 4 February 1941, 11; JARD: CSO 1B/5/77/220 1940, Memorandum on the Administration of Gibraltar Camp, 9 December 1940.

14. Stanton, *Escape from the Inferno of Europe*, 202. Other reports do not rule out both typhus and dengue fever.

15. "Criticism of Mr Hart's Recent Letter", *Gleaner*, 30 July 1941.

16. Donovan Davis, E-mail correspondence with author, 18 September 2005. He noted that a switch was where tram cars coming from opposite directions would meet. Rosie Johnston, a small child during the war, recalled seeing them when on walks as did another wartime child quoted in http://www.jamaicanfamilysearch.com/Samples/milww1-2.htm (accessed 10 February 2008).

17. *Gleaner*, 6 September 1939.
18. "Governor Cheered on Visit to Camp Gibraltar", *Gleaner*, 5 November 1940; "Lady Richards Pay Visit to Evacuees Camp", *Gleaner*, 8 November 1940.
19. "Life Gets More Orderly at Camp Gibraltar Daily", *Gleaner*, 5 November 1940.
20. *Jamaica Times*, 23 November 1940 in Finlayson, *The Fortress Came First*, 79.
21. "Dictatoritis", *Gleaner*, 17 January 1941.
22. Letters Page, *Gleaner*, 21 January 1941. Letter written 18 January.
23. Finlayson, *The Fortress Came First*, 83.
24. Noel Fraser, Conversation with author, Kingston, Jamaica, 2 June 2005.
25. "Film of life at Camp Gibraltar is Well Produced", *Gleaner*, 9 June 1941, 7.
26. TNA: CO 875/12/15, PR Films and CO 875/17/3, PR Films Gate of Gibraltar 1942–43. However, an enquiry in Gibraltar drew a blank.
27. "Anti-Malaria Plan Just Beyond Mona", *Gleaner*, 19 September 1940.
28. JARD: CSO 1B/5/77/220, Report on the organisation of Gibraltar Camp as at 30 September 1941.
29. "Mayor for Tax on Water Commission's Property" - subhead: "August Town Slums", *Gleaner*, 13 November 1940.
30. "Mayor Penso...Aid for August Town", *Gleaner*, 10 December 1940.
31. "Many Matters before KSAC", *Gleaner*, 14 January 1941.
32. "Better Water Supply for August Town", *Gleaner*, 17 December 1940.
33. "Water Commission, K.S.A.C. and August Town Supply", *Gleaner*, 16 May 1941.
34. "Councillors Demand Reason for Excess", *Gleaner*, 13 May 1941.
35. "August Town Seeks Better Water Supply", *Gleaner*, 19 June 1941.
36. Ibid.
37. Letters' Page, *Gleaner*, 16 May 1941.
38. "Typhoid Outbreak Checked", *Gleaner*, 15 July 1944.
39. The importance of local citizens' associations and other civil organisations, starting in the 1930s, was discussed by Iveroll Davis in Chapter 4, 26–27 of Patrick Bryan and Karl Watson, eds., *Not by Wages Alone: Eyewitness Summaries of the 1938 Labour Rebellion in Jamaica* (Jamaica: The Social History Project UWI, 2003). James Robertson, *Gone Is the Ancient Glory. Spanish Town, Jamaica, 1534-2000* (Kingston, Miami: Ian Randle Publishers, 2005), 280–81 states that Governor Edward Denham, Governor of Jamaica from 1935-1938, declined to recognise their input.
40. "Citizens' Associations Renewed Interest in the Federation", *Gleaner*, 22 June 1940. The meeting was chaired by President, Hon. E.E.A. Campbell, with Mr S.A. Miller, 2nd Vice-President and Mr S. McFarlane, Secretary.
41. "August Town To Ask Bridle Path Away from River Course", *Gleaner*, 30 November 1940.

42. JARD: CSO 1B/5/77/301, 30 November 1940, McFarlane to Colonial Secretary.

43. JARD: CSO 1B/5/77/301, 21 December 1940, Director of Public Works to Colonial Secretary.

44. JARD: CSO 1B/5/77/301, 30 December 1940, Colonial Secretary to Sam McFarlane.

45. JARD: CSO 1B/5/77/301, 28 January 1941, Sam McFarlane to Officer Administering the Government of Jamaica. A committee from the Federation had visited the site of the proposed bridle path on 24 January and agreed with the August Town association that the planned road was pointless as it would wash away in heavy weather. This was reported in "Matters before Federation of Citizens' Association", *Gleaner*, 10 February 1941.

46. "Legislative Council", *Gleaner*, 4 April 1941.

47. "August Town Citizens Assocn", *Gleaner*, 16 October 1943.

48. "The Feeding of the Nine Thousand", *Gleaner*, 21 October 1940, with reference to the Food Controller reassuring the public.

49. "Kellits Settlers Spurred to Food Production Drive", *Gleaner*, 25 November 1940, 5.

50. "Food Controller", *Gleaner*, 18 February 1941, 16.

51. "Governor's Message and Report of Committee on Pegging of the Cost of Living", *Gleaner*, 20 March 1942.

52. Ibid. The Message was dated 18 March 1942.

53. Table of Newspaper Stories Relating to the Beef Shortage, in Francis-Brown, "Gibraltar Camp, 1940-1947", 246.

54. "Where the Cattle Go", *Public Opinion*, 16 May 1942.

55. *Gleaner* reports on initiatives at Gibraltar Camp, from 13 July 1942, 16 July 1942 and 30 September 1942.

56. SFA: Camp Report, Mona Family Camp, 5 February 1945. Also Uwe Zitzow, E-mail correspondence with author, 24 January 2006.

57. "Mona, Haven of the Evacuees", *Gleaner*, 7 October 1940.

58. "Rum Sale Draws Fine", *Gleaner*, March 7, 1941.

59. Harold Ramdeen, Interview with author, 10 June 2007.

60. Inez Baker, E-mail correspondence with author.

61. Louise Bennett, "Jamaica Patois", in *Jamaica Labrish* (Kingston, Jamaica: Sangsters, Jamaica, 1972) and HartleyNeita, "The Benefits of Foreign Occupation", *Gleaner*, 6 September 1998.

62. Uwe Zitzow, E-mail correspondence, 23 January 2006.

63. Harold Ramdeen, Interview by author, Kingston, Jamaica, 10 June 2007.

64. Anthony Lara, E-mail correspondence with author. Lara put questions to former evacuee Oscar Alvarez, who was a teenager which living in the camp with his mother. His mother died while in the camp and was buried at Calvary Cemetery.

65. Finlayson, *The Fortress Came First*, 83.
66. Gibraltar Camp photographs taken in 1941 by the Colonial Office (CO1069/371) have been put online as part of The National Archives' Jamaica series, https://www.flickr.com/photos/nationalarchives/sets/72157630743140716/. Many can also be seen on https://commons.wikimedia.org/wiki/File:Gibraltar_Evacuee_Camp,_Jamaica.
67. Frank Tucker, Interview with Ruth Francis on behalf of author, London, UK, 26 January 2007.
68. Joan Arnay Halperin, E-mail and verbal correspondence with author.
69. Harold Ramdeen, Interview by author, Kingston, Jamaica, 10 June 2007. A 'ganzee' is a sleeveless undershirt.
70. Priscilla Harris, Interview by author, Kingston, Jamaica, 21 March 2004.
71. A wooden miniature ship, of a sort long a tradition among sailors, now in the collection of the UWI Mona Library, was gifted to the wife of Camp Commandant Ernest Rae. One of the Finns also made a decorative box for Priscilla Harris, interviewee and then wife of the Commissary Officer.
72. Jean DaCosta, Interview by author, Kingston, Jamaica, 2 October 2007.
73. JOINT: File 884–885, 17 December 1942, JOINT Report by Charles H. Jordan.
74. Manne Aronovsky Eckstein, Unpublished memoir, shared by her daughters.
75. Marshall, *The Caribbean at War*, 20.
76. Leo Fabritius, ex-internee and Gibraltar Camp resident, correspondence with author.
77. Classified advertisement, *Gleaner*, 28 August 1943, 10.
78. "Use of Italian Internees", *Gleaner*, 25 September 1945, 13; "Year's Record of Ja. Imperial Assn"., *Gleaner*, 29 April 1946, 13.
79. JARD: CSO 1B/5/77/1, 19 January 1944, Gibraltar Camp Commandant's Office to CS.
80. TNA: WO 176/24 Jamaica Garrison War Diary 18 May 1945 reported that due to water shortage, a large proportion of the troops at the Newcastle Hill Station were withdrawn to Kingston.
81. Correspondence with Rose Sharpley, 2004–2007.
82. "No Permanent Residence Here for Internees", *Gleaner*, 4 June 1946.
83. *Gleaner*, 13 September 1946.
84. "Italian Craftsman Back", *Gleaner*, 24 December 1949.
85. Rose Sharpley, Correspondence with author, 7 April–8 May 2004.
86. "From MoBay to Pt. Antonio: The Biggest Building Boom Is Underway", *Gleaner*, 14 June 1955.
87. TNA: FO371/4084, Letter from Prime Minister's Office to Gladwyn Morton, Foreign Office, 17 July 1944.
88. Ian Fleming, "Where Shall John Go? – Jamaica", December 1947.
89. Peter Simple, "It Seems to Me...", *Gleaner*, 12 October 1944.

90. The 75 attending Bishop Emmet's Jubilee consisted of the Girl Guides, the entire church choir and various officials. "Work of Bishop Emmet in Jamaica Praised at Golden Jubilee Mass", *Gleaner*, 27 September 1943.

91. Harold Ramdeen, Interview with author.

92. Interviews with Merrick Needham, Donald Lindo and Daphne Rae.

93. JOINT: File 884–885, Jamaica 1941–1944, 17 December 1942, JOINT Report by Charles H. Jordan.

94. Sister Paschal Figueroa, Interview by author, Kingston, Jamaica, 16 January 2007.

95. Frank Tucker, Interview with Ruth Francis on behalf of author, London, UK, 26 January 2007.

96. Oscar Alvarez, Interviewed by Anthony Lara, Gibraltar, intermittently 18 March 2005–21 September 2007.

97. Finlayson, *The Fortress Came First*, 78.

98. "Critical of Verboten's now in Force", *Gleaner*, 24 February 1941.

99. Allen Buchanan, E-mail correspondence with author, 6 December 2005–2 October 2007.

100. Frank Tucker, Interview with Ruth Francis on behalf of author, London, UK, 26 January 2007.

101. Frank Tucker, ibid.

102. Frank Tucker, ibid.

103. Daphne Rae Morrison, Interview with author, 2006.

104. "Jamaica Patois", Bennett, *Jamaica Labrish*, 87.

105. Aileen Gordon, "Family Chronicle", unpublished; shared with author.

106. Competition winners from Gibraltar Camp were among those listed on advertisements in the *Gleaner* over time, including: "Brodies' Users", *Gleaner*, 23 May 1941; "Sweepstake Winners", 10 December 1942; "Ernestina Costa Won a Pair of Leghorn Fowls at the Holy Cross Christmas Carnival", 11 December 1943; "Jubilee Xmas Fair prizewinners", 29 December 1943; "Sweepstake Winners", 7 August 1944.

107. "Gibraltar Evacuees will be Returning Home Before Long", *Gleaner*, 23 September 1944.

108. Interviews with Daphne Rae Morrison, Priscilla Harris, Allan Rae, all of whom lived in Gibraltar Camp as teenagers or young adults, as well as Donald Lindo and Merrick Needham. Allan Rae and Daphne Rae Morrison were the children Camp Commandant Ernest Rae. Lindo was an eleven-year-old schoolboy at the start of the war. His mother ran the Green Gables Hotel in St Andrew. Needham was a child who was evacuated from England with his mother during World War II, living in Kingston with his mother's aunt who entertained some of the refugees.

109. Stanton, *Escape from the Inferno of Europe*.

110. Manne Aronovsky Eckstein, Unpublished memoir, shared by her daughters.

111. Several letters related to Dr Arthur Steigler were published in the *Gleaner*, including those on 10 December 1943, 8 February 1944 and 27 January 1946.

112. Regina Inez Baker, E-mail correspondence with author, 27 December 2004–15 March 2006.

113. *Gleaner*, 8 September and 12 September 1946, and 23 November 1946.

114. Rose Sharpley, Correspondence with author, April 2004.

115. It should be noted that many of Jamaica's traditional secondary or 'high' schools were established by various denominations or by Trusts. However, these later became grant-aided by government.

116. Frank Tucker, Interview, 2007.

117. Information from Eddie & Joanne Power who interviewed Adelaide in Gibraltar; Eddie is Adelaide's grandnephew. His mother, Maria, was born to Adelaide's eldest sister, at Gibraltar Camp in 1941.

118. Manne Eckstein, Autograph book, in possession of Eckstein's daughters, shared in 2019 at UWI Museum.

119. Jenny Weinshel.

120. Inez Regina Schpektor Baker.

121. Eileen Scott, Conversation with author, Kingston, Jamaica, 31 December 2006.

122. Yvonne Legay, E-mail correspondence with author, 13 June–25 August 2005.

123. Stanley Carter, Telephone conversation with author, September 2005.

124. Gibraltar Archive: Letter from Commandant's Office, Gibraltar Camp to Chamber of Commerce, Gibraltar, 8 March 1944; Response from Gibraltar Chamber of Commerce to Secretary, Resettlement Board, Colonial Secretariat, 4 July 1944; Letter to Gibraltar Chamber of Commerce from Colonial Secretariat, 12 July 1944.

125. Potworowski, "The Evacuation", 180.

126. Regina Inez Baker, E-mail correspondence with author, 27 December 2004–15 March 2006.

127. TNA: FO371/42826 Details of numbers in, arrivals, births and departures from Camp 2, Polish Group.

128. R.W. Thompson, *Black Caribbean* (London: MacDonald & Co (Publishers), 1946).

129. "Polish-Dutch Bridal at Jewish Synagogue", *Gleaner*, 16 December 1943.

130. *Gibraltar Magazine*, May 2015.

131. Sister Bernadette Little, Telephone Interview by author, 15 January 2007; Jim McGillvray, E-mail correspondence with author, 16 April 2008.

132. Myrnelle McIntosh, "Nostalgia. Each One Teach One", *Sunday Gleaner*, 27 June 1993.

133. Jamaica Civil Registration records for marriages during 1946. Also interviews and correspondence with Frank Tucker, Jim McGillvray.

134. Email correspondence with Maurice Xiberras, 2009, 2015, 2017.

135. Connie Mark in Marshall, *The Caribbean at War*, 20.
136. Karen Barsoe-Adderley author Email Correspondence with author, May 2004.
137. Uwe Zitzow. E-mail correspondence with author.

Chapter 5

1. "Colonial Co-operation", *Gleaner*, 10 February 1941 reprinted from the *West India Committee Circular*, London.
2. JARD: 1B/5/77/270 Minute 98, 2827 April 1944.
3. JARD: 1B/5/77/270, From Gibraltar Camp Committee to Colonial Secretary, 13 March 1944.
4. JARD: 1B/5/77/270 Minute 97 From Attorney General to Colonial Secretary, 31 March 1944.
5. JARD: 1B/5/77/270 JR 29.4.44 From Governor Jamaica to SoS Colonies, 30 April 1944.
6. "Evacuees Need a Haven and New Township Is Born", *Gleaner*, 21 September 1940.
7. Interviews with Harold Ramdeen, Myrtle Gallow, Ram Ragbeir, all 2007.
8. "Britain Took Advantage in Land Sale – JLP", *Gleaner*, 19 August 1960.
9. "War Department Tender – Old Internment Camp Building, Up Park Camp", *Gleaner*, 28 August 1959.
10. Suzanne Francis-Brown, "History & Heritage of the UWI Mona Campus", MA Heritage diss., 2001; and Francis-Brown, *Mona Past and Present*, passim.
11. "Recalling The Jamaica Evacuees", and "Gibraltarians in Jamaica", *Gibraltar Chronicle*, 5 March 2007, 1 and 3. "The Making of the Gibraltar Monument at The UWI Mona", *Sunday Gleaner*, 29 April 2007. "Gibraltar Monument", *Sunday Gleaner*, 6 May 2007. Also "Rock of Gibraltar at Mona", CARIMAC, *The Insider* (UWI Student Publication) March 2007, Volume 1, Issue 1, 1 and 3.
12. University Library, Mona Campus, UWI: Raymond Priestley, "1944 Diary" (unpublished), Tuesday 4/4/44, 10.
13. Francis Brown, *Mona Past and Present*, 34–35.
14. *Sunday Gleaner*, 3 October 1948.
15. Zachary Beier and Clive Grey, "Campus Archaeology at the Gibraltar Camp", Poster, Archaeology Lab, Mona Campus, UWI.
16. Catholic Chancery: Sacred Heart Church Diary.
17. Catholic Chancery, Kingston, Jamaica.
18. https://www.cwgc.org/visit-us/find-cemeteries-memorials/cemetery-details/2024319/KINGSTON%20(UP%20PARK%20CAMP)%20MILITARY%20CEMETERY/.
19. UWI Mona Main Library collection. The stone was presented by then Gibraltarian minister Maurice Xiberras, who was married to a

Jamaican-Gibraltarian. The model ship was presented to the Library by Norman Rae.

20. Derek Walcott, "Gib Hall Revisited", quoted in Caribbean Quarterly, Vol.15, Nos. 2 and 3, 1969, University of the West Indies.

21. Memmi, *The Colonizer and the Colonized*, 92–93.

22. Correspondence with Ainsley Henriques, 2020.

23. Many of these visitors have visited the UWI Museum, which has recorded and communicated these stories through social media. These include <uwimuseum.wordpress.com>

24. Interviews and correspondence with Aileen Mansfield Gordon (2015–), Anthony Lara (2005–) and Joan Arnay Halperin (2013–).

25. "Chronicle of My Family", unpublished memoir by Aileen Mansfield Gordon, Gibraltar; shared with Author.

26. "A Jamaican Studies Gibraltar Camp", *Gibraltar Chronicle*, 9 January 2009.

27. Halperin, *My Sister's Eyes: A Family Chronicle of Rescue and Loss During World War II*. Halperin was first in touch with this author in 2013.

28. Stanton, *Escape from the Inferno of Europe*, 218–19. Stanton developed close ties with the Matalon family and other local Jewish families. However, she was unusual among the Polish Jews, most of whom appear to have eschewed contact according to the JOINT Charles H. Jordan Report (JOINT Archive). The Dutch Jews visited with local Jewish families, but no indications of close, long-term relationships were found.

29. Conversation with Ainsley Henriques; also Stanton's niece, Francoise Rabin, who visited the Mona site in 2018.

30. Feedback during lecture titled "From Rock to Rock", Suzanne Francis-Brown, 2015 at the Gibraltar Library during celebrations of the seventy-fifth anniversary of the Evacuation. Also interviews at the UWI Museum with Gibraltarian visitors interested in visiting the site. https://uwimuseum.wordpress.com/2018/04/18/gibraltar-camp-memories-come-alive/; https://uwimuseum.wordpress.com/2017/09/18/video-land-of-my-birth-new-spin/.

31. "From Rock to Rock", lecture by Dr Suzanne Francis-Brown, Curator of the University of the West Indies (UWI) Museum, Jamaica, May 2015.

32. "Twinning Visit to Kingston, Jamaica", *Gibraltar Chronicle*, 18 October 2018, https://www.chronicle.gi/twinning-visit-kingston-jamaica/ (accessed 18 October 2020).

33. https://uwimuseum.wordpress.com/2019/03/15/gibraltar-journey/ (accessed 18 October 2020).

Selected Bibliography

Ashton, S.R., and S.E. Stockwell (eds.). *Imperial Policy & Colonial Practice, 1925-1945*. Vol. 2, British Documents on the End of Empire. Series A. London: Institute of Commonwealth Studies in the University of London, 1996.

Bartrop, Paul R. "From Lisbon to Jamaica: A Study of British Refugee Rescue during the Second World War". *Immigrants & Minorities* 13, no. 1 (1994): 48–64.

Bennett, Louise. *Jamaica Labrish*. Kingston, Jamaica: Sangsters Book Stores, Jamaica, 1972.

Blackburne, Kenneth. *Lasting Legacy. A Story of British Colonialism*. London: Johnson Publications, 1976.

Brock, Esme. *An Evacuee in Jamaica, 1940-1945*. Buriton, Hampshire: Titchfield Publishers, 1990.

Bryan, Patrick E., and Karl Watson, eds. *Not for Wages Alone. Eyewitness Summaries of the 1938 Labour Rebellion in Jamaica*. Jamaica: The Social History Project, Department of History, University of the West Indies, 2003.

Bustamante, Lady Gladys. *The Memoirs of Lady Bustamante*. Kingston: Kingston Publishers Limited, 1997.

Cameron, Linda D. (ed.). *The Story of the Gleaner: Memoirs and Reminiscences*. Kingston, Jamaica: The Gleaner Company Limited, 2000.

Canessa, Eric. *They Went to War, the Story of Gibraltarians Who Served in His Majesty's Forces in World War*. Gibraltar: Eric Canessa, 2004.

Cesaire, Aime. *Discourse on Colonialism*. Translated by Joan Pinkham. New York and London: Monthly Review Press, 1972.

Cohen, David, and Robert Lemm. *één Rembrandt voor vijfentwintig levens* (One Rembrandt for 15 lives). Amsterdam: Uitgeverij Aspekt, 2013.

Eccles, Karen, and Debbie McCollin (eds.). *World War II in the Caribbean*. Jamaica, Barbados, Trinidad and Tobago: UWI Press, 2017.

Finlayson, T.J. *The Fortress Came First*. Gibraltar: Gibraltar Books, 2000.

Francis Brown, Suzanne. "Finnish Sailors among World War II Internees". *Jamaica Journal* 29, no. 3 (December 2005–April 2006): 60–62.

Francis-Brown, Suzanne. "Jamaica: Fixed-Time Haven and Holding Tank during World War II", in *World War II and the Caribbean*, edited by Karen E. Eccles and Debbie McCollin. Jamaica, Barbados, Trinidad and Tobago: UWI Press, 2017.

Francis Brown, Suzanne. *Mona Past and Present: The History and Heritage of the Mona Campus, University of the West Indies*. Jamaica, Barbados, Trinidad and Tobago: University of the West Indies Press and Department of History & Archaeology, UWI, 2004.

Grantham, Alexander. *Via Ports. From Hong Kong to Hong Kong*. Hong Kong: Hong Kong University Press, 1965.
Halperin, Joan Arnay. *My Sister's Eyes: A Family Chronicle of Rescue and Loss during World War II*. USA: JMA Press, 2019.
Hart, Richard. *Towards Decolonisation. Political, Labour & Economic Development in Jamaica. 1938-1945*. Barbados, Jamaica, Trinidad and Tobago: Canoe Press, UWI, 1999.
Henriques, Fernando. *Family and Colour in Jamaica*. London: Eyre & Spottiswoode, 1953.
Henry, A.E.T. *Sheets in the Wind. A Collection of Humorous Articles and Satires*. Kingston, Jamaica: The Gleaner Company, 1942.
Huggins, Molly. *Too Much to Tell*. London, Melbourne, Toronto, Cape Town and Aukland: William Heinemann, 1967.
Jeffery, Keith. "The Second World War". In *The Oxford History of the British Empire: The Twentieth Century*, edited by Judith M Brown and Wm. Roger Louis, 306–28. Oxford and New York: Oxford University Press, 1999.
Johnson, Howard. "The British Caribbean from Demobilization to Constitutional Decolonization". In *The Oxford History of the British Empire: The Twentieth Century*, edited by Judith M Brown and Wm. Roger Louis, 597–622. Oxford and New York: Oxford University Press, 1999.
Kelshall, Gaylord T.M. *The U-Boat War in the Caribbean*. Annapolis: Naval Institute Press, 1988, 1994.
Kwik, Christian, and Verena Muth. "European Refugees in the Wider Caribbean", in *World War II and the Caribbean*, edited by Karen E. Eccles and Debbie McCollin. Jamaica, Barbados, Trinidad and Tobago: UWI Press, 2017.
Lee, J.M., and Martin Petter. *The Colonial Office, War & Development Policy: Organisation and Planning of a Metropolitan Initiative, 1939-1945*. London: Institute of Commonwealth Studies, 1982.
Legislative Council Minutes, Jamaica 1939-1944.London, Louise. *Whitehall & the Jews, 1933-1948: British Immigration Policy & the Holocaust*. Cambridge: Cambridge University Press, 2000.
MacMillan, W.M. *Warning from the West Indies: A Tract for Africa and the Empire*. London: Faber & Faber, 1936.
Marrus, Michael R., and Anna C. Bramwell. *Refugees in the Age of Total War*. London: Routledge, 1988.
Marshall, O. *The Caribbean at War: 'British West Indians in World War II'*. London: The North Kensington Archive at the Notting Dale Urban Studies Centre, 1992.
Maunier, Rene. *The Sociology of Colonies: An Introduction to the Study of Race Contact*. Translated by E.O. Lorimer. Vol. 1. 2 vols. International Library of Sociology and Social Reconstruction, ed. Dr Karl Mannheim. London: Routledge & Kegan Paul, 1949.
McFarlane, W.G. *The Birth of Self-Government for Jamaica & the Jamaica Progressive League, 1937-1944*. Kingston, Jamaica: W.G. McFarlane, 1974.

Memmi, Albert. *The Colonizer and the Colonized*. Translated by Howard Greenfeld. Boston: Beacon Press, 1965.

Metzgen, Humphrey, and John Graham. *Caribbean Wars Untold*. Jamaica, Barbados, Trinidad and Tobago: UWI Press, 2007.

Moore, Bob, and Kent Fedorowich. *The British Empire & Its Italian Prisoners of War, 1940-1947*. Basingstoke: Palgrave, 2002.

Newman, Joanna. *Nearly the New World, The British West Indies and the Flight from Nazism, 1933-1945*. New York and Oxford: Berghahn Books, 2019.

Osborne, Francis J. *History of the Catholic Church in Jamaica*. Chicago: Loyola University Press, 1988.

Osterhammel, Jurgen. *Colonialism. A Theoretical Overview*. Translated by Shelly L. Frisch. Princeton and Kingston: Markus Wiener Publishers, Ian Randle Publishers, 1997.

Peel, Richard. *Old Sinister. A Memoir of Sir Arthur Richards, GCMG, First Baron Milverton of Lagos and Clifton in the City of Bristol, 1885-1978*. Cambridge: Privately Published, 1986.

Post, Ken. *Arise Ye Starvelings: The Jamaican Labour Rebellion of 1938 and Its Aftermath*. The Hague: Institute of Social Studies, 1978.

Post, Ken. *Strike the Iron: A Colony at War. Jamaica, 1939-1945*. The Hague: Institute of Social Sciences, 1981.

Potworowski, Tomasz. "The Evacuation of Jewish Polish Citizens from Portugal to Jamaica 1941-1943". *Polin* 19, no. 2007 (2007): 155–82.

Roberts, W. Adolphe. "The Future of Colonialism in the Caribbean: The British West Indies". In *The Economic Future of the Caribbean*, edited by Eric Williams, 37–39. Dover: The MajorityPress, 2004.

Stanton, Miriam. *Escape from the Inferno of Europe*. London: M. Stanton, 1996.

Stolberg, Claus, and Katja Fullberg-Stolberg. "Jewish Exiles in the British Colonial Empire - Gibraltar Camp Jamaica 1942-1947 (Translation)". *Hannoversche Schriften* Band 11 (1996): 85–102.

Sutcliffe, A.P.D. *The Military Mail of Jamaica. A Philatelic History*. Roses Caribbean Handbook No. 5, Published by Roses Caribbean Philatelic Society, UK, 1982.

Thompson, Dudley with Margaret Cezair Thompson. *From Kingston to Kenya: The Making of a Pan-Africanist Lawyer*, The Black World Series. Dover: The Majority Press, 1993.

Thompson, R.W. *Black Caribbean*. London: MacDonald & Co (Publishers), 1946.

Thurston, Anne. *Sources for Colonial Studies in the Public Record Office, Volume 1: Records of the Colonial Office, Dominions Office, Commonwealth Relations Office & Commonwealth Office*. Vol. 1. London: HMSO, 1995.

Index

Note: *Italic* page numbers refer to figures and page numbers followed by 'n' refer to notes.

ACIJ. *See* African Caribbean Institute of Jamaica (ACIJ)
administration, 85, 146–147, 184
African Caribbean Institute of Jamaica (ACIJ), 262n54
Air Raid Precautions (ARP), 48, 55
Air Raid Wardens, 47
Alderman, Kingston, 222
Alien Restriction Regulation, 126, 127
Alpha Academy, 103, 104
Alvarez, Oscar, 298n64
Amateur Theatre Movement, 155
American base, 5, 52, 75
American Jewish Joint Distribution Committee (JOINT), 15, 71–73, 87, 96, 110, 111, 248
Anderson, E.A., 205
anti-Semitism, 71, 83
Archer-Straw, Petrine, 26
Armistice (1943), 7, 115
Armond, A.V., 226
Arnay, Helene Krakowiak, 111, 225
ARP. *See* Air Raid Precautions (ARP)
Arrigo, Levi, 127
Aryan internees, 178
Ashenheim, Leslie, 40, 225
Aub, Rudolph, 129, 136, 137
August Town, 86, 87, 91, 107, 204–208, 220, 221
Austin-Cathie, B.D., 108
authoritarian, 3, 18, 32, 38
authoritarianism, 18, 38
Auxiliary Territorial Service (ATS), 215
Azzopardi, Adelaide, 104, 227
Azzopardi, Charles, 252

'backra,' 268n157

Bailey, Samuel, 25
Baker, Regina Inez, xiv, 276n113. *See also* Schpektor
banana industry, 21
Baptiste, Fitzroy, 47
Bartrop, Paul, 72
Battershill, William, 38
BBC broadcasts, 59
Bennett, Louise, 41, 211, 223, 246
Bennett, Rustel E., 23
Bergh, Van Den, 226
Bermuda Conference, 274n69
birth, in the camps, 228–231
Bismark, 57
BITU. *See* Bustamante Industrial Trade Union (BITU)
Blackburne, Kenneth, 24
Black Out Order, 47–48
blockade, 1, 5, 45
Bournemouth Bath, 25, 48, 221
Brereton, Bridget, 6–7
Briggs Park Military Cemetery, 243, 282n21
British armed services, colour bar in, 56–57
British Auxiliary Territorial Service, 53
British Cameroon, 138–139
British Documents on the End of Empire, 24
The British Empire and Its Italian Prisoners of War (Moore & Fedorowich), 121
British Ministry of Information, 204
British Nationality and Status of Aliens Act of 1914, 124
British Pathe (1939), 132
Brown, H.M., 80

Bryan, Patrick, 56
burials, 107, 242
Bustamante, Alexander, 39, 130, 237
Bustamante, Lady Gladys, 54–55, 131
Bustamante Industrial Trade Union (BITU), 34, 130, 131
Bustamante monument, 238
Busuttil/Mansfield romance, 68

Calvary Catholic Cemetery, 107
Cameroons, 135
Camp Report of September 1942, Male Internment Camp, 122
Canessa, Eric, 103
Cargill, Morris, 56, 57
The Caribbean at War, 231
Caribbean Wars Untold (Graham and Metzgen), 6–7, 20
Carreras, Angel P., 108
Catholic community, 233
Catholic Opinion, 9, 39, 58, 67, 68, 201, 221
Cattaneo, Umberto, 217, 246
Cesaire, Aimé, 4
Chapman, Esther, 94
charitable people, 225
Churchill, Winston, 37, 70, 111, 126
citizens associations, 207, 297n39
civil liberties, 39–40, 116
Clay Tile and Brick factory, 51, 217, 218
Clerk, Astley, 225
CO. *See* Colonial Office (CO)
Cohen, David, 8, 104
Cold Supper Shop, 268–269n177
Colonial Development and Welfare Act (1940), 22, 51
Colonial Development Fund, 19
The Colonial Empire, 50
The Colonial Empire at the Outbreak of War, 56
Colonial Office (CO), 1, 3, 20, 30, 35, 61, 67, 70, 72, 74, 98, 99, 107, 115, 124, 128, 134–136, 139, 180
Commonwealth Graves Commission, 289n196
concrete benches, Italian, 245
Convoy TAG-70, 46

Cooper-Clark, Diana, 8, 250
Cost of Living Index, 49–50
Creech-Jones, Arthur, 42
cross-faith marriage, Gibraltar Camp, 84, 107
Crown Colony government, 19–20
cultural performance, 235–246
Cwik, Christian, 8, 124
Czarnecki, Beta, 126
Czech refugee, 210

Daily Gleaner, 12, 18, 23, 25, 41, 43, 45, 48, 62–63, 67, 69, 77, 108, 123–125, 127, 131–133, 165, 173, 196, 197, 203, 204, 208, 220, 224, 225, 230, 237, 241, 259n2
daily life, Gibraltar Camp, 147–151
Dallin, Col John, 25
Daly, D. Denis, 46
Darling, Lt Col N.J., 116
Davis, Donovan, 287n141, 296n16
Davis, Iveroll, 297n39
death, wartime camp residents, 228–231
decision-making, 27, 232
defeatism, 57
Defence Regulations, 18, 20, 25, 33, 35, 38–45, 50, 139
Defence Security Office, 159
DeMercado, Lascelles, 93
Denham, Sir Edward, 18, 20, 21
detainees: Jamaican/political, 11, 130–131; long-term, 165–167
Deters, Theo A., 49, 123
Diederich, Max, 184
Dietrich, 48–49
divide et impera, 35
Domingo, W.A., 26, 39, 41, 131
Doro, Rinaldo, 127
Doro, Salvatore, 126, 128
Dozy, C.M. (Dutch Consul), 76
Dreams of Re-Creation in Jamaica (Cooper-Clark), 8, 250
drought, 52, 81, 146, 217
Dutch refugees, 96, 111, 112, 114, 114, 211, 226, 228, 233, 248
Dutch West Indian colonies, 76, 233
Duval, T., 206

Ebersohn, Max, 125
Eckstein, Manne, 85, 104, 111, *113*, 215, 225, 227, 276nn109, 114
economic interface, camp and community, 208–212
Economist, 57
Edwards, J., 184
én Rembrandt voor vijfentwintig levens (Cohen and Lemm), 114
Emergency Powers (Defence) Act, 38
Emmet, Thomas A., 220
Emmy Friedrich, 46, 132
Empire Audacity, 132
employment, wartime camps, 212–219
enclave, 6, 61, 66, 198, 200, 204, 232
enemy aliens, 1, 8, 13, 25, 43, 49, 117, 121, 126, 137, 201; locally interned, 130–137; women and children, 167–168
Epsworth Lara, Elizabeth, 249, 250
Escape from the Inferno (Stanton), 78
Escoffery, C.A., 225
Evacuation monument, Gibraltar camp, 252
evacuees, 1, 62–63, 66–69, 82–85
Evacuees (Defence) Regulations 1940, 99, 198
Ewen, W.V.G.S., 184
"exercise of patience," 56

Fabritius, Leo, 138, 276n115, 299n76
family camp, 183–184, 189
Fanon, Franz, 4
farm: areas, 152; irrigation, 152; Men's Camp, 210; vegetable gardens, 105–106, 146, 148, 151–152, 210
Farm Work programme, 267n147
Federation of Citizens' Associations (FCA), 36, 207
Fedorowich, Kent, 121, 122
Feeney, Thomas, 193
Feeney, William, 62, 197, 276n123
female aliens, 126
female internees, 2, 173, 174, 188
Female Internment Camp, 116, 179, 184, 202
filaria, 176

Filisetti, Antonio, 218
Finlayson, T.J., 66, 222
Finns, 1, 85, 138, 201, 215
fistball, 153, 154, 193
Fleming, Ian, 219
Foreign Office, 124, 134, 178, 181
The Fortress Came First (Finlayson), 66, 222
"Four H's," 131
Fox, John P., 124
Franco, General Francisco, 66
Frayman, Jose, 123
Frome Sugar Factory, 21
Füllberg-Stolberg, Katja, 78

ganzees, 215
Garvey, Marcus, 21, 23
gasolene shortages, 50, 54, 55
Gates of Gibraltar, 203
gender-differentiated camps, 1
Geneva Convention, 117, 121, 122, 190
German and European Jewish Refugees 1933–1945, 124
German companies, 134
German immigrants, Jamaica, 124
German internees, 133–138, 140, 148, 156, 165, 167, 174, 213, 231
German Red Cross, 150
Gertig, Willy, 125
Gibraltar Camp, 2–3, 11–13, 27–29, 44–45, 53, 131, 138, 164, 181, 188, 195, 198, 228, 229, 232, 235, 236, 270n12; administration, 97–98; barracks and bathroom layout, 97; camp conditions, 107–114; Camp I and Camp II, 63–64; Catholic Church, 92, 98; chief guard, 91; church, 255; closed, 64; construction of, 62–63, 87, 88, 89; corruption, 140; cross-faith marriage, 84; cultural group, 112, 156; Czechs, 80; deaths and burials, 107; dining halls, 93–97; Dutch refugees, 76–78, 96, 111, *112*, 114, *114*, 273n64, 274n69;

establishment, 61–62;
Evacuation monument,
252; evacuees, 7–8, 62–63,
66–69, 82–85, 98–99, 249;
expenditure, 79–80, 102;
Finlayson, 280n203; Finnish
sailors, 80–81; Finns, 85;
Gibraltarian population, 66;
health, 272n51; health of
the community, 106; Italian
collaborators, 81; Italians,
81–82; Jewish refugees,
71, 78; Lara family at, 224;
letters from, 108, 272n47;
living in, 101–107; location,
85–87, 86; meals, 105; media
coverage of, 202; New York
investigators, 109; non-
physical barriers, 83–84;
November 1940–October
1944, 68; nuns/nunnery,
92, 277n136; organization
of, 92; penalties, Jamaicans,
100, 100; Poles, 73; police
station, 91; Polish refugees,
74, 110–111; PWD layout,
89, 90, 91, 97; recreation
room, 93; refugees, 68–80,
98–99; regulations, 97–101;
reimbursement, refugees,
77; residential rooms,
93–94; section repurposed
as military facility, 63–64;
setup, 61; Spanish refugees,
68–70, 75–76, 271n30;
staff at, 213–214 ; tank, 255;
timeline, 65; weddings, 107;
young Gibraltarian women,
102
Gibraltar Camp Church Diary,
295n326
Gibraltar Evacuees Camp, xiv, 69, 205.
See also Gibraltar Camp
Gibraltarian Evacuees Fund, 109
Gibraltar Library, 254
Gibraltar Magazine, 230
Gibraltar Resettlement Board (1944),
69

Gleaner. See Daily Gleaner
"gloomy portals", 203
Gomez, Celia Mary, 270n18
Gordon, Aileen Mansfield, 223, 249
Gore, James F., 51
Graham, John, 6–7, 20
Grantham, Alexander, 21, 51, 121
Grinan, John, 269n181
The Growth of the Modern West Indies
(Lewis), 38
guards, 39, 82, 91, 116, 123–125, 132,
134, 136, 145, 147, 169, 173,
174, 176, 180, 182–184, 211,
212, 242

Hall, George, 42, 282n39
Halperin, Joan Arnay, 243, 250
handwork for sale, 215
Hart, Ansell, 41–42, 131
Hart, Richard, 11, 31–32, 37–38, 42,
51, 58–59, 131, 142, 143, 237,
268n177, 284n62
health, Male Internment Camp,
157–161
Heise, Martin H., 124
Henriques, Fernando, 23
Henry, A.E.T., 247
Henry, Arthur, 131
heritage, traces in camps, 232–256
Herrera, Juan, 91
Hill, Frank, 131
Hill, Ken, 131
History of Modern Trinidad, 1783-1962
(Brereton), 6–7
History of the Catholic Church in
Jamaica (Osborne), 102
HMS Ajax, 21
HMS Caradoc, 132
HMS Hood, 57
Hoffmann, Conrad, Jr, 15, 138, 158,
180, 216
holding tanks, 2, 7
Home Office, 124, 179
Hope Botanical Gardens, 87, 111, 245
Hope River, 86, 89, 204, 206, 207
Howell, Imelda Williams, 50
Huggins, Lady Molly, 26, 259n17
Huggins, Sir John, 19, 26, 69, 159, 234

"imperial obligation," 13
incomers, 257n4
interaction: employment, 212–219; social, 219–228
interface: economic, 208–212; media, 201–204; physical, 204–208
inter-group relationships and divisions, 138–141
internal management, Male Internment Camp, 147
International Committee of the Red Cross, 182. *See also* Red Cross
International impact of conditions at Women's Camp, Kingston, 116–117, 183
interned enemy aliens, 123–130
"Internment & P. of W. Camp, Jamaica," 122
internment of German and Italian civilians, British West Africa, 1
internment order, 126, 135
internment policy, 128
interviewees, 5, 34, 44, 47–49, 54, 55, 58, 64, 76, 82, 84, 87, 103, 105, 148, 161, 183, 200, 203, 211, 212, 215, 221–223, 227–229
isolating friends, 196–200
Italian internees, 15, 27, 29, 81, 115, 127, 134–138, 148, 149, 151, 153, 160–162, 165, 216, 229, 234, 242, 248

Jamaica: Britain's RAF, 6, 12, 24, 47, 53, 56, 64; British colonial context, 18; class superiority, 4; colonial authorities, 3; controlled environments, camps, 13; Cost of Living Index, 49–50; cultural nationalism, 26–27; dominion status, 37–38; education, 23–24; elections, 19; exports and imports, 266n132; gender considerations, 29–30; Germany and Japan, 58–59; Gibraltar Camp, 27–29; global recession, local impacts, 21; governor Richards. *See* Richards, Sir Arthur; governor's power, 20; impact of war, 45–54; imperial camps, *14*; implications for freedom, 38–45; imports and exports, 50–51; Jewish community, 31; journalistic style, 9–10; labour contracts overseas, 52; large-scale construction projects, 52; Legislative Council, 27–28; literacy, 5; local activists, 3; local heritage, 17; local impressions of the camps, 11–12; local industrial development, 51; local media, 5–6; local perceptions, war, 54–60; locations of camps, 2, *2*; loyalty, 4–5, 58; nationalist agitation, 31–38; newsprint restrictions, 9; official church, 31; political agitators, 20, 34; political and labour organizations, 18; population, 22–23; poverty, 9; race, 4, 6, 11; race-related factors, 23, 24; racial consciousness, Governor Richards, 26–28; regulations, 17; revenue, 4; riots, 21; risks, 265n112; safety hazards, 7; "settler ideology," 21; shortages, 47, 50; short-term employment, 4; society, 22–31; socio-economic context, 16–17; unemployment, 47, 50, 52; volunteer for the war, 12; wave of loyalty, 33; "white bias," 23; working-class confraternity, 29
Jamaica Defence Force (JDF), 151
Jamaica Defence Regulations, 130, 283–284nn61–62

Jamaica Defence Scheme (1939), 45
Jamaica Engineer Corps, 38
Jamaica Gleaner. See Gleaner
Jamaica Infantry Volunteers, 38, 64
Jamaica Militia Artillery, 38
Jamaican detainees, 130–131
Jamaican public, 89, 201, 202
"Jamaica Patois," 223
Jamaica Producer, 132
Jamaica Progressive League (JPL), 22, 37, 41, 131
Jamaica's Defence Regulations, 18–20, 25, 28, 33–35, 38–45, 47, 50, 61, 84, 126, 130, 139, 234
Jamaica's Legislative Council, 19, 24, 27, 34, 37, 41, 57, 59, 62, 74, 115, 121, 167, 195, 202, 208, 217
Jamaica Times, 9, 127, 201, 202
Jamaica Trade Union law, 43
Jamaica Welfare Limited, 216
Jeffery, Keith, 59
Jeffery-Smith, M., 58
Jewish community, Jamaica, 1, 8, 13, 31, 70, 71, 74, 77, 78, 92, 98, 106, 110, 123, 128, 194, 198, 224, 225, 229, 248, 250, 251
Johnson, Howard, 21, 32
Johnston, Rosie, 287n141, 296n16
JOINT. *See* American Jewish Joint Distribution Committee (JOINT)
Jordan, Charles H., 15, 87, 274n76
journalistic style, 9–10
Judah, Braham T, 41

Kahn, Wolfgang, 125
Kelshall, Gaylord, 5, 6, 46–47, 265n117
Kings Shropshire Light Infantry, 38
Kingston Public Hospital (KPH), 103, 106
Kingston & St. Andrew Corporation (KSAC), 25, 176, 205, 206
Kohler, Albrecht, 226
Koth, Bernard, 126, 128
Krakowiak, Ignas, 214, 280n185
Krakowiak, Yvonne, 250
KSAC. *See* Kingston & St. Andrew Corporation (KSAC)

Lackenbach, Fritz, 125, 282n26
Lara, Anthony, 239, 249, 300n96
Lara, Elizabeth Epsworth, 244
Lassig, R., 166, 179
layout, Male Internment Camp, 141–146
Legislative Council. *See* Jamaica's Legislative Council
Levy, Earl, 197
Lewis, Gordon, 38
Liddell, Sir Clive, 61–62
Liebenau Camp, 180–182
Lindo, Archie, 197
literacy, 5
living conditions, Women's Internment Camp, 173–177
Livingston, Sir Noel, 97
Lobbenberg, Ernest, 123, 125, 283n26
Local Defence Committee, 117
local industrial development, 51
Loffler, Alfred, 123, 125
London, Louise, 71, 124, 126
Longbridge, Gladys, 54, 131
Lopez, H., 176
Lopez, Kaiane Aldorino, 239, 252
Lord Haw Haw's German propaganda, 58–59
Lowe, A.B, 57
Lowi, Walter, 123
loyalty, 57, 58
Luppe, Herr, 135

MacMillan, W.M., 21, 24
Maffessanti, Andrea, 218
Magnus, Pauli, 179
Maier, Frieda, 188
Mais, Roger, 41, 225, 263n92, 283n61
male internees, 2, 144, 147, 155, 165, 169, 175, 186, 190, 191, 235
Male Internment Camp, 1, 5, 11, 13, 15, 81; administration, 146–147; band, 155; camp population, 161–165; Camp Reports, 122, 285n83; daily life, 147–151; escapes, 160–161, 226; fencing, 145; Finns, 138; football team, 154; German internees, 134–138; guard

on duty, 145; health, 157–161; inter-group relationships and divisions, 138–141; interned enemy aliens, 123–130; Italian internees, 134–138; Jamaican detainees, 130–131; location and layout, 141–146; long-term detainees, 165–167; merchant seamen, 132–134; oversight, 146–147; population of, *118–120* ; prisoners of war (POWs), 121, 122; Red Cross, 140; work and play, 151–157
Male Internment Centre, 115, 116
Manchester Guardian, 57, 166
Manley, Norman, 34–35
Mark, Connie, 231
Marquis, Samuel, 25, 39, 130, 131, 263n83
marriage, 228–231; Jamaica Civil Registration, 301n133. *See also* cross-faith marriage
Martin-Cooper, P., 196
material heritage, 235
Maunier, René, 3
May, Elsie Lillian, 214
Mayers, Henry, 234
McCabe, H., 141, 146
McCauley, Peter, 161
McFarlane, Sam A., 207, 298n45
McHugh, Lloyd Henry, 142
McMorris, Vayden, 266–267n124
media, 5, 9, 10, 18, 24, 25, 32, 51, 63, 196, 198, 201, 203
media articles, 25
media interface, 201–204
media reports, 9, 115
Medwen, R.G., 240
Memmi, Albert, 4, 247
Memorandum on the Administration of Gibraltar Camp, 101, 108–109
memorialization, 9, 17, 238, 250, 251
memories, 10, 236, 251
mental health of internees, 121
merchant mariners/seamen, 1, 5, 132–134. *See also* Male Internment Camp

Metzgen, Humphrey, 6–7, 20
Military Auxiliary Pioneer Corps, 68, 103, 107, 129, 137, 230, 234, 249
Military Detention Barracks, 123
Military Internment Camp. *See* Male Internment Camp
Mills, M.M., 169, 177
Mona Family Camp, 116, 183–194; Frau Berger layout of, *187*; initial population of, 187; layout and conditions, 188–194; painting of, 191, 246; residents of, *192*; Uwe Zitzow layout of, and index, *185*, 185–186, *186*, 189; young children at, *192*. *See also* Married Families Camp
Moore, Bob, 121, 122
Morrison, Daphne Rae, 276n107
Mortimer, P.E.N., 97
mosquitoes, 145, 189, 199, 204
Moxy, A.R., 179
Moyne, Lord, 22, 36
Moyne Commission report, 36
musical instruments, 154–155, *155*
Muth, Verena, 8, 124
My Sister's Eyes (Halperin), 250

Nazi concentration camps, 116
'N' Compound, 140–142, 160
Nearly the New World, The British West Indies and the Flight from Nazism (Newman), 8, 124, 235
Neita, Hartley, 211
Nethersole, Noel, 205
Newcastle Hill Station, 15, 147, *162*
Newman, Joanna, 8, 76–77, 124
newsprint restrictions, 9
Noel-Baker, Philip, 139
non-enemy aliens, 136
Norman, U.L.C., 123
Norman Manley International Airport, 52
nuns/nunnery, Gibraltar Camp, 92, 277n136
nursing, Gibraltarian trainees, 103

OCT. *See* Officer Commanding Troops (OCT)
Officer Commanding Troops (OCT), 116, 121
Operation Felix, 66
oral testimony, 142, 210
Osterhammel, Jürgen, 4
outings/recreational, 13, 49, 153, 170, 173

Palisadoes Aerodrome, 52
Papine, 64, 86, 87, 89, 104–106, 174, 198, 205–208, 210, 211, 215, 221, 228, 236, 244
Papine market, 105, 211
Paracchini, Giovanni, 127, 284n48
"parasitical individuals," 111
Parkinson, Sir Cosmo, 20
Peel, Richard, 20, 57–58
People's National Party (PNP), 33–34, 42
People's Political Party, 21
Petitions of Repatriation, 159
physical interface, Gibraltar Camp and neighbouring communities, 204–208
Pioneer Auxiliary Corps, 68, 103, 107, 129, 137, 230, 234, 249
PNP. *See* People's National Party (PNP)
Poelau Roebiah, 46
Polish refugees, 8, 63, 73, 74, 78, 83, 84, 87, 104, 106, 110, 111, 113, 200, 214, 225, 229, 233, 243, 250
'Po' Mufeena, 53
Post, Ken, 11, 23
Potworowski, Tomasz, 73, 272–273n54
POWs. *See* prisoners of war (POWs)
"Prisoner of War Code," 161
prisoners of war (POWs), 2, 12, 13, 15, 46, 63, 103, 117, 121, 122, 132, 142, 151, 165, 181, 229, 232, 236, 266
Protecting Power, 15, 115, 121
Public Opinion, 9, 25, 26, 33–34, 40, 43, 44, 51, 56, 57, 174, 201, 209, 210, 262n60, 284n61

Public Works Department (PWD), 62, 163

quarantine, 108
Quo Vadis Domine - In Poloniam, 225

Rae, Allan, 10
Rae, Ernest, 10, 24, 63, 242
RAF. *See* Royal Air Force (RAF)
Ramdeen, Harold, 215
Rastafarian community, 21, 23, 32
Rebecca, 156
Red Cross, 140, 172. *See also* International Committee of the Red Cross
Red Fence, 281n8
refugees in Cuba, 76
Reibnegger, Horst, 179
Reisch-German, 292n258
Ricci, Osvaldo, 217
Richards, Sir Arthur, 3, 18–20, 24, 26, 50, 62, 66, 71, 73, 130, 164, 178, 202, 209, 236, 283n53
Richter, Carol, 127
Roberts, W. Adolphe, 37, 131
Robitzsch, J.L., 147
Roerden, Felix, 147
Roosevelt, Eleanor, 26, 32–33
Rose, Phillip, 25
Royal Air Force (RAF), 4–6, 12, 64, 267n150
Royal Commission (1938), 19
Royal West India Commission, 3

Sabio, David, 271n36
Schoenbeck, Paul, 123
Schonbeck, Edward Paul, 125
Schpektor, 85, 96, 97, 112
Scotter, George St. C., 28, 39, 108, 131
scupper, 1, 45, 46, 132
securing enemies, 200–201
"seditious literature," 39
Segregated Compound, Male Internment Camp, 140, 142, 143, 149, 237
Seivwright, W.M., 206
Selva, Ercole F., 147
semi-internment camp, 222

Sharpley, Rose, 244, 290n222
Sherlock, P.M., 48
Silverman, Rabbi Henry, 84
Silverman, Samuel, 139
Simms, H., 196
Simple, Peter, 80
Smith, Egbert Charles, 23
Smith, F.E.V., 97
Smith, J.A.G., 27, 28, 41, 62, 195
social and race divisions, Jamaica, 23
social interaction, 219–228
social restrictions, 224
Sosúa, Dominican Republic, 194
Soulette, Alderman John, 44, 264n105
Spanish refugees among Gibraltar Camp evacuees, 67–69, 230
spies, 5, 48, 266
"sports model concentration camp," 131, 203
Spotlight, 9, 25, 57, 201, 203, 212
SS *Bergensfjord*, 165
SS *City of Benares*, 67
SS *Duchess of Richmond*, 68, 234
SS *Dusseldorf*, 126, 132
SS *Emmy Friedrich*, 132
SS *Esperance*, 165
SS *Esperance Bay*, 194
SS *Hannover*, 132
SS *Idarwald*, 132, 133
SS *Marques de Comillas*, 75, 77
SS *Neuralia*, 66
SS *Pennland*, 137
SS *Phrygia*, 133
SS *Rhein*, 132, 133
SS *San Thome*, 72
SS *Serpa Pinto*, 71, 72, 113
SS *Thysville*, 66
SS *Troja*, 132
SS *Yiloum*, 138
Stamm, Hans, 126, 128
Stanley, Oliver, 234
Stanton, Miriam Sandzer, 8, 78, 83, 200, 225, 250, 272n52
Steigler, Arthur, 80, 225, 275n92
Stevens, Joseph, 126
Stockdale, Sir Frank, 51
Stolberg, Claus, 78
"strict pass system," 108

Strike the Iron and *Arise Ye Starvelings* (Post), 11, 52
submarine, 5, 10, 38, 45–49, 67, 208, 265, 266
Swiss Consulate, 15, 115, 121, 140, 170

Taylor, S.A.G., 266n124
Tempelsman, Maurice, 72
Thomas, David, 212
Thompson, Briton R.W., 229
Thompson, Dudley, 24, 29
Thompson, Ralph, 130
Towards Decolonisation. Political, Labour & Economic Development in Jamaica. 1938–1945 (Hart), 11
Transatlantica, 75
Trinidad, camps in, 74–75
Trinidad Guardian, 258n2
Tucker, Frank, 279n168
typhoid, 200, 206
typhus, 72, 200

U-Boat War in the Caribbean (Kelshall), 5, 46, 265n117
UK government, unwillingness to accept refugees, 163
Ulffers, Enno, 147
Umuahia Camp, Nigeria, 134, 149
Umuahia Government College, 284n80
undue exercise of power, 116
"Unfortunate Victims of Hitler," 124
United Negro Improvement Association (UNIA), 21
United Service Organizations (USO) Canteen, 25
universal adult suffrage, Jamaica, 36, 37
University of the West Indies (UWI), 64, 236, 238, 240, 241
Up Park Camp, 93, 103, 117, 125, 137, 142, 143; Bustamante monument, 238; military detention barracks, 168; Military Hospital, 158; World War I Detention Centre, 281n6

Up Park Camp War Diary, 46, 136
UWI. *See* University of the West Indies (UWI)
UWI Mona Campus, 242, 249, 253
UWI Museum, 242, 252, 253, 303n23

Vaccino, Domenico, 218
vegetable gardening scheme, 151, 152
Victoria Jubilee Lying-In Hospital, 106
View from Mount Diablo (Thompson), 130
visas, onward, 110, 235
visits (between married internees), 182Vittel Camp, 180
Von der Porten, Gerhard Paul, 123, 125
Von Porten, Arnold, 123, 125, 133, 139, 158

WAAF. *See* Women's Auxiliary Air Force (WAAF)
Waeckerlin, Helen, 170
Waeckerlin, R.J., 15, 115, 140, 170
wages, 32, 52, 53, 76, 100–102, 122, 187, 199
war camps, 44–45
Ward, S., 157
Warning from the West Indies (MacMillan), 24
War Office, 182, 184; document, 122; request, 12
War Risks Insurance, 265n112
wartime camps, 10–11, 30–31
wartime evacuation experience, 252
Water Commission, 206
water supply, 206, 208
Watts, Lt Col R.A.B.P., 146
West India Committee Circular, 58, 264n98
West Indian sugar exports, 19
West India Royal Commission, 18, 22
Whitehall and the Jews (London), 71, 124

Williams, Delroy, 252
Williams, Margaret, 103, 279n166
Williams, Wilfred A., 39, 130
Willson, Gladstone, 127
Winkler, Hans, 123
Witte, F. Von, 166
Woehr, P., 179
Women's Auxiliary Air Force (WAAF), 47, 53
Women's Camp, Hanover Street, 15, 115, 134, 161, 167–183; challenges, 177–183; living conditions, 173–177; outline drawing of, 171; security at, 173; Zitzow family on, 172
wooden miniature ship, 299n71
Woolley, Sir Charles Campbell, 22
workshop, Italian, 82
World War I Detention Centre, 281n6
World War II camps, 115, 232, 242. *See also* individual entries
Worlledge, J.L., 24

Xiberras, Maurice, 302n19

YMCA. *See* Young Men's Christian Association (YMCA)
YMCA's War Prisoners Aid, 186
Young, Sir Herbert, 74
Young Men's Christian Association (YMCA), 15, 155, 156
Young Women's Christian Association (YWCA), 15, 121, 169
YWCA Report, 175

Zammitt, Josephine Mary, 270n18
Zitzow, Gerhard, 154
Zitzow, Uwe, 189–191, 193, 194
Zitzow family's recollection, 10
ZQI, 48, 59, 269nn181, 182

www.ingramcontent.com/pod-product-compliance
Lightning Source LLC
Chambersburg PA
CBHW030733230426
43667CB00007B/701